AUTOBIOGRAPHICAL,

SCIENTIFIC, RELIGIOUS, MORAL,

AND LITERARY WRITINGS

JEAN-JACQUES ROUSSEAU

AUTOBIOGRAPHICAL, SCIENTIFIC, RELIGIOUS, MORAL, AND LITERARY WRITINGS

THE COLLECTED WRITINGS OF ROUSSEAU
Vol. 12

TRANSLATED AND EDITED BY
CHRISTOPHER KELLY

ROGER D. MASTERS AND CHRISTOPHER KELLY
SERIES EDITORS

DARTMOUTH COLLEGE
PUBLISHED BY UNIVERSITY PRESS OF NEW ENGLAND
HANOVER AND LONDON

Dartmouth College Press
Published by University Press of New England,
One Court Street, Lebanon, NH 03766
www.upne.com
© 2006 by the Trustees of Dartmouth College
First Dartmouth College Press paperback edition 2014
ISBN for the paperback edition: 978-1-61168-645-6
Printed in the United States of America
5 4 3 2 1

All rights reserved. No part of this book may be reproduced in any form or by any electronic or mechanical means, including storage and retrieval systems, without permission in writing from the publisher, except by a reviewer, who may quote brief passages in a review. Members of educational institutions and organizations wishing to photocopy any of the work for classroom use, or authors and publishers who would like to obtain permission for any of the material in the work, should contact Permissions, University Press of New England, One Court Street, Lebanon, NH 03766.

This project has received generous support from
the Florence Gould Foundation

Library of Congress Cataloging-in-Publication Data for the hardcover edition:

Rousseau, Jean-Jacques, 1712–1778.
[Selections. English. 2007]
Autobiographical, scientific, religious, moral, and literary writings / Jean-Jacques Rousseau ; translated and edited by Christopher Kelly.
p. cm. — (The collected writings of Rousseau ; vol. 12)
Includes bibliographical references and index.
ISBN-13: 978-1-58465-599-2 (cloth : alk. paper)
ISBN-10: 1-58465-599-2 (cloth : alk. paper)
1. Rousseau, Jean-Jacques, 1712–1778. I. Kelly, Christopher, 1950– II. Title.
PQ2034.K45 2007
848'.509 — dc22   2006025076

Contents

Preface ix

Chronology of Works in Volume 12 xi

Introduction xv

Note on the Text xxvii

Autobiographical Writings 1

Autobiographical Poems 3

The Orchard of Madame the Baronne de Warens 3
Letter to M. Bordes 9
Enigma 13
Letter to Monsieur Parisot 13
Quatrain for One of His Portraits 21

The Banterer 22

Biographical Fragment 30

My Portrait 36

Response to the *Letters Written from the Mountain,* Published at Geneva, under this title: *Sentiment of the Citizens* 45

Notes for the *Reveries* 50

On the Art of Enjoying and Other Fragments 57

Various Writings 62

Travel Notebook 62
[Declaration Intended for a Journal] 62
Memorative Note on the Illness and Death of M. Deschamps 63
Sentiments of the Public Toward Me in the Various Estates that Compose It 67
Declaration Relative to Different Reprints of His Works 67
Memorandum Written in the Month of February 1777 68

Writings on Science 73

Course on Geography 75

Response to the Anonymous Memorandum 84

Memorandum Presented to M. de Mably
on the Education of M. his Son 91

Plan for the Education of Monsieur de Sainte-Marie 116

Rousseau to the abbé Guillaume-Thomas-François Raynal 130

Treatise on the Sphere 134

The New Daedalus 147

Writings on Religion and Morality 155

Fragments on God and Revelation 157
On God 157
Prayers 157

Memorandum Delivered April 19, 1742,
to Monsignor Boudet, Antonine 162

Fiction or Allegorical Fragment on Revelation 165

Fragment on the Infinite Power of God 174

Moral Letters 175

Notes on Helvétius's *On the Mind* 204

Literary Works 213

Queen Whimsical 215

The Loves of Claire and Marcellin 228

The Little Savoyard; or, The Life of Claude Noyer 234

On Eloquence 238

Contents

Idea of Method in the Composition of a Book 239

Lexicological Remarks 244

On Women 245

A Household on rue Saint-Denis 247

Essay on the Important Events of Which Women
Have Been the Secret Cause 248

Advice to a Curate 250

Funeral Oration for His Most Serene Highness
Monseigneur The Duke of Orléans 252

Letters to Sara 264

Remarks on the *Letters on the English and the French* 271

Various Fragments 275

Notes 287

Index 329

Preface

Although Jean-Jacques Rousseau is a significant figure in the Western tradition, there is no standard edition of his major writings available in English. Moreover, unlike those of other thinkers of comparable stature, many of Rousseau's important works have never been translated or have become unavailable. The present edition of the *Collected Writings of Rousseau* is intended to meet this need.

Our goal is to produce a series that can provide a standard reference for scholarship that is accessible to all those wishing to read broadly in the corpus of Rousseau's work. To this end, the translations seek to combine care and faithfulness to the original French text with readability in English. Although, as every translator knows, there are often passages where it is impossible to meet this criterion, readers of a thinker and writer of Rousseau's stature deserve texts that have not been deformed by the interpretive bias of the translators or editors.

Wherever possible, existing translations of high quality have been used, although in some cases the editors have felt that minor revisions were necessary to maintain the accuracy and consistency of the English versions. Where there was no English translation (or none of sufficient quality), a new translation has been prepared.

Each text is supplemented by editorial notes that clarify Rousseau's references and citations or passages otherwise not intelligible. Although these notes do not provide as much detail as is found in the critical apparatus of the Pléiade edition of the *Oeuvres complètes,* the English-speaking reader should nevertheless have in hand the basis for a more careful and comprehensive understanding of Rousseau than has hitherto been possible.

The works contained in this penultimate volume of the *Collected Writings of Rousseau* cover a wide range of subjects and were written over a very long period of time. The final volume will contain *Emile* and related writings. At this point in the series it is useful to state what parts of the Pléiade edition of the *Oeuvres complètes* have not been included in this series. The only omissions from Volume I of the Pléiade are Rousseau's account books and assorted documents (pp. 1192–1226). The only omissions from Volume II are the majority of the poems and romances (pp. 1115–1173) and the "Pensées d'un sprite droit et sentimens d'un coeur vertueux" (pp. 1299–1314), which are of very dubious authenticity. The only omissions from Volume III are the dispatches from Venice from the time Rousseau was secretary to the French ambassador from 1743 to 1744 (pp. 1045–1234). Aside from *Emile* and related writings (which will conclude this series) the only omission from Volume IV is the reproduction of Rousseau's "Characters of Botany" (pp. 1194–1195). The omissions from Volume V are Rousseau's writings on coding and decoding (pp. 553–583), portions of the *Dictionary of Music* (pp. 605–1191) and his translations of Seneca, Tacitus, Tasso, and Plato (pp. 1214–1298). This series has included a number of works and letters not found in the Pléiade edition.

We would like to thank the National Endowment for the Humanities for a research grant that allowed Christopher Kelly to complete this volume and the Florence Gould Foundation for a grant that allowed its publication. One piece in this volume, "Fiction or Allegorical Fragment on Revelation" previously appeared in *Interpretation* 23, no. 3 (Spring 1996). We thank Hilail Gildin for permission to reprint the translation. Sam Silverman graciously consulted on technical aspects of Rousseau's scientific writings. Natalie Wills Culp was very helpful in the preparation of the manuscript.

Chronology of Works in Volume 12

1712
June 28: Rousseau is born in Geneva.

1729
September: Occurrence of the miracle testified to by Rousseau in the "Memorandum to Monsignor Boudet."

1735
Possible date of "On God."
Probable date of the fragment "On Eloquence."

1736
Probable date of the composition of the "Course on Geography."

1738
September 28: Date of the "Response to the Anonymous Memorandum."
Earliest likely date of the prayers.

1739
Rousseau publishes "The Orchard of Madame the Baronne de Warens."

1740
April: Rousseau becomes the tutor to the children of M. de Mably in Lyon.
Probable date of the "Epistle to M. Bordes."

1741–42
Probable date of "Enigma."

1742
April 19: Date of "Memorandum to Monsignor Boudet."
July 10: Completion of the "Letter to M. Parisot."

1745
Approximate date of "Idea of Method in the Composition of a Book."
Likely date of the "Essay on the Important Events of Which Women Have Been the Secret Cause."

1749
Probable date of "The Banterer."

1752
Earliest possible date of the composition of "Advice to a Curate."
Composition of "Funeral Oration for His Most Serene Highness Monseigneur The Duke of Orléans."

1753
Rousseau writes the "Letter to Raynal" on the use of copper cooking utensils.

1754
September: During his stay in Geneva Rousseau takes the trip described in the "Travel Notebook."

1755–56
Probable date of "Biographical Fragment."

1756
In a letter Rousseau mentions having completed "Queen Whimsical."
Rousseau works on "The Loves of Claire and Marcellin" and "The Little Savoyard or the Life of Claude Noyer."

1756–57
Possible date of the composition of the "Fiction or Allegorical Fragment on Revelation."
Rousseau reads *Letters on the English and the French* by Béat de Muralt.

1757–58
Composition of the "Moral Letters."

1758
Publication of *On the Mind* by Helvétius.
Publication of "Queen Whimsical" without Rousseau's permission.

1762
Possible date of the composition of the "Letters to Sara."
June 9: The Parlement of Paris condemns *Emile* and a warrant is issued for Rousseau's arrest. He flees France.

1765
January: Rousseau publishes the "Response to the *Letters Written from the Mountain*" along with his notes.

1766
January 13: Rousseau arrives in London accompanied by David Hume.

1766–67
Rousseau writes the "Declaration Intended for a Journal."

1767

May 21: Rousseau leaves England.
Probable date of the "Quatrain for one of his Portraits."
Probable date of the "Treatise on the Sphere."

1768

April: Rousseau writes the "Memorative Note Upon the Illness and Death of M. Deschamps."

September: Rousseau writes "Sentiment of the Public Toward Me in the Various Estates that Compose it."

1776–78

Rousseau works on the *Reveries*.

1778

July 2: Rousseau dies at Ermenonville.

Introduction

It is very common to divide Rousseau's life into two parts with the "illumination" that led to the writing of the *Discourse on the Sciences and the Arts* marking the dividing point. The first part can be seen as a sort of picaresque novel in which Rousseau wandered around Europe in an extremely unsettled life of few accomplishments. The second part is the period in which he produced his great works. The widely varied writings in this volume shed new light on both parts of Rousseau's life. They show, first of all, that a large part of his early life was devoted to study and, second, that his immensely productive literary career produced interesting short works often overshadowed by his more famous books. This volume is divided into sections, not by chronology, but by topic: before discussing the topics separately, however, it will be useful to cast a glance at the two halves of Rousseau's life.

When he was twenty-one years old, Rousseau wrote a letter to his father claiming to have found himself at last after a period of what he refers to as irregular conduct. After discussing his projects, he concludes, "It is not to be feared that my taste might change; study has a charm that makes it so that once one has tasted it, one can no longer separate oneself from it."[1] The earliest of the writings contained in this volume dates from several years later; it, and others written before the *First Discourse*, show the extent of the young Rousseau's intellectual activity. It is necessary to show care in looking for the seeds of his mature thought in this early writings. In the *Confessions* Rousseau described his resolution during this period, "Let's begin by giving myself a storehouse of ideas, true or false, but clear, while waiting for my head to be well enough equipped to be able to compare and choose them."[2] The early writings in this volume give a very good view of the contents of this storehouse and of the serious issues that preoccupied Rousseau at this time.

Once he began his mature literary career he produced most of his significant works in a very short period of time. Between 1750 and 1762 he published the two *Discourses,* his opera *The Village Soothsayer,* the *Letter to d'Alembert, Julie, Emile,* and the *Social Contract.* These works would be enough to make the reputation of three writers: a musician, a novelist, and a political thinker. They were not, however, all that Rousseau wrote during this period and later. This volume contains some little-known works from Rousseau's maturity that show his astonishing inventive capacity. Some of these show him at work, as it were, on projects that lead to published writings. Others are complete short works that deserve more attention.

Autobiographical Writings

Rousseau's autobiographical project is usually associated with the last fifteen years of his life, the period in which he wrote the *Confessions, Dialogues,* and *Reveries.* Nevertheless, twenty-five years earlier he wrote three lengthy autobiographical poems and made other occasional autobiographical statements throughout his life. The majority of the later statements came in response to criticism, real or perceived, ranging from his republication of the pamphlet "Sentiment of the Citizens" (published anonymously by Voltaire) along with his own commentary to his "Memorative Note upon the Illness and Death of M. Deschamps," defending himself when he suspected that he was being accused of poisoning a neighbor.

One of the works in this section, "The Banterer" is included here because it is usually considered as fascinating autobiographical statement. In it the presumed author of this piece describes his immense changeability, saying, "Nothing is so dissimilar to me as myself, that is why it would be useless to attempt to define me other than by that singular variety."[3] The author continues by describing his two predominant dispositions (which he calls his "weekly souls") and says that "from one I find myself wisely mad, by the other madly wise."[4] Although many commentators have taken this as Rousseau's description of his rather unstable personality, because it occurs in the draft of a periodical that he was proposing to write along with his friend Diderot it seems more likely that it is meant to capture the two authors who will be publishing under the single name of "Banterer." Even so, the reader is still invited to speculate over which of the two friends was "wisely mad," and which "madly wise."

The early autobiographical poems are of considerable interest as a supplement to the account Rousseau gives of his youth in the *Confessions.* The later account places a great deal of emphasis on what the young Jean-Jacques did and felt during this period. These poems, however, also focus on what he was thinking and studying. They give the most detailed account of the intellectual life of what could be called the pre-Rousseauian Rousseau, the Rousseau before the "illumination" on the road to Vincennes in 1750 during which he claimed to discover his mature system of thought. "The Orchard of Madame the Baronne de Warens" provides an impressive list of the authors that Rousseau studied during his self-education. Along with the "Letter to M. Bordes" and the "Letter to Monsieur Parisot," this poem also gives some indication of the issues that were troubling the young man, issues that he spent the next decade trying to resolve. Above all, what is even clearer in the early autobiographical writings than in Rousseau's later accounts of his youth is an emphasis on inquiry as a guiding passion. The young Rousseau has not arrived at the conclusions of his mature "system," but he is turning himself into one of those who know how to think.

These poems were joined together along with others in a manuscript that Rousseau gave the title, "The Allobrogian Muse; or, The Works of Tom Thumb." As the Allobrogians were the ancient ancestors of the Genevans, Rousseau indicated a link and a possible tension between the rusticity of his origins and his poetic inspiration. The tension is underscored by his choice of an epigraph: "Here I am the barbarian, for they do not understand me / And the stupid Getae laugh at my Latin." Later the first line of this epigraph almost became a motto for Rousseau in that it framed his major literary output by serving as an epigraph to both the *First Discourse* (published in 1750) and the *Dialogues* (completed in 1776). His source for the epigraph is Ovid's *Tristia*, written when the poet was in exile from Rome, a subject that formed one of the acts of Rousseau's opera *The Gallant Muses*.[5] Ovid's meaning is quite clear: although he is a sophisticated poet from the center of civilization, his exile puts him in the position of a barbarian among people who would themselves be considered as barbarians at Rome. Rousseau's use of the epigraph in the *First Discourse* makes the statement more complex. First, the use of a quotation from Ovid at the head of the work qualifies the criticism made of the poet later in the text.[6] Second, Rousseau indicates that he appears to be a barbarian, not to the barbarous Getae among whom Ovid was exiled, but to the sophisticated Parisians who would be likely to look down upon a citizen of Geneva who dares to attack the arts and sciences. Rousseau's use of the epigraph helps to pose the basic question of the *Discourse:* whether the sophisticated Parisians should be so proud of their cultivation. Years later, in the *Dialogues,* this opposition is radicalized because Rousseau presents himself as someone who is misunderstood everywhere, not merely in Paris.

When Rousseau first made use of the epigraph, almost a decade before writing the *First Discourse,* he had not yet reached his conclusions about the corruption of Paris and what it represented. Moreover he was living first in Savoy and then in the provincial city of Lyon. Consequently he more directly identifies himself with the sophisticated poet living among a rustic tribe incapable of understanding his merit. This identification is made abundantly clear in a letter that Rousseau wrote during the same period which he closes with the same lines from Ovid. Just before citing the Roman poet at the end of this long letter analyzing the optimism of Pope and Leibniz, Rousseau remarks, "I notice, Sir, that in wanting to write you a letter, I have almost written a dissertation; I ask you for forgiveness, but in truth it is your fault, why are you not like the others, and what caused you to take it into your head to want to be reasonable here? Is Chambéry the country of reason, and when a man who thinks happens to meet another one there, is it possible not to abuse such a rare advantage?"[7] In other words, far from citing Ovid as part of a complicated criticism of sophistication, here Rousseau presents himself as a thinker in exile who seeks a kindred soul.

The young Rousseau's complaints about the society in which he lived as he approached the age of thirty involved more than its lack of sophistication. The early autobiographical poems repeatedly refer to pressure to "crawl" to curry favor with the rich. As he says in the "Letter to Monsieur Parisot," "Doubtless poverty is horrible to all eyes / But for those who know how to think it is much more tangible. / A coward can leave it as a result of crawling / The decent man cannot consent to this price."[8] In short, both because of the absence of intellectual equals and because of social and economic inferiority Rousseau is someone who keenly feels himself to be outside of the place in which he belongs. This raises the question of what his proper place is. In the "Letter to M. Bordes" he refers to himself as a "proud republican who wounds arrogance."[9] This certainly sounds like the Citizen of Geneva of the later writings who defends austere republicanism against the pretensions of luxury, commerce, and monarchy. Nevertheless, the letter concludes with praise of the city of Lyon that "[q]uenches needs by the path of luxury."[10] Lyon is characterized by commerce that "makes up one of the strong bonds of Society." In this poem Lyon is the place where talents shine. In the contest between unsophisticated but inegalitarian Chambéry and (relatively) sophisticated and open Lyon, the city of opulence and the arts wins hands down. In other words, for the young Rousseau, pride moves him away from Geneva rather than toward it.

In the "Letter to Monsieur Parisot" Rousseau makes it clear that Lyon wins in a direct comparison between it and his birthplace. He elaborates on his proud republican background by giving an account of his education. He says, "I was also taught that having by my birth / The right of sharing the supreme power / Small though I was, weak obscure Citizen /

I nevertheless made up a member of the sovereign."[11] He adds that this early education taught him that the luxury characteristic of powerful nations was "only a frivolous splendor that hides their chains from them." This statement could certainly be read as an early draft of the beginning of the *First Discourse*. There Rousseau says, "While Government and Laws provide for the safety and well-being of assembled men, the Sciences, Letters, and Arts, less despotic and perhaps more powerful, spread garlands of flowers over the iron chains with which men are burdened, stifle in them the sentiment of that original liberty for which they seemed to have been born, make them love their slavery and turn them into what is called civilized peoples."[12] Nevertheless, here Rousseau immediately claims that he has left such austere opinions behind, claiming, "Thus these insane speeches disturbed my soul, / I held on to them then, today I blame them: / Wiser lessons have formed my mind."[13] His newfound wisdom makes him more tolerant of both luxury and inequality. More significant, perhaps, Rousseau says that it leads him to call into question a stoic view that "[c]laimed to make us happy by virtue alone." He concludes, "I recognized how charming it is / To join a little amusement to wisdom."[14] Rather than attempting to triumph over his passions, he learned "the practice of innocent pleasures." If one wants to look for anticipations of the mature Rousseau in these early writings, they are not to be found in a preference for egalitarian republicanism over inegalitiarian monarchy; rather, they are to be found in a serious reflection on the relation between devotion to austere virtue and the pursuit of pleasure that he later called goodness. His preliminary reflections on this relation led him to a clear preference for the latter.

Scientific Writings

One of the most noteworthy features of Rousseau's account of his self-education in "The Orchard of Madame the Baronne de Warens" is the amount of scientific literature he consumed along with his readings in literature, history, and philosophy. In particular, he shows a well-developed interest in astronomy and physics. In the *Confessions* he says that he turned to astronomy after becoming disgusted with "the obscurities of chronology," apparently at least in part concerning the difficulty of reconciling sacred and secular history. Abandoning this pursuit, he became interested in "the exact measurement of time and the path of the celestial bodies"[15] His stargazing, however, led to rumors about sorcery from which Rousseau was rescued by two Jesuit priests. In this volume his early interest in astronomy and geophysics is shown by the "Elements of Astronomy" and the "Response to the Anonymous Memorandum." His continued interest is shown by his account of astronomy in Book III of *Emile* and the "Treatise on the Sphere" in this volume.

Although the time Rousseau spent as a tutor for the Mably family in 1740–41 managed only to demonstrate his unsuitability for that profession, he did write two memoranda to Mably containing his thoughts about education. In one of these he details his acquaintance with natural science and expresses his skepticism, not only about the rival Cartesian and Newtonian systems, but also about systematic physics as such. He says, "I have never been able to conceive how a philosopher could seriously imagine a System of Physics; the Cartesians appear ridiculous to me to want to give an account of all natural effects by their assumptions, and the Newtonians even more ridiculous to give their assumptions as facts: Let us be satisfied with knowing what is, without wanting to seek out how things are, since that knowledge is not within our grasp." In this case, at least, his youthful view remained his mature view and his later writings are filled with these doubts about the possibility of a completely successful natural science.

There is one very curious example of Rousseau's scientific thought in this volume, the section of the "New Daedalus" that was preserved. During Rousseau's life the one hint concerning the existence of such a work was contained in a discussion of Rousseau in Grimm's *Correspondence littéraire* in June 1762. When discussing Rousseau's life prior to his achievement of fame, Grimm says that "he was occupied with a machine with which he counted on learning to fly; he persisted in attempts that did not succeed at all; but he was never sufficiently disillusioned with his project to put up coolly with anyone treating it as chimerical. Thus his friends, if they are faithful, can expect to see him floating in the air someday."[16] It should be kept in mind that Grimm wrote this passage after his quarrel with Rousseau and included it as part of a rather unflattering character sketch. Moreover, Grimm is describing a period of Rousseau's life before the two of them met. Nevertheless, this testimony to a serious interest on Rousseau's part in the mechanical problems involved in flight is substantially confirmed by the "New Daedalus." Contrary to Grimm's account, however, Rousseau presents his interest as tempered by a healthy dose of skepticism.

Collectively, these writings testify to Rousseau's competence as an amateur scientist and, in the next decade, he went on to increase this competence with the serious study of chemistry. A small sign of this interest can be found in his letter to the abbé Raynal on the use of copper cooking utensils. Here, as elsewhere, Rousseau is particularly attentive to issues involved in the public dissemination of scientific knowledge. Much work remains to be done to understand the place of science in Rousseau's thought, particularly in relation to his thought about religious matters: nevertheless, the scientific writings contained in this volume allow one to make a beginning.[17]

Writings on Religion and Morality

The majority of the writings on religion and morality included here prepare the way for "The Profession of Faith of the Savoyard Vicar" in *Emile*. At the time of its publication the "Profession" was by far the most controversial of Rousseau's writings. It was largely this part of *Emile* that led to the issuing of a warrant for Rousseau's arrest in 1762 and caused him to spend years looking for a safe refuge. The religious views expressed in the "Profession" made Rousseau the target of the defenders of religious orthodoxy (both Protestant and Catholic) without winning him many allies among the more radically antireligious intellectuals.

Rousseau's journey to this position was eventful. Aside from some prayers (also included here), his earliest religious writing was the certification of a miracle, the "Memorandum Delivered April 19, 1742." When this work was unearthed years later, after Rousseau had attacked miracles in the *Letters Written from the Mountain*, he himself felt the use of the "Memorandum" to be a good joke at his expense. In the *Confessions* he says that, even at the time, he should not have attested to the miraculous character of the events he described, but adds, "Nevertheless, as far as I can recall my ideas, which were sincerely Catholic at that time, I was in good faith. The love of the marvelous so natural to the human heart, my veneration for this virtuous Prelate, the secret pride at having perhaps contributed to the miracle myself, helped to seduce me."[18] All of the later writings on religion are marked by the skepticism about miracles (coupled with the view that it is impossible to refute their possibility) indicated in this passage.

The most significant of the works contained here leading up to the "Profession of Faith" are the "Fiction or Allegorical Fragment on Revelation," the "Moral Letters," and Rousseau's marginal notes to Helvétius's *On the Mind*. The "Fiction" deals with the same issues as the "Profession of Faith," but from a very different perspective. The "Moral Letters," contain passages that found their way into the "Profession." Finally, Rousseau's reading of Helvétius led him to make his attack on materialism in the "Profession."

While the "Profession of Faith" is presented as the reflections of a

Catholic priest to a young but disillusioned convert, the "Fiction" portrays the reflections of a philosopher who, after reaching his philosophic conclusions, literally dreams about the appropriate means to teach these conclusions to mankind. His dream reveals that a direct presentation of these conclusions would be both dangerous to himself and harmful to the public. It concludes by showing that a presentation in religious guise, while still dangerous, would be more effective. It is easy to see this reflection as leading to the form Rousseau chose to give the "Profession of Faith." In *Emile* he stops short in his direct treatment of metaphysics and religion and entrusts this subject to his character, the Savoyard Vicar. Most scholars argue that Rousseau probably wrote the "Fiction" a couple of years before he started writing *Emile:* even if those who place it either much earlier or much later are correct, however, the "Fiction" remains an important statement about the relation between philosophic reflection and public action that is consistent with Rousseau's entire literary project.[19]

In the case of the "Moral Letters" Rousseau presents what he says as his own "profession of faith," expressed to the woman he loves who has rebuffed his advances, but asked for moral guidance.[20] It is, of course, possible to wonder whether a man in this position who wishes to reestablish his relationship with the woman on a new footing will state his opinion on all matters with complete openness. Nevertheless, it remains the case that Rousseau here addresses in his own voice many of the issues raised in the "Profession." Any definitive effort to establish how closely the Vicar's opinions reflect Rousseau's own must begin, although it will surely not end, with a close comparison with this work.

While both the "Moral Letters" and the "Profession of Faith" begin with expressions of doubt about the possibility of knowledge, the former is probably the most skeptical of Rousseau's works. For example, it gives a more radical critique of the reliability of sense perception than can be found in *Emile,* which stresses training the senses and judgment together to make them more trustworthy. In the "Moral Letters" Rousseau declares, "We do not know anything, my dear Sophie, we do not see anything; we are a band of blind men, cast at random in this vast universe."[21] This radical position is at the basis of an attempt to humble intellectual pretension in the name of "a worthier and more legitimate pride" in the feeling[22] of attachment to justice. This feeling, in turn, serves as the basis for a new attempt to gain philosophic knowledge. As Rousseau says, "Do you think that philosophy teaches us to return into ourselves. . . . It is entirely the opposite, my charming friend, it is necessary to begin by returning into oneself in order to learn to philosophize."[23] The "Moral

Letters," then, are concerned with the preconditions for genuine philosophic activity. Although they do not present anything like the whole of Rousseau's system, they may well be the best introduction to it.

The marginal notes to Helvétius present none of the issues concerning the intended audience posed by the "Moral Letters." They are notes that Rousseau did not intend for anyone but himself. Helvétius's *On the Mind* (*De l'esprit*) caused an immense uproar upon its publication in 1758 and its author quickly made a formal disavowal of its contents. Rousseau briefly considered writing a refutation of the work, but abandoned this project when he saw Helvétius being persecuted. While he frequently attacked the doctrines of *On the Mind*, he did so without naming either the book or the author. These notes, then, contain the germ of one of the numerous works that Rousseau considered writing, but abandoned. The most famous of these, *Sensitive Morality; or, The Wise Man's Materialism*, would doubtless have had a close relation to the refutation of Helvétius and these notes indicate something about what its content might have been.

There are certainly variations among these works on morality and religion, but their general lines of inquiry follow a similar pattern that makes detailed comparison possible. While the "Profession of Faith" is the starting point for consideration of what Rousseau has to say about these questions, these works stand on their own in providing important pieces of the puzzle.

Literary Works

While there is a certain unity of both orientation and substance throughout the writings on religion and morality, diversity is the hallmark of the literary works. At one extreme is the extremely serious funeral oration for the duke of Orléans that Rousseau was commissioned to write. At the other extreme is the very lighthearted fairy tale "Queen Whimsical," in which even death is treated as a joke. It is difficult to find the unity in such different works. The problem is compounded if one tries to determine the relation between these works and Rousseau's other writings. Here it is possible only to give some preliminary indications about how some of the works relate to each other and to Rousseau's other works.

Two of the works, "The Loves of Claire and Marcellin" and "The Little Savoyard; or, The Life of Claude Noyer" are fragments. By all appearances Rousseau's work on them was overwhelmed, as it were, by the composition of his great novel, *Julie*. Seen in the light of the novel, these sketches look like experiments at finding the right form and set of themes for his novel. Each of them leaves the action hanging at a turning point that makes it difficult to speculate about how they might have continued. The first of them has a narrator and the second is written in the first person. When he abandoned these works for *Julie* Rousseau also abandoned both forms of novel in favor of the epistolary form.[24]

Two other works were written in response to dares. One of the dares was to show that a man of fifty could avoid being ridiculous while being in love with a woman of twenty. The "Letters to Sarah" attempt to show that such a man could write at least four love letters (but not as many as six) before he dishonored himself. In the case of "Queen Whimsical" the challenge was "to write a tolerable and even merry Tale, without intrigue, without love, without marriage, and without lewdness."[25] One of its early readers found in the result a "spirit of singularity, itch for rebelling against accepted practices, and irreverence for sacred things."[26] This is, indeed, a merry tale that, as one of the characters says, is in danger of turning into a treatise on politics. It attacks the foundation of hereditary monarchy, questions gender identity, and mocks religious customs. Rousseau quickly concluded that this story could not be published in France, although he did allow manuscripts to circulate and it was published clandestinely without his permission in 1758.

Like these works the "Funeral Oration for his Most Serene Highness Monseigneur the Duke of Orléans First Prince of the Blood of France" was inspired by someone other than Rousseau. The abbé who commissioned Rousseau to write it never delivered it because he was not selected as the funeral orator. This is a moving and unsettling work, moving because of the great praise of the prince and unsettling because it implicitly (and sometimes explicitly) criticizes the way of life of all of its presumed listeners.

Finally, one of Rousseau's earliest works, the "Idea of Method in the Composition of a Book" is a sort of outline for his future literary career. In this work Rousseau carefully reflects on how to construct "a work of reasoning" independent of the subject to be treated.[27] Victor Goldschmidt has argued quite persuasively that he followed his own advice quite faithfully when he came to write his *Discourse on the Sciences and the Arts*.[28] In the "Idea" Rousseau pays particular attention to the difficulties involved in introducing new opinions and correcting well-established prejudices. A partial solution he recommends is for any author to demonstrate that he is both well informed and "upright and sincere." As he says in one of the numerous fragments collected here, "Doubtless it was necessary to say some good things, but in order to say them usefully it was necessary to begin by getting oneself listened to."[29] Rousseau's success in getting himself listened to was unrivaled partly because he thought so deeply about how to accomplish this.

How to get oneself listened to is the subject of another fragment, one that makes a fitting conclusion to this introduction. Rousseau says, "In the bosom of superstition where reason has no force philosophy must necessarily take on a mysterious air in order to gain credence. Without which all the truths that are merely demonstrated would not find any sectaries at all."[30] Rousseau lived in circumstances that he thought were both too superstitious and too philosophic. He often thought of himself as standing alone between the party of the devout and the party of philosophers. Perhaps this apartness explains some of the diversity of his works as he alternately seeks to demonstrate truths and to find supporters for them.

Note on the Text

Three of the works included in this volume are not in the Pléiade edition of Rousseau's works. They are (1) the letter, "Rousseau to the abbé Guillaume-Thomas-François Raynal," which is from *Correspondance complète de Jean-Jacques Rousseau*, edited by R. A. Leigh (Oxford: The Voltaire Foundation, 1965–1991), vol. 2, 221–225; (2) "Response to the *Letters Written from the Mountain*, published at Geneva as *Sentiment of the Citizens*," which is from *Résponse aux Lettres Exrites de la Montagne; Publiée à Genève, sous ce titre: Sentiment des Citoyens* (Paris: Duchesne, 1765); and (3) *The New Daedalus*, which is from *Le Nouveau Dédale: A Reproduction of the First Edition* (Pasadena, Calif.: Institute of Aeronautical History, n.d.).

AUTOBIOGRAPHICAL WRITINGS

Autobiographical Poems

The Orchard of Madame the Baronne de Warens[1]

Rara domus tenuem non aspernatur amicum:
Rareque non humiliem calcat fastosa Clientem.[2]

Foreword

In the past I had the misfortune of refusing some verses to persons whom I honor and whom I respect infinitely, because I had already forbidden myself to write any. I dare to hope, nevertheless, that the ones that I am publishing today will not offend them, and I believe I can say, without too much subtlety, that they are the work of my heart and not of my mind. It is even easy to notice that this is an impromptu enthusiasm, if I can speak this way, in which I hardly thought about shining. Frequent repetitions in the thoughts and even in the turns of phrase, and much negligence in the diction, do not proclaim a man extremely eager for the glory of a good Poet. I declare, in addition, that if I am ever found writing gallant verses or those sorts of beautiful things that are called witticisms, I willingly give myself over to all the indignation I shall have deserved.

It would be necessary to excuse myself with certain people for having praised my Benefactress, and with persons of merit for not having said enough good about her: the silence I am maintaining with regard to the former is not without foundation: As to the others, I have the honor of assuring them that I shall always be infinitely satisfied to hear the same reproach made to me. It is true that, while congratulating Madame de W*** about her inclination for doing good, I could elaborate on many other truths no less honorable for her. I have not claimed to be a Panegyrist here, but simply a sensitive and greatful man who is amusing himself by describing his pleasures.

Someone will not fail to cry out, "A sick man writing verses! A man within an inch of the tomb!" It is precisely for that reason that I have written verses: if I were less ill, I would believe myself to be accountable for my occupations to the good of society; the condition I am in allows me to labor only for my own satisfaction. How many people who abound with possessions and health do not pass their entire life any other way? It would also be necessary to know whether those who make this reproach to me are disposed to employ me for anything better.

The Orchard of Madame de Warens[3]

Orchard dear to my heart, abode of innocence,
Honor of the finest days that heaven to me does dispense
Charming solitude, Refuge of peace;
Happy orchard, may I never leave you.

Oh delightful days that flowed by beneath your shade!
The languishing song of Philomela in tears
The flattering murmur of a fleeting brook
Upon your speckled ground I learn to enjoy life:
I learn to meditate without regrets, without envy
About the frivolous tastes of insane mortals.
Their frivolous days with one being pushed by the other
Do not inflame my heart with the desire to follow them.
I set the value of living on greater pleasures;
Pleasures ever charming, ever sweet, ever pure,
You are always certain for my enchanted heart.
Whether at the first appearance of a fine day ready to burst forth
I go to see the knolls gilded by a rising Sun;
Or hunted by its ardor at noon,
I seek coolness under a bushy tree;
Carrying Montagne or la Bruiére there with me,[4]
I calmly laugh at human misery;
Or with Socrates and the Divine Plato
I practice walking in the footsteps of Cato:[5]
Or a shining night in extending its wings
Unveils to my gaze the Moon and the stars,
Then, following la Hire and Cassini from afar,[6]
I calculate, I observe, and near the infinite
Upon these various worlds that the Ether contains for us
I urge on in reasoning, Huyghens and Fontenelle:[7]
Or finally surprised by an unforeseen storm,
While running I reassure the frantic Shepherd,
Frightened by the winds that blow on his head;
The whirlwinds, the lightning, the thunder, the storm;
Always equally happy and satisfied,
I desire no more perfect happiness.

Oh you, wise WARENS, student of Minerva!
Pardon these outbursts of an indiscreet verve;

Although I might have promised never to rhyme,
Here I dare to sing the fruits of your benefits.
Yes, if my heart enjoys the most tranquil fate,
If I follow virtue in an easy path,
If I taste an innocent repose in these places,
I owe such a rare gift only to you alone;
Vainly a base heart,[8] mercenary souls,
By cruel, rather than salutary advice,
Have tried to deprive me of your kindnesses a hundred times.
They do not know the good you taste
In making people happy, in wiping away tears,
For them these delicate pleasures have no charms.
The liberal hands of Titus and Trajan[9]
Stir up nothing but inhuman laughter in their hearts.
Why do good in the century in which we live?
Is anyone found in the race of men,
Worthy of being drawn out of the rank of indigents?
Can there be honorable people in poverty?
And is it not worth more to use one's wealth,
And[10] enjoy pleasures than to make generous gifts?
Let them follow these horrible sentiments as they will;
I shall take good care not to ask them for anything.
I shall not go to crawl nor to seek to please them;
My heart knows how to face poverty if it must,
And more delicate than they are, more sensitive to honor,
Looks more closely at the choice of a Benefactor.
Yes, today I give public assurance of it,
This writing will be its authentic witness,
That if ever fate tears your benefits from me,
My needs will never have recourse to them.

[Let the contemptible pack of envious people[11]
Attack the virtues whose luster overwhelms them:
Disdain their plots, their hatred, their rage,
Peace is no less at the bottom of your heart for it,
While, vile playthings of their own furies,
Food for the serpents they have nourished,
Crime and remorse bring to the bottom of theirs
The sad punishment of their black horrors.
Similar in their rage to the malignant wasp
Incapable of labor and unworthy of aid

Who sees only thefts and finally whose fate
Is to do evil in giving itself death,
Let them exhale in vain their impotent anger,
Their threats have nothing in them that make me frightened for you;
They would like for a great King to deprive you of benefits:[12]
But nobler efforts make his projects illustrious.
Their low jealousy and their unjust rage
Will never reach his August Throne,
And the Monster that reigns in their dejected hearts
Is not made to brave the luster of his virtues.
This is how a good King makes his empire lovable,
He maintains the virtue that misfortune overwhelms:
When he must threaten, lightning is in his hands.
Without raising himself above humans, every King
Can throw the thunderbolt against criminals,
But if he makes people happy, he is a God on earth.
Charles, your empire is recognized by these traits;
Your hand brings joy and benefits everywhere:
Your subjects rendered equal, experience justice,
By a shameful caprice, one no longer lays claim to
An odious principle proscribed by equity,
Which, wounding all the rights of society,
Breaks the sacred knots by which it was united
Refuses its best part to its needs,
And claims to exempt from its most just Laws
Those it makes enjoy its richest rights.
Ah! If it had been enough for you to make yourself terrible,
What other could be more invincible than you,
When Europe saw you guiding its standards
Alone among all its Kings shining in the field of Mars!
But it is not enough to frighten the earth;
There are other duties than the cares of war,
And it is by them, great King, that your people today
Finds in you its avenger, its Father, and its support.
And you, wise WARENS, whom this Hero protects
In vain does calumny besiege you in secret,
Fear little its effects, brave its vain wrath,
Virtue defends you, and this is enough for you:
This Great King esteems you, he knows your zeal,
Always to his word he knows how to be faithful,
And to say it all, in sum, warrant of his kindnesses
Your Heart answers to you that you deserve them.

I am known well enough and my severe Muse
Knows not how to dispense mercenary incense;
The affected language of a vile flatterer never
Has sullied August truth in my verses.
You yourself despise an insipid praise,
Your sincere virtues do not have pride as a guide.
With your enemies let us agree, if necessary,
That wisdom does not exclude every defect in you.
On this Earth, Alas, such is our misery
That perfection is only error and chimera!
To know my failings is my foremost wish
And I make little account of every perfect man.
Hatred sometimes gives useful advice:
Blame that too gentle and too sweet kindness
That in their eyes has often caused your misfortunes.
Acknowledge in yourself the weaknesses of good hearts:
But know that in secret eternal wisdom
Hates their false virtues more than your weakness,
And that it would be a hundred times better to show oneself to its eyes
Imperfect as you are, than virtuous as they are.

From my childhood, then, devoted to instructing me, you
Who believed you read through my misery, Alas,
That Heaven had provided me with some talents,
Who deigned to form my heart to virtue,][13]
You whom I dare to call by the tender name of Mother,
Accept today this sincere homage,
This legitimate and too well deserved tribute
That my gratitude offers to the truth.
Ah![14] if some sweet things give zest to my life;
If I have been able to shield myself from envy until now,
If, the heart more sensitive, and the mind less coarse,
I have been seen to rise above the common;
In sum, if each day I take joy in myself;
Sometimes by soaring up to the supreme Being,
Sometimes in a profound repose by meditating upon
The errors of humans and their goods and their evils
Sometimes philosophizing about natural Laws,
I enter into the secret of eternal causes,
I seek to fathom all the various springs;
The hidden principles that move the Universe;
If, say I, in my power I have all these advantages;

I repeat it again those are your works,
Virtuous WARENS it is from you that I obtain
The true happiness of man, and solid possessions.

Without fear, without desires, in this solitude
I let my days pass exempt from uneasiness;
Oh! That my moved heart might to its taste be able to
Depict on this paper in a just measure
The perfect voluptuousness of the pleasures that it feels.
The present I enjoy, past that I regret,
Moments so precious![15] I shall no longer waste you
On bizarre projects, on superfluous worries.
In this charming orchard, I share its space,
Under a cool shade, sometimes I relax,
Sometimes with Leibnitz, Mallebranche, and Newton
I raise my reason upon a sublime tone,
I examine the Laws of bodies and of thoughts:
With Locke I compose the history of ideas:
With Kepler, Wallis, Barrow, Rainaud, Pascal,[16]
I outstrip Archimedes, and I follow[17] Hôpital*[18]
Sometimes applying my problems to Physics,
I give a free rein to the systematic spirit:
I tentatively follow Descartes and his wanderings
Sublime, it is true, but frivolous Novels.
I soon abandon the unfaithful Hypothesis,
Content to study natural History.
There Pliny and Nyeuventit[19] aiding me with their knowledge
Teach me to think, open my eyes, and see.
Sometimes descending from these vast intelligences,
I follow the characters of different mortals.
Sometimes amusing myself even with fiction,
Telemaque[20] and Sethos[21] give me their lesson,
Or indeed in Clévéland[22] I observe nature
Which is shown to my eyes as touching and always pure.
Sometimes also skimming over Spon's notebooks[23]
I reread the dangers of my fatherland in tears!
Geneva wise in days gone by, oh my dear Fatherland!
What Demon produces frenzy in your bosom?[24]
Remember that in bygone times you gave Heroes,

---

*The marquis de l'Hôpital, author of *Analysis of the Infinitely Small* and several other works of mathematics.

Whose blood purchased you the sweetness of repose!
Today transported by a sudden rage,
Blind Citizens, are you searching for slavery?
Too soon, perhaps, Alas, you might find it.
But if there is still time, it is up to you to ponder it.
Enjoy the benefits that Louis is granting you,
Call back into your walls that ancient concord.
Happy! If taking back the faith of your forbears,
You never forget to be free as they were.
Oh you tender Racine! Oh you lovable Horace!
In my leisure times you too find your place:
Claville, St. Aubin, Plutarch, Mezerai,[25]
Despréaux, Cicero, Pope, Rollin, Barclai,[26]
And you too sweet la Motte,[27] and you touching Voltaire,
Your reading will always remain dear to my heart.
But my taste turns aside from all frivolous writing,
Whose author's goal is merely pleasing[28] the mind.
He might well lavish the brilliant Antithesis,
Scatter flowers everywhere, seek a turn of phrase that pleases,
With me the heart more than the mind has needs,
And if it is not melted, rebuffs all your efforts.

It is thus that my days flow away without alarms:
My eyes shed no tears over my misfortunes:
If crying sometimes impairs my repose
It is for other subjects than my own ills.
Vainly do pain, fears, misery,
Want to dishearten the end of my life,
The stoic pride of the enslaved Epictetus
Teaches me to bear ills, poverty.
I see the languishing that overwhelms me without grieving;
The approach of death is not at all frightening to me,
And the illness from which my body feels itself almost prostrate,
For me is only a subject for strengthening my virtue.

Letter to M. Bordes[29]

You whom Apollo himself guides to the games of Parnassus,
You deign to incite a timid muse;
Too indulgent judge of my weak attempts,

In encouraging me your taste cedes to your goodness.
But, alas! for giving myself scope, I do not have
The warlike assurance of a lively athlete;
And from the first steps, anxious and astonished,
Breath abandons me and I give up the prize.

Bordes, worthy to judge my just alarms:
See what are the struggles, and what are the arms.
These laurels are very sweet, certainly,[30] to carry off:
But what audacity for me to dare to contend for them!
What! I would proceed upon the tone of my rustic lyre
To make a Helvetic muse swear in verse:
And harshly preaching the sad truth,
Rouse up against me the disgusted reader![31]
Happier, if you wish, although reckless,
If my feeble talents would find the art of pleasing;
If, by chance[32] saved from public hisses,
My verses could be approved by people with taste,
Tell me upon what subjects my muse will exert itself.
Every poet is a liar and the profession excuses him;
He knows how to make, by pompous words, a rich fop
Into a new Maecenas, a pillar of the State.
But I, who am little acquainted with the customs of France,
I, proud republican who wounds arrogance,
I disdain the support of the impertinent rich man,
If it is necessary to beg while crawling before him,
And know how to give applause only to you, to true merit:
Mad[33] vanity disgusts and irritates me.
The rich man despises me; and in spite of his pride,
We often see each other in just about the same way.
But, whatever hatred the failing inspires in me,
My sincere and frank[34] heart abhors satire;
Too uncovered perhaps and never a criminal[35]
I tell the truth without steeping it in bile.
Thus, my pen, always the implacable enemy
Of both flattery and calumny,
Knows not how to betray the truth in its verses;
And always granting a deserved tribute,
Always ready to give earned praises,
Never flattered a vile Croesus with foolishness.

Oh you³⁶ who in the bosom of a humble obscurity
Nourish virtues along with poverty,
Whose desires limited in wise indigence³⁷
Without pride disdain a vain abundance,
Too precious remnants of those ancient times
Where, of the slightest affectation, our ancestors content,
Select in their morals, simple in their adornment;
Felt no need of any but those of nature;
Unfortunate illustrious people, in what places do you live?
Say, what are your names? It will be too sweet for me
To exercise my talents by singing your glory,
In making you eternal in the temple of memory;
And if my feeble verses could not attain it,
These so respected names would³⁸ be able to preserve them.

But why occupy myself with an empty chimera?
There is no³⁹ wisdom where misery reigns;
Under the weight of hunger beaten down merit
Lets virtue be extinguished in a sad heart.
So many pompous⁴⁰ speeches about happy indigence
To me have very much the air of being born in the bosom of abundance:
Convenient philosopher, one always takes great care
To preach the virtues one does not need.⁴¹

Bordes, let us seek subjects for my muse elsewhere;
The pity it gives, often the poor abuse,
And decorating with the name of sacred charity
The gifts with which one nourishes their vile idleness,
Under the aspect of virtues that misfortune oppresses,
Hides the love of vice and the inclination to crime.⁴²
I honor merit in the most abject ranks;
But I find few such subjects to praise.⁴³

No, let us rather celebrate innocent industry
That knows how to multiply the sweet things of life,
And, salutary to all in its useful efforts,
Quenches needs by the path of luxury.
It is for⁴⁴ this charming art that ceaselessly enriches,
One sees your happy fatherland shining from afar.*

* The city of Lyon.

Its Commerce in all places, and always respected,
Makes up one of the strong bonds of Society;
And in all the Universe its fertile abundance
Proceeds to bring adornment and magnificence.

Precious works, superb ornaments,
One would say that Minerva in her amusements,
With gold and silk has, with a knowing hand,
Formed the fabric of your designs.
To contend with you, Turin, London, in vain,
Wish to imitate you with jealous efforts:
Your charming mixtures, matched by the graces,
Leave them very far behind exhausted in your tracks.
Good taste disdains them and triumphs among you;
And while dragged by their jealous spite,
They force nature in their cold works,
Your vivacity, always shining and pure,
Gives a more refined eye to what it adorns
And lends more luster even to beauty.

Happy city which makes up the ornament of France,
Treasure of the Universe, source of abundance,
Lyon, charming abode of the children of Plutus,
In your tranquil walls, all the arts are received:
The taste of a wise protector gathers them together there;
Apollo and Plutus, surprised at being together,
From their long contentions have trouble returning,
And ask what god could have joined them together.
One recognizes your efforts, Pallu:*[45] you restore to us
The renowned ages of Tyre and Athens:
Lyon shines with a thousand diverse outbursts at a time,
And its opulent people seems to be a people of kings.
You, worthy citizen of this illustrious city,
You can contribute to giving it luster;
By your happy talents, you can decorate it,
And to defer any longer is to make a theft from it.
How do you dare to propose that I write,
You, whom Minerva herself has taken care to instruct,
You, negligent possessor of her divine gifts,

*Intendant of Lyon

Who come to speak for her again by insulting her?
Ah! if of the divine fire that shines in your work,
At least a spark had been my share,
My muse, some day, softening hearts,
Perhaps on the stage might have made tears flow.
But I speak to you in vain, insensible to my complaints,
By cruel refusals you confirm my fears,
And I see that impotent to bend your rigor,
Blanche*[46] has not yet exhausted her misfortunes.

Enigma.[47]

Child of Art, Child of Nature,
Without prolonging days, I keep from dying:
The truer I am, the greater an imposture I make,
And I become too young as a result of growing old.

Letter to Monsieur Parisot[48]

Completed July 10, 1742

Friend, deign to allow that to your eyes today
I unveil this heart full of trouble and worry.
You who formerly knew my soul entirely
In whom alone I found a tender friend, a Father
Recall again your first kindnesses for me,
Give my heart your care, it has deserved it.

Do not believe that, alarmed by frivolous fears,
I am complaining to you about your silence here,
That from false suspicions unworthy of both
I might accuse you of an odious disdain:
No, you would vainly persist in being silent,
I can explain this severe Language too well,
About this sad plan that I unveiled to you[49]
Your silence has spoken without having answered me.
I do not excuse myself when a friend blames me.

**Blanche of Bourbon*, tragedy by M. Bordes, which, to the great regret of his friends, he perseveres in refusing to let be staged.

Vile pride is not my soul's vice,
Sometimes I have received solid advice
Given with kindness, followed with Zeal:
I am unacquainted with those dodges whose empty ruses
Transform our weaknesses into so many virtues,
And never under false colors could my mind
Conceal its errors from your gazes;
But might I be allowed by a legitimate effort
To preserve at least some rights to your esteem,
Weigh my feelings, my reasons, and my choice
And decide my fate for the last time.

Born in obscurity, since my childhood I have made
The sad trial of the caprices of fate
And if there is some good of which it has not deprived me
It has persecuted me even by its favors.
It caused me to be born free, Alas, for what use?
How very dearly has it sold me such an empty advantage!
I am free in fact: but from this cruel possession
I have received more troubles than from a real misfortune.
Ah if it was necessary one day to depart from my fatherland
To drag my languishing life to a Foreign home
If it was necessary to crawl basely before the Great
Why did I not learn that art from my youngest years.
But my youth was formed on other lessons
I was told to fulfill my duties without baseness
To respect the Great, Magistrates, Kings,
To cherish humans and to obey the Laws:
But I was also taught that having by my birth
The right of sharing the supreme power
Small though I was, weak obscure Citizen
I nevertheless made up a member of the sovereign,
That such a noble advantage must be maintained
By a Hero's heart, by a wise man's virtues,
That in the end freedom, that dear gift of the Heavens
Is only a fatal scourge for vicious hearts.
Among us one takes in these maxims along with milk
Less to pride oneself about our Legitimate rights
Than one day to be able to give oneself both
The best Magistrates and the most just Laws.

Do you see, I was told, these powerful nations
Rapidly furnishing their brilliant courses?
All that empty apparatus that delights the Universe
Is only a frivolous splendor that hides their chains from them:
By their own valor they forge their shackles,
They play at conqueror, they are vile slaves
And their vast power that art had produced
Soon finds itself destroyed by Luxury.
A very different concern interests us here
Our greatest force is in our weakness
We live without regret in humble obscurity
But at least one is free within our walls.
There we are unacquainted with haughty arrogance
No showy titles, no unjust power
Wise magistrates established by our votes
Judge our contentions, make our Laws observed.
Art is not at all the support of our Republic
To be just is the only policy among us;
All ranks separate, but not unequal
Each keeps the rank that is assigned to it:
Simple in their adornment, our leaders, our magistrates
Here without displaying Luxury and Gilt
Nevertheless are not at all merged among us,
They are distinguished: but it is by their virtues.

May this charming union always be able to endure,
Alas! one sees so little constant probity!
There is nothing that time does not corrupt in the end
Everything, even wisdom, is subject to decline.

Exercised by these reflections, my reason
Taught me to despise that insane pomp
By which the pride of the Great shines in every direction
And attracts the glances of the imbecilic People;
But how dearly it cost me when for my entire life
Faith removed me from my homeland's bosom
When I saw myself, in sum, without support, without aid
Constrained to have recourse to these same Great.

No, I cannot think without shedding tears
About those frightful moments full of trouble and alarms

When I experienced that in the end these fine feelings,
Far from softening my fate, irritated my torments.
Doubtless poverty is horrible to all eyes
But for those who know how to think it is much more tangible.
A coward can leave it as a result of crawling
The decent man could not consent to this price.
Again if some truly Great received my homage
Or if, at least, they had a share of merit,
By its nobly granted respects, my heart
Would acknowledge gifts that it did not possess:
But here must my humble submission
Nourish the arrogance of these proud Country Folk?
What vile Parchments obtained by favor
Will give them the right to live without virtues?
And in spite of my efforts, without my servile reverences
My zeal and my talents will remain useless.
Ah! let us see the end of my sad days rather
Than ever to undergo such a cowardly destiny.

Thus these insane speeches disturbed my soul,
I held onto them then, today I blame them:
Wiser lessons have formed my mind
But my reason is the fruit of many misfortunes.

You know, dear Parizot, what generous hand
Came to dry up the unfortunate source of my tears,
You know it and your eyes have been the witnesses
Of whether my heart can feel what it owes to her efforts.
But can my enflamed zeal ever claim
To pay for the benefits of that tender mother?
If one can aspire to it by feelings
Ah! at least by mine I have the right to hope so.

I can count her willing kindnesses for little
I owe her other, more estimable goods,
The goods of reason, the feelings of the heart,
Even some rights to honor from talents.
Before her goodness from the bosom of misery
Deigned to shield me from the saddest needs
I was a low child abandoned by fate

Perhaps destined to perish in the mire.
Conceited abortion whose burlesque pride
Comically mixed childhood with subjects of Novels
Made the good pity, made madman laugh,
And sometimes stirred up the wrath of fools.
But men are only what one makes them.
I had hardly dared to appear before her gazes
Than, learning my errors from my benefactress,
I felt the need to correct my morals.
I abjured forever those ferocious maxims
Bitter and precious fruits of native prejudice
Which from early years by their acrid Leavens
Nourished the pride of Republican hearts:
I learned to respect an illustrious Nobility
That could add Luster even to virtue.
In society it would not be good
For less inequality to enter into ranks.
In my empty jester's cap shall I play here
The great declaimer, the new Don Quixote,
On the earth destiny has put order into stations
And surely will not change them for my sake.
Thus from my reason, languishing for so long,
I then formed a nascent reason,
Ceaselessly led by the cares of a Mother
I soon gathered the fruit of her kindness:
I knew above all that savage inflexibility
Would be of a sad use in the world today;
Modesty then became dear to my heart
I loved humanity: I cherished gentleness
And respecting the rank and the birth of the great
I endured their haughtiness with that hope
That in spite of all the luster with which they are clothed
At least I could equal them in virtues
Finally during two Years in the bosom of your fatherland
I learned to cultivate the sweet things of life.
In the past the sad austerity of the Stoa
Mixed its harshness with my barely formed taste:
Epictetus and Zeno in their Stoic pride
Made me admire that Heroic courage
Which, causing a generous disdain for false goods,

Claimed to make us happy by virtue alone.
For a long time the brilliant chimera of that ardor
Seduced my mind, made my character inflexible;
But in spite of so many efforts have these empty fictions
Banished the passions from my heart?
Only God is allowed, only the Supreme Essence
To be always happy both alone and by itself;
For man, such as he is in mind and heart,
Remove the passions, there is no longer any happiness.
It is you, dear Parisot, it is your lovable commerce
That made me tractable from the coarse man I was
Then I recognized how charming it is
To join a little amusement to wisdom.
Some more refined friends, a less wild climate
Taught me the practice of innocent pleasures.
I saw with rapture that enchanting sight
That can go to the heart by the path of the senses:
Mine which had been peaceful until then
Finally became sensitive for the first time,
In spite of my happy efforts to lead myself astray Love
Taught me to sigh near two beautiful eyes.
Witty sayings, elegant verses, lively conversations,
A meal made gay by likable guests
Little games of commerce and from which sorrow flees
Where one relaxes the mind without risking the Purse.
In a word the attractions of an opulent life
That to the wishes of the Foreigner offers its wealth
All the pleasures of taste, the charm of the fine arts,
To my enchanted eyes shone from all directions.
It is not, nevertheless, that my soul gone astray
Gave way to an exaggerated softness.
Innocence is the good most dear to my heart,
Debauchery and excess are objects of horror:
Guilty pleasures are the torments of the soul
They are purchased too dearly if they are worthy of blame.
Doubtless, in order to be a real good, pleasure
Must make man happy and not criminal:
But it is no less true that of the course of our life
Heaven does not forbid us to soften the misery.
And to conclude this point debated too long
Nothing should be exaggerated, not even virtue.

That is a faithful summary of my errors;
It is for you to judge, friend, upon this model
If I can, imploring support from the Great,
Have recourse to fortune again today.
Is it time to seek the Luster of Glory
Here I am almost at the end of my sixth Lustrum.
[50]Half of my life has been passed in oblivion,
And already my wits are weary from labor.
Eager for knowledge, eager for wisdom
I have not lavished my youth at all on pleasures
I dared to make a better use of such valuable time
Study and virtue were the only Law
That I proposed to myself to order my conduct:
But one does not acquire merit by art;
What use is an empty labor disdained by heaven
If one always sees oneself far from one's goal?
Counting on securing my fortune by means of my talents
I neglected those efforts, that importunate intrigue,
That subtle stratagem by which a hundred ignoramuses
Steal away the favor and the benefits of the Great.

Success, nevertheless, betrays my confidence
From my feeble progress I feel little hope,
And I see that to judge from such slow effects
Other talents are needed to shine in the world.
Ah! What would I do, I whose timid aspect
Cannot put on that intrepid audacity,
That self-satisfied air, that proud and pretty tone
That rescues the refined man from the rank of Bystanders?
Must I today move into the world then
To vaunt my profound science impudently
And always secretly given the lie by my heart
Lavish on myself the flattery and the ranks of honor?
Will it be necessary, affecting the grimaces of a Devout person,
To make Heaven serve for gaining a place
And assuring my projects by hypocrisy
Swell the happy swarm of those perfect men
Of those humble devout people whose modesty
Recounts their virtues all the days of their life:
To glorify God their mouth has in turn
Some new grace to give each day:

But in vain does the proud man with a Christian cunning
Under the glory of God want to display his own.
The truly sensible man gives the disdain he owes
To the lies of the conceited, and the fool who believes them.

No, I cannot force my mind, born sincere,
To disguise my own Character this way
It would cost too much constraint to my heart
I renounce happiness at that unworthy price.
Moreover, it would then be necessary for a cowardly and mercenary son
Unworthily to betray the kindness of a mother
And, paying as an ingrate for all the benefits received
To leave to other hands the cares that are due to her.
Ah, these cares are too dear to my gratitude
If heaven put nothing more in my power
At least the too well deserved wishes of a pure Zeal
Will be presented to her each day by my heart.
I know too well, it is true, that this useless Zeal
Cannot procure a more tranquil destiny for her.
In vain do I wish to succor her in her languishing
To share it is not to cure it.
Alas the fatal sight of her torments
Will soon stifle the remnants of my courage
It is too much to see her brought by eternal efforts
Both troubles of the soul and pains of the body.
What use to her is it to seek in this solitude
To flee the dazzle of this world and its uneasiness
If, even in this wilderness destined for peace
Fate, relentless to harm her, still gives her
The horrible proximity of a frightful Prosecutor
Nourished by ink and bile, whose terrible claw
Is a hundred times more feared by his sad neighbors
Than the cruel Hussar by the poor Bavarian.

But this is to burden you too much with the account of our troubles:
Deign to pardon me, friend, for these empty complaints;
The last good left to the unfortunate is
To see their woes pitied by generous hearts.

Such is the naïve depiction of my woes.
Judge the future from that Perspective,

See if I still should by impotent efforts
Offer a useless flattery to fortune:
No, glory is not my soul's idol,
I do not feel burning in it that divine flame
Which enlivening the resilience of a fortunate genius
The force to exalt itself by noble efforts.
What does it matter to me, after all, what men think?
Their honors, their disdain, do they make us what we are,
And the one who does not know the art of getting himself admired
To what felicity can he aspire?
Ardent ambition has luster in share
But the pleasures of the heart form the wise man's happiness.
How sweet these pleasures are to the one who can taste them!
Happy the one who knows them and can be content with them!
To enjoy their sweetness in a peaceful station
This is the dearest desire that I feel.
A good Book, a friend, Freedom, peace,
Must other wishes be formed in order to live?
Great passions are the sources of pain:
I avoid the dangers where their inclination drags;
If one sees me fall into their skillful traps
At least I do not make succumbing to them a glory.
My heart is not the accomplice of my going astray
Without being virtuous I detest vice,
And happiness persists in hiding itself in vain,
Since in the end I know where I must seek it.

Quatrain for One of His Portraits

Men learned in the art of feigning
Who lend me such sweet features,
However much you wanted to depict me,
You will never depict anything but yourselves.

The Banterer[1]

As soon as I was informed that the writers who had been charged with examining new works, had, by various accidents, successively resigned their employment, I took it into my head that I could replace them extremely well, and since I do not have the bad vanity of wanting to be modest with the public, I frankly admit that I found myself very capable of it; I even maintain that one should never speak in any other way about oneself unless one is very sure of not being taken in by it. If I were a known author, perhaps I would pretend to reel off some untruths to my disadvantage in order to try skillfully under their cover to put the defects I was forced to admit into the same class: but at present the stratagem would be too dangerous, as a preliminary judgment the reader would infallibly play me the trick of taking everything literally: now I ask my dear colleagues, is that what is due to an author who speaks ill of himself?

I feel very well that it is not quite enough for me to be convinced of my great capacity and that it would be rather necessary for the public to share that conviction halfway: but it is easy for me to show that this reflection, even taken as it must be, turns almost entirely to my profit. For note, I beg you, that if the public does not have any proofs that I am provided with talents suitable for succeeding in the work that I am undertaking, one cannot say, either, that it has any to the contrary. Thus, I already have a considerable advantage over the majority of my competitors; with regard to them truly I am relatively far ahead by all the distance they have gone backward.

Thus I am providing for a favorable prejudice and I am confirming it by sufficient reasons, very capable, in my opinion, of dissipating forever every sort of disadvantageous suspicion on my account.

1st For a great number of years there have been published an infinite number of journals, newspapers, and other periodical works in every country and in every language, and I have applied the most scrupulous attention to never reading any of all that. From which I conclude that, since my head is not at all stuffed with that jargon, I am in a condition to draw from it productions that are much better in themselves, although perhaps in smaller quantity. This reason is good for the public, but I have been forced to reverse it for my publisher by telling him that the judgment engenders more things to the extent that the memory is less burdened with them, and that, therefore, materials would not be lacking to us.

2nd I have not found it appropriate either, and for just about the same reason, to lose much time with the study of the sciences or with that of ancient authors. For a long time systematic Physics has been relegated to the country of Novels, experimental physics does not appear to me to be anything more than the art of nicely arranging pretty baubles,* and Geometry that of

*See M. the Abbé Nolet's collection.[2]

I ask you to fill this lacuna, but in good faith and without skimping.[3]

As to the ancients, it seemed to me that, in the judgments that I would have to bring to bear, probity would not wish me to lead my readers astray as our scholars used to do by substituting, in my opinion fraudulently, for what they would expect, something from Aristotle or Cicero which they have no need to do; thanks to the spirit of our moderns this scandal has ceased for a long time and I will very much keep myself from bringing back its unwelcome fashion. The only thing I have applied myself to is reading Dictionaries and I have profited from it so much that, in less than three months, I have seen myself in a condition to settle everything with as much assurance and authority as if I had studied for two years. In addition, I have acquired a little collection of Latin passages drawn from various Poets, in which I shall find material to embroider and embellish my sheets, by handling them with economy so that they will last for a long time. I have already put one of them at the head of this sheet;[5] I know how much appropriately cited Latin verses enhance a philosopher, and for the same reason I have provided myself with a quantity of philosophic axioms and adages in order to adorn my dissertations when it is a question of Poetry. For I am not unaware that it is an indispensable duty for anyone who aspires to the reputation of a famous Author to speak pertinently about all the sciences, aside from the one with which he is concerned.

Moreover, I do not at all feel the necessity of being extremely learned for judging the works that we are given today. Would one not say that it is necessary to have read Father Petau, Montfaucon, etc. and to be profound in mathematics etc. in order to judge Tanzai, gri gri, Angoba, misapouf, and other sublime productions of this century.[4]

3rd My final reason, and at bottom the only one I need, is drawn from my very object. The aim that I am proposing for myself in the meditated work is to analyze the new works that will be appearing, to add to this my sentiment, and to make both known to the public; now, for all this, I do not see the slightest necessity to be learned; to judge soundly and impartially, to write well, to know one's language; those are, it seems to me, the only sorts of knowledge necessary in such a case: but who boasts about possessing these sorts of knowledge better than I do and to a higher degree? In truth, I could not demonstrate very well that what I am saying is completely true, but precisely because of that I believe it even more strongly: it is impossible to feel too strongly oneself what one wants to persuade others of. Would I then be the first who, as a result of believing himself to be an extremely skillful man, made the public believe it also? And if I succeed in giving it a similar opinion of myself, isn't whether it is well or ill founded just about the same thing for what concerns me in the case at issue?

Thus one cannot deny that I am very justified in raising myself up as an Aristarchus[6] and judging new works in a sovereign manner, praising, blaming, criticizing, at my whim without anyone having the right to accuse me of recklessness, but each and every one can avail themselves of the right of reprisal against me which I grant them very wholeheartedly, desiring only that it please them to speak ill of me in the same manner and in the same sense that I take it into my head to say good.

It is by a consequence of this principle of equity that, not being at all known by those who might become my adversaries, I declare that all personal criticism or observation will be banished from my journal forever: books are the only things that I am going to examine, for me the word "author" will be only the spirit of the book itself, it will not extend beyond and I positively give notice that I shall never make use of it in any other sense; so that if in my days of ill humor I sometimes happen to say: there is a fool, an impertinent writer, it is the work alone that will be accused of impertinence and foolishness, and I in no way understand its author to be any less of a genius of the first order, and perhaps even a worthy academician. How do I know, for example, whether someone will not take it into his head to treat my sheets with the epithets about which I just spoke: now one sees very well right away that I will not cease, for that, to be a man of much merit.

Since everything that I have said up to the present would appear a little vague if I did not add anything to set forth more clearly my plan and the manner in which I propose to execute it, I am going to warn my reader about certain peculiarities of my character that will inform him about what he can expect to find in my writings.

When Boileau said about man in general that he changed from white to black,[7] he sketched my portrait in two words; as an individual, he would have made it more precise if he had added to it all the other colors along with the intermediate nuances. Nothing is so dissimilar to me as myself, that is why it would be useless to attempt to define me other than by that singular variety; it is such in my mind that it even influences my feelings from time to time. Sometimes I am a harsh and fierce misanthrope, at other moments, I go into ecstasy in the midst of the charms of society and the delights of love. Sometimes I am austere and devout, and for the good of my soul I make every effort to make these holy dispositions last: but soon I become a frank libertine, and since I then occupy myself much more with my senses than with my reason, I constantly abstain from writing in those moments: this is what it is good for my readers to be adequately forewarned about, out of fear that they not expect to find in my sheets things that they certainly will never see there. In a word, a Proteus, a Chameleon, a woman, are less fickle beings than I am. Which from the beginning ought to deprive the curious of all hope of recognizing me someday from my character: for they will always find me under some particular form that will not be mine except during that moment; and they cannot even hope to recognize me from these changes, for since they have no fixed period, they sometimes happen from one moment to another, and at other times I shall remain in the same condition for entire months. It is this very irregularity that makes the basis of my constitution. Much more; the return of the same objects usually renews in me dispositions similar to those in which I found myself the first time that I saw them. That is why I am rather consistently in the same mood with the same people. So that, to listen separately to all those who know me, nothing would appear less varied than my character: but proceed to the final clarifications, one will tell you that I am playful, the other, serious, this one will take me for an ignoramus, the other for an extremely learned man; in a word, as many heads as opinions: I find myself so bizarrely disposed in this regard that, one day being accosted by two people at the same time, with one of whom I had been accustomed to be gay to the point of madness, and more gloomy than a follower of Heraclitus with the other, I felt myself so powerfully unsettled that I was constrained to leave them abruptly out of fear that the contrast of opposite passions might make me fall in a faint.

With all that; as a result of examining myself, I have not failed to unravel in myself certain dominant dispositions and certain almost periodic repetitions that would be difficult to note for anyone other than the most attentive observer, in a word for myself: it is just about the same way that all the vicissitudes and irregularities of the air do not keep sailors and inhabitants of the country from noting some annual circumstances and some phenomena that they have reduced to a rule in order to predict approximately the weather that will occur in certain seasons. I am subject, for example, to two principal dispositions which change rather consistently every eight days and which I call my weekly souls, from one I find myself wisely mad, by the other madly wise, but in such a manner nevertheless that, since the madness overshadows the wisdom in both cases, it manifestly has the upper hand particularly during the week in which I call myself wise, for then, the basis of all the material that I am treating, however reasonable it might be in itself, is found almost entirely absorbed by the futilities and extravagances in which I am always careful to dress it up. As for my mad soul, it is much wiser than that, for although it always draws the text about which it is arguing from its own depths, it puts so much art, so much order, and so much force into its reasoning and into its proofs that a madness disguised this way is in almost no way different from wisdom. Based on these ideas, which I guarantee to be precise, or almost so, I find a small puzzle to propose to my readers and I urge them to be good enough to decide which of my two souls it is that has dictated this sheet.

Thus do not at all expect to see only wise and serious dissertations here, doubtless one will see some of them, otherwise where would the variety be: but I do not at all guarantee that in the midst of the most profound metaphysics I might not be taken suddenly by an extravagant flash of wit, and, putting my reader into the icosaèdre,[8] I might suddenly transport him to the moon. Just as on the subject of Ariosto and the hypogriff, I could extremely well cite Plato, Locke, or Malebranche to him.[9]

What is more; all matters will be within my competence, I spread out my jurisdiction indiscriminately over everything that will leave the press, when the case arises I shall even arrogate to myself the right of revision over my colleagues' judgments; and not satisfied with subjecting to myself all the printing houses of France, I also propose from time to time making some good excursions outside of the Kingdom, and to make tributary to me Italy, Holland, and even England each in its turn, promising, traveler's faith, the most precise veracity in the proceedings that I will be reporting about them.

Although doubtless the reader cares rather little about the details that I am giving him here about myself and my character, I have resolved not to spare him a single line of them, I am acting this way as much for his profit as for my convenience. After having begun by bantering about myself I shall have all the time to banter about others, I shall open eyes: I shall write what I see, and one will find that I shall have acquitted myself of my task rather well.

It remains for me to apologize in advance to the Authors that I might wrongly treat badly, and to the public for all the unjust praises that I could give to the works that are presented to it. I will never commit such errors voluntarily; I know that, in a journalist, impartiality serves only to make enemies for him out of all authors for not having said to the taste of each of them enough good about him or enough bad about his colleagues: it is for that reason that I want always to remain unknown, my great madness is to want to consult only reason and to speak only the truth: so that, following the extent of my intelligence and the dispositions of my mind, one will find in me sometimes an amusing and playful critic, sometimes a severe and surly censor, not a bitter satirist nor a puerile adulator. The judgments can be false, but the judge will never be iniquitous.

I urge you, my dear fellow, to read this privately, and to correct it before having it read to those gentlemen.[10]

Biographical Fragment[1]

How many prejudices and errors and evils did I begin to notice in everything that causes men's admiration, this view touched me with pain and inflamed my courage, I believed that I felt myself animated by a finer zeal than that of amour-propre, I took up the pen and, having resolved to forget myself, I consecrated its productions to the service of truth and virtue.

This resolution seemed to inspire me with genius and a new soul. The lively persuasion that dictated my writings gave them a warmth that sometimes was able to take the place of force of reasoning; exalted me, so to speak, above myself by the sublimity of my subject, I was like those lawyers, more famous than eloquent, who are taken for great orators because they plead great cases, or rather like those evangelical preachers who preach artlessly but who move because they are moved. What makes the majority of modern books so cold along with so much wit, is that the authors do not believe anything they say, and do not even care about making others believe it. They want to shine and not convince; they have only one object, which is reputation, and if they believed that a sentiment opposed to theirs might lead them to it more surely none of them would hesitate to change it. But saying what one thinks is always a great advantage for speaking well, good faith serves as rhetoric, honesty as talent, and nothing is more similar to eloquence than the tone of a man who is strongly persuaded.

I was attacked from all directions and how would I not have been? I had had some success in the world and treated the learned people badly. Moreover people were so accustomed to confusing wisdom with knowledge that even good people were alarmed at seeing what they had admired for such a long time being accused. Zeal for virtue put the pen into one of those redoubtable hands that held the sword; the same zeal made me take it up again in my turn. As a Philosopher a great Prince deigned to attack me, I dared to respond as a free man, happy at doing good with so little risk. What would it cost to tell the truth to Kings, if it cost them so little to listen to it?[2]

Nevertheless the dispute flared up in the public; my adversaries multiplied. I was weighed down with refutations without ever being refuted, because the truth is not refuted. One can hardly conceive the thoughtlessness with which a crowd of authors vied with each other in taking up the pen and turned over three or four commonplaces from school in a thousand manners; neither reasoning nor reflection was ever seen in their writings, while they believed they were uniting against me, they did nothing but destroy each other, the proofs of one would haved served me as a reply to the other and it would have been enough for me to put them in opposition to each other to defeat them. A single one deserves to be excepted.[3] He knew how to think and wrote well, he took a position in the quarrel, he published—not against me as the others did, but against my sentiment—two discourses full of intelligence and perspectives and very pleasant to read, but it is certain that in that he did nothing but graft his genius onto his prejudices and give a fine coloring to vulgar errors.

I responded with all the warmth given by love of the truth and, if one wants, the zeal for our own opinions to people of bad faith whose interest makes them speak against their intelligence. I wondered how anyone could write with so little discretion and no reflection about matters that I had meditated about almost my whole life without having been able to clarify them adequately, and I was always surprised not to find in my adversaries' writings a single objection that I had not seen and rejected in advance as unworthy of attention. I let my disdain be seen in my replies, and I defended the truth with an anger little worthy of such a good cause; at least I did not imitate my adversaries in their personal attacks, and I did not return invectives to them for the ones they lavished on me, I always limited myself to showing that they were reasoning badly. But restrict myself to my subject as I might, I could never lead them back to it; they always found it more to their advantage to attack my person than my reasons or they quite lost themselves in vague declamations that had nothing to do with the subject and the dispute ended without my ever having been able to lead any of them back to the genuine state of the question.

While the crowd of fine wits and artists troubled themselves over this quarrel in a puerile manner, as if wealth and idleness could do without their talents and as if it were a question of morals in such a corrupt age, while Philosophers, who were not afraid that true genius might ever stop shining, digested these new questions in secret, I made efforts to go more deeply into them and to go back to the unique and fundamental principle that ought to serve to resolve them. I studied man in himself and I finally saw or believed I saw in his constitution the true System of nature which they have not failed to call mine, although in order to establish it I did not do anything but take away from man what I showed that he had given himself: but I did not at all rush to develop these new perspectives, the example of my adversaries taught me how necessary it is to reflect and to meditate before producing and I have always believed that it is a sort of respect that authors owe to the public never to speak to it until after having thought out well what they have to say. Thus for two or three years I enjoyed the pleasure of seeing them ceaselessly watering the leaves of the tree whose root I had secretly cut.

. . . and even more the conversations of that virtuous Philosopher whose friendship already immortalized in his writings constitutes the glory and the happiness of my life, of this genius, astonishing, universal, and perhaps unique whose age is unaware of his value but in which the future will find it hard to see a mere man . . .[4]

[But it is necessary to cast the veil of forgetfulness over these moments of error and to keep oneself from imputing to a hospitable and decent nation the delirium of some madmen. As for me how could I be sorry about having spoken about French Music with no more respect than I had about the sciences, Philosophers, the great, and even sovereigns, for not having abandoned the veracious and frank tone that nature gave me in order to take on that of a devotee of the opera of Paris.[5] How, I say, with the respect that I owe to the French people, could I ever think that it wanted to make common cause with a band of buffoons consecrated to the eternal jeering of all foreigners and three-quarters of the French, their compatriots? How would I believe that a People that shines with so much enlightenment, that possesses so many estimable talents, that enriches Europe with so many immortal Writings, and whose society appears preferable to me to that of the rest of men could have believed its glory to be at stake in the pretensions of a music that is unbearable even to those who hold its language in admiration and of a talent that is refused to it at the same time, by that same language, reason, nature, the ear, and the unanimous judgment of all the peoples of the world?

I know how to distinguish the honor of the French name, from both the low interests of the Buffoons and opera writers, and the vanity of women and young people who pride themselves in excelling in a ridiculous song. I shall never think, and although French urbanity might have forgotten itself rather harshly with regard to me more than once . . .]

[At just about the same time I had the misfortune to find myself implicated in a contention of a complete different consequence for my repose and all the more dangerous since its subject was more frivolous. It was a question of Music, a matter more important than all philosophy among people who sing more than they reason. As for myself I was certainly in that position, and I admit to my shame that for my whole life I have been occupied with music much more than is suitable for a wise man and that art of rendering feelings by sounds has always inspired in me a passion that well deserved to be punished and moderated by a little uneasiness. From my childhood I loved French Music, the only one that I knew, in Italy I heard Music and I loved it more without taking a dislike to the other, the preference was always for the one that I heard last. It was only after having heard both the same day in the same Theater that the illusion disappeared and I felt how much habit can fascinate nature and make us find good what is bad and beautiful what is horrible. Nevertheless, I heard it said that each language has its harmony, its accent, its sounds, and a music that is suited to it; and that was the discourse of the wisest people, for to the liking of the others there was no bearable music other than the French. Very astonished at not finding French arias in Italian song, the great number reasoned like that bourgeois of Molière who believed that the whole secret of the languages that he does not understand is to speak words that have no sense.]

I know how difficult it is to protect oneself against the illusions of the heart and not to lead oneself astray over the motives that make us act. I am simply giving an account of what I believed I felt, without affirming that vanity has not imposed on me in it, but I have always regarded as hardly dangerous all the emotions that are brought to us only by decent things and that make us do with pleasure what we would do equally from the purest intentions.

of those idle people with whom Paris abounds, who by inaction make themselves into the arbiters of the beautiful which they have never felt, pass their life in being occupied with Music without loving it, with painting without knowing anything about it, and taking for taste for the arts, the vanity of being adulated by flatterers and of shining in the eyes of fools.

It was just about at the same time that I had the misfortune of finding myself implicated in a contention of a completely different consequence for my tranquillity and all the more dangerous since its subject was more frivolous. The taste for an art which I had loved and cultivated more than is suitable for a wise man, and in which I believed I had made some discoveries made me speak about Music and mountebanks with the same freedom as about science and the Learned, about government and Kings.

But I soon learned at the risk of my repose, my life, and my freedom, that there are times and places in which trifles ought to be treated more circumspectly than serious things, and that in general the intolerance of bad taste is hardly less cruel than that of false Religions. It is necessary to cast the veil of forgetfulness over these moments of error and keep oneself from imputing to a hospitable and decent nation the delirium of some madmen. I know how to distinguish the honor of the French name from the base interest of Buffoons, and Opera writers, and from the vanity of some women and young people who prided themselves at excelling in a ridiculous song. Although French urbanity might have forgotten itself in my regard for several moments, I shall never think that such a gentle People, who shine with so much enlightenment, who possess so many estimable talents, who enrich Europe with so many immortal works, and whose society appears to me preferable to that of the rest of men could have believed its glory concerned by the pretensions of a Music unbearable to every ear that was not predisposed, and by a talent that is refused to it at the same time by its own language, reason, nature, the ear, and the unanimous judgment of all the peoples of the world.

On the occasion of that *Letter on French Music,* the public saw itself inundated with polemical writings of a new sort. I soon became acquainted with the difference there was between this quarrel and the preceding one, and between the tone of Literary People and that of Musicians. I kept myself from returning to a dispute in which it was a question of everything, aside from the question, and which appeared to me more in the jurisdiction of public order than of reasoning. In fact, how could I prove to others that I was not a fool, a conceited fellow, a dunce, an ignoramus, I who would have been extremely perplexed to prove it well to myself.

Among all these lampoons there appeared some pamphlets that the enemies of a Famous Artist dared to attribute to him: One among others which contained some truths, and whose title began with these words, *Errors on Music.*[6] In it the Author (doubtless some bad joker) rather mischievously criticizes the obscurity of the writings of that great Musician. He reproaches me, as if for a crime, for making myself understood, he gives that clarity as a proof of my ignorance, and gives as a proof of M. Rameau's great knowledge, his obscure arguments, all the more useful, according to the author, as fewer people understand them. From which it follows that the Philosopher who has deigned to make evident the system so learnedly concealed in M. Rameau's writings does not display any less ignorance in his luminous elements of music than I do in my articles for the *Encyclopedia.*[7] In following this maxim one can say that the author of the pamphlet surpasses M. Rameau himself in knowledge and surpasses Rabelais in capacity from the most unintelligible gibberish that any ill-formed head ever produced. Nevertheless at intervals in it several interesting questions are set forth, for example, this one *whether melody is born from harmony* and this other one *whether the accompaniment ought to represent the sonorous body*. Questions which, better treated, would seem to announce some perspectives and which I shall have the occasion to examine in my *Dictionary of Music*.

What ought invincibly to clear M. Rameau of having any part in the banter of this pamphlet, where in order to hold him up to ridicule they pretend to have him ceaselessly praised by himself, is an old fact that is cited in it about my Opera the *Gallant Muses* and the memory of which it is to be believed that he would keep himself from recalling. At least I do not know whether he is humble enough to speak about it himself, what I do know, is that the work and the witnesses still exist; as for myself I have forgotten everything.[8]

That is too much about songs, let us return to more serious things; so many ceaselessly reborn quarrels inspired me with reflections which it might have been better to make sooner but which finally had their effect even though belatedly. What did I see in that hailstorm of writings that were thrown against me every day? ceaseless invectives and clumsy pleading in which Literary people maintained that literature is the support of the State, French Musicians that nothing is as beautiful as French Music, writers for the French Opera that French opera is the masterpiece of the human mind, and in which, shamelessly and unrestrainedly, self-interest and animosity did not even deign to borrow the mask of verisimilitude in order to impose on the public. I saw that in all literary disputes it is never a question of being right but of speaking last nor of truth but of victory, and that some scribbler whom his adversary does not deign even to look at does not fail to put himself in the ranks less to combat than to be in view for a moment.

My Portrait[1]

1

Readers, I willingly think about myself and I am speaking as I think. Dispense yourself then from reading this preface if you do not like anyone to talk about himself.

2

I am approaching the end of life and I have not done any good on earth. I have good intentions, but it is not always as easy as one thinks to do good. I conceive a new sort of service to render to men: it is to offer them the faithful image of one among them so that they might learn to know themselves.

3

I am an observer and not a moralist. I am the Botanist who describes the plant. It is up to the doctor to regulate the usage.

4

But I am poor and when I am on the verge of lacking bread I do not know any more honest means for having it than to live from my own work.[2]

There are many readers who will be kept from continuing by this idea alone. They will not conceive that a man who needs bread might be worthy of being known. It is not for them that I am writing.

5

I am well enough known for what I am saying to be easily verified, and for my book to protest against me if I am lying.

6

I see that the people who live most intimately with me do not know me, and that they attribute the majority of my actions, either for good or for evil, to completely different motives than the ones that produced them. This made me think that the majority of character studies and portraits that one finds in the historians are only chimeras that, with intelligence, an author easily makes credible and that he inscribes upon a man's principal actions just as a painter adjusts an imaginary face upon the five points.

7

It is impossible for a man ceaselessly moving about in society and endlessly occupied with disguising himself with others not to disguise himself a little with himself and, if he had the time to study himself, it would be almost impossible for him to know himself.

8

If even Princes are depicted with some uniformity by historians, it is not, as is thought, because they are in view and easy to know; but because the first who depicted them is copied by all the others. There is hardly any likelihood that Livia's son resembled the Tiberius of Tacitus, nevertheless that is the way that we all see him, and one prefers to see a beautiful portrait than a good likeness.

9

All copies from the same original resemble each other, but have the same face drawn by various painters, all these portraits will have hardly the slightest relation to each other; are they all good, or which is the true one? Judge about portraits of the soul.

10

They claim that one speaks of oneself out of vanity. Well then, if this feeling is in me why would I hide it? Is it out of vanity that one shows one's vanity? Perhaps I would find favor before modest people, but it is the vanity of readers that is going to introduce subtleties about mine.

11

If I depart from the rule for a moment, I move a hundred leagues away from it. If I touch the purse that I saved up with so much difficulty, soon all is squandered.

12

For what purpose was that good to say? To make the most of the rest, to put harmony into the whole; the features of the face make their effect only because they are all there; if one of them is lacking, the face is disfigured. When I write, I do not think about that ensemble, I think only about saying what I know and that is from what results the ensemble and the resemblance of the whole to its original.

13

I am persuaded that it matters to the human race that my book be respected. In truth I believe that it is impossible to act too honestly toward its author. One must not chastise men for speaking sincerely about themselves. Moreover the honesty that I am demanding is not painful. If one never speaks to me about my book I shall be satisfied. Which will not keep everyone from being able to say to the public what he thinks about it, for I shall not read a word of all that. I have the right to believe myself capable of that restraint; it will not be my apprenticeship.

14

I do not care at all about being noticed, but when I am noticed I am not sorry for it to be in a slightly distinctive manner, and I would prefer to be forgotten by the whole human race than regarded as an ordinary man.

15

On that point I have an unanswerable reply to make; it is that from the manner in which I am known in the world I have less to gain than to lose in showing myself as I am. Even if I did want to set myself off to good advantage, I pass for so singular a man that, since everyone takes pleasure in amplifying, I have only to rest myself upon the public voice; it will serve me better than my own praises. Thus, consulting nothing but my own interest, it would be more clever to let others speak about me than to speak about me myself. But perhaps by another return of amour-propre I prefer for less good to be said about me and that I be spoken about more. Now if I let the public, which has spoken so much about me, act, it would be much to be feared that soon it would no longer speak about me.*

16

I do not let others off any more than I do myself; for, not being able to depict myself realistically without depicting them, I shall be acting, if you please, like devout Catholics, I shall make my confession for them and for me.

17

Moreover, I shall not wear myself out by protesting my sincerity: if it is not perceived in this work, if it does not testify for it by itself, it must be believed that it is not there.

18

I was made to be the best friend that ever was, but the one who should have responded to me has yet to come. Alas, I am at an age at which the heart begins to shut itself and no longer opens itself to new friends. Farewell then, sweet feeling that I have sought so much, it is too late to be happy.

19

I have been a little acquainted with the tone of societies, the matters treated there and the manner of treating them. Where is the great marvel at passing one's life in idle conversations by subtly discussing the pro and the con and by establishing a moral skepticism that makes the choice of vice and of virtue indifferent to men?

20

For the wicked, hell is to be reduced to living alone with oneself, but that is the good man's paradise, and there is no spectacle more agreeable for him than the one of his own conscience.

* That is plausible, but I do not feel it clearly.[3]

21

A proof that I have less amour-propre than other men or that mine is made in another manner is the facility that I have at living alone. Whatever they say about it, one seeks to see the world only in order to be seen by it, and I believe that one can always estimate the importance a man sets on the approval of others by his eagerness at seeking it. It is true that one is very careful to cover the motive for the eagerness with the paint of fine words, society, duties, humanity. I believe that it would be easy to prove that the man who takes himself away from society the most is the one who harms it the least and that the greatest of its inconveniences is to be too numerous.

22

The civil man wants others to be satisfied with him, the solitary is forced to be so with himself or his life is unbearable to him. Thus the second is forced to be virtuous, but the first can be only a hypocrite, and perhaps he is forced to become one if it is true that the appearances of virtue are worth more than its practice for pleasing men and making one's way among them. Those who will want to discuss the point can cast their eyes on the speech of[4]   in the second book of Plato's Republic. What does Socrates do to refute this speech? He establishes an ideal Republic in which he proves very well that each will be estimated in proportion to how estimable he will be and that the most just will also be the happiest. Good people who are seeking out society, go then to live in Plato's. But may all those who are pleased to live among the wicked not flatter themselves for being good.

23

I believe that there is no man upon whose virtue one could count less than the one who most seeks out the approval of others; it is easy, I admit, to say that one does not care about it; but on this point what a man says must be relied upon less than what he does.

24

In all this I am not speaking about myself, for I am solitary only because I am sick and lazy; it is almost certain that if I were healthy and active I would act as the others do.

25

Perhaps this house contains a man made to be my friend. Perhaps a person worthy of my homage takes a walk in this park every day.

26

They are always ready for money or services; I might well refuse or receive poorly, they are never rebuffed and ceaselessly importune me with solicitations that are unbearable to me. I am overwhelmed with things that I do not care about at all. The only ones that they refuse me are the only ones that would be sweet for me. A sweet feeling, a tender effusion is yet to come from their direction and one would say that they lavished their fortune and their time in order to economize their heart.

27

Since they never speak to me about themselves, I must speak to them about myself for all I can do.

28

So many other bonds chain them, so many people console them for me that they did not even notice my absence; if they complained about it, it is not that they suffer from it, but it is that they know well that I suffer from it myself and[5] that they do not see[6] that[7] it is less hard for me to regret them in the country than to not be able to enjoy them in the city.

29

I acknowledge as true benefits only those that can contribute to my happiness and it is for those that I am full of gratitude; but certainly money and gifts do not contribute to it, and when I give way to the lengthy importunities of an offer repeated a hundred times, it is a discomfort with which I burden myself in order to get some peace rather than an advantage that I am procuring for myself. Of whatever value a present offered might be and whatever it costs the one who is offering it, since it costs me even more to accept it, the one from whom it comes is indebted to me, it is up to him not to be an ingrate; it is true that this assumes that my poverty is not at all onerous to me and that I do not seek out benefactors and benefits; these feelings which I have always loudly professed will bear witness to what is the case. As for genuine friendship, that is a completely different thing. What does it matter which one of two friends gives or receives, and that the common goods pass from one hand to another, they remember that they love each other and everything is said, they can forget all the rest. I admit that such a principle is rather convenient when one is poor and one has rich friends. But there is this difference between my rich and poor friends, that the former have sought me out and I have sought out the others. It is up to the former to make me forget their opulence. Why would I flee a friend in opulence when he knows how to make me forget it; is it not enough that I slip away from him at the moment I remember it?

30

I do not even like to ask for the street where I have to go, because in that I am depending on the one who is going to answer me. I prefer to wander for two hours uselessly searching for it; I carry a map of Paris in my pocket with the aid of which and of glasses I find my bearings in the end, I arrive covered with mud, worn out, often too late but completely consoled at owing nothing to anyone but myself.

31

I count past suffering for nothing, but I still enjoy a pleasure that no longer exists. I appropriate only the present pain, and my past labors seem so alien to me, that, when I take away the price for it, it seems to me that I am enjoying someone else's labor. What is bizarre in that is that if someone seizes hold of the fruit of my efforts all my amour-propre is awakened, I feel the privation of what they have deprived me of more than I would have felt its possession if they had left it to me; to my personal harm is joined my rage against all injustice, and to be unjust toward me is, to the taste of my anger, to be doubly unjust.

32

Insensitive to covetousness, I am extremely attached to possession; I do not care at all about acquiring but I cannot bear losing, and that is true in friendship as well as in possessions.

33

... From certain states of soul that depend, not only on the events of my life, but also on the objects that had been most familiar to me during these events. So that I could not recall one of these states without at the same time feeling my imagination being modified in the same manner that my senses and my being were when I experienced it.

34

The readings that I made while I was sick no longer gratify me in health. It is an unpleasant local memory that brings back to me, along with the ideas of the Book, those of the ills that I suffered while reading it. For having leafed through Montaigne during an attack of the stone, I can no longer read him with pleasure in my moments of respite. It torments my imagination more than it satisfies my mind. This experience makes me so foolishly restrained that out of fear of depriving myself of a comforter I refuse them all, and, when I am suffering, almost no longer dare to read any of the books I love.

35

I never do anything except while taking a walk, while in the country and while in my dressing room; the sight of a table, some paper, and books bores me, the apparatus of labor discourages me, if I sit down to write I find nothing and the necessity of having wit deprives me of it. I throw my scattered and disconnected thoughts on scraps of paper, afterward I stitch all that together somehow or other and that is how I write a book. Judge what a book! I have pleasure in meditating, seeking, inventing, the distaste is in putting into order and the proof that I have less reasoning than intelligence is that the transitions are always what costs me the most, that does not happen for me if the ideas are well linked in my head. Otherwise my natural obstinacy makes me struggle intentionally against this difficulty, I have always wanted to give some sequence to all my writings and this is the first work that I have divided by chapters.[8]

36

I remember having been present once in my life at the death of a stag, and I also remember that, at this noble spectacle, I was struck less by the joyous fury of the dogs, the beast's natural enemies, than by that of the men who were striving to imitate them. As for me, upon considering the final yelps of that unfortunate animal and its affecting tears, I felt how plebian nature is, and I promised myself firmly that I would never again be seen at such a festival.

37

It is not impossible for an author to be a great man, but it will never be by writing books either in verse or in prose that he will become such.

38

Never were Homer or Virgil called great men although they were very great Poets. During my life some authors wore themselves out calling the Poet Rousseau the great Rousseau. When I am dead the Poet Rousseau will be a great Poet. But he will no longer be the great Rousseau. For if it is not impossible for an author to be a great man, it is not by writing books either in verse or in prose that he will become such.

Response to the Letters Written From the Mountain *Published at Geneva, under this title:* Sentiment of the Citizens[1]

LETTER FROM J. J. ROUSSEAU TO THE BOOKSELLER

From Môtiers, January 6, 1765

I am sending you Sir, a Piece printed and made public at Geneva and which I am urging you to print and publish in Paris, so as to put the Public in a condition to hear the two Parties, while waiting for the other more crushing Responses that are being prepared against me at Geneva. This one is by M. Vernes, Minister of the Holy Gospel, and Pastor at Séligny: I recognized it at first from its pastoral style. If, however, I am mistaken, it is necessary only to wait in order to become clear about it; for if he is its Author, he will not fail to acknowledge it loudly in accordance with the duty of a man of honor and a good Christian; if he is not, he will disavow it in the same way, and the Public will soon know what to make of it.

I know you too well, Sir, to believe that you would want to print such a Piece, if it came to you from another hand: but since I am the one who is urging you, you ought not to make any scruple for yourself about it. I salute you with all my heart,

Rousseau.

Sentiment of the Citizens

After the Letters from the Country,[2] have come those from the Mountain. Here are the sentiments of the City.

One has pity for a madman; but when dementia turns into rage, one ties him up. Tolerance, which is a virtue, would then be a vice.

We have pitied Jean-Jacques Rousseau, formerly Citizen of our City,[3] as long as he limited himself, in Paris, to the unfortunate profession of a Buffoon who received snubs at the Opera and someone prostituted him walking on four paws on the Comic Stage.[4] In truth these disgraces fell back, in some fashion, upon us: it was sad, for a Genevan arriving in Paris, to see himself humiliated by the shame of a Compatriot. Some of us warned him, and did not correct him. We pardoned his Novels, in which decency and modesty were spared as little as good sense was. Previously our City was known only from pure morals and from some solid Works that attracted Foreigners to our Academy: this is the first time that one of our Citizens made it known from Books which shock morals, which decent people despise, and which piety condemns.

When he mixed irreligion into his Novels, our Magistrates were indispensably obliged to imitate those of Paris and of Bern,[a] from which the first issued a warrant for him, and the others expelled him. But the Council of Geneva, still listening to its compassion in its justice, left a door open for the repentance of a wild guilty man who might return to his Fatherland and deserve its clemency there.

Today is patience not worn out when he dares to publish a new Lampoon in which he insults, with rage, the Christian Religion, the Reformation which he professes, all the Ministers of the holy Gospel, and all the Bodies of the State? Dementia can no longer serve as an excuse when it causes crimes to be committed.

He might well say at present: recognize my malady of the brain from my inconsistencies and my contradictions. It will not remain any less true that this madness has pushed him to the point of insulting Jesus Christ, to the point of publishing that *the Gospel is a scandalous, reckless, impious Book, whose morality is to teach children to repudiate their mothers and their brothers, etc.*[5] I shall not repeat the other words: they make one shudder. He believes he is disguising their horror by putting them into the mouth of a Contradictor; but he does not respond to this imaginary Contradictor at all. There never was one forsaken enough to make these disgraceful objections, and to twist so wickedly the natural and divine sense of our Savior's Parables. *Picture an infernal soul analyzing the Gospel this way.* Eh! Who has ever analyzed it this way? Where is that infernal soul?[b] La Métrie,[6] in his Man a Machine, says that he knew a dangerous Atheist, whose arguments he relates without refuting them: one sees

[a] I was expelled from the Canton of Bern only one month after the warrant issued by Geneva.

[b] It appears that the Author of this Piece could respond to his question better than anyone. I urge the Reader not to fail to consult what precedes and what follows in the place that he cites.

well enough who that Atheist is; assuredly one is not allowed to spread such poisons without presenting the antidote.

It is true that, in this very place, Rousseau compares himself to Jesus Christ with the same humility that he said that we ought to erect a statue to him. It is known that this comparison is one of the fits of madness. But can a madness that blasphemes to this point have any other Doctor than the same hand that has done justice to his other scandals?

If, in his obscure style, he believed he was preparing an excuse for his blasphemies, by attributing them to an imaginary Police Informer, he can have none for the manner in which he speaks of the miracles of our Savior. He says clearly, in his own name: *there are some Miracles in the Gospel, that it is not possible to take Literally without renouncing good sense.*[7] He turns to ridicule all the wonders that Jesus deigned to operate in order to establish Religion.

Here we admit again the dementia that he has in calling himself a Christian, when he is undermining the first foundation of Christianity; but this madness only makes him more criminal. To be a Christian and to want to destroy Christianity is to be not only a Blasphemer, but a Traitor.

After having insulted Jesus Christ, it is not surprising that he shows disrespect to the Ministers of his holy Gospel.

He calls one of their professions of faith a *Piece of Nonsense*,[8] a low term, and from slang, which signifies unreason. He compares their declarations to Rabelais's Speakers for the defense; they do not know, he says, either what they believe, or what they want, or what they are saying.

We know neither what they believe nor what they do not believe, nor what they pretend to believe.[9]

There he is then accusing them of the blackest hypocrisy, without the slightest proof, without the slightest pretext. This is how he treats those who have pardoned him for his first Apostasy,[10] and who did not have the slightest share in the punishment of the second, when his blasphemies, poured out in a bad Novel, were given over to the Executioner. Is there a single Citizen among us who, in thinking coolly about this behavior, is not indignant against the Calumniator?

Is a man born in our City allowed to offend to this point our Pastors, the majority of whom are our relatives and our friends, and who are sometimes our consolers? Let us consider who is treating them this way; is it a Scholar who is disputing against Scholars? No, it is the Author of an Opera and of two Comedies that were hissed at. Is it a good man who, deceived by a false zeal, is making indiscreet reproaches to virtuous men? We admit with pain, and while blushing, that this is a man who still bears the fatal marks of his debaucheries, and who, disguised as a mountebank, drags with him from Village to Village, and from Mountain to Mountain, the unfortunate woman whose mother he caused to die, and whose children he exposed at the door of a hospital, while rejecting the cares that a charitable person wished to have for them, and while abjuring all the feelings of Nature, as he casts off those of honor and religion.[a]

There, then, is the one who dares to give advice to our Fellow Citizens! [We shall soon see what advice.] There, then, is the one who talks about the duties of society!

Certainly he does not fulfill these duties when, in the same Lampoon, betraying a friend's confidence,[b] he has one of his Letters printed[12] in order to set three Pastors against each other. It is here that one can say, along with one of the foremost men of Europe, about this same Writer, Author of a Novel of Education, that in order to bring up a young man, it is necessary to begin by having been well brought up.[c]

Let us come to what regards us in particular, our city, which he would like to turn upside down because he has been given a Judicial reprimand there. In what spirit does he remind us of our assuaged disturbances? Why does he reawaken our old quarrels and speak to us about our misfortunes? Does he want us to slaughter each other[d] because a bad Book

[a] I wish to make the declaration that this item seems to require of me with simplicity. Never has any malady among those about which the Author is speaking here, either small or great, ever sullied my body. The one with which I am afflicted does not have the slightest relation to them: it was born with me, as is known by Persons still living who took care of my childhood. This malady is known to Messieurs Malouin, Morand, Thyerri, Daran, Brother Come. If there is found in it the slightest mark of debauchery, I urge them to confound me, and to put me to shame for my motto. The modest and generally esteemed Person who tends to me in my illnesses and consoles me in my afflictions, is unfortunate only because she shares the fate of an extremely unfortunate man; her mother is at present full of life, and in good health in spite of her old age. I have never exposed, nor caused to be exposed any child at the door of any hospital, or elsewhere. A Person who would have had the charity that is being talked about, would have had that of keeping its secret; and everyone feels that it is not from Geneva, where I have not lived at all, and from where so much animosity is poured out against me, that one should expect faithful information about my behavior. I shall add nothing about this passage, other than that, aside from murder, I would rather have done what this Author is accusing me of, than to have written such a passage.[11]

[b] I believe I ought to notify the Public that the Theologian who wrote the Letter from which I gave an extract is not, nor ever was my friend; that I have seen him only once in my life, and that he does not have the slightest bone to pick, either for good, or for bad with the Ministers of Geneva. This notice appeared to me to be necessary in order to prevent reckless applications.

[c] Everyone will grant, I think, to the Author of this Piece, that he and I do not have the same education any more than we have the same Religion.

[d] One can see, in my behavior, the painful sacrifices that I have made so as not to disturb the peace of my Fatherland, and in my Work, with what force I exhort the Citizens never to disturb it, whatever the extremity to which they are reduced.

has been burned at Paris and Geneva? When our freedom and our rights will be in danger, we shall defend them well without him. It is ridiculous that a man of his sort, who is no longer our Fellow Citizen, might say to us:

You are neither Spartans, nor Athenians; you are Merchants, Artisans, Bourgeois, occupied with your private interests and your gain.[13] We were nothing different, when we resisted Philip II and the Duke of Savoy; we acquired our freedom by means of our courage and at the price of our blood, and we shall maintain it the same way.

Let him stop calling us *Slaves*,[14] we never shall be. He calls Tyrants, the Magistrates of our Republic, the first of which are elected by ourselves. He says, *In the Council of the Two Hundred little enlightenment and even less courage has always been seen.*[15] By means of these accumulated lies, he seeks to stir up the Two Hundred against the Small Council; the Pastors against these two Bodies; and finally, all against all, in order to expose us to the disdain and the mockery of our neighbors. Does he want to enliven us by insulting us? Does he want to overturn our Constitution by disfiguring it, as he wants to overturn Christianity, the profession of which he dares to make? It is enough to give notice that the City that he wants to disturb, disavows him with horror. If he believed that we would draw the sword for the Novel of Emile, he can put that idea into the number of his absurdities and his follies. But he must be taught that, if one lightly chastises an impious Novelist, one punishes capitally a low seditious person.

Post-scriptum of a Work by Citizens of Geneva, entitled: *Response to to the Letters written from the Country.*

Several days ago there appeared a Brochure of eight pages in octavo, under the title of *Sentiment of the Citizens;* no one was deceived by it. It would be beneath the Citizens to clear themselves of such a production. In conformity with Article 3. of title XI or the Edict, they have thrown it into the fire as an infamous Libel.

END.

Notes for the Reveries[1]

1

In order to fulfill the title of this collection well I should have begun sixty years ago: for my entire life has hardly been anything but a long reverie divided into chapters by my walks each day.

I begin it today, even though belatedly, because there is nothing better left for me to do in this world.

I already feel my imagination becoming frozen, all my faculties becoming weaker. I expect to see my reveries becoming colder from day to day until the boredom of writing them deprives me of the courage to do so; thus if I continue it, my book must naturally end when I approach the end of my life.

2

It is true that the most impassive man is subjected by his body and his senses to impressions of pleasure and pain and to their effects. But, by themselves, these purely physical impressions are only sensations. They can only produce passions, even sometimes virtues, either when the deep and lasting impression is prolonged in the soul and outlives the sensation; or when the will, moved by other motives, resists the pleasure or consents to the pain; also it is necessary that this will always remain prevalent in the act[2]   for if the sensation, being more powerful, finally uproots the consent, all the morality of the resistance vanishes and the act becomes again, both by itself and by its effects, absolutely the same as if it had been fully consented to. This rigor appears harsh but also is it not, then, from it that virtue bears such a sublime name? If the victory costs nothing what crown would it deserve?

3

Happiness is too constant a condition and man too mutable a being for the one to suit the other.

***

Solon cited to Croesus the example of three happy men, less because of the happiness of their life than from the gentleness of their death, and did not at all grant that he was a happy man as long as he was still alive.[3] Experience proved that he was right. I add that if there is some truly happy man on the earth, he will not be cited as an example of it for no one other than himself knows anything about it.

A continuous movement that I perceive informs me that I exist for it is certain the sole affection that I experience then is the weak sensation of a slight, even, and monotonous noise. What, then, is it that I enjoy: myself. From . . .

4

It is true that I do not do anything on the earth; but when I no longer have a body I shall not do anything either, and nevertheless I shall be a more excellent being, more full of feeling and life than the most active of mortals.

5

A modern makes them smaller to his own measure and I, I make myself bigger to theirs.

6

And what error, for example, is not worth more than the art of detecting false friends when this art is acquired only as a result of showing us as such all the ones that one had believed genuine.

7

These Gentlemen act like a band of buccaneers who, torturing a poor Spaniard at their ease with red-hot pincers, benignly consoled him by proving to him by very stoic arguments that pain was not at all an evil.

8

But I did not want either to give her my address or to take hers, being certain that as soon as I had turned my back, she was going to be interrogated, and that by transformations familiar to these Gentlemen they would know how to draw from my known intentions an evil much greater than the good that I would have desired to do.

9

And if my finally acknowledged innocence has convinced my persecutors, if the truth shines more brilliantly than the sun to all eyes, far from quelling its rage, the public would only become more relentless from it; it would hate me more then for its own injustice than it hates me today for the vices it likes to attribute to me. It would never pardon me for the indignities with which it has burdened me. They would henceforth be for it my most unpardonable heinous crime.

10

I ought always to do what I ought to do, because I ought to, but not from any hope of success, for I know very well that this success is henceforth impossible.

11

I portray to myself the astonishment of this generation, so haughty, so prideful, so proud of its so-called knowledge, and which counts with such a cruel self-importance on its enlightenment with regard to me.

12

There is no longer either affinity or fraternity between them and me, they have repudiated me as their brother and I, I have made it into a glory for myself to take them at their word. But nevertheless if I could still fulfill some duty of humanity toward them I would doubtless do so, not as with my fellows, but as with suffering and sensitive beings who need help. In the same way and even more wholeheartedly I would help a dog that is suffering. For, being neither a traitor nor a scoundrel and never affectionate from duplicity, a dog is much closer to me than a man of this generation.

13

The sovereign himself does not have the right to give a pardon until after the guilty person has been judged and condemned in accordance with all formalities. Otherwise that would be to leave on him the stain of the crime without having convicted him of it, which would be the most flagrant of all inequities.

If they want to nourish me with bread, it is while steeping me in ignominy. The charity of which they want to make use with regard to me is not beneficence, it is opprobrium and insult; it is a means of debasing me and nothing more. Doubtless, they would like me dead; but they like me even better alive and defamed.

14

And I will receive their alms with the same gratitude that a passerby could have for a thief who, after having taken his purse, gives him back a small portion to finish his trip. Also, there is this difference that the intention of the thief is not to debase the passerby, but solely to help him.

I am the only one in the world who gets up each day with the perfect certainty of not experiencing any new pain during the day and of not going to bed any more unhappy.

15

The expectation of the afterlife softens all the ills of this one and makes terrors about death into almost nothing; but in the things of this world, hope is always mixed with uneasiness and there is no true repose other than in resignation.

16

As Cardinal Mazarin said, it will happen from a condition that is neither less extended nor more necessary that it will be ridiculous not to have it and even more ridiculous to have it.

Who consult self-interest before justice and prefer the one who is speaking to their advantage over the one who has spoken best.[4]

17

Reverie
From which I have concluded that this condition was pleasant to me more as a suspension of the pains of life than as a positive enjoyment.

***

But, with my body and my senses, not being able to put myself into the position of pure minds. I have no way of judging well their genuine manner of being.[5]

Do I want to avenge myself on them as cruelly as possible? For that I have only to live happily and contentedly; that is a sure way to make them miserable.

By giving themselves the need to make me unhappy they make their destiny depend on me.

18

I would quite think that the existence of intelligent and free beings is a necessary consequence of the existence of God, and in the divinity itself I conceive an enjoyment outside of its plenitude, or rather which complements it, that is to reign over just souls.

19

They have opened up between them and me an immense abyss that nothing can any longer either fill up or cross, and I am as separated from them for the rest of my life as the dead are from the living.

That makes me believe that of all those who speak of the peace of a good conscience, there are very few who are speaking about it with knowledge, and who have felt its effects.

If there is henceforth some chance that can change the condition of things, which I do not believe, it is very certain at least that this chance can only be in my favor; for nothing worse is possible.

20

Some seek me out eagerly, weep with joy and emotion at my sight, embrace me, kiss me with rapture, with tears, the others grow heated at my sight with a rage that I see sparkling in their eyes, others spit, either on me or very close to me, with so much affectation that their intention is clear to me. Such different signs are all inspired by the same feeling, that is no less clear to me. What is this feeling that manifests itself by so many contradictory signs? It is the one, I see, of all my contemporaries with regard to me; otherwise it is unknown to me.

21

Shame accompanies innocence, crime no longer knows it.

I state my feelings, my opinions, however bizarre, however paradoxical they might be in a completely naïve manner; I do not argue or prove because I am not seeking to persuade anyone and because I am writing only for myself.

22

Henceforth all human power is without force against me. And if I had impetuous passions I could satisfy them at my ease and as publicly as I could with impunity. For it is clear that dreading all explanation with me more than death, they will avoid it at any price whatsoever. Moreover what will they do to me, will they stop me? That is all that I ask and I cannot obtain it. Will they torment me? They will change the type of my sufferings, but they will not increase them. Will they make me die? Oh, they will be very careful not to. That would end my pains. Master and King on the earth, all those who surround me are at my mercy, I can do anything to them and they can no longer do anything to me.

23

But when these Gentlemen have reduced me to the condition I am in they knew very well that I did not have a hateful and vindictive soul: without which they would never have exposed themselves to what could happen from it.

24

How powerful one is, how strong one is when one no longer hopes for anything from men. I laugh at the foolish ineptitude of the wicked, when I consider that thirty years of efforts, of labors, of worries, of pains have served them only to put me fully above them.

25

Let them state only how they have known all those things and what they have done to learn them, if they perform this point faithfully I promise not to make any other response to all their accusations.

26

Everything shows me and persuades me that providence does not meddle in any way with human opinions nor with everything that pertains to reputation, and that it abandons entirely to fortune and men everything that is left here below of the man after his death.

27[6]

1 Know yourself
2 Cold and sad reveries
3 Sensitive morality[7]
How ought I to conduct myself with my contemporaries
On lying
Too little health
Eternity of punishments
Sensitive morality

28

Will, then, a sensible man never come who notices the malignant skill with which they speak about me, either directly or indirectly, in almost all modern books, in a treacherously foreign tone, with perfidious allusions, with forced parallels, with ironic citations, equivocal and shifty phrases, and always avoiding direct applications, but all artfully leading the malignity of readers.

29

But this tranquillity which they[8] cannot deprive me of without losing the fruit of their conspiracy, they are very careful to poison it with everything that can make it unbearable for a man of honor. And since they are unacquainted with the resources of innocence they have not taken care to foresee those that I would find to bear the bitterness of my situation.

30

While death advances with slow steps and forestalls the progression of years while it makes me see and feel its sad advances at leisure . . .[9]

On the Art of Enjoying and Other Fragments[1]

I
On the Art of Enjoying

Consumed by an incurable illness that is dragging me with slow steps toward the tomb, I often turn an interested eye toward the course of life I am leaving and, without groaning about finding its end, I would willingly begin it again. Yet, what have I experienced during that interval that deserves my attachment? Dependency, errors, vain desires, indigence, infirmities of every sort, some brief pleasures and some long-lasting pains, many real ills, and some goods in smoke. Ah, doubtless to live is a sweet thing, since a life so little fortunate nevertheless leaves me regrets.

But what I hear every day the happy people of the world . . .

2

Cherished solitude, in which I still pass with pleasure the remnants of a life given over to suffering, forest without woods, marsh without waters, furze bushes, reeds, sad heaths, inanimate objects that can neither speak nor listen to me, what secret charm ceaselessly draws me back into your midst? Insentient and dead beings, this charm is not at all in you, it could not be there, it is in my own heart that wants to relate everything to itself. Commerce with men takes me away from the commerce that is dearest to me, and it is only in your refuges that I can be at peace with myself.

3

See at dinner a convalescent devoured by an appetite that he is forced to restrain, voluptuously savoring all the bits that he is allowed and covetously counting those he can still allow himself to have. He seasons each bit with a greater measure of pleasure than another puts into a whole meal; while eating half as much as you do he enjoys twice as much.

4

Let us not seek true pleasures on earth; for they are not there; let us not at all seek there the soul's delights, the desire and the need for which it has; for they are not there. We have a dull instinct for the plenitude of happiness only in order to feel the void in ours.

5

In saying to myself, I have enjoyed, I enjoy again.

6

I believe I see pure minds,[2] ministers of the most high, at its word putting everything into order in nature, being eager to carry out the laws of its providence here below. The intellectual world seems to come together around me in order to animate and people the sensible world for my eyes.

7

They are afraid of dying and are bored with living.
Fear of death does not keep them from complaining about life, and, from their boredom with everything that makes it pleasant, one sees that they feel the ill that they do not say about it.

8

And it is this way that Homer, speaking about an ivory ornament dyed red, says that it was stained with dye.[3]

9

As for me, I would believe, on the contrary, that it is only to the extent that one loves to live alone that one is truly sociable; for in order not to hate men it is necessary to see them only from afar and it is only then that one does not demand from them preferences that it is not in the human heart to grant.[4]

10

I have the internal feeling which does not organize itself by means of syllogisms, but which convinces more than reasoning does.

11

I have much more than proofs, I have certainty.[5]

12

I have lost if they are only just, but if they dare to be equitable I am the winner.

13

I think that all the disasters of his destiny since the fatal period of his fame are the fruits of a long-standing plot formed in great secrecy among a few people who found the art of including gradually all the Grandees, all the fine wits, that it . . .[6]

14

The French do not hate me at all, my heart tells me that that cannot be. I do not impute to France the insults of several writers which its equity condemns and which its urbanity disavows. The true French do not write in that tone, above all against unfortunate people; doubtless they have mistreated me, but they have done it reluctantly. The very affront they have given me has debased me less than the efforts that have atoned for it honor me.

15

. . . It is possible that they might have responded to what I said, but they have certainly not responded to what I wanted to say. Thus everything that their writings prove, supposing that they have indeed refuted mine, is that I have not been able to make myself understood, since they refute nothing of what I have thought. If, then, someone takes the trouble to seek out my true sentiments through my bad fashion of stating them, he might indeed be able to find that I am wrong, but he will certainly not find it by means of my adversaries' reasons, for they do nothing at all against me.

16

When I entered into the perilous career that I am daring to traverse, I did not know the dangers with which it was surrounded; in consecrating my pen to the truth, I foresaw . . . I foresaw from afar all the evils that I had to fear; and I was reckless enough to brave them, at least I was not so imprudent as to be mistaken about them.

17

In the Autumn of 1768, having resolved to return to England, I inspected the papers that I had left with the plan of burning the greatest number as a useless encumbrance that I was dragging behind me. I began that operation with the present collection, when, upon leafing through them mechanically, by chance I fell upon a gap that had hardly struck me until then, but, since other circumstances reminded me of its importance at that moment, and its authors gave me the first idea of the frightful plot of which I am the victim. From that point, renouncing the project of burning this collection, on the contrary, I resolved to preserve it carefully, strongly persuaded that, in spite of the things it contains and which appeared to be opposed to me, sooner or later it will provide sufficient indications to put any impartial and attentive man unto the path of the truth. It was also at this very moment that, although I had a passport from M. de Choiseul,[7] I renounced the project of leaving the Kingdom and resolved to expose myself to all the consequences of the plot hatched against me armed only with my innocence. I put some brief notes at the end of some letters in order to put those into whose hands this collection will fall onto the path of the truth. It is up to them, if they love justice, to do, with the aid of this guide, the research necessary to render it someday to the innocence of the most unfortunate of mortals and to avenge his memory for the outrages of his persecutors.

18

I have always regarded and I still do regard the republican state as the only one worthy of man, I have always said so with the audacity and the pride that a virtuous heart draws from the uprightness of its feelings, I do not doubt at all that De Layre,[8] who at bottom thought as I did, but who liked to irritate me, and push me into an argument, often made me speak with disdain about the condition of subjects. If this is a crime for a Republican, I declare myself very guilty of it. I have spoken as I have written, loudly, publicly, and always with a petulance that I have not been able to conquer, pushing my sentiment to the extreme against anyone who comes to attack it. But all that does not excuse the very extraordinary tone that reigns in De Layre's letters and for which he alone can explain the motive. I hope he will survive me; may one learn from him what brought him to write to me in this manner, I am as sure in advance that Diderot and d'Holback will be found as the prime movers as if he had already told me.

19

Married Therese Le Vasseur on September 11, 1768, at Bourgoin in the presence of M. de Champagneux, Mayor of Bourgouin and of M. de Rosière, an officer in the Artillery.[9]

Various Writings

I
Travel Notebook[1]

1754

Sunday dined on the grass near Hermance.
Slept at the Chateau of Coudrée.
Monday dined on the grass near Ripailles.
Slept at Meilleraie.
Tuesday slept at Bex.
Dined at Pisse-Vache.
Slept at Saint-Maurice.
Dined at Aigle.
Frugal repast of hospitality.
Isn't there something in Homer worthy of my trip?
Tuesday dined at Villeneuve.
Slept at Vevai.[2]
Wednesday dined at Cuilli.
Slept at Lausanne.
Thursday dined and slept at Morges.
Friday dined at Nion and slept at Eaux-Vives.

2
[Declaration Intended for a Journal][3]

J.-J. Rousseau begs all those with whom he had some relations, it does not matter whether they are friends or enemies provided that they love justice and truth, to declare whether they have ever heard him boast directly or indirectly about having refused some pensions or benefits either from any Prince or from any private individual. If he has said this to anyone, if he has ever even spoken about it in any manner, aside from when he might have been forced to defend himself after having been accused of having dishonorably refused it, let him name himself. If he wrote it, let his letter be shown. He sincerely asks forgiveness from the public for daring to bother it again about him, but it is important for him and someday it will be important to the honor of his memory that the truth or falseness of an accusation brought so publicly be verified publicly and promptly.

3
Memorative Note on the Illness and Death of M. Deschamps[4]

From his arrival at Trye,[5] and even the very first day, M. Deschamps always complained that he was suffering very much; speaking without cease to everyone about killing himself, about throwing himself out the windows, etc. This very language even rendered suspect to me the good faith of a supposed dropsical patient, whose legs I did not see swell up nor face change. Although he consulted many people, took many drugs, and would have consulted me myself as if I had been a doctor, upon which I sent him away very curtly, I saw him little or not at all.

Nevertheless, he stopped going out. Soon they said he was in danger. Finally based on the proposal that M. Manory[6] made him about it, he consulted M. Laubel, a Doctor from Gisors, who, finding him extremely ill in fact, judged puncture indispensable, and told me so. Since I could not recover from my prejudice, I told him that in spite of the extreme pain I had at enduring such sights, I would desire to be present at that operation. Soon afterward, M. Laubel no longer insisted on the puncture, already judging it to be too late and henceforth useless for the cure of the sick man, who moreover was very much afraid of it. M. Laubel spoke about him so decidedly as a sick man without recourse and near death, even insisting that he be immediately administered the sacraments that his affirmative tone finally unsettled me, and I desired to see the sick man's condition myself. I was with him for the first time in a very long while along with M. Laubel on Thursday morning, March 17. This time I found him as ill as they had said. Great pains in the side, considerable swelling and straining in the lower abdomen, fever, and an extremely changed face. I was sorry that my incredulity had kept me for so long from fulfilling the duties of humanity toward a close neighbor, and from then I went to see him at least twice every day.

Upon that visit and the following one M. Laubel insisted anew upon the sacraments and finally induced the sick man to receive them. I offered him everything that depended on me for his relief, and two or three days afterward I sent him two bottles of Burgundy wine still sealed and packed in straw, as they had come from Rouen. I joined to them a jar of barberry jam of which I had two, and I kept one of them for myself. This wine, which I recommended that he drink only several spoonfuls of from time to time in order to revive him, was drunk in his home both by him and by others; I drank some of it myself, in the same way I ate from his jar of barberry. His daughter also ate it. Neither the wine nor the jam did any harm to anyone.

The sick man got perceptibly worse, bile took over him, he became jaundiced, the attacks to the spleen increased and became unbearable. He received the viaticum on Holy Wednesday, March 30. The same day, speaking about the choice of his foods, he told me that he very much liked fish, which I have always regarded as an extremely healthy food and I told him so; he answered me that he did not know where to buy it and that he had not tasted it since his arrival; in which he was lying; for, while appearing to be on quite bad terms with him, M. Manoury provided him with it secretly, along with game. The next morning M. Manoury sent me a pike that my sister* cooked in a wine sauce for our dinner. Upon sitting down at the table I thought that a little of this fish would give great pleasure to my neighbor, and right away through my sister I sent him a piece completely dry and without sauce. Although the piece was small he told his servant that he would not eat all of it without her, and in fact afterward she told my sister that she had eaten it and had found it excellent. He was the same: but instead of eating it dry as I had sent it to him he seasoned it with chives and vinegar. Nevertheless he did not have an upset stomach or intestinal aches; but his attack resumed during the day, and he continued to have short respites and to get worse; always persuaded, as he testified to me and to others by a thousand signs, that he was not dying from dropsy but from that fish, and without even remembering that he had received the viaticum the day before.

Six or seven days later, namely April 6 in the morning, he received Extreme Unction, and the puncture—to which, feeling himself suffocating, he finally consented—was done an hour after. They drew from him five or six pints of a reddish and bilious water that M. Manoury found very extraordinary. He had some relief as to respiration; but the fever increased; bilious vomiting came, and finally he died the next morning, April 7.

*M. the Prince de Conti had obtained from my too easy obligingness a submission that I would change my name, and that I would call my Governess my sister; but this was only after my return from England for at Calais they had me write my name; and I wrote Rousseau and I kept the name Rousseau at Amiens and for the whole journey, not wanting to have the air of a man who was concealing himself.

Everything that I saw and heard during the course of that day, the equivocal and insidious remarks of M. Manoury, of the scrubber, of the wigmaker, those who spread out secretly in the neighborhood, the countenance that the deceased had toward me the final days, everything told me that I was being accused of having poisoned him. Then I finally made my decision. On the morning of the 8th I wrote to M. Manoury to propose to him an autopsy of the cadaver offering to pay the expenses for it, and in order to beg him to furnish me on the spot with a express for Isle-Adam, in conformity to the orders he had received here from His Highness.

He came, promised to have the autopsy done: he told me; I will take Misters Laubel, father and son. I answered him: *and others; the first ones to be found.*

With regard to the express, he refused to give it to me before the autopsy was done, claiming that I could have nothing to say to the Prince until that time. That was said to me in so many words, and confirmed, because I assured him that this autopsy was not at all an issue in what I had to write to His Highness. So that, thanks to M. Manoury's dilly-dallying and obstinacy at not wanting to take anyone but the Misters Laubel, the autopsy was not done until the next day and I could not obtain any express for that day.

Upon this clear refusal I made the decision to address myself to the tenant farmer. The letter with which I charged him for His Highness contained a declaration that I wanted to go clear my warrant,[7] an entreaty to have me driven there the next day, very certain that if I prepared to go there myself, the people with whom I had to deal would not fail to accuse me of wanting to escape, and finally a resolution on my part if I had no news on Saturday, to confine myself on Sunday in the prison of Trye in order to stay there until it pleased His Highness to have me brought to my judges.

I also pointed out that it would have appeared suitable to me also to check on M. Deschamps's servant in order to verify the truth of the facts more easily.

M. Manoury sent the scrubber to Gisors to look for Misters Laubel, father and son; he found neither of them, but he left a notice. Two or three hours later the surgeon's assistant came and wanted to speak to me; he was referred to M. Manoury; the master came later and wanted to speak to me; he was referred the same way. Since the doctor did not arrive that day, the autopsy was put off to the next day.

Saturday morning M. Laubel, the doctor, came again to ask me what needed to be done, and in whose name? I told him that only M. Manoury was charged with everything, even with the payment, and that I would not[8] take a hand in anything but in reimbursing him for the expenses. Mlle. Deschamps who was in the other room could hear this short conversation which was made aloud, with the door open, and M. Laubel, whom I did not even have sit down, left a half a minute after having entered.

Finally they proceeded to the autopsy the third day after the death. M. Manoury put guards at the room's entrance: this was not for the people, since the operation was supposed to be and was public; this should not have been, either, for me, since instead of keeping me from being a spectator of an operation that I was having done, in good order they should have invited me to it.

It should be noted that, although no one other than myself had spoken about an autopsy until the moment when the body was ready to be buried, and in spite of my very positive letter, M. Manoury did every sort of trick to insinuate that it was Mlle. Deschamps who was asking for the autopsy of her father's body, and to engage her to speak in the same way. When it was a question of knowing in whose name the report would be drawn up, Mme. Manoury said to her husband that she did not want him to be found to be involved in such business, nor the report to be drawn up in his name. Afterwards she asked what a great lord I was then that the report should be drawn up in mine? The conclusion had been to appeal to Mlle. Deschamps to know whether she wanted it to be drawn up in hers, to which she was not opposed. If this arrangement took place it will be funny that the report of the autopsy was made in the name of a person who did not even consider asking for it, and that it does not make any mention of the one who did ask for it and who paid for it. That is what it means not to be a great enough lord to the taste of Mme. de Manoury.[9]

Another remark. Changing their tone suddenly about M. Deschamps's servant, M. and Mme. Manoury have begun to entice her to their home, and have extremely praised her great merit: although formerly both of them had spoken about her a hundred times to everyone and to myself as a hussy, a drunkard, and the lowest of sluts. Moreover, M. and Mme. Manoury are doing all of that only with pious intentions, since two days ago they did their Easter duties and they say so to everyone so that they might have confidence in them.

Note on the illness and death of M. Deschamps at Trye.

4
Sentiments of the Public Toward Me in the Various Estates that Compose It.[10]

Kings and the Great do not say what they think, but they will always treat me generously.

The true nobility, which loves glory and which knows that I am an expert in it, honors me and keeps silent.

The Magistrates hate me because of the wrong they have done to me.

The Philosophers, whom I have unmasked, want to ruin me at any cost and will succeed.

The Bishops, proud of their birth and of their station, esteem me without fearing me and honor themselves by showing consideration for me.

The Priests, minions of the philosophers, bay after me in order to pay their court.

The fine wits avenge themselves by insulting me about my superiority which they feel.

The people, which was my idol, sees in me only an ill-combed wig and a man with a warrant out for him.

The women, dupes of two cold fish who despise them, betray the man who deserved the best from them.

The Swiss will never forgive me for the evil they have done to me.

The Magistracy of Geneva feels its wrongs, knows that I forgive it for them, and would atone for them if it dared.

The leaders of the people, raised up on my shoulders, would like to hide me so well that they might be the only ones seen.

The authors filch from me and blame me, the knaves curse me, the rabble hoot at me.

The good people, if any still exist, bemoan my fate under their breath; and I, I bless them, if they can instruct mortals some day.

Voltaire, whom I keep from sleeping, will parody these lines. His crude insults are homage that he is forced to render me in spite of himself.

6[11]
Declaration Relative to Different Reprints of His Works[12]

When J. J. Rousseau discovered that people were concealing their actions from him in order to print his writings furtively in Paris, and that it was being affirmed to the public that he was the one who was directing these printings, he easily understood that the principal aim of this maneuver was the falsification of these same writings, and he did not delay, in spite of the efforts that were being made to hide the knowledge of this from him, in being convinced of this falsification with his own eyes. His confidence in the bookseller Rey did not allow him to assume that he was participating in these faithless acts, and upon having sent him his protest against the works printed in France, still being done under the name of said Rey, he joined to it a declaration in conformity with the opinion he continued to have of him. Since then he has also been convinced, by his own eyes, that Rey's reprintings contain exactly the same alterations, suppressions, falsifications as those of France, and that both have been done on the same model and under the same directions. Thus since his writings, as he composed and published them, no longer exist in the first edition of each work which he did himself, and which disappeared from the public's eyes a long time ago, he declares all the old or new books that are being printed and will be printed henceforth under his name, in whatever place it might be, to be either false, or altered, mutilated and falsified with the most cruel malignity, and disavows them, some as no longer being his work, and the others as being falsely attributed to him. His powerlessness for making his complaints reach the public's ears is making him attempt, as final recourse, to hand over to various persons copies of this declaration, written and signed by his hand, certain that if in the number he finds a single honest and generous friend who has not sold himself out to iniquity, such a necessary and just protest will not remain stifled, and posterity will not pass judgment about the sentiments of an unfortunate man based on books disfigured by his persecutors.

Written at Paris, this January 23, 1774.

J. J. Rousseau

7
Memorandum Written in the Month of February 1777, and Since Then Handed Over or Shown to Various Persons[13]

My wife has been sick for a long time, and the progression of her illness, which puts her in no condition to take care of her small household, makes someone else's cares necessary to her when she is forced to keep to her bed. Until now I have looked after and taken care of her in all her maladies, old age no longer allows me to perform the same service. Moreover, the household, very small though it is, does not go along all by itself; it is necessary to provide the things necessary for existence from outside and to prepare them; it is necessary to maintain cleanliness in the house.* Being unable to fulfill all these cares alone, in order to provide for them I have been forced to try to give a servant to my wife. Ten months of experience have made me feel the inadequacy and the inevitable inconveniences of this resource in a position such as ours. Reduced to living absolutely alone and nevertheless in no condition to do without someone else's service, in infirmities and abandonment there is only one way left to sustain our elderly days. That is to beg those who are disposing of our destinies not to mind disposing of our persons also and to open some refuge to us where we could continue to live at our expense, but exempt from a labor that henceforth surpasses our strength, and circumstances and efforts of which we are no longer capable.

Furthermore, in whatever fashion I am treated, whether I am kept in express enclosure or in apparent freedom, in a hospital or in a desert, with people who are gentle or harsh, false or frank (if there are still any of those), I consent to everything provided that my wife is given the care that her condition requires, and I am given lodging, the simplest clothing, and the most sober nourishment until the end of my days without my being obliged to get involved in anything. We shall give for that what we might have of money, effects, and revenue,[14] and I have reason to hope that that will be able to suffice in the provinces where commodities are cheap and in houses intended for this purpose, where the resources of economy are known and practiced, above all by submitting as I do wholeheartedly, to a regimen proportionate to my means.

In this I believe I am asking nothing that in such a sad situation as mine, if there can be one, is refused among humans, and I am even very certain that this arrangement, far from being burdensome to those who dispose of my fate, would be worth considerable savings to them both in trouble and in money. Nevertheless, the experience I have of the system that is being followed with regard to me makes me doubt that this favor will be granted to me, but I owe it to myself to ask for it, and if it is refused to me, I will bear more patiently in my old age the anguish of my situation, by bearing witness to myself of having done what depended on me to soften it.

*My inconceivable situation of which no one has the idea, not even those who have reduced me to it forces me to enter into these details.

8[15]

Whoever without urgent necessity, without indispensable business seeks out, even to the point of importunity, a man of whom he thinks ill, without wanting to clarify with him the justice or the injustice that he is bringing to it, whether he is deceived or not in this judgment, is himself a man about whom one must think ill.

To cajole a man when he is present and defame him when he is absent is certainly the duplicity of a traitor and very likely the maneuvering of an impostor.

To say, while concealing one's actions from a man in order to defame him, that it is out of consideration for him that one does not want to overwhelm him, is to tell a lie that is no less inept than it is cowardly. Defamation being the worst of civil evils and the one whose effects are the most terrible, if it was true that one wanted to treat this man considerately, one would overwhelm him, perhaps one would threaten him with defamation, but one would not do anything. One would reproach him for his crime in private while concealing it from everyone: but to say it to everyone while concealing it from him alone, and also to feign having an interest in him is the refinement of hatred, the summit of barbarity and heinousness.

To give alms out of deceit to someone in spite of him is not to serve him, it is to debase him; it is not an act of kindness, it is one of malignity: above all if, while making the alms paltry, useless but noisy, and unavoidable to the one who is its object, one acts discreetly so that everyone is informed about it except him. This double-dealing is not only cruel but base. By covering oneself with the mask of beneficence, it dresses up wickedness as virtue, and, on the rebound, the indignation of insulted honor as ingratitude.

The gift is a contract that always assumes the consent of the two parties. A gift made by force or by ruse, and that is not accepted, is a theft. It is tyrannical, it is horrible to want treacherously to make a duty of gratitude for the one whose hatred one has deserved and by whom one is justly despised.

Since honor is more precious and more important than life, and nothing makes life more burdensome than the loss of honor, there is no case possible in which it is allowed to conceal from the one whom one is defaming, no more than to the one whom one is punishing with death, the accusation, the accuser, and his proofs. Evidentness itself is subject to this indispensable law: for if everyone in town had seen one man murder another, still one would not cause the accused to die without interrogating and hearing him. Otherwise there would no longer be any security for anyone and society would crumble at its foundations. If this sacred law is without exception, it is also without abuse; since all the skill of an accused cannot keep a demonstrated offense from continuing to be so, nor to guarantee him against being convicted in such a case. But without this conviction the evidentness cannot exist. If depends essentially on the answers of the accused or on his silence; because one cannot presume that enemies, or even indifferent people, will give to the proofs of the offense the same attention to grasping the weakness of these proofs, or the clarifications that might destroy them that the accused can naturally give to them; thus no one has the right to put himself in his place in order to strip him of the right of defending himself by taking it upon oneself without his admission; and it will even be a great deal if sometimes a secret disposition does not make those people who have so much pleasure in finding the accused guilty see that so-called evidentness, the imposture of which he himself might have demonstrated if he had been heard.

From this it follows that this very evidentness is against the accuser as long as he persists in violating this sacred law. For this cowardice of an accuser who sets everything to work in order to conceal his actions from the accused, under whatever pretext one covers it, cannot have any true motive other than the fear of seeing his imposture unveiled and the innocent person vindicated. Thus all those who in this case approve the maneuvers of the accuser and lend themselves to them, are henchmen of iniquity.

We undersigned acquiesce wholeheartedly in these maxims and believe every reasonable and just person bound to acquiesce in them.

Le Mierre[16]

WRITINGS ON SCIENCE

Course on Geography[1]

Geography is a Science that treats the knowledge of the terrestrial Globe, and that teaches the position of all regions, with regard to each other and in relation to the Heavens. The word, Geography, comes from Greek, and signifies precisely, description of the earth.

This Science contains Hydrography, which treats waters in general, that is to say the sea, rivers, and Islands. Chorography which is the description of a Kingdom, a state, a nation, or a province; and Topography which describes a city, a castle, or some particular place.[2]

One can divide it again into Cosmographic and Historic; the Cosmographic divides the terrestrial globe by Circles, oppositions, shadows, Zones, and Climatic zones; the historic considers the government, forces, religion, and the morals of the different people who inhabit it.

There is also another Science that is named Astronomy which treats the extent, distance, motion, and position of the Heavenly bodies; and although it makes up a separate and entirely detached study from the one that treats our earth in particular, we shall not fail, nevertheless, to say something about it at the beginning of this Geographic course because these two Sciences have a sort of analogy with each other, and because one could not possess this last one quite precisely unless one has some knowledge of the other.

Elements of Astronomy

Astronomers assume to start with that this immense space that we discover around us, in which our eyes lose their way, and in which the sun and the stars are situated, is filled with a material that is extremely fluid and much more subtle than the air that we breathe. The extent of this space is indefinite because we cannot discover its limits, either by simple sight, or with the aid of Telescopes.

They assume, afterward, that the Celestial and fluid material about which we spoke and which they name Ether, forms several Vortices, that each moves extremely rapidly around a star that they call fixed because no perceptible motion is noticed in it.[3]

The Sun that gives us light is one of these fixed stars which is, consequently, the center of a vortex which carries along with it around the Sun numerous other bodies in which is included the earth that we inhabit. They call these bodies Planets from a Greek word that means to wander, because they wander, so to speak, through the air; we shall see below that this word should not be taken in all its force because their paths, although very great and rapid, do not fail to be regular.

These planets are of the number of seven[4] including in it the Sun that is called a planet by an old manner of speaking, even though the Copernican Hypothesis, which is the one that we are following in these elements, establishes it as a fixed Star. Here are their names with the figures by which they are ordinarily designated:

The Sun,   Mercury,   Venus,   The Earth,
   Mars,   Jupiter,   Saturn.

All these bodies move in an orbit with the Vortex of the West and East and each finishes its orbit in more or less time in proportion to the Greatness of the Circle it traces around the common Center.

Aside from this Circle, which is extremely large, each planet also traces another, smaller one on its axis, just about like a ball which, rolling from one place to another, covers its path while continuously rotating. With regard to the earth, this motion is called diurnal because it accomplishes its rotation in one day, and the other is named annual because it takes a year to make its Circular revolution around the Sun; we shall explain this more fully.

The planets do not trace a perfect circle around the Sun. For all the radii drawn from the center of a circle to its circumference ought to be equal, but the planets are sometimes closer to the Sun and sometimes farther away and, by this means, trace a sort of Oval that is called an ellipse.

The Aphelion of a planet is its greatest distance from the Sun, and its greatest proximity is called Perihelion. With regard to the earth a planet is in Apogee when it is at its greatest distance and in perigee when it is at its closest.

One ordinarily calculates the distance of the planets from the Sun by their average distance from that star.

Following that manner, Mercury is distant from the Sun by four thousand Diameters of the earth, Venus by 7,000, the earth 12,000 and beyond, Mars 15,000, Jupiter 51,000, and Saturn 95,000. Since Astronomers are not absolutely in agreement about these distances, here we take the mean of their various opinions.

Now it is necessary to see the size, the relation, and the motion of each planet. Following the best observations, one finds that the Diameter of the Sun must [be] 110 times greater than that of the earth, 308 times that of Mercury, 84 times that of Venus, 166 times that of Mars, 5½ that of Jupiter, and $62\,5/44$ that of Saturn not including the ring.

As to the revolution of the planets around the common center, the Sun rotates in approximately 25 and a quarter days.

Mercury accomplishes its turn around the Sun in 88 days, Venus in 225 days.

The Earth in 365 days, 5 hours and 49 minutes and this time is the extent of the year.

Mars in one year and 321 days.

Jupiter in 11 years 313 days and 19 hours.

Saturn traces a circle so far that it accomplishes it only in the space of 29 years and 169 days.

Now examining the motion of the planets each upon its axis, by observations of the most famous astronomers we find that Venus rotates in 23 hours 56 minutes, the earth also 23 h. 56 min. and 49 seconds (one ordinarily says in 24 hours given the smallness of the difference), Mars in one day 40 min. Jupiter according to Mr. Neuvton in 9 hours 56 min. and following Mr. Cassini in 5 h. 56 min.[5] Mercury and Saturn are unknown with regard to this motion, the first because it is too near the Sun which most often obscures it by the gleam of its light and the second because of its great distance. As to the Sun we have already said above that it accomplishes its revolution on its axis in 25 days and 6 hours.

Observe that this movement of the planets on their axes is the cause of days and nights from their different exposure to the Sun's rays.

Here for a moment let us make an assumption that will serve to clarify what we have left to relate in detail about these astronomical principles.

First, if one imagines a man in the Sun occupied with examining the path and the revolution of the heavenly bodies, it is clear that, to him, the earth will appear to turn around it by a continuous motion from the west to the east, as is in fact the case. Moreover, he will see all the fixed stars positioned from all sides as in the concave of a Sphere of which his eye is the center and, by the same means, he will consider the earth as moving among these stars and always approaching the easternmost point until the point that, its annual revolution being accomplished, it begins again to proceed through the same path without interruption. Now the plane of the circle that he will see traced this way for the earth is called the ecliptic because it is when the sun and the moon find themselves in conjunction or in opposition in this plane that eclipses are formed, as we shall say below, and now if he divides the circumference of this circle into 12 equal parts distinguished from each other by the different stars that are found situated in them he will have the Zodiac, named this way from a Greek word that signifies animal because they gave the names of numerous animals to 12 signs or figures composed of 12 stars that are found in each of the 12 parts of its division.

The twelve signs of the Zodiac are:

Ares, Taurus, Gemini, Cancer or Crawfish.
Leo, Virgo, Libra, Scorpio.
Sagittarius, Capricorn, Aquarius, Pisces.

Each of these signs is also subdivided into 30 other equal parts that are called degrees, which makes 360 Degrees for the whole Zodiac. One knows that the Geometric division of the Circle is always into 360 degrees.

Now if one assumes the observer to be transported from the Sun to the earth, and that the earth, for example, is the place in the Zodiac that corresponds to the sign of Ares, the Sun will appear to him in the other point of the diameter contrary to the sign of Libra and, since the earth moves from west to east toward Taurus, the Sun will appear to move from east to west toward Sagittarius; this is obvious and does not need any other explanation; it is from this apparent motion that one says that the Sun is in such or such sign, which properly signifies that the earth is in the opposite sign.

The same Phenomena are also found respectively between the Sun and every other planet: for they all have, as the earth does, a particular circle of revolution that is called their orbit and from which they never deviate.

These Orbits do not follow the path of the orbit of the earth and of the ecliptic in a parallel manner; but they are inclined to it, some more, others less, each following its particular direction.

Now, the two points in which the orbit of each planet intersects the ecliptic are called the nodes of the planet, and the angle that its orbit makes with the ecliptic is called its latitude, from which it appears that while a planet is in the nodes its latitude is zero. As for the Longitudes of the planets, it is their distance from the sun which is sometimes greater and at others less, by reason of the elliptical shape of their orbits.

But, we do not want to enter into a detailed account that would take us too far. On these slightly abstract matters we send the Reader who wants to be more amply instructed to the authors who have treated this Science in particular. We are going to complete in a few words what there remains for us to say, after which we shall pass to another subject.

The planes of the orbits of each planet are inclined to that of the Ecliptic in the following manner

Mercury makes an angle of 6 degrees with the ecliptic

Venus	3 degrees 30 minutes
The Earth	———
Mars	1 degree 50 minutes
Jupiter	2 degrees 30 minutes 50 seconds
Saturn	2 degrees 30 minutes 50 seconds

There are three planets that have Satellites, that is to say other small planets that revolve around them, as the planets themselves revolve around the Sun. Saturn has five of them the discovery of which is rather modern. Jupiter has four of them, and the earth one, which we call the moon.

We shall not speak here about the Satellites of Jupiter and Saturn; our plan does not lead me to these matters which are entirely foreign to my subject. But as for the Moon, since its effects are perceptible to us, and since for this reason the knowledge of it interests us more here, we shall explain in a few words the mechanics of its principal phenomena.

The globe of the Moon is 60½ terrestrial diameters away from us in its mean distance; as to is size, it is nearly one-fiftieth that of the earth.

The Moon turns around the earth in 27 days, 7 hours, and 43 minutes: this is what is called its periodic revolution.

Conjunction happens when the moon is found at the point in its circle or its Ellipsis which is between the sun and the earth, and when the earth is between the moon and the sun, then it is said that the moon is in opposition with that heavenly body.

Now, although the moon makes the entire circle around the earth in around 27 and a half days, this is not to say, because of that, that it returns from one conjunction to the other in the same space of time: for, since during this time the earth has advanced almost one sign or 30 degrees in the ecliptic, the Moon requires just about two more days in order to reattain the same point of position between the earth and the sun from which it had left, and this addition, which makes just about 29 and a half days, makes up the synodical month that makes up the measurement of space and times by which we count the lunar months.

The different Phases of the moon are divided into four quarters; the first Quarter begins at the point of its conjunction with the Sun, which then illuminates the Hemisphere of the moon that we do not see at all, so that the moon is then entirely dark for us. Upon leaving the perpendicular line from the sun, it presents the other Hemisphere to it little by little, to the extent that it gets farther away from it, so that at the end of a little more than seven days, half of the hemisphere that is turned toward us is illuminated, and this is what is called the first quarter from which the second phase begins. From that, always getting farther away from the sun, and always being illuminated more on the side that it presents to us, it arrives at the full, when, being in precise opposition to the sun, the whole hemisphere that is turned toward the earth reflects the rays of the sun back to us, from which, drawing nearer, and gradually presenting it the side that we do not see at all, it diminishes the light, until having lost half of it, it enters into its final quarter which lasts until the new conjunction.

Once this revolution of the moon is understood, it is easy to conceive that its eclipse happens when the mass of the earth is found interposed between the sun and the moon, and the moon, having entered into the shadow of the earth, no longer receives rays from the sun.

Now, during the course of a year, the moon is twelve times in conjunction and twelve times in opposition to the sun; from which it would follow that each year we should have twelve Eclipses of the moon, and as many of the sun if the revolution of these two heavenly bodies took place in the same plane.

But that is very far from being the case; eclipses of the moon are rare and those of the Sun even more so, the reason for which is that the moon, having five degrees of latitude, that is to say having that much of a gap from the ecliptic, it cannot deprive us of the sight of the sun, nor reciprocally can the earth deprive the moon of that heavenly body except when it is in the nodes, that is to say when the three globes are found disposed in a straight line: for as soon as the moon takes on some latitude, and it begins to move away from the plane of the ecliptic, it is clear that, then, making an angle with the two other bodies, it can no longer be found interposed precisely between the earth and the sun in conjunction, nor the earth between the sun and the moon in opposition.

That is enough to give the reader an idea about the disposition and the motion of the planets. As for the fixed stars, astronomers place them at an immense distance, since the prodigious distance from Saturn to the Sun is very small in comparison to the one that is found between Saturn and the fixed stars. They are obliged to make this assumption in order to adjust all the parts of their systems; but there is nothing repugnant in that assumption, if one pays attention to the infinite power of the creator of the universe. "I hold," says Monsieur de Fénélon, "the key to all the mysteries of nature, as soon as I discover its author."[6]

There would have been too much trouble retaining the name of each fixed star, if one had been given to each one; thus they took it into their heads to make several collections of them that are called constellations or asterisms, and the Pagans, Greeks, and Latins have given them names that are for the most part drawn from their fables.

We have retained these names, and we have even added others since we have taken the trouble to pass to the other side of the equator in order to discover the stars that are around the South Pole, and which the ancient astronomers had not seen at all.

There are 60 Constellations that are divided into those of the Zodiac which are 12, those that are to the north of the Zodiac of the number of 21, fifteen which the ancient astronomers had known to the south of the Zodiac, and the 12 that the Moderns have made out of the stars that are around the South Pole.

The 12 Constellations of the Zodiac have been named above on page ———.[7]

The names of the 21 Constellations from the signs of the Zodiac up to the North Pole are:

The Ursa minor or Cynosure, Ursa major or Helix, Draco, Cepheus, Cassiopeia, Perseus, Andromeda, Triangulum, the Charioteer or Erichthonius,[8] Coma Berenices, the Cowherd or Boötes or Architophilax, Corona borealis or Ariane, Hercules or the Giant, the Swooping Vulture,[9] Cygnus, Pegasus, Equuleus, Delphinus, Aquila, Antinoüs, Serpentarius or Ophiuchus.

It should be noted that the star that makes the farthest end of the tail of Ursa minor is the Pole Star.

Here are the names of the 15 constellations that the ancients knew to the south of the Zodiac:

Cetus, the Nile or Eridanus, Orion, Lepus, Canis major, Canis minor, Hydra, Crater, Corvus, Argo or Noah's Ark, Pisces australis, Centaurus, Lupus or the Wild Beast, Corona australis, and Ara or the Censer.

And here are the 12 Constellations that the modern astronomers have discovered around the South Pole:

Columba, Pavo, Grus, Phoenix, Indus, Avis Paradisi, Dorado, Chameleon, Pisces volans, Toucan, Hydra minor,

The Names of the Constellations and the Planets Put into Latin Verse

Insunt Signifero bis sex Coelestia Signa;
Suntque, *Aries, Taurus, Gemini, Cancer, Leo, Virgo,*
Libraque, Scorpius, Arcitenens, Caper, Amphora, Pisces.

Ad Boream verò ter septem conspiciantur;
Ursa minor, major, Draco, Cepheus, atque *Corona,*
Herculeum sidus, Lyra, Cassiopeia, Bootés,
Perseus, Andromede, Deltotum, Auriga, Caballus,
Sectio equi, Cignus, Delphin, Aquila, Anguitenenesque
Hinc *Coma,* et *Antinoüs,* quem forma ad sidera vexit.

Denique converti terquinque notantur ad austrum;
Cetus, et *Eridanus, Lepus,* et nimbosus *Orion,*
Sirius, et *Procion, Navis, Triquetrum, Hydraque, Crater,*
Corvus, Centaurus, Lupus, atque hinc Thure sabaeo
Ara calens, *Piscis, Fomalhaut* insignis in Ore

Sidera jam pando quae non novére vetusti;
Pavo, Grus, Phoenix, hinc *Indus, Avis paradise*
Piscis qui occiduo *Dorada* est dictus Ibero,
Musca, Chamoeque-leon, Piscis de Stirpe volantum,
Hydra minor, Toucan, necnon sine felle *Columba;*

Sed Vaga preterea dicuntur lumina septem;
Luna, et *Mercurius, Venus* ac *Sol, Mars* quoque fulgens.
Hinc, *Jovis* et sidus super omnia lucens,
Celsior his *Saturnus,* tardier omnibus astris.

Let us pass to another subject. We are stopping our rapid trip through the vast extent of the Heavens, in the midst of which the earth is only a point. Let us come to this point, Theater of disputes, and of men's ambition. But since everything is great or small only by comparison, we are going to consider it from a very different perspective. We have seen it make up an almost imperceptible part of the Universe; we are going to see it divided up into immense spaces, which are divided into other spaces for the possession of which miserable humans mutually tear each other to pieces.

On the Sphere

After having given an idea of the mechanical system of the universe, we are going to treat the sphere, where we will have occasion to take up again and to explain in a more tangible manner the essence of what we have said touching the shape, the order, and the position of all the parts of this vast machine, and particularly the relation that the earth has with the other parts of the universe.

We urge the reader not to be at all surprised if henceforth we sometimes attribute motion[10]

Response to the Anonymous Memorandum Entitled, "Whether the World that We Inhabit is a Sphere etc." inserted in the Mercury *of July, p. 1514*[1]

Sir,

Attracted by the title of your memorandum, I read it with all the voracity of a man who has been impatiently waiting for several years along with all of Europe for the result of those famous voyages undertaken by several members of the Royal Academy of sciences under the auspices of the most magnificent of all Kings. I shall admit frankly, Sir, that I had some regret at seeing that what I had taken for the abstract of these great men's observations was actually only a conjecture hazarded, perhaps a little inappropriately. I do not claim, for that reason, to depreciate the ingenious things that your memorandum contains: but you will permit me, Sir, to avail myself of the same privilege that you granted yourself, and of which, according to you, every man ought to be in possession, which is to state his thought freely on the subject at issue.

First, it appears to me that you chose the least suitable time to announce your sentiment to the public. You assure us, sir, that you did not at all have the intention of tarnishing the glory of the observers from the academy, nor of diminishing the value of the King's generosity. I am certainly very inclined to vindicate your heart on this point, and, from reading your memorandum, it also appears that in fact such low feelings are very distant from your thought. Nevertheless, you will agree, Sir, that if you had in fact solved the difficulty, and you had shown that the shape of the earth is not at all the cause of the variation that has been found in the measurement of the different degrees of latitude, all the value of the efforts and toils of these Gentlemen, and the expenses that they cost, and the glory that ought to be their fruit, would be very close to being annihilated in public opinion. I do not claim for that, Sir, that, out of private considerations, you should have disguised or hidden the truth from men if you believed you found it; I would be speaking contrary to my dearest principles. The truth is so precious to my heart, that I do not make any other advantage enter into comparison with it.

But, Sir, here it was only a question of delaying your memorandum for several months, or rather of moving it forward by several years. Then, you could with seemliness have made use of the freedom that all men have of saying what they think about certain matters, and doubtless it would have been very sweet for you, if you had been found to be accurate, to have spared the King the expense of two such long voyages, and those Gentlemen the pains they have suffered, and the dangers they have confronted. But today now that they have just returned, before being informed about the observations they have made, the conclusions they have drawn from them; in a word before having seen their accounts and their discoveries, it appears, Sir, that you ought to be less hasty in proposing your objections, which, the more force they might have, the more they would also be suited to lessen the eagerness and the gratitude of the public, and to deprive these Gentlemen of the legitimate glory due to their labors.

It is a question of knowing whether the earth is spherical, or not. Based on several arguments, you decide for the affirmative. To the extent that I am capable of bringing my judgment to bear on these matters, your arguments are sound. The conclusion from them, however, does not appear to me inevitably necessary.

In the first place, by associating yourself with the ancients, the authority with which you fortify your cause is, in my opinion, very weak. I believe that the preeminence that they have very justly preserved over the moderns as regards poetry and eloquence does not extend to physics and astronomy, and I doubt that one dares to put Aristotle and Ptolemy in comparison with Sir Isaac Newton and Monsieur Cassini: thus, Sir, do not flatter yourself on drawing a great advantage from their support: without offending the memory of these great men one can believe that something escaped their intelligence. Deprived, as they were, of the necessary experiments and instruments, they should not have laid claim to the glory of having known everything, and if one puts their dearth of aids in comparison with the ones that we enjoy today, one will see that their opinions ought not to be of a very great weight against the sentiments of the moderns; I say, of the moderns in general, because in fact you gather them all together against you, by declaring yourself against the two nations that without contradiction hold the first rank in the sciences in question: for at the head of the list you have the French on one side, and the English on the other, which, in truth, are not in agreement among themselves about the shape of the earth, but who are united on this point, of denying its spherical character. In truth, Sir, if the glory of triumphing increases in proportion to the number and the value of the adversaries, your victory, if you carry it off, will be accompanied by a very flattering triumph.

Your first proof, drawn from the equal tendency of the water toward its center of gravity appears to me to have a great deal of force, and I admit in good faith that I do not know any satisfactory answer to it. In fact, if it is true that the surface of the sea is spherical, it must necessarily be, either that the entire Globe follows the same shape, or that the lands bordering must be horribly steep in the places of their elongation. Moreover (and I am surprised that this escaped you) one could not conceive that the course of rivers could tend from the equator toward the poles,* that is to say, from the low places toward the more elevated parts, principally to the environs of the polar latitudes, and in the cold regions where the elevation would become more perceptible: nevertheless, experience teaches us that there are numerous rivers that follow this direction.

What could one reply to such strong instances? I know nothing at all about it. Note, nevertheless, Sir, that your demonstration, or that of Father Tacquet,[2] is based on this principle, that from their weight all the parts of the terraqueous mass tend toward a common center which is only a point, and consequently has no length; and doubtless it is not probable that such an evident axiom, which makes up the foundation of two considerable parts of mathematics, could become subject to being contested; but when it is a question of reconciling contradictory demonstrations with reliable facts, what will one not be able to contest? I have seen in the Preface of the *Elements of Astronomy* by M. Fizes, Professor of Mathematics at Montpélier,[3] an argument that tends to show that in the Hypothesis of Copernicus, and following the principles of weight established by Descartes, it would follow that the center of gravity of each part of the earth ought to be, not the common center of the Globe, but the portion of the axis that corresponds perpendicularly to that part, and that consequently the shape of the earth would be found to be cylindrical. I certainly have no intention to wish to support such an astonishing paradox, which taken strictly is very evidently false: but who will answer us that once the earth has been demonstrated to be oblate by repeated observations, some Physicist, more subtle and more bold than I am would not adopt some similar Hypothesis? "For in the end," he would say, "it is a necessity in Physics that what ought to be should be found to be in agreement with what is."

But let us not quibble; I wish to grant your first argument. You have demonstrated that the surface of the sea, and consequently that of the

---

*Following the hypothesis of M. Cassini; that of M. Newton would also be subject to the same difficulties: but in an opposite direction.

earth, must be spherical; if by experiment I demonstrate that it is not so at all, could all your reasoning destroy the force of my conclusion? Let us assume for a moment that a hundred precise and repeated proofs happen to convince us that a degree of latitude always has more length as one approaches the equator; will I have less right to draw a conclusion from it in my turn: thus, the earth is actually more curved toward the poles than toward the equator: therefore, it is elongated in this direction: therefore it is a spheroid. Would my demonstration, founded on the most reliable operations of Geometry, be any less evident than yours, established on a universally granted principle? Where the facts speak, is it not up to reasoning to fall silent? Now, it is to establish the fact in question that numerous members of the Academy have undertaken voyages to the north and to Peru: therefore it is up to the Academy to settle it, and your argument will have no force at all against its decision.

In order to evade in advance a conclusion whose necessity you feel, you attempt to cast uncertainty on operations performed in various places, and repeatedly by Messieurs Picart, de la Hire, and Cassini,[4] in order to trace the famous meridian which crosses France, which first gave the occasion for M. Cassini to be the first to suspect some irregularity in the roundness of the Globe when he was certain that the degrees measured toward the north were somewhat less long than those that advanced toward the south.

You distinguish two manners of considering the surface of the earth; viewed from afar, as for example, from the moon, you establish it as spherical; but regarded from up close, it no longer appears to you as such, because of its irregularities: for, you say, radii drawn from the center to the summit of the highest mountains will not be equal to those that will be limited to the surface of the sea; thus, the arcs of the circle although proportional among them, being unequal following the inequality of the radii, it might very well be that the differences that have been found between the degrees measured (even though with all the exactitude and precision of which human attentiveness is capable) come from the different elevations at which they have been taken, which must have given arcs unequal in size although equal portions of their respective circles.

I have two things to respond to that. In the first place, Sir, I do not at all believe that the inequality of the altitudes at which the observations have been made by itself was enough to give very perceptible differences in the measurement of the degrees. To be convinced of it, one must consider that, following the common sentiment of Geographers, the highest mountains are not capable of changing the shape of the earth, spherical or other, more than some grains of sand or gravel cast on a ball of two or three feet in diameter. In fact, today it is generally agreed that there is no mountain that has a height of a league above the surface of the earth; a league, nevertheless would not be a great thing, in comparison with a circumference of 8 or 9,000. As to the altitude of the surface of the land even over that of the sea, and again of the sea above certain lands, as for example of the Zuiderzee above North Holland, it is known that they are hardly considerable. The moderate course of the majority of rivers and watercourses can only be the effect of an extremely gentle incline. Nevertheless, I shall admit that, taken strictly, these differences would be very capable of introducing some difference into the measurements: but in good faith, would it be reasonable to draw an advantage from the entire difference that can be found between the summit of the highest mountain, and the lands lower than the sea; have the observations that have occasioned the new conjectures about the shape of the earth been taken at such enormous distances? Doubtless you are not unaware, Sir, that care was taken in the construction of the great meridian to establish stations on the most equal altitudes possible: this was even an occasion that contributed a great deal to the perfection of the levels.

That is it, Sir, assuming along with you that the earth is spherical, it now remains for me to show that this assumption, in the manner in which you take it, is a pure petitio principii. One moment of attention and I shall explain myself.

Your entire reasoning turns upon this Theorem, demonstrated in Geometry, that when two circles are concentric, if one takes the radii to the circumference of the large one, the arcs intersected by these radii will be unequal and proportionately larger as they are portions of larger circles. To this point all is good, your principle is incontestable: but you appear to me less fortunate in the application that you make of this to the degrees of latitude. If one divides a terrestrial meridian into 360 equal parts by radii taken from the center, according to you, these equal parts will be degrees by which the elevation of the pole will be measured. Sir, I dare to dispute the validity of such a sentiment, and I maintain that that is not at all the idea that one must give oneself about the degrees of latitude.

In order to convince you in an incontestable manner, let us see what would result from that, by supposing for a moment that the earth is an oblate spheroid. In order to make the division of the degrees, I inscribe a circle into an Ellipsis that will represent the shape of the earth, the small axis will be the equator, and the large will be the axis of the earth itself, I divide the circle into 360 degrees so that the two axes pass through four of these divisions. Through all the other divisions I draw radii which

I extend to the circumference of the Ellipsis, the arcs of that curve included between the extremities of the radii will give the extent of the degrees which will evidently be unequal, (*A figure would make all this more intelligible, I omit it so as not to frighten the eyes of the Ladies who read this journal,*) but in an opposite direction from the one that should be: for the degrees will be longer toward the poles, and shorter toward the equator, as is manifest to anyone who has some smattering of Geometry. Nevertheless, it is demonstrated that if the earth is oblate, the degrees ought to have more length toward the equator than toward the poles. It is up to you, Sir, to rescue the contradiction.

What then is the idea that one ought to form for oneself about the degrees of latitude? The very term Elevation of the pole teaches you. From different degrees of this elevation, drawn on one and the other hand from tangents at the surface of the earth; the intervals included between the points of intersection will give the degrees of latitude. Now it is very true, that if the earth were spherical, all these points would correspond to the divisions that would mark the degrees of the circumference of the earth considered as circular; but if it is not spherical at all, this will no longer be the same thing. Completely contrary to your system, where the poles, being more elevated, the degrees ought to be greater in it, here the earth being more curved toward the poles, the degrees are smaller. It is the greater or less curvature, and not the distance from the center that influences the length of the degrees of elevation of the pole. Thus, then, since your reasoning is accurate only as long as you assume that the earth is spherical, I have the right to say that you are basing yourself on a petitio principii;[5] and since it is not from the greater or lesser distance from the center that the length of the degrees of latitude results, I conclude once again that your argument does not have any solidity in any of its parts.

It might be that the term *degree*, equivocal in the matter in question, has led you into error. A degree of the earth considered as one 360th part of a circular circumference is one thing, and a degree of latitude considered as the measure of the elevation of the pole over the horizon is another. And although one can take the one for the other in the case in which the earth is spherical, one is far from being able to do the same if its figure is irregular.

Take care, Sir, that when I said that the earth does not have a considerable slope, I understood it, not in relation to the spherical shape, but in relation to its natural oblong or other shape; a shape which I regard as determined from the beginning by the laws of gravity and motion, and to which the equilibrium or the level of fluids can very well be subject;

but on these matters, there is no reasoning that one can hazard that is better known to us than the fact itself.

As for what is from the inspection of the moon, it is very true that it appears spherical to us, and it probably is so: but it does not at all follow that the earth also is so. By what rule would its shape be subject to that of the moon, rather than, for example, to that of Jupiter, a Planet of a completely different importance, and which nevertheless is not spherical? The reason that you draw from the shadow of the earth is hardly any stronger, if the circle would show itself in entirety, it would be unanswerable; but you know, sir, that it is difficult to distinguish a small portion of the curve from the arc of a larger or less large circle. Moreover, it is not at all believed that the earth departs so extremely from the spherical shape that that ought to occasion a perceptibly irregular shadow on the surface of the moon, all the more so since, because the earth is considerably larger than the moon, only a very small part of its circumference ever appears on it.

I am etc.

ROUSSEAU.

Chambéri, September 20, 1738.

Memorandum Presented to M. de Mably[1]
on the Education of M. His Son

Sir, you have done me the honor of entrusting me with the instruction of Messieurs your Children and; it is up to me to respond to this with all my efforts[2] and with the entire extent of the little enlightenment that I might have, and to do so I believed that my first object should be to be well acquainted with the subjects with whom I shall be concerned: That is how I have principally employed the time that I have had the honor of being in your household, and I believe I am adequately informed in that regard to be able to settle the plan for their education. It is not necessary for me to pay you a compliment, Sir, upon the advantageous things that I have noticed there, the affection that I have conceived for them will manifest itself by more solid signs than praises, and a Father as tender and as enlightened as you are does not need to be instructed about his Children's fine qualities.

At present it remains to me, Sir, to be enlightened by you yourself about the particular views that you might have about each of them, about the degree of authority that you have the intention of granting me with regard to them[3] and about the precise limits that you will give to my rights.

It is likely that, having accepted me in your house with an honest salary and marked distinctions, you have expected from me effects that correspond to such advantageous conditions, and one sees very well that such expense and behavior were not necessary for giving Messieurs your Children an ordinary Preceptor who might teach them Basic Grammar, Spelling, and the Catechism. I also intend very well to justify the favorable hopes that you have been able to conceive on my account with all my power and I feel sufficiently sure of myself to answer in advance that you will never for a moment find me to fail in the Zeal and attachment that I owe to my students.

But, Sir, whatever efforts and whatever troubles I might take, success is very far from depending on me alone. It is the perfect harmony that ought to reign between us, the confidence that you will design to grant me, and the authority that you will give me over my Students that will determine the effect of my labor. I believe, Sir, that it is completely manifest to you that a man who has no rights of any sort over Children either for making his instructions likeable or for giving them some weight will never acquire ascendancy over minds which, at bottom, however precocious one might wish to assume them to be, at a certain age always determine their operations based on the impressions of the senses. You also feel that a teacher who is obliged to file an accusation over all a Child's faults will, if he can, very much keep from making himself unbearable by ceaselessly renewing vain lamentations. Besides, a thousand small decisive occasions for making a correction or for flattering appropriately escape in the absence of a Father and a Mother, or in the moments when it is impossible to interrupt them in such a disagreeable manner and it is too late to return to them at another moment when a Child's change of ideas would make pernicious to him what would have been salutary. Finally a Child, who does not delay in taking note of a Teacher's impotence with regard to him, seizes the occasion to take little account of his prohibitions and his precepts and to destroy irrevocably the ascendancy that the teacher would strive to acquire. You should not believe, sir, that in speaking in this tone, I am seeking to procure for myself the right to mistreat Messieurs you Children with blows: I have always held that brutal method in horror, I detest it more than ever and certainly I am not made to make use of it. Even threats, if I am to be believed about it, will never strike M. de Ste. Marie's ears, and I dare to promise myself to obtain from him everything that will be required, by less harsh and more suitable means if you savor the plan that I have the honor of proposing to you. Moreover, speaking frankly, if you think, Sir, that there would be ignominy in M. your son being struck by foreign hands, on my side I also find that an honorable man could hardly put his to a more shameful use than to employ them in mistreating a Child. But with regard to M. de Ste. Marie, we do not lack ways of mortifying him by punishments that would produce better effects: For in a Mind as lively as his the idea of blows will be erased as soon as the pain is, while that of a marked disdain, of a convincing reason, or of a perceptible privation will remain there much longer.

    A teacher ought to be feared, for this it is necessary that the Student be completely convinced that he has the right to punish him: but above all he ought to be loved. What means does a Preceptor have to make himself loved by a child to whom he has never anything to propose but occupations contrary to his taste, if moreover he does not have the power to grant him certain small particular pleasures that cost almost no expense nor loss of time and, being appropriately managed, do not fail to be felt infinitely by a Child and attach him very much to his Teacher?

Nevertheless I shall rely rather little on this point, because, judging from the first effects of my Zeal, I dare to count on M. de Ste. Marie not being able to refuse his Friendship to me, and, taking everything into account, I believe that without inconvenience a Father can reserve for himself the exclusive right to grant favors provided that he brings the following precautions to it, above all necessary for M. de Ste. M. whose liveliness and inclination for being undisciplined require more dependency.

Before giving him any gift, to learn secretly from the Governor whether there is occasion to be satisfied with the Child's behavior; to declare to the young man that when he has any favor to ask, he ought to do it by his Teacher's mouth and that if he should happen to ask on his own initiative that alone will be enough not to allow it to him; sometimes to take the occasion from that to reproach the Preceptor for being too kind, because this excessive easiness will harm his Student's progress, and that it is up to his prudence to correct what is lacking in a Child's moderation. Moreover, it will not be at all necessary to explain to the young child in the event that one does grant him some favor that it is precisely because he has done his duty well, it is better for him to conclude that pleasures and enjoyments are the natural consequences of wisdom and good behavior, than for him to regard them as arbitrary recompenses that might depend on caprice and that at bottom ought never to be proposed as[4] the object or the reward for study and for virtue.

There, at least, are the rights that you ought to grant me over M. your son if you wish to give him a fortunate education and one that answers to the fine qualities that he shows in many respects but which at present are obscured by many bad habits that need to be corrected right away and before time has made it impossible to do so. That is so true that it is very far from being the case for so many precautions to be necessary with M. de Condillac. He has as much need to be pushed as the other has to be held back, and I will be very capable of taking all the necessary ascendancy over him by myself: But for M. de Ste. M. it is a decisive point for his Education to give him a bridle that he feels and that is capable of holding him back. In the state things are in, the feelings that you will wish him to have on my account, Sir, depend very much more on you than on myself.

We are approaching the end of the year. You will not be able to find a more natural occasion than the beginning of the new one to give M. your son[5] a little speech within the grasp of his age which, setting before his eyes the advantages of a good education and the regrettable consequences of a neglected childhood, disposes him to lend himself willingly to what the knowledge of his interest well understood will make us require from him henceforth. After which you would have the kindness to declare to me in his presence that you are making me the depository of your authority over him, and that you are granting me without reserve the right to oblige him to fulfill his duty by the means that will appear suitable to me, in consequence ordering him to obey me as he does you yourself under penalty of all your indignation: moreover, this declaration, which will take place only in order to make more of an impression on him, will have no effect other than in conformity to what you will have taken the trouble of prescribing to me in private.

There, Sir, are some indispensable preliminaries for being assured that the efforts that I will be giving to M. your Son will not be wasted. Now I am going to trace the sketch of his education as I had conceived its plan based on what I have known up to now about his character and your intentions. I do not at all propose it as a rule to which one must be attached: but as a project that, needing to be recast and corrected by your enlightenment and by that of Monsieur the Abbé de M.[6] will serve only to give him some idea of the genius with which we are dealing.

The goal that one ought to propose for oneself in the education of a young man is to form his Heart, judgment, and Mind, and to do so in the order that I name them. Most Teachers, especially the Pedants, regard the acquisition and heaping up of types of knowledge as the sole object of a fine education without thinking that often, as Molière says,

> A learned fool is more of a Fool than an ignorant fool.[7]

From another side, many Fathers, rather despising everything that is called studies and saying that they do not want to make their children into *Scholars,* care about hardly anything but perfecting them in the exercising of the body and what is called knowledge of the world: Between these extremes we will take a middle in order to lead M. your son. The sciences ought not to be neglected, I shall soon speak about them, but they ought not to precede morals, above all in a mind that is sparkling and full of fire hardly capable of attention up to a certain age and the character of which will be found to be determined very early. Of what use to a man is the knowledge of Varro[8] if otherwise he does not know how to think accurately? If he had the misfortune to let his heart be corrupted, in his head the sciences are like so many weapons in the hands of a madman. Of two Persons equally committed to vice, the less skillful will always do the less evil, and the sciences, even the most speculative and the ones in appearance farthest removed from society do not fail to exercise the Mind and, by exercising it, give it a force which it is easy to abuse in the commerce of life when one has a bad Heart.

There is more with regard to M. your son; he has conceived such a strong distaste against everything that is called study and application that a great deal of time will be needed to destroy it, and it would be regrettable if this time were wasted for him, for there would be too many inconveniences in constraining him to it, and it would be even better for him to be eternally ignorant about what studies and sciences are than to know them only in order to detest them.

I cannot resolve to move on from this point without admitting to you, Sir, how much the manner in which they go about teaching Children appears insane and ridiculous to me. They make them waste three or four years composing wretched Themes while one is very certain that they will not find the occasion to write in Latin twice in their lives. Afterward they teach them to made Amplifications, that is to say, that after having given them an Author's thought they order them to spoil it by drawing it out by means of the most useless words they can find. They exercise them very much about Greek and Roman history and they leave them in the most abysmal ignorance about that of their country; they let the worst French pass provided that they speak Latin well. They speak to them about a God in three persons none of which is the other and of which each is nevertheless the same God; about the mystery of the Eucharist in which a space of five feet is contained in a space of two inches; about original sin for which we are very justly punished for faults that we did not commit; about the Effectiveness of the sacraments which put Virtues into operation in the Soul by means of a purely corporal application; all matters about which the best head does not have enough strength to conceive anything; in a word, at the very time in which one is beginning to cultivate their reason, at the very beginning of things, one makes them make the strangest exceptions against the most evident concepts, and to cap it all, one overwhelms them with a multitude of dry and sterile precepts conceived in terms whose very grammatical construction is not within their grasp. On the other hand one says nothing to them either about the principles of Christianity, or about the foundations of Morality, one leaves them in the most abysmal ignorance about the general duties of humanity and one believes that one is performing wonders by getting them used to taking,[9] like imbecilic Monks, the will of their Teachers as the sole rule of virtue. After fifteen years of such an education reason begins to pierce through all that undergrowth; one is completely astonished at finding oneself in the midst of so many impertinences. One makes it a point of honor to forget them as quickly as one can. At twenty-five years one has finally arrived at the same point of ignorance one was in upon being born; and as for Religion, in recalling the absurd speeches one made to them about it and the unintelligible Lessons that one gave them about it, they regard it as all Old Woman's tale, putting Jesus Christ and the Virgin into the ranks of Cinderella and Tom Thumb and end by having no principle of reason or behavior at all in the mind or in the heart.

These reflections have occupied me for a long time and, based on the consequences I have drawn from them, I had formed a plan of education very different from the one that is in practice. I do not know how successful it would be; what I can say is that it is too much opposed to both received ideas and established customs for me to be obliged to propose it to you. It is one of those attempts that one is not permitted to attempt upon a Child who is not one's own, and besides, an entirely natural reflection is enough to render it extremely suspect even to myself. As a result of turning an object over, a heated-up imagination can find new and singular things: But would a young and inexperienced man have the grace to flatter himself for having imagined something really better than what a practice of two thousand years has caused to be accepted unanimously by the most learned and experienced men?

Everything well considered; I believe then that, aside from several differences, we could not do better than to keep to the established System for M. your son's type of Studies: we shall only attempt to remedy the principal defects of the ordinary education by changing something in the method and detail of his. With regard then to Religion and Morality, one will not be able to succeed in inspiring him with solid principles that serve as a rule for his behavior for his entire life by multiplying precepts. Aside from the indispensable Elements that are within the reach of his age, at first one ought to consider less tiring out his memory with a detailed account of Laws and duties without principle and unconnected to each other than to disposing his mind and his heart to knowing them and to relishing them to the extent that the occasion presents itself for developing[10] them in him. These preparations are completely within the reach of his age and his mind because they contain nothing but curious and interesting subjects about civil commerce, about the arts and professions, and about the varied manner in which Providence has made all men useful to each other. Some stories chosen with discernment, some Fables from which one will remove the moral in order to give him practice in finding it by himself: all these Subjects, which are matters for conversations and Promenades rather than ordered studies, will have more advantages whose effect appears infallible to me.

First; not affecting his mind in a disagreeable way by means of the ideas of constraint and ordered study, and not demanding from him a painful and continuous attention, they will not have anything harmful to his health. In the second place they will accustom his Mind early to reflection and to considering things from their effects and their consequences. Third; they will make him curious and inspire him with the taste for the natural Sciences.[11]

Here I ought to anticipate an impression that one might receive about my project by imagining that I am only seeking to enjoy myself and to rid myself of what is dry and boring in lessons in order to procure a more pleasant occupation for myself. I do not believe, Sir, that you could happen to think this way about me. Perhaps a man has never made a more important and more serious business for himself than the one that I am making of Messieurs your Children's education if you want to second my Zeal; up to the present you have no occasion to notice that I am seeking to flee labor; but I do not at all believe that, in order to give himself an air of Zeal and occupation, a teacher ought to pretend to overburden his Students with a serious and unappealing labor, always to show them a severe and angry arrogance and to purchase this way the reputation of a precise and Hardworking man at their expense. For myself, Sir, I declare it once and for all: scrupulous to the utmost extent over the performance of my duty, I am not capable of ever neglecting it. Neither my taste nor my principles ever lead me to either laziness or relaxation: but out of the two ways of assuring myself of the same success I shall always prefer the one that costs the least trouble and unpleasantness to my Students and I dare to assure, without wanting to appear to be a very busy man, that the less they are working in appearance the more I shall be working for them.

If there are some occasions in which severity might be necessary with regard to Children it is in cases connected to morals or in those in which it is a question of correcting bad habits. Often the more wit a Child has the more the knowledge of his advantages makes him indocile about the ones that remain for him to acquire. From that, disdain toward inferiors, disobedience to superiors, and rudeness with equals: when one believes oneself to be perfect what shortcomings does one not give oneself? M. de Sainte Marie has too much intelligence[12] not to feel his fine qualities: but if one does not provide for it early he will count too much upon them and will neglect to draw all the advantage that one ought to hope from them. These seeds of vanity have already produced in him many little inclinations that must be corrected. It is in this respect, Sir, that we cannot act in too coordinated a manner, and it is very necessary that whenever there is occasion to be dissatisfied with him, from every direction he finds an appearance of indifference and disdain that will mortify him all the more since these signs of coldness will not be at all ordinary for him. This is punishing pride by its own weapons and attacking it in its very source, and one can rest assured that M. de Sainte M. is too well born not to be infinitely sensitive to the esteem of Persons who are dear to him.

When it is reinforced by reasoning, rectitude of heart is the source of aptness of Mind; a decent man almost always thinks aptly, and when one is accustomed from Childhood not to dizzy oneself over reflection and not to abandon oneself to present pleasure until after having weighed its consequences and set its advantages into balance with the inconveniences, with a little experience one has acquired almost everything necessary for forming the judgment. In fact, it seems that good sense depends even more on feelings of the heart than on Enlightenment of the mind, and one has the experience that the most learned and the most enlightened are not always the wisest and those who conduct themselves best in the business of life. Thus after having filled M. de Sainte Marie with good principles of morality one could regard him as advanced enough in the science of reasoning: but if there is an important point in education without contradiction it is that one, and when it is time for it, one could not be too devoted to teaching him to be acquainted with men; to know how to take them by their virtues and even by their weaknesses in order to lead them to his goal and always to choose the best course in difficult occasions. This depends in part on the manner in which one gives him practice in considering objects and turning them over on all their facets, and in part on experience of the World. As to the first point, you can contribute very much to it, Sir, and with very great success by sometimes pretending to consult him about the manner in which you should behave in hypothetical Cases;[13] That will flatter his vanity, and he will not at all regard as labor the time that is put into deliberating over a piece of business in which his voice will be counted for something. It is in such conversations that one can inspire him with a consistent and judicious mind and, by this means, he will learn more in two days than he would in two years by formal instructions: But it is necessary to watch out at first not to present him with anything but matters proportionate to his age and above all to give him practice for a long time on Subjects in which the best course can be easily seen: Both for the goal of leading him more easily to find it by himself and for keeping him from regarding the business of life as a series of problems in which, the various courses of action appearing equally reasonable, it would be a matter of indifference to decide for one rather than for the other, which would lead him to indolence in reasoning and indifference in conduct.

Experience of the world also appears to be to be absolutely necessary and even more so for M. de Sainte M. since, born timid, he needs to see company often in order to learn to find himself at liberty in it and to behave in it with those graces and that ease that characterize the man of the World and likeable man.

I will venture, Sir, to make a digression here in order to develop some reflections that appear to me worthy of being examined.

What is the true goal of the education of a young man? It is to make him happy. All the detailed aspects that one proposes to oneself in its regard are only so many means for arriving at this end; this principle is incontestable. But how can one lead him to this happiness? What paths make one attain it? To almost all eyes, these quite uncleared routes have imperceptible Tracks, and it hardly appears possible to indicate to others what one has not been able to find for oneself. We would more easily show them the footpaths to avoid: we know only too well, for example, that this precious felicity is not at all found on the other sides of these forests of Conjugations, of Themes, of catechisms and of impertinences through which one makes these poor Children pierce with so many tears and troubles, and it seems that one undertakes at first to gather into these young hearts all the displeasures to which their age is susceptible.

What happens as a result of that? Soon abandoned to themselves; they throw themselves into pleasures with all their might; they do not have any idea of them, novelty makes them more piquant, carried away by the passions, age fortifies the taste for them, and they abandon themselves to them with so little caution that, after having used up their heart[14] and destroyed their Temperament, this precipitous enjoyment makes them pass the end of their life in sufferings equal to those at the beginning but that are no longer softened by the same hopes.

Nothing is so sad as the fate of men in general; nevertheless in themselves they find a devouring desire to become happy that makes them feel at every moment that they were made to be so. Why aren't they at all? They accuse destiny or they mutter against their Fathers and their Preceptors. As for myself, Sir, I ardently desire to make your memory and mine always dear to M. de Sainte Marie, not only from the ordinary feelings of love, of respect, and of gratitude, but also by a recurrence of pleasure based on the enjoyments of his first years and on the advantageous influence that they spread out over the others.

I conceive two ways of attaining felicity. One by satisfying one's passions and the other by moderating them: by means of the first one enjoys, by means of the second one does not desire at all, and one would be happy by means of both of them if the one did not lack that duration and the other that vivacity that makes up true happiness.

The routes for attaining these two conditions are entirely opposed, one must then choose, and the choice is easy if one compares the effects of both of them. One could not deny that a man who savors pleasure and voluptuousness with long drafts is actually happier and enjoys the charms of life better than the one who neither desires nor possesses them at all. Nevertheless, two things seem to me to make the condition of the latter preferable. In the first place; the more lively the activity of pleasure is, the less it endures: this is an uncontested fact; Thus one loses in time what one gains in feeling; up to this point everything is compensated for: but here is how the thing is not equal: It is that the ardent taste for pleasures acts in such a manner on the imagination that it remains moved even after the effect of the feeling and this way prolongs the desire longer than the possibility of satisfying it, from which I conclude that the immoderate enjoyment of pleasure is a principle of uneasiness for the future.

On the contrary: the pains of a man who, without having enjoyed, has only a few desires to combat, diminishes to the extent that he gains time, and the long tranquillity of the soul gives him more force to preserve it forever: his happiness increases to the same extent that that of the other one diminishes.

Besides, where is the decent man who, like a Bear in society, would want to be continuously occupied only with satisfying his desires without regard for the proprieties or the repose of other someone else: would one be happy with such feelings and if there is a happiness reserved to men, do not honor and delicacy make up its base? Let us not consider ourselves as if we were alone in nature, lend ourselves to someone else's needs so that he might lend himself to ours reciprocally, sometimes sacrifice our pleasures to him, we shall enjoy those we have left with more relish and, taking everything into account, we shall be happier for it.

Thus for the reasonable man the Condition of a man who abandons himself to all his passions is a chimera. This respectable reason is doubtless a divine gift, but it has been given to us only in order for us to struggle with ourselves ceaselessly: perhaps it has been dearly sold to us. But in the end we enjoy it and it is no longer time to dispute over it.

On this basis, we differ only more or less from the one who resists his passions. In whatever condition we might be, we always have so many of them to combat that, in truth, it will hardly cost us any more to take on the whole task: but let us not impose anything impossible on ourselves and let us see in what condition the mind ought to be in order to be able to subdue the emotions of the heart.

It is here that I shall dare, Sir, to propose to you this surprising Paradox that there are no people tranquil and moderate in their desires other than those who get out and about in the social world. I say that they are tranquil, not absolutely, but in comparison to those who, nourished in retirement and distance from pleasures, have known them only through an imagination all the more active since its springs have not been at all weakened by the continuous activity of the organs.

A solitary person abandoned to himself very soon conceives that other men than himself exist in nature; even if he assumes that some of them live alone, he is not unaware that others live together, and by comparing this society with his solitude he does not delay in feeling how much there is to gain for the enjoyment of life in entering into relations with his fellows: from that his imagination departs and returns to him to depict objects that are increased and embellished by the leisure and freedom to enlarge and combine them without anything making him see how far he is distancing himself from the truth. Soon the heart joins in with these imaginations, it forms desires; far from exhausting it, these desires heat it up: for desire is the only feeling that duration does not weaken at all. From it is born uneasiness, melancholy, even regrets, and perhaps finally despair if the retirement still lasts and the imagination is too lively. Suddenly transport such a man into the midst of the world; I omit the fact that he will put up a foolish front there: but it is certain, at least, that at every new object he will find himself moved much more than a man who saw that object every day; doubtless in many respects he will find much to scale back in all that he had depicted to himself; but the great diversity of objects will add something to the impression of each of them, and will take away the freedom of reflections that could diminish the effect; he will be continuously agitated and abandoned to a torrent of alien feelings, each will have the value of novelty for him. Experience teaches us with what greediness one abandons oneself to them in such a case, and how dangerous is it, even with the greatest basis of Philosophy and reason, to pass suddenly from a long calm into such a violent agitation.

At present let us take a man abandoned to the social world from his Childhood. That crowd of pleasant and unpleasant objects acts upon him only with a degree of force tempered by long habituation. The heart eats its fill of them, because the Mind is accustomed to seeing them; for him the most piquant pleasures, the most marked tribulations are only ordinary events whose repeated experience almost takes the feeling away from him. He is not violently moved by anything because everything is familiar to him; he counts his pleasures rather than weighing them; and an always continuous slight agitation keeps his soul in a certain evenness in which it could not be with lively emotions. See a man who gets out and about an extreme amount; everywhere he bears an air of gaiety and cheerfulness, his Head is filled with Music, Painting, Shows, banquets, little verses, pretty women: rarely is there anything more. That forms such an amusing group that the soul has hardly any Leisure to distract itself upon other more serious objects, nor even to occupy itself strongly with each of those in particular. It touches them all lightly and it is satisfied. In order to be happy, at least in order not to be pitied, it would thus be necessary to enervate the passions and multiply tastes, and that is precisely the effect of commerce with the social world. It is usually imagined that the World is the Theater of great passions; on the contrary I think that it is only the theater of petty tastes and it is not necessary to be very experienced in order to convince oneself that the great strokes of Passion in every type have almost always been produced by solitary and melancholy hearts.

From all that, I conclude that a man destined one day to cut a figure in the world could not be introduced to it too early, not only in order to learn to conduct himself with ease, but also in order to accustom himself to know it and to prevent himself from being immoderately charmed by it when he finds himself abandoned into it by Station at the most impetuous age.

I would be rather of the opinion of those who claim that nothing is so easy for a young man as to form himself for society and to make himself likable even upon leaving the dust of School: This is the ordinary effect of a first attachment and there are few polite Knights who do not owe their education to the first Women who inspired a taste in them; also that is not the principal inconvenience that I see in delaying a young Man's introduction. It is with the dispositions of the Heart that I am concerned and with the passions that are their work. This young man who has left the hands of a Teacher lacking taste has never heard Rameau, Blavet, Coypel, nor Girardon spoken of.[15] He does not know whether there have been any Painters, Engravers, Sculptors, and Composers in the world since the Greeks; he is unacquainted with Racine, Molière, Corneille, or Voltaire except from some dry explanations from his Teacher and often he does not doubt that it would be impressive to forget all that very quickly: On the other hand, women have been depicted to him as wicked Animals and he already adores them, young people as Monsters of debauchery and he is burning to act the way they do: In general everything that one has said to him in order to distance him from love of pleasures is precisely what attracts him to them; thus he abandons himself to them without reserve at the first opportunity: but he abandons himself to them brutally like a man without feeling and without taste who, believing everything to be equally forbidden, runs to them all with equal ardor. The unworthy and base greediness of gambling, drunkenness, the coarsest rages of temperament abandon him to Usurers, to Panderers, and to the most despicable women. The Literature that he detests, the fine Arts that he is unaware of do not serve at all to calm the fits of his passions; delicacy and taste are chimeras for him, and his heart has not yet experienced the pleasures that he believes he has already exhausted.

In the end, if one is well born, the time will come when one makes reflections upon oneself. One goes into houses where politeness, taste, and seemliness, reign. One is completely astonished to find oneself there as if one were in another world; one hears a fine and delicate language spoken there that one does not understand at all; one sees gentle and polished manners reigning there. A thousand lovable tastes of which one was unaware seem to make up the charm of the most decent People there. Elegant conversations cast new lights into the mind and new feelings into the soul there. A woman comes to pose a Question to a young man on a point of science that one assumes he ought to know and about which he does not know a word. What would he not give at that moment to have something to say; he keeps silent and blushes; and finally he is completely astonished that the Lady who had interrogated him in order to give him the opportunity to shine discusses the question herself with as much wisdom and surely more Intelligence than his Professor would have done.

That is when one begins to change ideas; that is when, little by little, one gets over the frenetic prejudices of the earliest youth; finally one acquires a horror for riffraff, one leaves one's coarse friends and one's vile habits, and one no longer gives to the temperament anything but pleasures inspired by the heart: One simultaneously detests the disgusting education one has received and the bad use one has made of one's first freedom, and one wisely tempers the ardor of one's passions by means of the multiplicity of tastes that weaken them by dividing them.

There, I think, is the most common depiction of the introduction of young people into the social world; fortunate are those who get away from it with the shame of having taken such poor advantage of their finest years; fortunate, even, those to whom it costs only a portion of their health and their possessions; fortunate, above all, those whom a wise return to themselves brings them back from their going astray early enough to enjoy life with the status of honorable people; More fortunate those who, guided by moderate and judicious counsels, have been able to become reasonable men and men of the world without passing through such fatal tests. I hope, Sir, that M. de Sainte Marie, enlightened by your enlightenment and supported by my Zeal, will enter it by a charming and more honorable door, and will never have regrets to mix into the remembrance of his earliest years.

Such are the reasons that I have to propose to you, Sir, to give M. your son very early the taste for the society for which he is destined. I know that the premature sight of men and their defects presents to Children a Spectacle very capable of ruining them as soon as one abandons them to their own reflections. I know, furthermore, that it is extremely dangerous to make them Philosophers and reasoners too soon, and to accustom them to dissect someone else's behavior with an air of curiosity and of criticism that would not fail to make of them in the long run wits, makers of epilogues, sarcastic, and ill-humored.

A harsh and fierce teacher who begrudges to others[16] pleasures that are not within his reach believes that he is performing wonders by taking note for his Student's eyes of all the faults that he sees committed, all the shortcomings that he notices and, under the pretext of teaching him to avoid the same imperfections, upon leaving a gathering one does not fail to pass in review everything bad one believed one saw in it, and to exhort him to draw, from the behavior of M. or Madame such and such, good Lessons so as never to imitate them; it is based on these fine instructions that every day are formed those petty makers of satires and Epigrams and that crowd of furies whose dangerous tongues and pens, after having been in fashion for a time, in the end become the horror and the scourge of society.

Perhaps this detestable method found its source in the pulpits of our Preachers, where they take on the task of depicting all men to us as monsters to be stifled, as victims of the Demon whose commerce is made only to corrupt the heart and cast one into Hell: What is singular in this is that, after all these fine declamations, the same man comes gravely to teach us love of the neighbor, that is to say of that entire band of Rogues for whom he inspired us with so much horror.

I hope that more sensible maxims will form M. de Sainte M's judgment. Let him be acquainted with the world as an assembly of decent people for whom he owes great consideration, doubtless subject to vices and weaknesses, but all bearing in themselves a basis of probity and principles of honor which are never effaced and which sooner or later ought to bring them back to wisdom and virtue. It is necessary to be born very unhappily witty to find in all men only subjects for satire; as for me, although I have hardly any wit to praise myself for, I love to bear this satisfying witness to myself of never having left a gathering without having noticed something estimable in it. Thus it is not necessary to believe that one cannot form a young man other than by making him eternally the critic of the human race. So many commentaries about the secret motives of men's actions usually make minds difficult and punctilious, rarely just and penetrating: in the commerce of life it is the same as in politics, an excess of refinement makes us give in to chimeras and distances us from our goal by the roundabout paths that we believe ought to lead us there sooner.

The Actions that are most upright in appearance do not always have the most praiseworthy motives; I admit it, and it is not necessary, in fact, for a young man to take more confidence in someone else's good faith than prudence allows. One must employ this part of their instruction on general Lessons supported only by examples taken from history: but let these examples never be applied to subjects that are alive and too close to us: For, aside from the fact that scandal mongering is very despicable by itself, a sad experience teaches us too well that the spectacle of vice is more suited to seducing than to correcting.

Thus by inspiring M. de Sainte M. with the taste for the social world and good company it will not be at all necessary to be in a hurry to show him all the recesses of the human heart, and even less necessary since, by the selection of the Houses into which one will lead him, he will see only objects and hear only speeches capable of exciting in him a noble emulation for acquiring merit that alone suffices for giving it.

This way I will follow a method completely opposed to the one that I have seen employed by other teachers, and instead of criticizing other people's proceedings in order to perfect him[17] at their expense, on the contrary I will make him notice in them all the things that will appear to me worthy of praise and I shall attempt to put them in a light for him that will please him and give him some taste for them.

As for what is ridiculous, when it is coarse it is impossible for it to escape children's eyes and, since one willingly laughs at it and that pleases them, it is good not to leave them in doubt about the principle of an effect that is so strongly to their taste. Besides, the laws that have established judges and punishments to punish vice deprive us of the right to meddle in it; but for their whole punishment ridiculous people are abandoned to public raillery, and it is not completely unjust that they undergo the only sort of punishment that suits them for the inconvenience they cause in society.[18] Thus I believe that, in this regard, one can, but only extremely carefully, relax some of the attentiveness that one ought always to have with Students of not criticizing Anyone: Above all one must add a necessary corrective to this and, after having let them enjoy themselves for some time, one must skillfully attempt to make them make a little reflection of comparison upon themselves in which their amour-propre will not make out well, so that they might learn to have some indulgence for others from the indulgence they will need, and so that they might accustom themselves always to looking at themselves before blaming someone else.

A young man brought up this way among decent people would not delay in finding his place among them, he would acquire some taste for society, he would learn politeness and the regard that people owe each other reciprocally in life; he would cultivate that multitude of tastes that are opposed to the progress of the passions and in a more advanced age, without changing his pace and almost without noticing it he would already find himself completely initiated into this so dangerous world, the apprenticeship of which costs the majority of young men so dearly.

I admit that these counsels would appear suspect from a teacher whom one could suspect of giving them only for his own interest: but very far from being taxed with loving the social world and dissipation, I know, Sir, that more than once people have tried to make me pass with you as a sad and misanthropic character, as a man little suited to giving gentleness and manners to M. your son, in a word as a shy and Pedantic mind who, in no condition to know the social world, was in even less of one to form a young Student in it. All these accusations appeared so plausible that I could not find it strange if they issued from people Zealous for the education of M. your son: However that might be, I joyfully see that they have not produced much of an effect on your mind, and I shall try to make them appear more unjust to you every day. It is not that I do not feel extremely well all that I am lacking in certain respects: a constrained and perplexed manner, conversation that is dry and without attractiveness, a foolish and ridiculous timidity are defects that will be difficult for me to correct. Three powerful obstacles will always oppose my efforts to succeed in doing so. The first is an invincible inclination toward melancholy that makes up the torment of my soul in spite of me; whether it is temperament or a habit of being unhappy, I bear in myself a source of sadness the origin of which I would not know how to unravel. I have almost always lived in solitude: an invalid and listless, considering the end of my short life as the closest object, a lively degree of sensitivity in a soul[19] that has never been open to anything but suffering, continuously carrying in my bosom both my own pains and those of all that were dear to me, that was only too much to strengthen my natural sadness.

The second obstacle is an insurmountable timidity that causes me to lose my composure and deprives me of freedom of mind, even in front of People as foolish as I am. I ought to have been cured of this defect by the harm it has done me, nevertheless I cannot keep myself from imagining that this can be easily taken advantage of in order to despise me a little more than I deserve.

The third is a profound indifference for everything that is called brilliant. Men's opinion touches me little: not because I disdain it; but on the contrary because I do not regard it as worth their effort to think about me, and because, moreover, the most flattering distinctions would never produce an extremely sharp pleasure in my heart, unless the people from whom it came were extremely dear to me. With such dispositions it is very difficult to acquire the spirit of intercourse and society to a certain point: But do not do me the injustice of concluding from this that I have a harsh and fierce character, or that a base and servile anxiety makes me find myself out of my place among good company; however foreign I might appear in it, I have never seen any other, and in order never to put up with bad company I have learned to be alone when it is necessary, I even dare to add that I feel nothing in my inclinations that does not proclaim to me that I was born to live with the most honorable people.[20]

With regard to my mood; I believe I have the right to complain about those who accuse me of misanthropy and Taciturnity; it is apparently the case that none of them has considered it worth the trouble to examine me a little more closely; for I admit that I could not manage to throw myself at people: I can, nevertheless, bear witness to myself that there is no virtue more dear to me than gentleness of character, and, as a complete proof, I want only to appeal to the pleasure that M. de Sainte Marie shows at finding himself near me. Assuredly, however good his heart might be, at such a tender age it would not be possible for him to acquire a taste for a harsh and fierce Teacher and he must have found in me something that compensates him for the gaiety that I lack and that is so extremely to the liking[21] of Children. I shall not insist on all that any longer and, without a doubt, I shall gain at leaving the effort of my justification entirely to your goodness.

A man without intelligence and without feeling who, having left behind the dust of a College, finds himself suddenly transplanted[22] among the most polite social world is fit neither to feel its charms nor inspire a Pupil's taste. Another man, proud and gruff who, imagining himself to be above everything, believed that he was debasing himself by taking part in ordinary conversation would succeed in it even less. Nevertheless, in order to judge the pace of the social world and of human life in order to develop its resiliencies, and in order to guide a young man in it successfully, I do not believe that it is necessary to have an extremely subtle genius; to think rather precisely, to have good sense and a little taste, not to be singular either out of stupidity or fatuousness, with that alone a Zealous teacher ought to succeed in forming a Child and in making him into a Refined Knight and a decent man which makes up the double object of education.

It is up to you, Sir, and to Madame his Mother to see what is suitable on this point and up to you to take the trouble of taking M. de Sainte Marie[23] with you sometimes if you judge that that would be more advantageous to him. It will also be good if when one has company one keeps him in the room sometimes and by questioning him appropriately about the subjects of the conversation one gives him the occasion to take part in it gradually. But there is one point upon which I fear that I do not find myself entirely in agreement with you. When M. de Sainte Marie finds himself in company before your eyes, he talks trifles and enjoys himself around you and has eyes only for his Papa: a very flattering and lovable mark of tenderness, but if he is constrained to confront someone else or talk to him, right away he loses his composure, he cannot walk or speak a single word, or he takes the extreme and lets out some indiscretion. That is pardonable at his age, but finally one grows up and what was suitable yesterday no longer is suitable today and I dare to say that he will never learn to present himself as long as he keeps this defect. The reason for it is that he is not at all in company even though he might have the world around him, out of fear of being constrained to bother himself he pretends not to see anyone and Papa serves him as an object for distracting himself from all the others. Far from destroying his timidity, this forced boldness will only make it take root more deeply as long as he does not dare to envisage a gathering or respond to those who address a word to him. In order to prevent this inconvenience, I believe, Sir, that it would be good sometimes to keep him away from you, either at Table, or elsewhere, and to give him over a little to Strangers in order to accustom him to familiarizing himself with them. Sir, you ought to pardon me for this excessive precaution against the progression[24] of timidity; I have more reasons than someone else to forestall it in my Students. Timidity is rarely the defect of fools, nevertheless it is clothed with all the ridiculousness of foolishness, and what is worse, of all the defects that one can carry into society it is the most difficult to cure and the only one that is good for nothing.

To all that, I would like, when it is time for it, to join some Reading that without spoiling his heart might make him know men well enough so as not to be completely a stranger among them. We would have a great need for a work of this sort written expressly for young people. Out of all those that we have at present I do not see any more suitable than Molière and la Bruière (I do not speak at all about the Abbé de Bellegarde[25] because I have not read it). These two authors, nevertheless, each have their defects: almost all of Molière's characters are too overdrawn, that very much diminishes the use that Children could draw from Reading him both because they will never see anyone made that way and because, accustomed to these vivid and sharp colors, in the world they will find only much less marked characters and the nuances of which their eyes will not know how to distinguish. Sometimes La Bruière has the same defect, he is even much less within the grasp of Children; as a result of wanting to be strong and concise, he often becomes obscure and stilted and I see almost as much danger for taste in wanting to imitate him as pleasure for the Mind in understanding him.

Besides, the defects of an Author never turn to the prejudice of the Child who reads him when he is dealing with a patient and judicious Teacher; On the contrary, he takes the opportunity to form his taste by making him observe the defective spots, not with that self-important and decisive air that characterizes Pedants, but with a Tone that is circumspect, modest, and suitable to the respect that we owe great men even in the examination of their faults, in a word with the tone of a man who is seeking the truth and who acknowledges himself to be subject to error. Thus one will not at all teach him to speak with the air of a Fop,[26] "That is too flowery," "That is too dry," "That Author thinks falsely," "This one chases after wit," "That one is given to neologisms;" Instead one will tell him simply that one believes that such a thing[27] would have been better that way for such and such reason; that, to tell the truth, the greatest men are subject to making mistakes, but that we who take part in judging them would regard ourselves as very fortunate to make them at the same price.

Now I pass to what concerns the cultivation of the mind, that is to say, to studies properly speaking.

Speak as one might to the disadvantage of Studies and try to annihilate the necessity for them; it will always be fine and useful to know, and as to Pedantry, it is not study itself that gives it but the bad disposition of the subject or the bad habits he has received. Truly Learned People are polite because they know what people owe each other reciprocally, and they are modest because knowledge of what they lack keeps them from acquiring vanity from what they have; it is only petty Geniuses and the half learned who, believing they know everything, proudly despise a thousand things that they do not know at all. Moreover, the taste for Letters is a great resource in life, even for a man of the sword. It is very charming not to always need the cooperation of other men in order to provide oneself with pleasures: so many injustices are committed in the world, one is subject to so many displeasures there that one often has the occasion to estimate oneself as fortunate to find friends and consolations in one's study for lack of [28] those that the world refuses us. I count for nothing the pleasure of shining and of attracting Praises to oneself, because, aside from the fact that it seems extremely frivolous and slight to me, it is directed so close to Pedantry that I would strongly wish not to make my Students too sensitive to it.

But it is not enough to agree about the advantages of study, the great point is to cause the taste for it to be born in M. your son who gives witness to a horrible aversion to everything that smells of application. I dare to say that up to now he has made the progress that he has neither out of obedience nor taste, but solely out of obligingness and friendship for me, and you are not unaware, Sir, how easy the obligingness of Children is to exhaust. Nevertheless, here violence ought not to enter into things at all, I have stated the reason above: but for that to come naturally it is necessary to go back to the source of this Antipathy. This source is an excessive taste for dissipation that he has acquired in fooling around with his brothers and his sister which makes it so that he cannot bear being distracted from it for a moment and he acquires a hatred for everything that produces this effect: For moreover I am convinced that he has no aversion for study in itself, and there are even dispositions from which one can promise oneself a great deal. In order to remedy this inconvenience it would be necessary to provide him with other amusements that detach him from the foolishness with which he occupies himself and for that to hold him a little apart from his brothers and his sister, which can hardly be done in a room like mine, too small for the movements of such a lively child and in which one would even run the risk of impairing his health if one wanted to constrain him to stay too closed in there; perhaps it would be more important, Sir, than you think to have a reasonable room for doing his studies and to be his ordinary place for staying. I would attempt to make it likable for him by means of everything that I could present him that is most pleasant, and it would already be gaining a great deal to make it so that he was pleased to be in the place where he is supposed to study. Then in order to detach him from all his puerile fooling around gradually I would put myself halfway into all his amusements, and I would provide him with the ones most suited for pleasing him and stirring up his curiosity. Some clippings, a little drawing, music, instruments, a prism, a microscope, a burning lens, a barometer, an Aeoliopyle,[29] a Syphon, a hiero fountain,[30] a magnet, and a thousand other little curiosities would continuously provide me with subjects to divert him, instruct him, even without him noticing it, and to attach him little by little to his apartment to the point of no longer taking pleasure everywhere else. From another direction care would be taken to send him to me as soon as he has gotten up without any pretext being able to dispense him from it, he would not be at all allowed to go slouching around the house or to seek refuge near you, nor near Madame his Mother during his working hours, and so as to make him regard study as having an importance that nothing could counterbalance, this time will be avoided for combing him, curling his hair, or giving him any other necessary care. Here, in relation to myself, is how I would go about leading him gradually to studying by his own motion. At the hours in which I wanted to keep him occupied I would take away from him every sort of amusement and I would propose work to him at that hour: If he did not give himself over to it willingly I would not even pretend to notice it, and I would leave him alone and without amusement to mope about until the boredom at being absolutely without anything to do led him by himself to what I was requiring of him; Then I would pretend to shower an enjoyment and a gaiety over his labor that would make him feel the difference a decent occupation has even for pleasure over idling about. If this means did not succeed, I would not treat him badly at all: but I would take all his amusements away from him for that day saying coldly that I do not at all insist on forcing him to study, but that, since entertainment is legitimate only when it is relaxation from labor, those who do not do anything could not have the right to take advantage of it. Beyond this, I would very much keep myself from telling him this with a sharp tone, on the contrary, I would otherwise pretend to act with him as I usually do, even bearing witness to him of being sorry that equity does not allow me to give him his daily amusements; I believe that this evenness of expression and word ought to be an inviolable maxim with Children; when one shows Anger to them, they willingly believe that one is punishing them more out of ill-humor than justice. My goal in this behavior would be to make him accustomed to linking together so well the ideas of Studying and pleasure on one side, and on the other those of idleness and boredom that in the end he might come to regard them as naturally inseparable: I am persuaded that that is the simplest and most certain way of inspiring the taste for study among Children: For, whatever one might do, the idea of constraint and application that studying carries with it will never become agreeable to them except by joining[31] some foreign and pleasant idea that can always be presented at the same time.

For M. your son to take his studies to heart; I believe, Sir, that you ought to bear witness to taking a great share in them yourself: for that, you will have the kindness of interrogating him about his progress sometimes, but only at times and on matters in which he will have done best, so as to have only contentment and satisfaction to show to him and by that to give him even more emulation. Sometimes also, but more rarely, your examination will cover matters he will have neglected; Then you would inform yourself about his health and the causes of his slacking off with signs of uneasiness that would not fail to communicate some of it to himself.

As to the order of his Studies itself, it will be very simple during the first two or three years. The Elements of Latin, of history and Geography will divide his time. With regard to Latin, I do not at all plan to practice it by too methodical a study and still less by the composition of themes. According to M. Rollin,[32] Themes are the cross of Children, and with my intention of making his studies likable I will very much keep myself from making him bear that cross and put into his Head my Latin of bad Gallicisms instead of that of Cicero, of Caesar, and of Titus Livius. Moreover, if he is destined for the Sword, a young man studies Latin in order to understand it and not in order to write it: Thus let him translate Ancient Authors and by reading them let him acquire the taste for fine Literature and for good Latinity, that is all that I will require from him in that regard.

I know that with the need one has to learn French methodically and in some way other than by use, at least if one wants to know how to write, many people prefer to have Children begin by French grammar following the most natural order: nevertheless I would not be completely of this opinion because it seems to me that this is imposing a double labor on them: For after French Grammar it is still necessary to come back to Latin, that is to say to the rudiment, whereas by beginning with that, they learn the Elements of both at the same time; Which furthermore has the advantage of settling their mind better than French Grammar the utility of which they do not feel at first. Thus after these first Elements, I would put the small *Abstract* by Restaut[33] into M. de Sainte Marie's hands and I would attempt to lead him gradually to make very well the distinction between the Genius and construction of the two languages until the time comes to make him read what Vaugelas, Desmarais, and Father Bouhours have written about French grammar and language.[34]

For History and Geography, at first it will be necessary only to give him an easy smattering, from which I shall banish everything that smells too much of dryness and study, reserving for a more advanced age the difficulties of chronology and of the Sphere. Besides, diverging a little from the ordinary plan of studies, I shall attach myself much more to modern than to ancient history, because I believe it to be much more suitable to an officer and because moreover, I am convinced about modern history in general of what M. the Abbé de M. says about that of France in particular,[35] that it does not abound any less in great features than Ancient history does and that it is only lacking better historians to put it in as fine a light.

It is my opinion that all those sorts of studies in which one makes young people languish for a number of years without any solid use should be suppressed for M. de Sainte Marie. Rhetoric, Logic, scholastic Philosophy are all, to my sense, very superfluous things for him: only when it is time for it will I make him read the *Logic* of Port Royal and *The Art of Speaking* by Father Lami:[36] But without amusing him on the one side with lengthy detailed accounts of tropes and figures nor on the other with rules of Syllogisms or with the vain subtleties of dialectic, it is enough to exercise him in precision and purity in style, in order and method in arguments, and in making for himself a spirit of exactness that serves him for disentangling errors and sophisms from the truth.

Thus instead of a formal course of Rhetoric, when M. de Sainte Marie is in a condition to explain pieces of Cicero and Virgil, I shall put into his hands the abridged Quintilian of M. Rollin which he ought to learn by heart,[37] the *Treatise on Studies* by the same Rollin, and the *Manner of Thinking Well*, by Father Bouhours.[38] I shall begin then by having him translate pieces of Titus Livius, Sallust, a little Tacitus, but much Caesar, if I am at least allowed to give something to my particular taste, for I admire the noble simplicity, the purity of style, and clarity of Caesar just as much as I have an aversion for Tacitus whose obscurity can be pierced through only with efforts that are only a pure loss for Readers. I cannot bear that excessive refinement or that fussy manner of seeking out all the subtle and mysterious motives and often as little solid as that of an Arruntius who killed himself out of policy.[39] To me Caesar appears admirable from his air of simplicity and indifference and from his very facility: this Candor and this truth[40] with which the greatest man in the World speaks about himself is a very strong Lesson for young people who might have a penchant for vanity. Perhaps one would wish for Caesar's glory that he had committed some faults, his naivety in recounting them to us would have made him even greater in our eyes.

Today from the manner in which it is treated, natural History can pass for the most interesting of all the sciences that men cultivate and the one that leads us most naturally from admiration for the works to love of the workman. I shall not neglect to make him curious about matters that relate to it, and I intend to introduce him to it in two or three years through the reading of *The Spectacle of Nature*,[41] which perhaps I shall have followed by that of Nyeuwentit.[42] In general, in that Science it is better to see and reason about what we see than to read; thus I shall remove Physics from the rank of our regular studies in order to make it a subject of recreation and promenades, by that means I shall gain time for our studies and our amusements will be more reasonable without being less pleasurable.

There are Systems of Physics that is to say hypotheses following which assuming that the World [has been] arranged, one departs from there to give an account of all Phenomena; I shall explain to him the two principal ones that are in fashion today, rather to make them known to him than to make him adopt them; I have never been able to conceive how a philosopher could seriously imagine a System of Physics; the Cartesians appear ridiculous to me to want to give an account of all natural effects by their assumptions, and the Newtonians even more ridiculous to give their assumptions as facts: Let us be satisfied with knowing what is, without wanting to seek out how things are, since that knowledge is not within our grasp.

One does not go far in physics without a little mathematics; I shall have him given a year of it, which will in addition teach him to reason consistently and to apply himself a little attentively, an exercise that he will very much need. That will also be advantageous for the Condition for which you intend him. That is when it will be necessary to make him reread Caesar, no longer as a Student, but as a warrior: We shall add the reading of Polybius with the comments of the Chevalier Follard, a work about which I have heard it said by people of the Profession that it has not been rendered justice.[43]

Finally if it happens that my Student remains in my hands enough time for that, I shall venture to give him a slightly more reasoned knowledge of Morality and Natural right through the Reading of Puffendorf and Grotius because it is worthy of a decent man and of an intelligent man to know the principles of good and evil, and the foundations upon which the society to which he belongs is established.

In making the sciences follow one after the other this way, I shall not at all lose sight of history as the principal part of his studies and the one whose branches extend the farthest over the other sciences. After several years I shall lead him to its first principles with more method and a more detailed account: It is then that I shall seek to make him draw all the profit that one can hope from that study, and to make him distinguish the genius and morals of the different nations, their vices and their virtues, the causes of their progress and their decadence, the great men they have produced, and the characteristics of the different historians. From all this detail I do not at all claim to give myself an air of erudition; I admit in good faith that although few men of my age have read as much as I have, there are few whose memory is less adorned because I have never had the opportunity to exercise it in conversation. Nevertheless, from all my Readings I have been left with general ideas precise enough perhaps to contribute to forming the taste of a young man, all the more so since the method for doing so appears simple to me: It consists, I believe, only in knowing how to suspend the pleasure of Reading in order to reflect on the Author's art, on the solidity of his thoughts, and on the selection, energy, and elegance of his expressions. The comparisons that one afterward makes of these different results determines the judgment that one brings to bear on different Authors, and these compared judgments are, ordinarily, precise enough if one is not in too much of a rush to make them.

I intend also to make an amusing recreation for him of what is called properly Belles Lettres, such as the knowledge of Books and Authors, of Poetry, Style, Theater, newspapers, and in a word everything that can contribute to forming his taste and showing him study under a smiling face.

I have not said anything about Academic exercises because that is hardly the item that one takes it into one's head to neglect. They are advantageous for several reasons. First, because it is absolutely necessary to know them. In the second place, because they give the Body an agitation that suits young People and which contributes to their health. Third, because they serve as relaxation and recreation from the labors of the Mind, and finally because they distract Children from the little games and other foolishness that narrows the Mind and which, at the very least, is a complete waste of time.

After having given a slight idea of the route that I intend to follow in my Student's Studies, I hope that M. your brother[44] will want to keep his promise to us and draw up a plan that can serve me as a guide in path that is so new to me. I beg him to be assured that I will conform myself to it with a precision that will convince him of my respect and my attentiveness for everything that comes from him. I flatter myself that with such good help and M. de Sainte Marie's fine dispositions, I shall have the joy of seeing him become a decent man, a polite Knight, a Brave Officer, and a good Citizen; the height of my happiness will be to have contributed to it.

Plan for the Education of Monsieur de Sainte-Marie

Sir, you have done me the honor of entrusting me with the instruction of Messieurs your children and; it is up to me to answer for this by all my efforts and by the entire extent of the enlightenment that I might have, and for that I believed that my first object ought to have been to be well acquainted with the subjects with whom I will be concerned: that is how I have principally employed the time that I have had the honor of being in your household, and I believe I am sufficiently informed in that regard to be able to settle the plan for their education. It is not necessary for me to pay you a compliment, Sir, upon the advantageous things that I have noticed there, the affection that I have conceived for them will manifest itself by more solid signs than praises, and as tender and as enlightened a father as you are does not need to be instructed about his children's fine qualities.

At present it remains to me, Sir, to be enlightened by you yourself about the particular views that you might have about each of them, about the degree of authority that you have the design of granting me with regard to them and about the precise limits that you will give to my rights as to rewards and punishments.

It is probable that, having done me the favor of accepting me in your house with an honest salary and flattering distinctions, you have expected from me effects that correspond to such advantageous conditions, and one sees very well that such expense and behavior were not necessary to give Messieurs your children an ordinary preceptor who might teach them basic grammar, spelling, and the catechism. I also intend very well to justify with all my power the favorable hopes that you have been able to conceive on my account and, though, in other respects, I am completely full of faults and weaknesses, you will never for a moment find me to fail in the zeal and attachment that I owe to my students.

But, Sir, whatever efforts and whatever troubles I might take, success is very far from depending on me alone. It is the perfect harmony that ought to reign between us, the confidence that you will deign to grant me, and the authority that you will give me over my students that will determine the effect of my labor. I believe, Sir, that it is completely manifest to you that a man who has no rights of any sort over children either for making his instructions likable or for giving them some weight will never acquire ascendancy over minds that at bottom, however precocious one might wish to assume them to be, at a certain age always determine three-quarters of their operations based on the impressions of the senses. You also feel that a teacher who is obliged to bring his accusations over all a child's faults will very much keep himself, if he could do so with seemliness, from making himself unbearable by ceaselessly renewing vain lamentations and, besides, a thousand small decisive occasions for making a correction or for flattering appropriately get away in the absence of a father and a mother, or in the moments when it would be unseemly to interrupt them in such a disagreeable manner and it is too late to return to them at another moment when a child's change of ideas would make pernicious to him what would have been salutary: finally a child, who does not delay in taking note of a teacher's impotence with regard to him, seizes the occasion to take little account of his prohibitions and his precepts and irrevocably to destroy the ascendancy that the other would strive to acquire. You should not believe, sir, that in speaking in this tone, I wish to procure for myself the right to mistreat Messieurs your children with blows; I have always declared myself against that method, nothing would appear sadder to me for M. de Sainte Marie than if that were the only way left for subduing him, and I dare to promise henceforth to obtain from him all that one will happen to require, by less harsh and more suitable means if you savor the plan that I have the honor of proposing to you. Moreover, speaking frankly, if you think, Sir, that there would be ignominy in M. your son being struck by foreign hands, on my side I also find that an honorable man could hardly put his to a more shameful use than to employ them in mistreating a child. But with regard to M. de Ste. Marie, ways are not lacking for punishing him at need by mortifications that would make even more of an impression, and that would produce better effects: for in a mind as lively as his the idea of blows will be erased as soon as the pain is while that of a marked disdain, or of a perceptible privation will remain there much longer.

 A teacher ought to be feared, for this it is necessary that the student be completely convinced that he has the right to punish him: but above all he ought to be loved, and what means does a governor have to make himself loved by a child to whom he has never anything to propose but occupations contrary to his taste, if moreover he does not have the power to grant him certain small particular pleasures that cost almost no expense nor loss of time and do not fail, being appropriately managed, to be felt extremely by a child and attach him very much to his teacher? I shall rely little on this point, without inconvenience a father can reserve for himself the exclusive right to grant favors provided that he brings the following precautions to it, above all necessary for M. de Ste. M. whose liveliness and inclination to lack discipline requires more dependency. (1) Before giving him any gift, to learn secretly from the governor whether there is occasion to be satisfied with the Child's behavior. (2) To declare to the young man that when he has any favor to ask, he ought to do it by his governor's mouth, and that if he should happen to ask on his own initiative that alone will be enough not to allow it to him. (3) Sometimes to take the occasion from that to reproach the governor for being too kind, that this too great easiness will harm his student's progress, and that it is up to his own prudence to correct what is lacking in a child's moderation. (4) That if the teacher believes he has some reason to be opposed to any gift that one wants to give his student, to refuse absolutely to grant it to him, until he has found the means to move his preceptor. Moreover, it will not be at all necessary to explain to the young child in the event that one does grant him some favor that it is precisely because he has done his duty well, but it is better for him to conclude that pleasures and enjoyments are the natural consequences of wisdom and good behavior, than for him to regard them as arbitrary recompenses that might depend on caprice and that at bottom ought never to be proposed as the object or the prize for study and for virtue.

There, Sir, at least, are the rights that you ought to grant me over M. your son if you wish to give him a fortunate education and one that answers to the fine qualities that he shows in many respects but that at present are obscured by many bad habits that require being corrected right away and before time has made it impossible to do so. That is so true that it is very far from being the case that so many precautions are necessary with M. de Condillac. He has as much need to be pushed as the other has to be held back, and I will be very capable by myself of taking all the ascendancy I shall need over him: but for M. de Ste. M. it is a decisive point for his education to give him a bridle that he feels and that is capable of holding him back. In the state things are in, the feelings that you will wish him to have on my account, Sir, depend very much more on you than on myself.

I am always assuming, Sir, that you would be very careful not to entrust the education of Messieurs your children to a man whom you did not believe worthy of your esteem, and do not think, I beg you, that by the decision that I have taken to attach myself unreservedly to your house in a delicate occasion, I claimed to engage you in any manner; there is a great deal of difference between us: in doing my duty as much as you will leave me the freedom to do so, I am not responsible for anything, and at bottom, as you are, Sir, the master and the natural superior of your children, I do not have the right to want to force your taste to relate itself to mine with regard to their education; thus after you have made the representations that appeared necessary to me, if it happened that you did not judge them the same way, my conscience would be easy in that regard, and the only thing left for me to do would be to conform myself to your will. But for you, sir, no human consideration can counterbalance what you owe to the morals and education of Messieurs your children, and I would not find it bad in any way that, after having discovered defects that you perhaps might not have noticed at first, and that might have a certain consequence for my students, you pursued a better subject elsewhere.

Thus I have reason to think that as long as you tolerate me in your house, you have not found anything in me to efface the esteem with which you have honored me. It is true, Sir, that I could complain that on the occasions when I might have committed some fault, you have not done me the honor of notifying me about it plainly, that is a favor for which I asked you upon entering your home, and that at least showed my good will: and if it is not in my own regard, at least it would be for that of Messieurs your children, whose interest would be for me to become a perfect man, if it were possible.

With these assumptions, I believe, Sir, that you ought not to give any difficulty over communicating to M. your son the good sentiments that you might have on my account, and that, since it is impossible for my faults and my weaknesses to escape eyes as clear-sighted as yours, it would be impossible for you to avoid too much discussing them in his presence: for these are impressions that strike a blow, and as M. de la Bruyère says, the first care of children is to seek out their teachers' weak points in order to acquire the right of despising them:[1] now, I ask what impression could be made by the lessons of a man for whom his schoolboy has disdain?

In order to flatter myself at a fortunate success in the education of M. your son, I cannot then require anything less than to be loved, feared, and esteemed by him. If one were to respond to me that all that ought to be my work, and that it is my fault if I have not succeeded in it, I would have to complain about such an unjust judgment; you have never explained to me the authority that you permit me to take with regard to him, which was all the more necessary since I am beginning a profession that I have never had, since having found in him from the beginning a perfect resistance to my instructions and an excessive negligence for me,

I have not known how to subdue him; and at the slightest discontentment he ran to seek an inviolable refuge with his papa, to whom perhaps he did not fail afterward to give an account of things as it pleased him.

Fortunately the evil is not great; at his age we have had the leisure to feel our way, so to speak, reciprocally, without this delay having yet been able to bring any great prejudice to his progress, which moreover the delicacy of his health would not have allowed to push very much* but since bad habits, dangerous at every age, are infinitely more so at that one, it is time to put some order into them seriously: not in order to burden him with studies and duties, but in order right away to give him a habit of obedience and docility that will be found to be completely acquired when it is time for it.

We are approaching the end of the year: you will not be able to find a more natural occasion, Sir, than the beginning of the new one to give a little speech to M. your son within the reach of his age which, setting before his eyes the advantages of a good education and the inconveniences of a neglected education, disposes him to lend himself willingly to what the knowledge of his interest well understood will make us require from him afterward. After which you would have the kindness to declare to me in his presence that you are making me the depository of your authority over him, and that you are granting me without reserve the right to oblige him to fulfill his duty by the means that will appear suitable to me, in consequence ordering him to obey me as he does you yourself under penalty of all your indignation. This declaration, which will only be in order to make a more lively impression on him, moreover will have no effect other than in conformity to what you will have taken the trouble of prescribing to me in private.

There, Sir, are the indispensable preliminaries for being assured that the efforts that I will be giving to M. your son will not be wasted. Now I am going to trace the sketch of his education as I had conceived its plan based on what I have known up to now about his character and your intentions. I do not at all propose it as a rule to which it is necessary to be attached: but as a project that, needing to be recast and corrected by your enlightenment and by that of Monsieur the Abbé de . . .[2] will serve only to give him some idea of the genius of the child with whom we are dealing, and I shall esteem myself only too happy for Monsieur your brother to want to guide me in the paths I should keep to: he can be assured that I shall make it an inviolable principle for myself to follow entirely, and in accordance with the entire small reach of my enlightenment and my

---

* It was extremely failing when I entered the house: today his health has visibly gotten stronger.

talents, the routes he will have taken the trouble of prescribing to me with your approval.

The goal that one ought to propose for oneself in the education of a young man is to form his heart, judgment, and Mind, and to do so in the order that I name them: most teachers, especially the pedants, regard the acquisition and heaping up of types of knowledge as the sole object of a fine education without thinking that often, as Molière says,

> A learned fool is more of a fool than an ignorant fool.[3]

From another side, many Fathers, rather despising everything that is called studies, care about hardly anything but forming their children in the exercising of the body and knowledge of the world. Between these extremes we will take a golden mean in order to lead M. your son; the sciences ought not to be neglected, I shall speak about them right away, but they also ought not to precede morals, above all in a mind that is sparkling and full of fire hardly capable of attention up to a certain age and the character of which will be found to be determined very early. What use is the knowledge of Varro to a man if otherwise he does not know how to think accurately: if he had the misfortune to let his heart be corrupted, in his head the sciences are like so many weapons in the hands of a madman. Of two persons equally committed to vice, the less skillful will always do the less evil, and the sciences, even the most speculative and the ones in appearance farthest removed from society do not fail to exercise the mind and, by exercising it, giving it a force that it is easy to abuse in the commerce of life when one has a bad heart.

There is more with regard to M. de Sainte Marie. He has conceived such a strong distaste against everything that bears the name of study and application that a great deal of art and time will be needed to destroy it, and it would be regrettable if this time were wasted for him, for there would be too many inconveniences in constraining him to it, and it would be even better for him to be entirely ignorant about what studies and sciences are than to know them only in order to detest them.

With regard to religion and morality; it is not at all by multiplying precepts that one will be able to succeed in inspiring in him solid principles that serve as a rule for his behavior for the rest of his life. Aside from the Elements that are within the reach of his age, at first one ought to consider less tiring out his memory with a detailed account of laws and duties than disposing his mind and his heart to knowing them and to relishing them to the extent that the occasion presents itself for developing them in him; and it is from that very thing that these preparations are all completely within the reach of his age and his mind, because they contain nothing but curious and interesting subjects about civil commerce, about the arts and professions, and about the varied manner in which Providence has made all men useful and necessary to each other. These Subjects which are more matters for conversations and promenades than ordered studies will have various advantages the effect of which appears infallible to me.

First; not disagreeably affecting his mind by means of the ideas of constraint and ordered study, and not demanding from him a painful and continuous attention, they will not have anything harmful to his health. In the second place they will accustom his mind early to reflection and to considering things from their consequences and their effects. 3rd. They will make him curious and inspire him with the taste for the natural sciences.

Here I ought to anticipate an impression that one might receive about my project by imagining that I am only seeking to enjoy myself and to rid myself of what is dry and boring in lessons in order to procure a more pleasant occupation for myself. I do not believe, Sir, that it could fall into your mind to think this way on my account. Perhaps a man has never made a more important business for himself than the one that I am making of Messieurs your children's education if you want to second my zeal: up to the present you have no occasion to notice that I am seeking to flee labor; but I do not at all believe that, in order to give himself an air of zeal and occupation, a teacher ought to pretend to overburden his students with an unappealing and serious labor, always to show them a severe and angry countenance and to make for himself this way the reputation of a precise and hardworking man at their expense. For myself, Sir, I declare it once and for all: scrupulous to the utmost extent over the performance of my duty, I am incapable of ever relaxing in it: neither my taste nor my principles ever lead me to either laziness or relaxation: but out of the two ways of assuring myself of the same success I shall always prefer the one that costs the least trouble and unpleasantness to my students and I dare to assure without wanting to appear to be a very busy man that the less they will be working in appearance the more I shall be working for them.

If there are some occasions in which severity might be necessary with regard to children it is in cases connected to morals or when it is a question of correcting bad habits. Often the more wit a child has the more the knowledge of his own advantages makes him indocile about the ones that remain for him to acquire. From that, disdain toward inferiors, disobedience to superiors, and rudeness with equals: when one believes oneself to be perfect what shortcomings does one not give oneself? M. de

Sainte Marie has too much intelligence not to feel his fine qualities: but unless one watches out for it he will count too much upon them and will neglect to draw all the advantage that would be necessary. These seeds of vanity have already produced in him many little inclinations that must be corrected. It is in this respect, Sir, that we cannot act in too coordinated a manner, and it is very important that, whenever there is occasion to be dissatisfied with him, from every direction he finds an appearance of indifference and disdain that will mortify him all the more since these signs of coldness will not be at all ordinary for him. This is punishing pride by its own weapons and attacking it in its very source, and one can rest assured that M. de Sainte M. is too well born not to be infinitely sensitive to the esteem of persons who are dear to him.

When it is reinforced by reasoning, rectitude of heart is the source of aptness of mind; a decent man almost always thinks aptly, and when one is accustomed from childhood not to dizzy oneself over reflection and not to abandon oneself to present pleasure until after having weighed its consequences and set its advantages into balance with the inconveniences, with a little experience one has acquired almost everything necessary for forming the judgment. In fact, it seems that good sense depends even more on feelings of the heart than on enlightenment of the mind, and one has the experience that the most learned and the most enlightened people are not always those who conduct themselves best in the business of life: thus, after having filled M. de Sainte Marie with good principles of morality, in a sense one could regard him as advanced enough in the science of reasoning: but if there is an important point in education without contradiction it is that one, and one could not teach him too well to be acquainted with men; to know how to take them by their virtues and even by their weaknesses in order to lead them to his goal and always to choose the best course in difficult occasions. That depends in part on the manner in which one gives him practice in considering objects and turning them over on all their facets, and in part on experience of the world. As to the first point, you can contribute very much to it, Sir, and with very great success by sometimes pretending to consult him about the manner in which you should behave in hypothetical cases; that will flatter his vanity, and he will not at all regard as labor the time that will be put into deliberating over a piece of business in which his voice will be counted for something. It is in such conversations that one can give him the most enlightenment about the knowledge of the world, and he will learn more by this means in two hours' time than he would in two years by formal instructions; but it is necessary to watch out not to present him with anything but matters proportionate to his age and above all to give him practice for a long time on subjects in which the best course can be easily seen, both for the goal of leading him more easily to find it as if by himself and for keeping him from envisaging the business of life as a series of problems in which, the various courses of action appearing equally probable, it would be almost indifferent to decide for one rather than for the other, which would lead him to indolence in reasoning and indifference in conduct.

Experience of the world also appears to be absolutely necessary and even more so for M. de Sainte M. since, born timid, he needs to see company often in order to learn to find himself at liberty in it and to behave in it with those graces and that ease that characterize the man of the world and likable man. For that, Sir, you would have the kindness to indicate to me two or three houses in which I could sometimes take him as a form of relaxation and recompense; it is true that, having to correct in myself the defects that I am seeking to forestall in him, I could appear little suited to this practice. It is up to you, Sir, and to Madame his mother to see what is suitable, and up to you to take the trouble of taking him with you sometimes if you judge that that would be more advantageous to him. It will also be good if, when one has a crowd over, one keeps him in the room and by sometimes questioning him appropriately about the subjects of the conversation one gives him the occasion to take part in it gradually. But there is one point upon which I fear that I do not find myself entirely in agreement with you. When M. de Sainte Marie finds himself in company before your eyes, he talks trifles and enjoys himself around you and has eyes only for his papa: a very flattering and lovable tenderness, but if he is constrained to confront someone else or talk to him, right away he loses his composure, he cannot walk or speak a single word, or he takes the extreme and lets out some indiscretion. That is pardonable at his age, but finally one grows up and what was suitable yesterday no longer is suitable today and I dare to say that he will never learn to present himself as long as he keeps this defect. The reason for it is that he is not at all in company even though he might have the world around him; out of fear of being constrained to bother himself he pretends not to see anyone and papa serves him as an object for distracting himself from all the others. Far from destroying his timidity, this forced boldness will only make it take root more deeply as long as he will not at all dare to envisage a gathering or respond to those who address a word to him. In order to prevent this inconvenience, I believe, Sir, that it would be good sometimes to keep him away from you, either at table, or elsewhere, and to give him over to strangers in order to accustom him to familiarizing himself with them.

One would be concluding very badly if, from everything that I have just been saying, one concluded that, wanting to rid myself of the trouble of instructing, or perhaps out of bad taste despising the sciences, I had no plan for forming M. your son in them, and that after having instructed him in the indispensable elements I will keep myself there, without putting myself to the trouble of pushing him in suitable studies. Those who know me will not reason that way, my declared taste for the sciences is known, and I have cultivated them enough that I should have made some progress in them however little disposition I might have had.

Speak as one might to the disadvantage of studies and try to annihilate the necessity for them, and to exaggerate their bad effects; it will always be fine and useful to know, and as to pedantry, it is not study itself that gives it but the bad disposition of the subject or the bad habits he has received. Truly learned people are polite and they are modest because knowledge of what they lack keeps them from acquiring vanity from what they have; it is only petty geniuses and the half learned who, believing they know everything, proudly despise what they do not know at all. Moreover, the taste for letters is a great resource in life, even for a man of the sword. It is very charming not to always need the cooperation of other men in order to provide oneself with pleasures, and so many injustices are committed in the world, one is subject to so many setbacks there that one often has the occasion to estimate oneself as fortunate to find friends and consolers in one's study for lack of those that the world takes away from or refuses us.

But it is a question of causing the taste for them to be born in M. your son, who at present gives witness to a horrible aversion to everything that smells of application. Already here violence ought not to enter into things at all, I have stated the reason above: but for that to come back naturally it is necessary to go back to the source of this antipathy. This source is an excessive taste for dissipation that he has acquired in fooling around with his brothers and his sister which makes it so that he cannot bear being distracted from it for a moment and he acquires an aversion for everything that produces this effect: for moreover I am convinced that he has no hatred for study in itself, and there are even dispositions from which one can promise oneself a great deal. In order to remedy this inconvenience it would be necessary to provide him with other amusements that detach him from the foolishness with which he occupies himself, and for that, to hold him a little apart from his brothers and his sister, which can hardly be done in a apartment like mine, too small for the movements of such a lively child and in which one would even run the risk of impairing his health if one wanted to constrain him to stay too closed in there. It would be more important, Sir, than you think to have a reasonable room for doing his studies and to be his ordinary place for staying; I would attempt to make it likable for him by means of everything that I could present him that is most pleasant, and it would already be gaining a lot to make it so that he was pleased to be in the place where he is supposed to study. Then in order to gradually detach him from that puerile fooling around I would put myself halfway into all his amusements, and I would provide him with the ones must fitting for pleasing him and stirring up his curiosity; little games, some clippings, a little drawing, music, instruments, a prism, a microscope, a burning lens, and a thousand other little curiosities would provide me with subjects to divert him and to attach him little by little to his apartment, to the point of no longer taking pleasure everywhere else. From another direction care would be taken to send him to me as soon as he has gotten up without any pretext being able to dispense him from it, he would not be allowed to go slouching around the house or to seek refuge near you, nor near Madame his Mother during his working hours, and so as to make him regard study as having an importance that nothing could counterbalance, this time will be avoided for combing him, curling his hair, or giving him any other necessary care. Here, in relation to myself, is how I would go about leading him gradually to studying by his own motion. At the hours in which I wanted to keep him occupied I would take away from him every species of amusement and I would propose work to him at that hour; if he did not give himself over to it willingly I would not even pretend to notice it, and I would leave him alone and without amusement to mope about, until the boredom at being absolutely without anything to do led him by himself to what I was requiring of him; Then I would pretend to shower an enjoyment and a gaiety over his labor that would make him feel the difference a decent occupation has, even for pleasure, over idling about. If this means did not succeed, I would not treat him badly at all; but I would take away from him all his recreation for that day saying coldly that I do not at all insist on forcing him to study, but that, since entertainment is legitimate only when it is relaxation from labor, those who do not do anything have no need for it: moreover you would have the goodness to agree with me from a sign by which, without apparent collusion, I could testify to you in the same way as to Madame his mother when I was dissatisfied with him. Then the coldness and indifference that he would find on every side, without nevertheless making him the slightest reproach, would surprise him all the more since he would not at all perceive that I complained about him, and he would bring himself to believe that just as the natural recompense for duty is the friendship and blandishments of his superiors, in the same way doing nothing and idleness bear with them a definite despicable character that makes itself felt right away and that cools off the entire world with regard to him.

I knew a tender father who did not trust a mercenary so much over the instruction of his children that he did not want to have an eye over it himself; in order not to neglect anything at all that could give some emulation to his children, the good father had adopted the same means that I am setting forth here. When he saw his children again, before greeting them he cast a glance at their governor: when the latter touched the first button of his outfit with the right hand, this was a sign that he was satisfied and the father caressed his son in his ordinary way; if the governor touched the second, then that was the sign of perfect satisfaction, and the father did not set any limits to the tenderness of his caresses and usually added to them some gift but without affectation; when the governor made no sign at all, that meant that he was poorly satisfied, and the coldness of the father corresponded to the teacher's dissatisfaction: but, when the latter touched his first button with his left hand, the father had his son taken from his presence and then the governor explained the child's faults to him. In a little time, I saw this young lord acquire such great perfections, that I believe that one cannot augur too well from a method that has produced such good effects: also it is only a perfect harmony and correspondence that can assure the success of a good education; and since the best father would vainly give himself motions in order to bring up his child well if otherwise he left him in the hands of an inattentive preceptor, even the most intelligent and most zealous of all teachers would be making wasted efforts if the father, instead of seconding him, destroyed his work by inopportune steps.

For M. your son to take his studies to heart; I believe, Sir, that you ought to bear witness to taking a great share in them yourself: for that, you will have the kindness of interrogating him about his progress sometimes, but only at times and on matters in which he will have done best, so as to have only contentment and satisfaction to show to him, not nevertheless by too great praises suited to inspiring him with pride and making him count too much on himself. Sometimes also, but more rarely, your examination will cover matters he will have neglected; Then you would inform yourself about his health and the causes of his slacking off with signs of uneasiness that would not fail to communicate some of it to himself.

When you, Sir, or Madame his mother has some gift to give him, you will have the goodness to choose the times when there will be the greatest occasion to be satisfied with him, or at least to notify me in advance, so that I might avoid during that time exposing him to giving me subject to complain about him; for at that age the slightest irregularities strike a blow.

As to the order of his studies itself, it will be very simple during the first two or three years. The elements of Latin, of history and geography will divide his time: with regard to Latin, I do not at all plan to practice it by too methodical a study and still less by the composition of themes; according to M. Rollin, themes are the cross of children, and with my intention of making his studies likable I will very much keep myself from making him bear that cross, nor to put into his head my Latin of bad Gallicisms instead of that of Titus Livius, of Caesar, and of Cicero. Moreover, above all if he is destined for the sword, a young man studies Latin in order to understand it and not in order to write it, a thing that it will never happen for him to need once in his life. Thus let him translate ancient authors and by reading them let him acquire the taste for good Latinity and for fine Literature, that is all that I will require from him in that regard.

For history and geography, at first it will be necessary only to give him an easy smattering, from which I shall banish everything that smells too much of dryness and study, reserving for a more advanced age the most necessary difficulties of chronology and of the sphere. Besides, diverging a little from the ordinary plan of studies, I shall attach myself much more to modern than to ancient history, because I believe it to be much more suitable to an officer and because moreover, I am convinced about modern history in general of what M. the Abbé de . . . says about that of France in particular,[4] that it does not abound any less in great features than ancient history does and that it is only lacking better historians to put it in as fine a light.

It is my opinion that all those sorts of studies in which one makes young people languish for numerous years without any solid use should be suppressed for M. de Sainte Marie: rhetoric, logic, scholastic philosophy are all, to my sense, very superfluous things for him: only when it is time for it I will make him read the *Logic* of Port Royal and at the very most *The Art of Speaking* by Father Lami, but without amusing him on the one side with lengthy detailed accounts of tropes and figures nor on the other with the vain subtleties of dialectic, I plan only to exercise him in precision and purity in style, in order and method in arguments, and in making for himself a spirit of exactness that serves him for disentangling the falsely ornate from the simple truth whenever the opportunity presents itself.

Today from the manner in which it is treated, natural history can pass for the most interesting of all the sciences that men cultivate and the one that leads us most naturally from admiration for the works to love of the workman. I shall not neglect to make him curious about matters that relate to it, and I intend to introduce him to it in two or three years through the reading of *The Spectacle of Nature*, which perhaps I shall have followed by that of Niuventyt.

One does not go far in physics without the aid of mathematics; and I shall have him given a year of it, which will in addition teach him to reason consistently and to apply himself a little attentively, an exercise that he will very much need. That will also put him within reach of making himself better considered among the Officers, for whom a smattering of mathematics and fortifications makes up a part of the profession.

Finally if it happens that my student remains in my hands long enough, I shall venture to give him a slightly more reasoned knowledge of morality and natural right through the Reading of Puffendorf and Grotius because it is worthy of a decent man and of a reasonable man to know the principles of good and evil, and the foundations upon which the society to which he belongs is established.

In making the sciences follow one after the other this way, I shall not at all lose sight of history as the principal object of all his studies and the one whose branches extend the farthest over all the other sciences. After several years I shall lead him to its first principles with more method and a more detailed account: It is then that I shall seek to make him draw all the profit that one can hope from that study.

I intend also to make an amusing recreation for him of what is called properly Belles Lettres, such as the knowledge of books and authors, of poetry, style, eloquence, theater, and in a word everything that can contribute to forming his taste and showing him study under a smiling face.

I shall not dwell any longer on this point; because after having given a slight idea of the route that I had intended to follow in my student's studies, I hope that M. your brother[5] will want to keep the promise he made you to draw us up a plan that can serve me as a guide in a path that is so new to me. In advance I beg him to be assured that I will conform myself to it with an exactitude and care that will convince him of the profound respect and my attentiveness for what comes from him, and I dare to answer to you for it that it will not be a result of my zeal and my attachment if Messieurs his nephews do not become perfect men.

Rousseau to the abbé Guillaume-Thomas-François Raynal[1]

I believe, Sir, that it will give you pleasure to see the enclosed extract from a letter from Stockholm which the person to whom it is addressed charged me to ask you to insert in the Mercury. Its object is of the utmost importance for men's lives; and the more excessive the public's negligence is in this respect, the more enlightened citizens ought to redouble their zeal and activity to overcome it.

All the Chemists of Europe have been warning us for a long time about the deadly qualities of copper, and about the dangers to which one exposes oneself in making use of this pernicious metal in sets of kitchen utensils. M. Rouelle,[2] of the Academy of Sciences, is the one who has demonstrated the fatal effects of this most tangibly, and who has raised the most vehement complaints about it. M. Thierri,[3] Doctor of Medicine, has gathered together in a learned Thesis, which he defended under the presidency of M. Falconet,[4] a multitude of proofs capable of frightening any reasonable man who attaches some importance to his life and that of his fellow citizens. These Physicists have caused it to be seen that the verdigris or dissolved copper is a violent poison, whose effect is always accompanied by horrible symptoms; that even the vapor of this metal is dangerous, since the Workers who work with it are subject to various fatal or chronic maladies; that all solvents, fats, salts, and even water dissolve copper and make it into verdigris; that the most precise plating only causes this dissolution to diminish; that the tin that is employed in this plating itself is not exempt from danger, in spite of the indiscriminate use that has been made of this metal up to the present, and that this danger is greater or lesser in accordance with the different sorts of tin that are employed, in proportion to the arsenic that enters into their composition, or the lead that enters into their alloy;* that, even assuming an adequate precaution in the plating, it is an unpardonable imprudence to make men's life and health depend on a very slender plate of tin that

---

* That dissolved lead is a poison is proved only too well by the fatal accidents caused every day by wines adulterated with litharge. Thus to use this metal safely it is important to know well which solvents attack it.

wears away very quickly,* and on the precision of Servants and Cooks who ordinarily reject recently plated vessels because of the bad taste that the materials used in plating give. They have caused it to be seen how many horrible accidents produced by copper are attributed every day to entirely different causes; they have proven that a multitude of people die, and that an even greater number are attacked by a thousand different maladies by the use of this metal in our kitchens and in our fountains, without them suspecting the genuine cause of their illnesses. Nevertheless although the manufacturing of utensils of beaten and plated iron, which is established at the Faubourg Saint-Antoine, offers easy ways to substitute in kitchens less costly sets of utensils, as convenient as those of copper, and perfectly healthy, at least as to the principal metal, men's usual laziness about things that are genuinely useful to them, and the little maxims that laziness invents about established practices, above all when they are bad, have so far allowed only a little progress to the wise warnings of the Chemists, and have proscribed copper from only a few kitchens. The repugnance of Cooks for using other vessels than the ones they know is an obstacle whose whole force is felt only when one is acquainted with the laziness and gluttony of the masters. Everyone knows that society abounds in people who prefer indolence to rest and pleasure to happiness; but one has trouble conceiving that there are people who prefer to expose themselves and their whole family to perishing in horrible torments, rather than to eat a burnt stew.

One must reason with wise men and never with the public. The multitude has been compared to a flock of sheep for a long time; it is necessary to give it examples instead of arguments, for everyone fears being ridiculed much more than being foolish or wicked. Moreover in all things that concern the common interest, since almost all people judge in accordance with their own maxims, they are less attached to examining the force of proofs than to penetrating the secret motives of the one who proposes them: for example, many honest readers would willingly suspect that the Head of the factory of beaten iron, or the Author of domestic fountains is animating my zeal with money on this occasion; a rather natural mistrust in this age of charlatanry, in which the greatest rogues always have public interest in their mouth. In this example is more persuasive than argument, because, since in all likelihood the same

* It is easy to demonstrate that, in whatever manner one goes about it, one could not, in the uses of kitchen utensils, be certain for a single day of the most solid plating. For since tin melts at a degree of heat extremely inferior to that of boiling grease, every time a Cook browns some butter, it is not possible for him to safeguard some part of the plating from melting, nor consequently the stew from contact with the copper.

mistrust must also have been in other people's minds, one is brought to believe that those whom it has not kept from adopting what one is proposing have found decisive reasons for doing so. Thus, instead of stopping to show how absurd it is, even in doubt, to leave utensils suspected of poison in the kitchen, it is worth more to say that M. Duverney[5] has just ordered a set of iron kitchen utensils for the Ecole militaire; that M. the Prince de Conti[6] has banished all copper from his kitchen; that M. the duc de Duras, Ambassador to Spain has done the same, and that his Cook, whom he consulted on this question, told him bluntly that all those of his profession who did not accommodate themselves to the set of iron kitchen utensils just as well as to those of copper were ignoramuses or people of ill will. Numerous private individuals have followed this example which the enlightened persons who handed over the enclosed extract to me have set for a long time, without their table feeling the effect of this change in the slightest except from the confidence with which one can eat excellent stews, very well prepared in vessels of iron.

But what can one put under the eyes of the public that would be more striking than this very extract? If there were in the world a Nation that ought to be opposed to the expulsion of copper, it is certainly Sweden, whose mines of this metal constitute its principal wealth, and whose peoples in general idolize their ancient customs. Nevertheless it is this Kingdom, so rich in copper, that is setting the example for others, of taking away from this metal all the uses that render it dangerous and that concern the life of citizens; it is these Peoples, so attached to their old practices, who are renouncing without difficulty a multitude of commodities that they would take away from their mines as soon as reason and the authority of wise men show them the risk that the indiscriminate use of this metal is making them run. I would like to be able to hope that such a salutary example will be followed in the rest of Europe, where one ought not to have the same repugnance at proscribing, at least in kitchens, a metal that one draws from outside. I would like the public warnings of Philosophers and literary People to awaken Peoples about the dangers of every sort to which their imprudence exposes them, and more often recall to all Sovereigns that care for the preservation of men is not only their first duty, but also their greatest interest.

I am, Sir, etc.

EXTRACT OF A LETTER WRITTEN BY A SENATOR OF SWEDEN TO A LADY OF PARIS[7]

From Stockholm, May 8, 1753

Madam, you have so well fulfilled the promise you had made me to send me the recipe for the plating of iron, that I do not know, in truth, how to bear witness to you of all my gratitude. I beg you to receive my very humble thanks for all the trouble that you deigned to take for this Country which, in a hundred years from now, will owe you the preservation of numerous hundreds of thousands inhabitants that the use of copper has been removing from us daily. I have had M. Amy's[8] book translated and printed in Sweden; I have had numerous Dissertations that have appeared in your country and elsewhere about the same matter inserted into our Gazettes and into our literary Journals; all this has had such a great effect here and in our Provinces that at present people are occupied with nothing but reforming old sets of kitchen utensils and other copper utensils in order to substitute other ones of iron for them. Nevertheless at first this reform will not be so universal as one would wish; there are some heads in which prejudices holds more strongly than in others, it will be very necessary to give them time to find their way. But, while waiting, what appeared most important to me has been to set the example for the private individual by a similar reform in all the establishments that depend immediately on the efforts and the public order of the Government. For this effect the King has already had a circular letter written to all the Colonels of the army for them to sell, without losing any time, the cooking pots, the decanters, and all other copper utensils that enter into the equipment of the troops, and henceforth for iron alone to be employed for all these uses. The same orders will be given to the Navy as soon as our new Factories are in a condition to furnish its needs. You see, Madam, that I am not losing any time at all to carry out what is in the order of possibilities. I shall have the honor of giving you an account of the remainder to the extent as I have new progress to convey to you.

Treatise on the Sphere[1]

[First Chapter]

In order to know how to act, let us learn how to think. To know how to think is the most universal talent of human life. It is by it alone that one can make good use for oneself of fortune, other people, and oneself. All things being equal, the one who thinks the best is the closest to happiness. To think is to have ideas and combine them; it is to see objects and compare them; it is to find the true relations that they have among themselves; it is to draw conclusions that lead to the knowledge of the truth; it is to fit them to the things that are useful to us. Thus the Art of thinking is the Art of making ourselves as happy as we can. Now that depends on us much more than is thought; and the majority of men are unhappy less from their own situation than because they do not know how to benefit from it.

To learn how to think is, then, to proceed to our primary destination in this life; it is to learn how to make us happy. But this knowledge presupposes many others. We do not generate our own ideas, they come to us from outside.

In order to succeed in knowing ourselves it is necessary to know many things that are not us. A man does not know himself well unless he knows other men well; and in order to know men, it is also necessary to know the things on which they are dependent. Thus everything is connected. Wisdom leads to happiness, knowledge leads to wisdom.[2] The best natural mind is nothing without instruction. With the best eyes, the most clearsighted man would not see anything, if he did not learn to see in his infancy.

In order to learn to know ourselves, let us then begin by studying what surrounds us. In order to know oneself, it is necessary to know man. In order to know man, it is necessary to study men; and to know men, it is necessary to study them in various times, in various places.[3] It is necessary to begin by seeing them in the great tableau of History. It is there that by contemplating them in all possible situations, given over to all the human passions, to all the vicissitudes of things, exposed to all the play of fortune, sometimes foolish and sometimes wise, sometimes good and sometimes wicked, in that prodigious variety of relations and differences, we learn to disentangle what is essential to man, what is inseparable, what one always finds in him, from what is only accidental to him, and which can change in him in accordance with Nations and in accordance with Ages. In contrasts of virtues and crimes, of weakness and strength, of greatness and pettiness, which will often strike us, we learn to separate man from his mask, and not to believe that we have known human Nature well enough by seeing the men that are around us.

Second Chapter

Before investigating the origin of the human race, let us cast a glance upon its abode; it is worthy of some attention. The abode of man and of all the animals, this earth covered with so many trees and plants, with so many Mountains and Valleys, with so many rocks and seas; this vast limitless and endless world, is a very great dwelling-place to our material eyes, but very small to the eyes of our reason, when they begin to open up. In the immense space of the air, in that frightening Expanse in which the imagination drowns itself, by means of thought I transport myself into one of those enormous and luminous masses that rotate majestically over our heads; and I perceive from afar a grain of sand, which floats in that aerial sea. It escapes from my sight by its smallness; I need a telescope to perceive it. Laughing, I ask whether there are mites small enough to inhabit this grain of sand? "Doubtless," a Philosopher of the place tells me, "it is covered with I know not what little insects that are called men, and who have divided its surface into Regions, Nations, Provinces. They have built Cities and Towns on it. They have founded Empires and Republics on it. They have established Kings, Magistrates, Grandees on it. They have erected Tribunals on it. They have formed Academies, Universities on it where they gravely dispute about whether we others, who are here, are something or nothing."—"There," I answer, "are arrogant and vain reptiles whose brood I would crush under my fingernail with great pleasure."—"Not so fast," resumes the Saturnian Philosopher, "let's not crush anyone, out of fear of being crushed ourselves under the fingernails of the inhabitants of those other Heavenly Bodies, incomparably larger than ours. These poor little animals with their five feet of height are as well founded in finding themselves large as we are with our twenty-five or thirty feet from those other Beings who perhaps have seven or eight hundred, who perhaps do not see any difference in the smallness of either, and who, perhaps also, are as small themselves in the eyes of the inhabitants of Boötes and of Sirius." "We are," continues my Philosopher, "and the inhabitants of the earth are just as we are, very big in certain respects, very small in others. Consequently there is no absolute Size at all. Let us not be proud nor humble ourselves about what is not. For every finite being, nothing is large or small except by comparison.

This World, then, is large, not in itself, but for us who are small; it is very large for our statures, for our strides, for measurement by our eyes. It would not be large for ogres who have seven-league boots with which they would make its circuit in a day, and it would be small for the Gods of Homer who cross the space of the heavens in three steps, and arrive with the fourth.

Third Chapter

The earth's size and shape have been known with precision for only a few centuries. Up to Christopher Columbus, who discovered America, only one side of the Globe was known, namely the one that we inhabit. Among the Ancients, the Vulgar believed that the earth was flat, and that the sun set in the sea; without troubling themselves about what became of this Heavenly Body during the night, nor how, having set on one side, it rose on the other. More enlightened people did not yet have anything but half-knowledge. As a matter of fact, they conceived that the sun turned around the earth, and that night for our hemisphere was day for the opposite hemisphere. But, nevertheless, they had not arrived at the point of thinking that the earth was populated all the way around, and that there might be Antipodes for us; that is to say people in the opposite hemisphere, who had their feet up against ours, for whom the Sun rose when it sets for us, and set when it is rising. The first who dared to put forward this truth was excommunicated by a Pope. Today the French, the English, the Dutch, have colonies in the Antipodes, and their Vessels go there and return every day. Thus it is a very certain fact that the globe of the earth is round, or just about, and that it has inhabitants everywhere whom the sun lights successively by revolving around it in twenty-four hours from East to West. I say that the sun revolves around the earth, in order to make use of the vulgar expression, and to conform to appearances. For it is acknowledged that the Sun is fixed, that it is the Globe of the earth, which, revolving around itself in twenty-four hours, successively presents all the points of its Circuit to the Sun (which makes up an ordinary day), and which, moreover, making a great revolution around the sun every three hundred and sixty-five days, marks a completed year upon its return to the same point. But so as not to enter into long explanations that would require spheres and figures, let us hold to the supposed Motion of the Sun, by which one explains in an easier and less involved manner the unevenness of the days and seasons.

Fourth Chapter

The circular trail of the diurnal path of the Sun separates the world into two equal parts, is called the Equator, or the equinoctial Line, or simply the Line. The two apparent points of the globe that make up the center of this Line from the two sides are called the Poles. If the World turned in the same direction on a pivot, these two ends of this pivot would be the two Poles, and this pivot would be called the earth's axis. From that it is easy to conceive that the countries through which the Line passes and that are perpendicularly under the sun's path are very hot countries; and that those, on the contrary, that are far from this path under the Poles and in the environs are very cold countries. Those that are intermediary between the Line and one of the Poles are temperate countries; such is France. The Pole that on our side is called the arctic or north Pole; the one that is on the other side of the Line is called the Antarctic or south Pole. This is the simple and crude reason for the Unevenness of Climates. That for the Unevenness of the seasons and days is a little more difficult to explain without a figure. Let us try.

Fifth Chapter

The sun does not make its daily Circle on the Line every day; on the contrary, it traces it exactly only two days in the year, at six months from one to the other, and these two days in which the day and the night are precisely the same duration, are called the equinoxes. The day after the Spring Equinox, the sun no longer traces its daily Circle on the line, but next to the line approaching our Pole and consequently us; and it continues to approach it every day for six months, until it has arrived at a Circle called tropical; after which, instead of approaching us again, it moves away while approaching the Line; and even passing it after the Autumn Equinox, in order to go to the other tropic, approaching the opposite Pole, and consequently moving away from ours and from us. The day that the Sun has reached our tropic is our Summer solstice, and the winter Solstice of those who are on the other side of the Line; reciprocally our winter Solstice is their Summer solstice. One conceives how the moving away and approaching of the Sun makes the seasons cold or hot. One also conceives why we have a shadow at noon, even in Summer, since the Sun never comes completely to the point over us. Only those who are between the tropics, in the zone called torrid or burning, having the sun directly over their head twice a year, have no shadow at all at noon on those two days.[4]

Sixth Chapter

From what I just said, one should conceive that the Sun turns daily from East to West on the Line, or on Circles parallel to the Line, on both sides up to the tropic. Its annual Path is marked from West to East on a Circle at an oblique angle to the equinoctial Line which it intersects at two Points, and in two other of these same Points this same Circle touches the tropics. This annual Circle is called the Ecliptic, because it is when the earth or the Moon meet each other in this Line along with the Sun that Eclipses are made. The band of Sky in the middle of which the Ecliptic is, and where the twelve Constellations into which the sun passes annually are marked, is called the Zodiac.

Let us now pass to the Unevenness of days and nights.

Seventh Chapter

If one placed one of the points of a large compass under my feet, and from the other point one drew around me a large Circle which divided the world into two domes or hemispheres, one of which is in part subject to my sight around me, and the other one of which, that is opposite it beneath me, is hidden to my sight; this Circle drawn this way would be called my horizon, and although it is not actually drawn, I assume it, and for that horizon I take approximately the extent that my eyes can discover completely around me. Each man thus has his particular Circle or horizon of which he is the Center. But in order to limit oneself to what is perceptible, one does not take things strictly this way, and since one can give a large Center to such a large Circle, one assumes the same horizon for a whole country. For, Trye[5] or Paris, for example, can, without perceptible error, be taken for the same Center when it is a question of a Circle of nine thousand leagues around.

Thus our horizon divides the world into two halves one of which is subject to our sight, and the other of which is hidden from it. While the Sun is above our horizon in its diurnal path, it is day for us, when it is below, it is night, and the moment when it reaches the horizon is the one of its rising or its setting. The diurnal Path of the Sun is a Circle. The horizon is another Circle which intersects the first; and it is the manner in which these two Circles intersect each other that makes the days long or short, the nights short or long, and both of them equal or unequal.

One cannot see these various intersections of the Circle very well except in a Sphere. But here is the result of that inspection.

All year long people who are at the Equator have days equal to each other and equal to the nights, consequently always of twelve hours. Why is that? Because in this Region during the whole year, the horizon cuts the daily Circle of the Sun into two equal parts; from which it follows that the Sun, which traces this Circle, stays above the horizon for as much time as below it.

At the two poles, on the contrary, in the whole year there is only one long day of six months, and one long night of six months. Why is that? Because in this position the Equator and the horizon merge into the same Circle, so that consequently during the six months that the Sun is on this side of the Equator, it is day at our pole, and night at the opposite pole, and so that during the six months when the Sun is on the other side of the Equator, it is exactly the opposite. Those who live between the line and the pole have long days and short nights in Summer, long nights and short days in winter; because their horizon intersects the daily Circle of the Sun obliquely and unequally. In order to conceive well how this happens, one has only to place the globe in accordance with our position. Then one will find that out of the three hundred sixty-five daily Circles, those that are above the Equator are intersected by our horizon in such a manner that the portion[6] of each of these Circles that is above the horizon is smaller than the portion that is below. From which it follows that the sun tracing the said Circles in the winter, resides below our horizon for longer than it does above, and that consequently the night lasts longer than the day.

On the contrary the daily Circles or parallels that are above the Equator, are intersected by the horizon in such a way that the greatest portion of the Circle is above, and the smaller below; from which it follows that when the Sun traces these Circles, namely in the Summer, the days are longer than the nights. But when the sun traces the Circle of the Equator itself, that is to say at the two Equinoxes, the day is equal to the night and of twelve hours; because the Equator is always intersected by the horizon into two equal semi-Circles, and because, consequently, the Sun uses as much time to trace the one as the other.

Eighth Chapter

After having spoken about the unevenness of the seasons and of the days, let us say several words about what is called latitude, longitude, and elevation of the Pole.

Every Circle, small or large, is conceived of as divided into three hundred sixty equal parts or small arcs, which are called degrees.

A Circle that passes perpendicularly to the Equator through the two Poles is called a Meridian, or rather, its two halves from one Pole to the other, are two Meridians, because at the same moment that the Sun passes into one point of this semi-Circle, it is noon at all the points, and midnight at all the points of the opposite semi-Circle.

One can make similar Circles pass through all the points of the Equator, and if one forms at least one of them for each degree, there will be as many Meridians as there are degrees in the Equator, that is to say three hundred sixty.

Let us assume in the same way a meridian Circle divided into three hundred sixty degrees by as many Circles parallel to each semi-Circle or Meridian, that is to say ninety degrees from the Equator to the Pole on each side.

We have said that all the semi-Circles that pass through all the degrees of the Equator and end at the pole on one side and the other are called Meridians.

The Circles parallel to the Equator, which divide the Meridian in its degrees are called parallels.

Thus there are as many Meridians or semi-Circles, as there are degrees marked on the Equator, that is to say, three hundred sixty.

And there are as many parallels or entire Circles, parallel to the Equator as there are degrees marked on a meridian, that is to say ninety, or, in counting from the Equator, ninety on each side up to the pole.

The Degrees or parallels, which are marked this way on the meridian by counting from the Equator to the pole, measure latitude. And the degrees or semi-Circles that are marked all around the Equator by Meridians, measure longitude. Latitude has its measure fixed because one counts it from the Equator.

But to find longitude, it is necessary to agree on a Meridian, from which one begins to count.

This agreed-upon prime Meridian is the one that passes through Ferro, one of the Canaries; it is from this prime Meridian that one counts the degrees of longitude, by turning from West to East.[7]

When one knows the latitude and longitude of any place whatsoever, one can mark this place very precisely on the globe. For it will be at the point of intersection of the two Circles.

One finds the latitude by taking the altitude of the pole, or that of the sun. One finds the longitude by the relation of the hours; but this operation has its difficulty.

The altitude of the Pole from any place whatsoever is the Arc of the Meridian comprised between the horizon of this place and the Pole.

The altitude of the Sun is the Arc of the Meridian comprised between the horizon and any place whatsoever and the Equator, which is measured by the Sun at the Equinoxes. Now the altitude of the Pole, equal to the latitude, and the altitude of the sun being always complementary to each other to ninety degrees, can always be found by each other.

Ninth Chapter

We have explained the apparent Path of the Sun by its assumed Motion around the earth in order to be able to make use of the armillary sphere, constructed in this system which is Ptolemy's; the same things can be explained in Copernicus's which makes the earth revolve around the Sun. In this system the obliquity of the axis of the world or of the Equator on the axis of the sun or of the Ecliptic is enough to explain the same unevenness of the seasons and the days. The Phases of the Moon and Eclipses are explained without much difficulty in both Systems. We shall continue to use Ptolemy's.

The Moon has a daily motion, from East to West, similar to that of the Sun. But given that it proceeds much faster, being much closer to us, and making a much smaller circuit, it passes through the Zodiac from West to East much sooner, and instead of taking a year as the sun does to make its circuit, it takes only a month. This month can be considered as the year of the Moon. During this month, in relation to us it has four different positions, which are called phases, which are occasioned by the manner in which the Sun lights up the Moon, and by which the Moon reflects this Light from the sun toward us.

Being a Globe just as the earth is, the Moon, just like the earth, always has one of its halves lit up by the sun, and the other in darkness.

When in its circuit of a month the Moon is found between the sun and the earth, then its side lit up by the sun is not at all the one that it is showing to us, and we have the new Moon.

When, proceeding faster, it has reached a quarter of a Circle to the West, then we see half of its lit-up half and this is the first quarter.

When it has reached yet another quarter of the Circle, and the earth is found between it and the sun, then the Moon shows us all of its lit-up half, and this is the full Moon.

When at last it has reached a third quarter of its Circle, we no longer see anything but the other half of its lit-up half and that is the final quarter.

Such are the reasons for the phases of the Moon. Let us pass to Eclipses.

In the new Moons, the Moon usually is not so directly interposed between us and the Sun that it hides its Light from us. But when that does happen, there is an Eclipse of the Sun, which is more or less great in accordance with whether the interposition is more or less direct.

In the same way in the full Moons, the earth usually is not so directly opposed between the Sun and the Moon that it intercepts the rays of the Sun, and keeps them from falling on the Moon; but when that does happen, there is an Eclipse of the Moon. When the Eclipse, either of the Moon or of the Sun, is such that the centers of the three Heavenly Bodies are exactly in the same line, which is rare, then the Eclipse is central.

It follows from what was just said that there is never an Eclipse of the sun except in the new Moons, and that there are never Eclipses of the Moon, except in the full Moons.

Since no Eclipse ever takes place except when the Heavenly Bodies that cause it meet each other, not only in the Zodiac, but precisely in the Circle that passes through the middle of the Zodiac, it is for that reason that this Circle is called the Ecliptic.

Since the Path of each Heavenly Body is precisely known and measured, one knows in advance what times and at what points they will meet in the Ecliptic, and it is for that reason that one can predict with certainty the moment in which Eclipses will happen.

Chapter Ten

After having spoken about the fictive Circles that the Explanation of the path of the Sun caused to be imagined, let us say a word about the astronomical Divisions of the earth marked by these same Circles.

The Globe of the earth is divided into five bands or belts called Zones, of which the one in the middle which is under the annual path of the sun, is called because of that the torrid or burning Zone. This Zone contains the space that is on each side of the Equator up to the tropic. Now this space [is] twenty-three and a half degrees, which is the quantity of the Angle that the Ecliptic forms on the Equator. Twenty-three and a half degrees on each side make together forty-seven degrees for the total size of the torrid Zone between the two tropics.

Taking the same size of twenty-three and a half degrees for each Pole on the Meridian and drawing a Circle around the Pole at this distance; this Circle is called the arctic Circle, and the dome of twenty-three and a half degrees that it encloses, is called the cold or glacial Zone, because of its extreme distance for the Sun. Since there are two poles, there are also two glacial Zones each of which bears the name of the Pole that is at its Center.

From the arctic Circle of each side up to the tropic, there remains a distance of forty-three degrees, which forms on the two sides two other Zones called temperate, because they are intermediary between the glacial Zones and the torrid Zone.

The total space of these five Zones comprises precisely that of the whole earth. For, counting from the Equator, toward one of the two Poles, one first has half of the torrid Zone making twenty-three and a half degrees; then a temperate Zone whose forty-three degrees added to the twenty-three and a half above, make sixty-six and a half degrees, and also twenty-three and a half degrees of the polar Circle to the pole form in all ninety degrees, which are exactly the total distance from the Equator to the pole, and as many on the other side of the Equator to the opposite pole, give in all the ninety degrees that divide the Meridian and the whole earth from one pole to another.

Before taking leave of the general inspection of the Globe of the earth, now we shall speak in brief about its real divisions by lands, seas, mountains, and rivers.

We have said above that the earth is divided into two demi-Globes or hemispheres. The one that we inhabit comprises what is called the Old world, because it has always been known; the other comprises the new World, discovered only three centuries ago.

Each of the two Hemispheres is composed of lands and seas; but this composition is such that the space of the seas is immense and much greater than that of the lands. The Continent or the land of each Hemisphere is like a large Island in the midst of these vast seas. The total quantity of the lands that make up the World is divided into four principal Parts of which our Continent makes up three; namely Europe, Asia, and Africa. The opposite Hemisphere or continent contains only one, namely America; but almost as large by itself as the three others together.

Of the three parts of which our World is composed, Europe and Africa are situated to the West or West, Asia to the East or East,[8] Africa to the South or *Midi*. The divisions of these three parts are made by seas or rivers in accordance with their position. As to America, its shape and its vast extent make it subdivided into two parts; the one South; the other North.

The great Sea in which the four parts of the World swim, so to speak, is called Ocean; its part that is between Europe and America to our West is called North sea; and its part that is between Asia and America to the

East, is called South Sea.⁹ There is a individual Sea that separates Europe from Africa and which communicates with the Ocean only by means of a rather narrow opening that is named Straits of Gibraltar. This Sea is called the Mediterranean; to the East it communicates with another, smaller sea called the Black Sea or Euxine Pont; and also to the East from that one, is another small sea in Asia, which does not communicate with any other, it is called the Caspian Sea. There are sea passages for going around the World by means of the southern direction. But it is not yet known whether there are passages for Vessels in the same way by the northern direction, since the ice prevents Navigation. There are rewards promised to those who will discover this passage, and it has been attempted by numerous Navigators, but without success up to now.

To the North of Europe there is another Sea called the Baltic Sea that communicates with the Ocean to the West by means of a Strait called the Sund. This Sea is divided into two principal Gulfs, the one toward the East called the Gulf of Finland, the other toward the North called the Gulf of Bothnia. Between Africa and Asia is another sea called the Red Sea that also communicates with the Ocean by means of a Strait. With regard to America there is only one sea there distinguished by a particular name, this sea almost entirely divides the northern part from the southern and this sea is called the Gulf of Mexico.

In the environs of the Continent are scattered various Islands some of which form immense countries. Such is the Isle of Madagascar to the East of Africa; the Isle of Japan to the East of Asia; the British Isles to the number of two, namely Great Britain, which comprises England and Scotland; and Ireland, which is one Island and an individual Kingdom. To the north of the British Isles is also a large Island called Iceland. America is also bordered by a great number of Islands to its West: among others the Antilles of which Cuba, Jamaica, and Santo Domingo are the most considerable. The Mediterranean also includes numerous Islands of which Sicily is the largest; then the Islands of Sardinia, of Corsica, etc.

The principal rivers of Europe are the Tagus in Spain; in France the Rhône which receives the Saône at Lyon and flows into the Mediterranean, the Garonne and the Loire which flow into the Ocean, the same as the Seine which passes through the Capital. The Rhine separates France from Germany and flows into the Ocean in Holland. After having crossed Germany and Hungary, the Danube flows into the Black Sea. The largest river in Italy is the Po; the most famous is the Tiber. The most famous in Africa is the Nile which crosses and enriches Egypt. Of the multitudes of rivers that flow in Asia, I shall speak only about the Ganges which flows to the south into the Indian Ocean, and the Don or

Tanais which also flows into the Black Sea, and forms one of the separations of Asia and Europe.

In its northern part America has for principal rivers the Mississippi which flows into the Gulf of Mexico, and the St. Lawrence which passes through Quebec and flows into the North Sea.

Of that infinity of Mountains which divide and variegate the various Regions of the Earth the tallest and the best known are: the Pyrenees which separate Spain from France; the Alps which separate France from Italy; the Apennines which cross the length of Italy. In Africa the chains of Mount Atlas, in Asia Mount Taurus, and in America the Andes.

Now in order to say several words about the situation of the different Peoples and about national Divisions; we shall begin with the West of Europe, where one finds in the south, drawing toward the East,[10] first Portugal; then Spain; then France; then Italy, which juts out into the Mediterranean in the form of a Boot that has Sicily at the end of its foot; and finally Greece, a small Region so renowned in Ancient History, and Constantinople which limits it to the East toward Asia.

Beginning again then by the West, but more to the North, one finds Holland, Germany, Hungary, and Poland, drawing toward the East. Completely to the North taking it up again from West to East, one finds Scandinavia which surrounds the Baltic Sea, and is composed of the Kingdoms of Denmark and Sweden. Then, Russia, an immense Empire, of which Petersburg in Europe is the Capital; but which extends into Asia up to the borders of Tartary and China.

Chapter Eleven

Based on these Elements of Cosmography, although unpolished and crude, one can trace for oneself some ideas about the economy that reigns in the Construction and the disposition of our Globe. One sees with what Art, sublime and worthy of its divine workman, this enormous [mass] is found distributed and lit up in such a manner that all the living Beings that cover it can live and continue to exist.

The Zone that is called torrid is tempered by continuous clouds and vapors that in the places over which the Sun passes pour long rains in order to moderate their heat. The glacial Zones, where the languishing rays of the Sun seem hardly to be able to reach, are heated up again in Summer by the extreme length of the days; so that in these hyperborean Countries it seems as if nothing should grow, seeds scatter themselves, rise, mature, and are harvested in the space of six weeks, while much more than double the time is necessary in our much warmer climates.

The long and terrible nights of winter are shortened there by long twilights, given that the Sun, setting much more obliquely than for us, does not descend so rapidly over the horizon. Aside from that during these long nights of winter these sad Regions are almost continuously lit up by the Aurora borealis and other luminous Phenomena that moderate the horror of the darkness, and put the inhabitants in a condition to discern objects.

Those great chains of Mountains that seem to be useless weights on the earth are the sources and reservoirs of the rivers and fountains that come to quench our thirst. Moreover the various Orientations of these Mountains give rise to almost continuous air currents and winds by which the mass of the Air is renewed and purified. These immense seas the Salinity of which protects them from Corruption[11] and whose bosom contains multitudes of fish for our use, far from cutting off communication among the various regions of the World, facilitates it by navigation. It is through it that the European, the American, the African, the Asian, whom Providence has[12] caused to be born so far from each other, are found continuously brought closer, and reciprocally enrich each other from the productions of the countries they inhabit.

The seasonal and trade winds, those that sailors call monsoons, constantly returning at the same seasons, facilitate their long voyages for Vessels, and provide Navigators with the means of expecting them and availing themselves of them.

In sum everything, if only one casts a reflecting eye on the great and magnificent objects with which the earth is covered and adorned, everything I say, shows us the powerful and beneficent hand that prepared this earth for our habitation, and which stupid and ungrateful man dares to disregard.

Oh, if in human life there reigned an order similar to the one that reigns in nature, by what touching and beautiful sight would the face of the earth not be struck? But unfortunate and barbarous men take pleasure in disfiguring it by their crimes and by their wickedness; they take their frightful pleasure in tormenting each other. Traitors and scoundrels even in their apparent endearments, they merge friends and enemies in the same malevolence, and make the heavenly spectacle of this world into the genuine image of Hell.

The New Daedalus[1]
by J. J. Rousseau

It is a spectacle worthy of admiration to see men risking their lives in the midst of the seas, and give themselves over to the most dreadful of the elements with so much assurance that entire armies go into action, put themselves into order, make their maneuvers, and fight at two or three hundred leagues from land and with the same boldness as if they felt very convenient and well drawn up camps behind them. As a result of seeing the navy and the vessels, one becomes accustomed to considering them without astonishment, in the same way that one does not show any at the sight of the sun and the most beautiful phenomena; but the eyes of[2] reason cannot cease admiring what those of the body see coolly; and to convince oneself that habit alone makes these objects familiar to us, one has only to consider the astonishment and admiration of the person who, getting onto a vessel for the first time, examines its construction, the rigging, and the handling.[3] What a spectacle to see a man seated with a small box in front of him, calm in the midst of the awful noise of the waves and storms, having an enormous mass move with all the lightness of a horse from Spain! Taming the sea and the winds with his voice, and making them serve in spite of themselves to push him in a contrary direction. The Americans took the vessels of Columbus for large birds,[4] and it is said that the Tartars regarded Doria[5] as a sorcerer upon seeing him steer against the wind on the Black Sea. In fact this is a very surprising paradox, and many men would be Tartar enough in that regard if this spectacle were less familiar.

If only one happens to reflect on the advantages that navigation procures for us, thoughts of admiration will change into lively feelings of gratitude for the first person who dared to open up the route of the sea for us; and very far from heaping insults on him, following the example of some thoughtless poet, antiquity which deified people so cheaply, should have raised altars to him. Consider what the condition of the world would be if crossing the water were closed to us; no commerce, no communications with the closest regions as soon as an arm of the sea passed between two of them. Our reciprocal scope would be really impoverished by the number of countries from which the sea separates us; England and Sicily would be worlds eternally unknown to us, and doubtless we would make fine arguments to prove that they can be inhabited, which would not fail to be made fun of as one might expect. The earth, as at the time of Herodotus, and even at the time of Pliny, was rather trifling. Two-thirds of Europe, Persia, Arabia, Egypt, Ethiopia, and Barbary, composed just about all the habitable regions. Did you advance toward the south? You were smothered, roasted by the fires of the torrid zone. Did you go to the north? You hit your head against the sky, which slopes downward too much on that side, or you were suffocated by the feathers that fly abundantly there; from the east or the west, you were stopped by the sea or by deserts. Great voyages were so rare in that time of ignorance and error that the Argonauts were immortalized for having made a trip of a hundred leagues into the Euxine Sea,[6] with this precaution that they drew their vessels unto land every night, and the next day put them back afloat in order to continue their trip. It does not appear that in all antiquity very considerable discoveries were made for geography, even by the Phoenicians. The reason for this is that their navy, being still very imperfect, and them finding themselves constrained, for lack of guides in the high seas, always to navigate from land to land on rather heavy vessels that also needed a prodigious crew; it was impossible for them to attempt those bold trips that make great discoveries and that we have been making so happily for almost three hundred years.

Waters are not navigable everywhere, nor at all times; sometimes enormous icebergs, sometimes reefs; here currents, there continuous storms; each sea has its contrary seasons during which it is not stable. It must be agreed, then, that voyages are lengthy, expensive, difficult, and often impossible; that those by land are dangerous and do not lead everywhere; from which it follows that it would be desirable for the good of the human race, that some new more universal means be found that joined the safety of land voyages to the convenience of those by sea, and the power of penetrating into the most remote continents.

If it is from such considerations that ingenious men have tried at different times and in various manners to open up a new path in the air, such noble intentions should justify even the most chimerical project. A wicked man is no less blameworthy for having succeeded in a bad undertaking by extremely clever means, and consequently a generous man who, blinded by his zeal, attempts a project that is useful, but impossible, should always be excused by his motives.

But is it entirely true that the impossibility of ascending into the air is demonstrated? And is one perfectly sure of the solidity of the reasons that establish it? If, in order to destroy a proposition, it was only a question of holding it up to ridicule, I admit that aerial navigation would not have a good chance. Its idea carries with it a certain air of paradox and chimera entirely suited to putting the scoffers in a good humor. Nevertheless, the most respectable evidence would not be sheltered from such attacks. The circulation of the blood had already been perfectly demonstrated when the old doctors and stubborn scholastics made extremely pretty jests about it that did not fail to attract the laughers onto their side. To believe that blood circulates would have been so many amusements lost. To be made fun of is almost always the fate of the truth. Irony and raillery are the genuine weapons of error. They are very much easier for it to find than reasons are.

We walk upon the earth, we sail upon the sea, we even swim in it and we skim through it. Why would the path of the air be prohibited to our industry? Is not the air an element like the others? And what privilege can the birds have in order to exclude us from their abode, while we are admitted into that of the fish? Air and water have a perfect analogy together; both are fluids, both are transparent, both are inhabited, with this difference that one has much more conformity with our organs, since we breathe in the air and we suffocate in the water. Thus there is no distinction between them other than a little more or less identity and weight; and in all that I do not see the slightest thing that ought to make the air more respectable to us, and make us regard the boldness of trampling it underfoot as a great crime.

Let us consider the thing in another sense, and assume that someone has found the means of perfecting the use of our aerial vehicles so well that one drives them with all the ease in the world, and that one can even carry weapons and provisions in them. There is a new source of advantages and conveniences in society. Is it necessary to prohibit it to us because a wretched bandit will perhaps be able to avail himself of it? From similar arguments we would be brought to take away what is most excellent on the earth; for what is not misused? No more horses, they favor the bad strokes and the flight of criminals; no more navigation, it supports pirates; no more clothing, it engenders luxury; what am I saying, even no more laws, nor religion, they are the sources of chicanery and fanaticism.

This response is trivial, because the blame of the best things, by means of the consideration of their misuses, is a sophism often combated and often renewed. Another reflection serves to remove every scruple on this matter: it is that every invention useful to the human race, although common to all men, nevertheless very truly provides advantages to the good against the wicked, by giving new weapons to the body of society to attack them or to defend oneself against them.[7]

Nota. After several other discussions about the possibility of aerial flight, J. J. transports his readers to Daedalus's labyrinth, and represents to them there this sublime genius creating wings for himself in order to escape from Minos's power and from the tedium of a prison that he had not made for him, for a great man's soul ought to have none other than the immensity of the universe. Several short digressions follow, then he says to his readers after having offered them such a good model of what they could do.

Let us return to our wings; thus when they will be well adjusted this way, they must be lightly anointed with oil in order to make them impenetrable to water. We shall attach them very neatly along the length of our arms, after fitting ourselves out as lightly as possible; nothing more is left but to have several trials, by balancing ourselves very carefully. At first we shall not do anything but skim over the earth like young starlings; but soon made bold by habit and experiment, we shall throw ourselves into the air with an eagle's impetuosity, and we shall divert ourselves by considering beneath us the puerile roundabout of all those little men who are crawling miserably on the earth.

Also that would be better than having oneself carried by two ducks, like the tortoise in the fable; and we, we shall be able to shout from up there as loudly as we can that we are the kings of the animals, without fearing to lose the gag or life from an unseasonable harangue, etc. etc.[8]

Or rather, to make use of a more gallant image, I believe I see our lovable youth transformed into so many little cupids, who, without fearing the perils of Leander,[9] will be able to chase success with the ladies; it would not even be very difficult to imagine more than one tender heroine equally bold, obliging and light, who would sometimes deign to spare them half the route.

Up to now everything is going as well as possible, and these imaginings certainly have nothing but what is extremely pretty. The bad thing is that the ideas of the least possible projects are precisely the ones that amuse us more. What a misfortune for us that the pleasure that one takes in it is not a degree of probability in their favor, or rather would it not be the greatest of misfortunes if things were different? The author of nature is not satisfied with engendering a crowd of positive goods under our steps, he has allowed us to find in the very weakness of our mind, and even in our frivolous imagination, the source of a thousand other paths, which although existing only in idea, are hardly less perceptible for it. If all chimeras were destroyed, we would lose an infinite number of real pleasures along with them.

This gives me some regret at laying hold of the supposed possibility of flying: but in the end the love of the truth is also my chimera; and since I have committed myself to this inquiry, it is all the less just to constrain myself to disguise its result, since the hope or desire to have wings is assuredly not among those passions that cause much uneasiness, and about which one fears to be disabused.

Following Borelli[10] the force of the muscles that move the wings of a bird surpasses the weight of that bird ten thousand times, and since, following the same Borelli, the force with which the deltoid is capable of acting is only seventy-one thousand three hundred and sixty pounds, by doubling this number and by compounding it with the force a man would need to make his wings act proportionally to those of the bird, it follows by an unanswerable reply, that if that man weighed only a hundred pounds, it would require eight hundred fifty seven thousand two hundred and eighty pounds, that is to say more than six times his actual force, that this force does not equal the one he would need in order to make use of the wings that we are assuming him to have.

I cannot, however, resolve to omit here the singular invention that Honoratus Fabri[11] proposes for raising oneself into the air. "You take," he says, "a cardboard canister; you fill it with a composition of cannon powder, iron filings, and crushed coal; you attach a stick to it and you set it on fire; that gives you a rocket that raises you up to the clouds. The rarefaction caused by the blazing of the powder and by the elasticity of the air, acts in all directions, makes the burning powder leave by the bottom hole of the rocket, and shoots this same rocket aloft. Now, Hiero-fountains,[12] wind sticks, and other similar instruments teach us that air, closed up, compressed, and squeezed into a small space has hardly less force than the powder itself, or rather that, at bottom, the force of the powder is only in the force of the air. Thus in the same case it ought to produce the same effects. Based on this reasoning, I suggest that one take, for example, a glass tube, that one fill it with much air introduced with force by a bellows, and constrained by a valve; that one attach a light stick (the stick must be of such a weight, that the center of gravity of the whole matter might be perceptibly lower than the tube) to this tube; that one give it a direction perpendicular to the horizon, and finally that one pierce it from underneath, with astonishment one will see this tube ascend and raise itself up by itself until all the superabundant air is worn down." Since the reason for this is the same as that of rockets, our physicist assumes that that has no need of demonstration.

"But this fact being granted, who will prevent us from pushing the consequences farther? Let us increase the length and the diameter of our tubes until we find one of them capable of a great enough quantity of air, to lift up some quintals,[13] beyond its own weight, solely by its elastic force. Then by suspending a chair from this tube, a man who will be seated in it will infallibly be raised up aloft; and if one adds to this a rudder with some bellows by which one can insert air into the tube over again, before the first has flowed out, you will be able to fly in the air with impunity for as long as you please. After having taught us this fine secret, Fabre[14] tells us coldly that although that might be very true theoretically speaking, up to now he has not found anyone foolish enough to want to attempt the experiment.

But without undertaking seriously to refute such a project, I shall only admit that I would be curious to see another tube strong enough to lift up a man; but the height of my admiration would be to see this man wandering for a long time to the right and to the left through the medium of the air, with an instrument that nevertheless would have no force other than the one for continuously climbing. *Hinc diu per multas horas pro medium aera ambulabit, quo nihil fere mirabilis esse potest.*[15] Fabri is right to say that one could not see anything more wonderful. Nevertheless after all these fine things it would still remain to be known how our man would finally set about coming down without breaking his neck. That has some relation to Harlequin's perplexity. He proposes to Pierrot an admirable invention that he has found to make him fly in the air. "I take," he says, "four good kegs of powder; I attach them together, I arrange on them very suitably a little deck on which you place yourself just as you like; I make a great trail, which connects with the kegs; I set the fire to it; and there goes Pierrot who is flying the best way possible." "Oh! But," says Pierrot, "that would kill me." "Ah!" answers Harlequin, "if one would not die I would have myself done up in gold." With that secret, in good faith is not Harlequin's secret still preferable to Father Fabri's? At least in it one sees only a single difficulty to overcome, after which, there would not be the slightest trouble in all the rest.

Let us leave aside the good Jesuit's tubes, then. Its invention appears all the less suited to producing the effect sought after, since the more one fills them with air, the more one increases their weight; they lose, then, in heaviness what they gain in force; and in spite of the experience of rockets, and, whatever explanation one gives, it is hardly natural to want, by making them heavier, to make them surpass the external air in lightness.

Here is another difficulty, almost as considerable, about the manner in which it would be necessary to navigate in the air. In order to float on the water, it is enough for a body to be lighter than it is; for the ballast, for example, is not intended to give the vessel a degree of heaviness, but to make it bear the sails and keep it trim. Now, if it were necessary for this vessel to swim through the water and at different depths at the pilot's will, having assumed that he could breathe in it, then it would be necessary for the vessel to be in a perfect equilibrium with that water, and, aside from that, that it be in the conductor's power to increase or diminish the weight of the vessel as much and as little as he would please, in order to make it rise and descend at his will.

That is exactly the case for aerial navigation. It is a question of sailing, not on the surface of the air, but in the middle of the air, by immersion. The question is reduced, then, to these two points that it is good to establish clearly:

First. To find a body lighter than a similar volume of air, for by one of the first principles of hydrostatics this body will rise, and by its excess of lightness will be able to support a weight and still stay in equilibrium with the air.

But as soon as one has made it light enough to rise, how to keep it from rising farther, and how to make it heavy enough to descend? This is a second difficulty that is hardly less perplexing than the first; but also it is clear that anyone who could resolve these two questions would have found the solution for the famous problem of aerial navigation.[16]

Nota. After this ingenious and surprising discussion by J. J. about aerial navigation there immediately follows a demonstration about the comparative heaviness of the air and mercury, and about the reason for which the first holds the second in equilibrium at various heights in the tubes that contain them.[17] In all these arguments one does not notice the pompous and scientific showing-off of our modern physicists, who, like the priests of antiquity, seem to take as their task to cloud up their explanations with enigmatic expressions, either to astonish the fools who love the marvelous, or also to impose their guidance on the blind; on the contrary in it everything is set forth with order, method, and simplicity. One believes that one sees a man who, the torch of the truth in his hand,[18] guides you in the obscure and tortuous meanderings of the abyss in which science seems to be hidden, puts your finger on the difficulty that you would despair of overcoming, and the solution of which constantly resists all your mind's efforts: he is also a man who, at each step that he makes in the path of truth, consults reason in order to account for his discovery, develops the doubts that it can engender; silences amour-propre whose obliging and deceitful avowal persuades presumptuous minds: these avoid the obstacles of difficulties in order to dissimulate to themselves how impossible it is for them to overcome them.

WRITINGS ON RELIGION AND MORALITY

Fragments on God and Revelation

[On God]¹

We all believe we are persuaded of the existence of a God; nevertheless it is inconceivable for us to reconcile this persuasion with the principles upon which we regulate our behavior in this life. The idea of God is inseparable from the ideas of eternal, infinite in intelligence, in wisdom, in justice, and in power. It would be easier to annihilate the sentiment of divinity in oneself than to conceive of a God without acknowledging in him those attributes the combination of which forms the only manner in which he can be represented to our mind. Now, from a necessary consequence of his infinite power, it must extend over us; and if it extends over us, since it is the source of all wisdom, it requires that we govern ourselves following the principles of wisdom that it put into our mind; then it is able to constrain us to do so, and to put us under the necessity of following the order of its decrees that are the foundations of virtue and Religion. But by casting one's eyes upon the manner in which men behave here below we are soon convinced that they do not at all follow this order, the principles of which are engraved in the depths of their hearts; thus it must be that God has not used his infinite power to force them to do so for it would be absurd to imagine that they could have avoided doing so in any manner; now if we examine what follows from that; we are going to discover the immense source of the benefits that it pleases God to pour over men and the means that he put into their hands in order to be able to become happy.

Since we did not give being to ourselves we must be someone else's work, this is a simple and clear argument by itself; whereas it would be impossible for us to conceive how something could be produced by nothingness.

Prayer²

We prostrate ourselves in your presence, divine, great God creator and preserver of the universe, in order to render you the homage that we owe you, in order to thank you for all the benefits that we have received from you and in order to address our humble Prayers to you.

Our Father etc.

We offer you, oh my God, our homage and our adoration, deign to accept them; we are only dust and ashes before you, and it is only while trembling that we should put ourselves into your formidable presence; but you have even more mercy than Majesty, we entrust ourselves to your infinite Clemency. You are our Creator, we are the work of your goodness, you are our Father, we are your children; receive then favorably, oh my God, our wishes, our prayers, and our acts of Grace.

We thank you for all the graces and all the goods with which you load men, and in particular for all those that we have received from you since our birth, we thank you for having created us, for having endowed us with a reasonable soul, for having given us knowledge of your Divinity, for having provided by means of your Holy Providence for the needs of our poverty, and for the relieving of our infirmities, and finally for having brought us together.

Continue all these graces for us, almighty God, but do not allow us ever to abuse them, give us the Enlightenment and the will to serve you in the manner that is most pleasing to you; lead us always in the path of virtue, do not allow us ever to go astray from it. Do not allow us, oh my God, ever to be unfortunate enough to doubt your divine existence for a single moment, stir up in our hearts the love that we owe to your paternal tenderness, and to all your benefits; the respect and the veneration that we owe to your immense Majesty, and your formidable power; and the charity that we owe to our neighbor. May your word be in our mouth, and your Law in our Heart; spread your holy Benediction over our union; may it serve to incite us mutually to serve you. In a word, oh my God, give us everything that you see as necessary to us to contribute to your[3] glory, and to labor for our Salvation.

For the Evening

Also give us a sweet and tranquil night, we commend our minds and our bodies to your divine Protection.

For the Morning

Also bless our labor of this day, and protect us by your divine providence from all that could harm us and principally from what could offend you.

[Prayer]

Almighty God, eternal Father, my heart raises itself up in your presence, in order to offer you the homage and adoration it owes you, my soul imbued with your immense majesty, with your formidable power, and your infinite greatness, humbles itself before you with the feelings of the most profound veneration and of the most respectful abasement. Oh my God, I adore you with all the extent of my force, I acknowledge you as the creator, the preserver, the master, and the absolute sovereign of all that exists, as the absolute and independent being who needs nothing but himself to exist, who has created everything by means of his power, and without the support of which all the beings would immediately return into nothingness. I acknowledge that your divine providence supports and governs the whole world[4] without these efforts being capable of altering your august tranquillity in the slightest, finally, whatever magnificence reigns in the construction of this vast universe, I conceive that it needed only an instant of your will in order to depart from nothingness in all its perfection, and that, very far from being the final effort of your power, all the vigor of the human mind is not even capable of conceiving how far you could extend beyond the effects of your infinite power. I adore so much greatness and majesty, and, since the weakness of my intelligence does not allow me to conceive the whole extent of your divine perfections, my soul, full of submission and respect, reveres its august and immense profundity, acknowledging itself to be incapable of fathoming it.

But oh God of Heaven, if your power is infinite, your divine goodness is no less so; oh my Father, my heart takes pleasure in meditating about the greatness of your benefits, it finds in them a thousand unfailing sources of zeal and benediction; what mouth could worthily make the enumeration of all the goods I have received from you? You have drawn me from nothingness, you have given me existence, you have endowed me with a reasonable soul, you have graven in the depths of my heart laws to the execution of which you have attached the reward of an eternal happiness, laws full of justice and gentleness and the practice of which tends to make me happy even in this life. You have attached gentleness to my fate on this earth, and by setting forth before my eyes the touching and magnificent spectacle of this vast universe, you have not disdained to destine a great part of it to my convenience and my pleasures. Oh sublime benefactor! Your benefits are infinite as you are; you are the King of nature; but you are the father of humans. What hearts will take fire enough to bear witness to you of a love and gratitude worthy of your kindnesses? Will my homage and my zeal, weak as they are, dare to offer themselves to you to fulfill my gratitude? Yes, my God, you deign to accept them, in consideration of my weakness, you accept feelings very unworthy of you in truth; but which are nevertheless the fruit of all the efforts of my heart: my gratitude, my zeal, and my love, weak as they are, are not disdained by your divine goodness. Oh my Creator, my heart warms up from the contemplation of all your graces and of all your benefits, to offer you proportionate acts of grace and thanks: accept them in the fullness of your mercy.

Oh my God,[5] pardon all the sins that I have committed up to today, all the aberrations into which I have fallen; deign to have pity for my weakness, deign to destroy in me all the vices[6] into which it has dragged me. My conscience tells me how guilty I am, I feel that all the pleasures that my passions had represented to me in neglect of wisdom, have become worse than illusion for me, and that they have been changed into odious gall; I feel that there are no true pleasures except those that are tasted in the exercise of virtue and in the practice of one's duties. I am filled with regret at having made such a bad use of a life and a freedom that you had granted me only to give me the means of making myself worthy of eternal felicity. Accept my repentance, oh my God; ashamed of my past faults, I am making a firm resolution to atone for them with a conduct full of rectitude and wisdom. Henceforth I shall refer all my actions to you, I shall meditate on you, I shall bless you, I shall serve you, I shall fear you; I shall always have your law in my heart, and all my acts will be the practice of it; I shall love my neighbor as myself, I shall serve him in all that depends on me both in relation to the body and in relation to the soul, I shall always remember that you do not want his happiness any less than my own; I shall have pity for the unfortunate, and I shall come to their aid with all my force; I shall attempt to know well all the duties of my station and I shall fulfill them attentively. I shall remember that you are the witness of all my actions and I shall attempt to do nothing unworthy of your august presence. I shall be indulgent toward others and severe toward myself, I shall resist temptations, I shall live in purity, I shall be temperate, moderate in everything, and I shall never allow myself any pleasures aside from those authorized by virtue; above all I shall repress my anger and my impatience, and I shall attempt to make myself gentle with regard to everyone, I shall speak ill of no one, I shall not allow myself either reckless judgments or bad conjectures about anyone else's[7] behavior; I shall separate myself as much as possible from the taste for the world, its joys, and the commodities of life, in order to occupy myself solely with you and your infinite perfections. From the bottom of my heart I shall always pardon all those who might offend me as I already pardon now without reserve all those who might have done me some offense, I beg you, oh my God, to pardon them the same way and to grant them your grace. I shall carefully avoid offending anyone, and if I had this misfortune I shall not blush at making the most satisfactory reparations to them. I shall always be perfectly submissive to everything it pleases your Divine providence to order me, and I shall always receive with a perfect resignation to your supreme will all the goods or ills that it will please you to send me. I shall prepare myself for death as for the day when I must give you an account of all my actions; and I shall wait for it without fear as the moment that must deliver me from subjection to the body and reunite me to you for ever; in a word, oh my sovereign master, I shall employ my life in serving you, in obeying your laws, and by fulfilling my duties; I implore your benedictions upon these resolutions that I am forming with all my heart, and with a firm purpose of putting them into practice, knowing by a sad experience that without the aid of your grace, the firmest plans fade away but that you never refuse it to those who ask you for it from the heart, and with humility and fervor.

I implore the same graces, oh my God, for my dear Mamma, for my dear benefactress, and for my dear Father. Grant them, Father of Mercies, all the aid they need, pardon in them all the evil they have done, inspire in them the good they ought to do, and give them the force to fulfill, both the duties of their station, and those that you demand from them, remember generally all my benefactors, make all the good things they have done for me fall back on their heads, in the same way grant your divine benedictions to all my friends, to my fatherland, and to all the human race in general, remember, oh my God, that you are the common father of all men, and have pity on us all in the fullness of your mercy.

*Memorandum Delivered April 19, 1742,
to Monsignor Boudet, Antonine,
Who is Working on the History of the
Late Monsieur de Bernex, Bishop of Geneva*[1]

With the intention of not omitting any of the considerable facts in M. de Bernex's history that can serve to put his Christian virtues in all their clarity, one could not forget the conversion of Madame the Baronne de Warens de la Tour, which was the work of this prelate.[2]

In the month of July of the Year 1726, the King of Sardinia Being at Evian, numerous persons of distinction from the Pays de Vaud proceeded there in order to see the Court. Madame de Warens was among the number, and this Lady, who had been brought by a pure motive of curiosity, was kept there by motives of a higher sort, and which were not any less effective for having been less foreseen. Having attended by chance one of the speeches that this Prelate pronounced with that Zeal and that smoothness that carry the fire of his charity into hearts, Mme. de Warens was moved by it to the point that one can regard this moment as the Time of her Conversion; the thing, nevertheless, must have appeared all the more difficult since this Lady, being very enlightened, kept herself on guard against the seductions of eloquence, and was not disposed to give way without being fully convinced: but when one has a precise mind and an upright heart, what could be lacking in order to taste the truth but the aid of grace, and was not Monsignor de Bernex accustomed to bring it into the most hardened hearts? Mme. de Warens saw the Prelate; her prejudices were destroyed; her doubts were dispelled and filled with the great truths that had been proclaimed to her, she decided to give back to the faith, by means of a striking sacrifice, the value of the enlightenment with which it had just illuminated her.

It did not take long for the rumor of Madame de Warens's plan to be spread through the pays de Vaud: there were mourning and universal alarms: this Lady was adored there and the love they had for her was changed into rage against what they called her seducers and her abductors. The inhabitants of Vevai spoke of nothing less than setting fire to Evian and carrying her away by force of arms in the very midst of the

Court. This insane project, the usual fruit of a fanatical Zeal, came to His Majesty's ears and it was on this occasion that he gave Monsignor de Bernex that so glorious reproach, that he made very noisy conversions. On the spot, the King had Mme. de Warens depart for Anneci escorted by forty of his Guardsmen. It was there that some time later His Majesty assured her of his protection in the most flattering terms and allocated to her a pension that must pass for a striking proof of the piety and generosity of this Prince, but that does not at all deprive Mme. de Warens of the merit of having abandoned great possessions and a brilliant rank in her fatherland in order to follow the voice of the Lord and to give herself over to his providence without reserve. He even had the kindness to offer her to increase this pension so that she could appear with all the splendor that she wished and to procure for her the most attractive position if she wanted to proceed to Turin to the Queen; but Mme. de Warens did not abuse the monarch's kindness, she went to acquire the greatest goods by participating in those that the Church spreads over the Faithful and the splendor of the others henceforth no longer had anything that could touch her. It is thus that she explained herself to Monsignor de Bernex, and it is upon these maxims of detachment and moderation that she has been seen to conduct herself constantly since then.

Finally the day arrived when Monsignor de Bernex was going to guarantee for the Church the conquest that he had acquired for it: He publicly received Madame de Warens's abjuration and administered to her the sacrament of confirmation on the 8th of September, 1726, the day of the nativity of Our Lady in the Church of the visitation before the relic of Saint Francis de Sales. This Lady had the honor of having as her godmother in this Ceremony Madame the Princess of Hesse, sister of the Princess of Piedmont, since, Queen of Sardinia. It was a touching spectacle to see a young Lady of an illustrious Birth favored by the graces of nature and enriched by the goods of fortune, and who a short time before, was the delight of her fatherland, tear herself from the bosom of abundance and pleasures in order to come to lay down the splendor and the voluptuous pleasures of the world at the foot of the Cross of Christ and renounce them forever. Monsignor de Bernex made a very touching and very moving speech on this subject; that day the ardor of his Zeal leant him new force, all of that numerous assembly melted into tears and, bathed in tears, the Ladies came to embrace Mme. de Warens, congratulate her, and to give thanks to God along with her for the victory he caused him to win. Moreover, the papers of the late Monsignor de Bernex have been searched in vain for the speech he pronounced on that occasion and which, by the testimony of all those who heard it, is a masterpiece of eloquence, and there is reason to believe that however fine it might have been, it was composed on the spot and without preparation.

From that day Monsignor de Bernex no longer called Mme. de W. anything but his daughter, and she called him her Father, in fact, he always preserved the kindness of a Father for her, and one must not be surprised that he regarded the work of his Apostolic efforts with some sort of self-satisfaction, since that Lady has always striven to follow as closely as she could the holy examples of this Prelate, whether in his detachment from worldly things, or in his extreme charity toward the poor, two virtues that perfectly define the character of Madame de Warens.

The following fact can enter among the proofs that verify the miraculous actions of Monsignor de Bernex.

In the month of September 1729, when Madame de Warens was residing in M. de Boige's house, the oven of the Franciscan Friars which adjoined the Courtyard of that house caught on fire with such a violence that this oven which enclosed a rather large Building entirely full of faggots and dried wood was soon completely ablaze. Carried by a violent wind, the fire caught onto the roof of the House and even penetrated into the apartments through the windows: Madame de Warens immediately gave her orders to stop the progress of the fire and to have her furnishings transported into her Garden: she was occupied with these efforts when she learned that Monsignor the Bishop had hastened at the noise of the danger that threatened her and that he was about to appear, she was in front of him; they entered the garden together, he got down on his knees and had all those who were present, in the number of whom I was, do so, and began to utter orisons with that fervor that was inseparable from his prayers: their effect was tangible; the wind that was carrying the flames above the house close to the garden, suddenly changed, and sent them away so well that the oven although adjacent was entirely consumed without the House having any other harm than the damage it had received hitherto. This is a fact known to all of Anneci, and which I the Writer of the present memorandum saw with my own eyes.

Monsignor de Bernex constantly continued to take the same interest in everything that concerned Mme. de W.; he had the Portrait of that Lady made saying that he wished that it remain in his family as an honorable monument of one of his happiest labors. In the end, although she was far away from him, a short time before dying he gave her tokens of his memory and even left them in his testament. After the death of this Prelate, Mme. de W. completely dedicated herself to solitude and retreat, saying that after having lost her Father nothing could attach her to the world any longer.

[Fiction or Allegorical Fragment on Revelation][1]

It was during a fine Summer night that the first man who attempted to philosophize, having abandoned himself to a deep and delightful reverie and being guided by that involuntary enthusiasm that sometimes transports the soul out of its abode and makes it embrace the entire universe so to speak, dared to raise his reflections up to the sanctuary of Nature and to penetrate by means of thought as far as human wisdom is permitted to reach.

The heat had scarcely subsided along with the sun, the birds (already withdrawn and not yet asleep) betokened the pleasure they were tasting in breathing a cooler air by means of a languishing and voluptuous warbling. An abundant and healthy dew was already reviving the greenery withered by the heat of the sun, the flowers were casting their sweetest perfumes from every direction. In all their adornment, the orchards and the woods were forming a less lively and more touching sight through the twilight and the first rays of the moon, than during the brightness of the day. Having been effaced by the tumult of the day, the murmur of the brooks was beginning to make itself heard, various domestic animals returning slowly were lowing in the distance and seemed to be enjoying the repose the night was going to give them, and the calm that was beginning to reign in every direction was all the more charming in that it betokened places that were tranquil without being deserts, and peace rather than solitude.

Touched by this combination of pleasant objects, as a sensitive soul always is in such a case where tranquil innocence reigns, the philosopher abandons his heart and his senses to their sweet impressions: to taste them more at leisure he lies down on the grass and leaning his head on his hand he lets his gazes move delightfully over everything that charms them. After several moments of contemplation, by chance he turns his eyes toward Heaven and, from this sight that is so familiar to him and that ordinarily strikes him so little, he is left seized by admiration, he believes he is seeing this immense vault and its superb adornment for the first time. He notices still in the west the traces of fire which the heavenly body that gives us heat[2] and light leaves after it; toward the east he perceives the gentle and melancholy gleam of the one that guides our steps and excites our reveries during the night; moreover he distinguishes two or three of them that make themselves noticed by the apparent irregularity of their path in the midst of the constant and regular disposition of all the other parts of Heaven; he considers with I know not what shivering the slow and majestic progress of this multitude of globes that are rolling in silence over his head and that ceaselessly cast a pure and unfailing light across the spaces of the Heavens. In spite of the immense intervals that separate them from each other, there is a secret correspondence among these bodies that makes them all move in accordance with the same guidance, and, with a curiosity mixed with uneasiness, between the zenith and the horizon he observes the mysterious star around which this common revolution seems to be made. "What inconceivable mechanic could have made all the stars submit to this law, what hand could have linked all the parts of this universe among themselves in this way; and by what strange faculty of myself are all these parts—united outside by this common law—also in a sort of system in my thought which I suspect without conceiving it?

"The same regularity of movement that I notice in the revolutions of the celestial bodies, I find again on the earth in the succession of the seasons, in the organization of the plants and animals. The explanation of all these Phenomena can be sought only in matter set into motion and ordered in accordance with fixed Laws: but who can have established these Laws and how do all bodies find themselves subjected to them? That is what I do not know how to understand. Moreover, the progressive and spontaneous movement of the animals, the sensations, power to think, freedom of will and action that I find in myself and in my fellows, all this surpasses the concepts of mechanism that I can deduce from the known properties of matter.

"That it might have some property that I do not know at all and perhaps never will know so that, ordered or organized in a certain manner, it becomes susceptible to feeling, reflection and will, I can believe without difficulty; but how can the rule of this organization that could have established it be something by itself or in what archetype can it be conceived as existing?

"If I assume that everything is the effect of a fortuitous arrangement, what will become of the idea of order and the relation of intention and end that I notice among all the parts of the Universe? I admit that in the multitude of possible combinations the one that exists cannot be excluded and that it must even have found its place in the infinity of successions; but these successions themselves cannot have happened except with the aid of motion and this is a source of new perplexity for my mind.

"I can conceive that there reigns in the universe a certain amount of motion which, successively modifying bodies, might always be the same in quantity; but I find that since the idea of motion is nothing but an abstraction and cannot be conceived apart from the substance moved, what force could have moved matter still remains to be sought, and if the sum of the motion was susceptible of augmentation or diminution the difficulty would become even greater.

"Thus here I am reduced to assuming the one thing in the world most contrary to all my experiences, namely the necessity of motion within matter: for on every occasion I find bodies indifferent to motion and to rest by themselves, and equally susceptible to either in accordance with the force that pushes them or holds them back; whereas it is impossible for me to conceive motion as a natural property of matter if only for lack of a fixed direction, without which there is no motion whatsoever, and which—if it existed—would eternally carry all bodies along in straight and parallel lines with an equal force, or at least an equal speed, without the smallest atom ever being able to meet another nor to swerve from the common direction for an instant."

Plunged into these reveries and abandoning himself to a thousand confused ideas that he could neither abandon nor clarify, the indiscreet Philosopher was striving vainly to pierce the mysteries of nature, its sight that had at first enchanted him was no longer anything but a subject of uneasiness for him and the whim of explaining it had deprived him of all the pleasure of enjoying it.

Weary at last of fluctuating with so much contention between doubt and error, discouraged at dividing his mind between unprovable systems and unanswerable objections, he was ready to renounce deep and frivolous meditations more fit to inspire him with pride than with knowledge; when all at once a ray of light happened to strike his mind and to unveil for him those sublime truths that it does not belong to man to know by himself and that human reason serves to confirm without serving to discover them. A new universe offered itself so to speak to his contemplation; he perceived the invisible chain that links all the Beings among themselves,[3] he saw a powerful hand extended over everything that exists, the sanctuary of nature was open to his understanding as it is to the celestial intelligences and all the most sublime ideas that we attach to this word *God* presented themselves to his mind. This grace was the reward for his sincere love for the truth and for the good faith with which, without wishing to show off his vain researches, he consented to waste the effort he had taken and to admit his ignorance rather than to consecrate his errors in the eyes of other people under the fine name of philosophy.

Instantly all the enigmas that had made him so very uneasy were made clear to his mind. The course of the Heavens, the magnificence of the stars, the adornment of the earth, the succession of Beings, the relations of conformity and utility that he remarked among them, the mystery of physical organization, that of thought, in a word, the action of the entire machine, all became possible for him to conceive as the work of a powerful Being, director of all things; and—if there were some difficulties left for him that he could not resolve, their solution[s][4] appeared to him beyond his understanding rather than contrary to his reason—he trusted the interior sentiment that was speaking to him with so much energy in favor of his discovery, in preference to some perplexing sophisms that drew their strength only from his mind's weakness.

His soul—seized by admiration by these great and ravishing lights[5] and raising itself so to speak to the level of the object that occupied it—felt itself penetrated by a lively and delightful sensation: a spark of that divine fire that it had perceived seemed to give him a new life; carried away with respect, gratitude and zeal he arose precipitously then, raising his eyes and hands toward Heaven and next bowing his face against the earth, his heart and his mouth addressed to the Divine Being the first and perhaps the purest homage that it might ever have received from mortals.

Set aflame by this new[6] Enthusiasm he would have wanted to communicate its ardor to all of nature, he would have wished above all to share it with his fellows and his most delightful thoughts turned upon the projects of wisdom and felicity that he contemplated making men adopt by showing them the source of the virtues they ought to acquire in the perfections of their common author, and the example and the reward of those they ought to spread in his benefits. "Let us go," he shouted carried away with zeal, "let us carry everywhere along with the explanation of the mysteries of nature the sublime Law of the master who governs it and who manifests himself in his works. Let us teach men to regard themselves as the instruments of a supreme will who unites them among themselves and with a greater whole; to despise the ills of this short life which is only a passage for returning to the eternal being from which they draw their existence, and to love everyone as so many brothers destined to be reunited one day in the bosom of their common Father."

It was in these thoughts so flattering for human pride and so sweet for every loving and sensitive being that he awaited the return of daylight, impatient to carry a purer and more striking one into the soul of other men and to communicate to them the celestial enlightenment that he had just acquired. Nevertheless, since the fatigue of a long meditation had exhausted his spirits and the coolness of the night was inviting him to rest, he dozed off insensibly still dreaming and meditating, and finally slept deeply. During his sleep the disturbances that contemplation had just excited in his brain gave him a dream that was as extraordinary as the ideas that had produced it. He believed he was in the middle of an immense edifice formed by a dazzling Dome supported by seven colossal statues[7] instead of columns. To look at them closely all these statues were horrible and deformed, but by the artifice of a clever perspective, viewed from the center of the Edifice each of them changed appearance and presented a charming form to the eye. These statues all had separate and emblematic poses. One, a mirror in her hand, was sitting on a Peacock whose vain and haughty countenance she imitated. Another with an impudent eye and a lascivious hand urged the objects of her brutal sensuality to share it. Another held serpents nourished from her own substance which she tore out of her bosom in order to devour them and one saw them reborn endlessly. Another, a hideous skeleton that one could distinguish from death only by the sparkling voracity of its eyes, shunned true food in order to swallow with long gulps cups of molten gold that parched it without nourishing it. Finally, all were marked by dreadful attributes that should have made them objects of horror, but that, seen from the point at which they appeared beautiful, seemed to be the ornaments of their beauty. On the keystone of the vault were written these words in large letters: *Peoples serve*[8] *the Gods of the earth*. Directly underneath, that is to say at the center of the building and at the point of perspective, was a large Heptagonal altar on which the humans came in crowds to offer their offerings and their vows to the seven statues which they honored with a thousand different rites and under a thousand bizarre names. This altar served as base to an eighth statue to which the whole edifice was consecrated and which shared the honors rendered to all the others.[9] Always surrounded by an impenetrable veil, it was perpetually served by the People and was never perceived by them;[10] the imagination of its worshippers depicted it to them in accordance with their characters and their passions and each—all the more attached to the object of his worship the more imaginary it was—place under this mysterious veil only the idol of his own heart.[11]

Among the crowd that flocked ceaselessly in this place, he[12] distinguished at first some singularly dressed men[13] who—through a modest and contemplative air—had in their physiognomy an indefinable something sinister that announced pride and cruelty at the same time. Occupied with continuously introducing Peoples into the edifice, they appeared to be the officers or the masters of the place and directed the worship of the seven statues in a sovereign manner. They began by blindfolding the eyes of all those who presented themselves at the entrance of the temple, then—having led them this way into a corner of the sanctuary—they gave them back the use of sight only when all the objects cooperated in fascinating it. If someone tried to remove his blindfold during the journey, they instantly pronounced over him some magic words that gave him the form of a monster under which, abhorred by all and unknown to his relatives, it was not long before he was torn apart by the assembly.

What was most surprising is that the Ministers of the temple who saw all the deformity of their idols fully did not serve them less ardently than the blind vulgar people. They identified themselves so to speak with their horrible divinities and, receiving in their name the homages and the gifts of mortals, each of them offered for his self-interest the same vows to them that fear tore from the peoples.

The continual noise of hymns and songs of gladness threw the spectators into an enthusiasm that set them outside of themselves.[14] The altar that stood in the middle of the temple was barely distinguished through the fumes of a thick incense that spread to the head and disturbed reason; but while the vulgar saw there only the phantoms of its agitated imagination, the calmer philosopher perceived enough of it to judge about what he did not discern, the apparatus of a continuous carnage surrounded that terrible altar, he saw with horror the monstrous mixture of murder and prostitution. Now tender infants were thrown into flames from cedar wood, now grown men were immolated through the falsehoods of a decrepit old man. While groaning denatured Fathers plunged the knife into the bosom of their own daughters. Young people in an elegant and pompous adornment that still enhanced their beauty were[15] buried alive for having listened to the voice of nature while others were ceremoniously abandoned to the most infamous debauchery, and by an abominable contrast one heard at the same time the sighs of the dying along with those of sensual pleasure.

"Ah,"[16] cried the appalled philosopher to himself, "what horrible[17] spectacle, why have my gazes been soiled by it? Let us hasten to leave this infernal abode." "It is not yet time," the invisible being who had already spoken to him[18] said to him while holding him back, "you have just contemplated the blindness of peoples; it remains for you to see what the destiny of the wise is in this place."

Instantly he noticed at the entrance of the Temple a man dressed exactly like him and whose features he was prevented from distinguishing by the distance.[19] This man whose bearing was grave and composed did not himself go to the altar, but—subtly touching the blindfold of those who were led there without causing any apparent displacement in it—he returned the use of sight to them. This service was soon discovered by the indiscretion of those who received it. For, seeing the ugliness of the objects of their worship while crossing the temple, the majority of them refused to go to the altar and attempted to dissuade their neighbors from doing so. Always vigilant for their interest, the Ministers of the Temple soon discovered the source of the scandal, seized the veiled man, dragged him to the foot of the altar and immolated him on the spot to the unanimous acclamations of the blinded troop.

Turning his eyes toward the nearest entrance, the Philosopher saw there an old man of a rather unimposing appearance but whose insinuating manners and familiar and profound discourse soon caused his physiognomy to be forgotten.[20] As soon as he presented himself to enter, the ministers of the temple brought the sacred blindfold. But he said to them, "Divine men, spare yourselves a superfluous care for a poor old man deprived of sight who comes under your auspices to seek to recover it here; condescend only to lead me to the altar so that I can give homage to the divinity and she can cure me." As he pretended to bump rather heavily against the objects around him, the hope of a miracle made them forget to verify the need for it any better;[21] the ceremony of the blindfold was omitted as superfluous and the old man was ushered in leaning upon a young man who served him as guide, and to whom no attention was paid.

Frightened by the horrible sight of the seven statues and by the blood that he saw streaming around the eighth, twenty times this young man tried to escape and to flee out of the temple, but, held back with a vigorous arm by the old man, he was constrained to lead him, or rather, to follow him all the way to the enclosure of the sanctuary in order to observe what he saw and to work one day for the instruction of men. All at once, lightly leaping onto the altar, the pretended blind man uncovered the statue with a bold hand and exposed it to all gazes without its veil. Depicted on its visage was seen ecstasy along with fury; under its feet it stifled personified humanity, but its eyes were tenderly turned toward Heaven: in the left hand it was holding an inflamed heart and in the other it was sharpening a dagger. This sight made the philosopher shudder, but far from revolting the spectators, instead of an air of cruelty they saw there only a celestial enthusiasm, and felt augment for the statue thus uncovered the zeal they had had for it without knowing it. "*Peoples,*" the intrepid old man who perceived this cried out to them with a tone full of fire, "*how mad are you to serve Gods who seek only to harm, and to adore beings even more maleficent than you? Ah far from forcing them by indiscreet sacrifices to think about you in order to torment you, endeavor rather to make them forget you, you will be less wretched for it; if you believe you please them by destroying their works, what can you hope from them other than that they destroy you in their turn? Serve the one who wants everyone to be happy if you wish to be happy yourselves."*

The Ministers did not permit him to proceed, and interrupting him with a great noise they asked the People for justice for that ingrate who as a reward for having, they said, recovered his sight upon the altar of the Goddess dared to profane her statue and to disparage her worship. At once the whole People threw itself upon him, ready to tear him to pieces, but seeing his death assured the Ministers wished to clothe it with a juridical form and caused him to be condemned by the assembly to drink green water, a type of death often imposed on the wise. While the liquor was being prepared the friends of the old man wished to take him away secretly, but he refused to follow them. "Let me," he said to them, "go to receive the reward for my zeal from the one who is its object. While living among these peoples, did I not submit to their laws, and ought I to transgress them at the moment they crown me? After having devoted my days to the progress of truth am I not only too happy still to be able to devote to it the end of a life that nature was going to ask back from me? Oh my friends, the example of my last day is the only instruction that I leave you, or at least the one that ought to give weight to all the others. I would be suspected of having lived only as a sophist if I were afraid to die as a Philosopher." After this speech he received the cup of the Wise Men and, having drunk with a serene air, he conversed peacefully with his friends about the immortality of the soul and the great truths of nature which the philosopher listened to all the more attentively because they were related to his preceding meditations. But the last speech of the old man which was a very distinct homage to that same statue that he had unveiled cast into the mind of the Philosopher a doubt and a perplexity from which he was never able to extricate himself very well, and he was always uncertain whether these words contained an allegorical sense or simply an act of submission to the worship established by the laws. "For," he said, "if all the manners of serving the divinity are indifferent to it, it is obedience to the laws that must be preferred." Nevertheless between this action and the preceding one there always remained a contradiction that appeared to him impossible to remove.

Struck by everything that he had just seen, he was reflecting deeply about these terrible scenes; when suddenly a voice made itself heard in the air pronouncing distinctly these words: *"Here is the son of man.*[22] *The Heavens are silent before him, earth listen to his voice."* Then lifting his eyes he perceived on the altar a personage whose imposing and gentle aspect struck him with astonishment and respect; his clothing was common and similar to that of an artisan, but his gaze was celestial, his bearing modest, grave, and less affected even than that of his predecessor;[23] his features had something undefinably sublime in which simplicity was allied with greatness and one could not envisage him without feeling oneself pierced with a lively and delightful emotion that had its source in no feeling known to men. *"Oh my Children,"* he said in a tone of tenderness that pierced the soul, *"I come to atone for and cure your errors, love the one who loves you and know the one who is."* Instantly seizing the statue, he threw it down effortlessly and climbing onto the pedestal with as little agitation, he seemed to be taking his place rather than usurping someone else's.

His air, his tone, his gesture caused an extraordinary fermentation in the assembly; the People were seized by them to the point of enthusiasm, the ministers were angered by them to the point of fury, but they were hardly listened to. Preaching a divine morality,[24] the popular and firm unknown man swept away everything, everything announced a revolution, he had only to say a word and his enemies were no longer: but the one who came to destroy bloodthirsty intolerance had no care to imitate it, he employed only the means that suited the things he had to say and the functions with which he was charged, and because of this the people—all of whose passions are furies—became less zealous for his defense.[25] After the testimony of strength and intrepidity that he had just given he took up his discourse again with the same gentleness as before; he depicted the love of men and all the virtues with such touching features and such lovable colors that aside from the officers of the Temple (enemies of all humanity by their estate) none heard him without being softened and without loving better his duties and the happiness of others because of them. His speech was simple and gentle and yet profound and sublime, without stunning the ear he nourished the soul, it was milk for children and bread for men,[26] he animated[27] the strong and consoled the weak and the least adequate geniuses among them all found him equally at their level, he did not at all harangue with a pompous and dignified tone but his familiar speeches shone with the most ravishing eloquence, and his teachings were fables and apologues, common conversations but full of justness and profundity. Nothing perplexed him; the most captious questions that the desire to ruin him caused to be proposed immediately had solutions dictated by wisdom; it was necessary to hear him only once to be certain of admiring him always, one felt that the language of the truth cost him nothing because it had its source within him.[28]

[Fragment on the Infinite Power of God][1]

Why does the sublime produce such a great effect? It is because this simplicity in great things makes one assume that they are familiar to the one who is speaking, and that they have nothing extraordinary for him. Nothing better proclaims an infinite power, than such ease at doing what surpasses human understanding. The imagination gets frightened and comes to a stop, seeking what might cost some effort to the one who does not put any effort into productions as incomprehensible as that one.

What! to make light is such a simple operation, that it is enough tranquilly to tell light to be for light instantly to be! . . .

Same simplicity in speech and execution. Neither the author nor the historian have seen anything astonishing in an operation that the reader cannot even imagine. What is, then, that unknown order of power, whose slightest operations are beyond the human mind; and what should one assume in those that would cost it some effort? . . .

Manez, Pharez, Tekel.[2] Sublime fearlessness in the spectator who would have tranquilly copied these words on his writing-tablet.

Moral Letters[1]

[Letter 1]

Come, my dear and worthy friend, listen to the voice of the one who loves you;[2] it is not at all, you know, that of a vile seducer; if my heart ever went astray in wishes about which you have made me blush, at least my mouth did not attempt to justify my going astray,[3] reason dressed up[4] in sophisms did not lend its service to the error;[5] humiliated vice fell silent at the sacred name of virtue;[6] faith, honor, holy truth were not insulted in my speeches; by abstaining from giving decent names to my faults I kept decency from leaving my heart, I kept it open to the lessons of wisdom that you deigned to make me hear: now it is my turn, oh Sophie,[7] it is up to me to render back to you the value of your efforts, since you have preserved my soul for the virtues that are dear to you. I want to insert into yours those that are perhaps still unknown to it.[8] How happy I consider myself for not having ever prostituted my pen or my mouth to lying, because of this I feel myself less unworthy of being the organ of truth near you today.

In recalling the circumstances in which you asked me for rules of morality for your use, I cannot doubt that at that time you were putting into practice one of the most sublime ones, and that, in the danger to which a blind passion was exposing me,[9] you were giving thought to my instruction even more than to your own. Only a scoundrel could set forth someone else's duties while trampling his own underfoot or bend morality to his passions and you, who honor me with your friendship, know very well that, with a weak heart, I do not have the soul of a wicked man. In striving today to fulfill the noble task that you imposed on me, I am offering you an homage that is due to you. Virtue is dearer to me since I received it from you.

By subjecting the feelings that you inspired in me to duty and reason, you have exercised the greatest, the worthiest[10] empire that heaven has given to beauty and wisdom. No, Sophie, a love like mine could give way only to itself,[11] like the Gods you alone could destroy your work and it rested only with your virtues to erase the effect of your charms.

In purifying itself, my heart was far from detaching itself from yours,[12] blind love gave way to a thousand enlightened feelings[13] which made it a charming duty for me to love you all my life, and you are only dearer to me for it since I stopped adoring you. Far from cooling off, upon changing their object my desires only became more ardent while becoming more decent. If in the confines of my heart they dared to make an attempt upon your charms, they have well atoned for that insult, they no longer yearn for anything but the perfection of your soul and to justify, if it is possible, everything that mine has felt for you. Yes, be perfect, as you can be, and I shall be happier than if I had possessed you. May my zeal be able to help to exalt you so far above me, that amour-propre will compensate me in you for my humiliations and console me in some manner for not having been able to attain you. Ah! If the efforts of my friendship can encourage your progress, consider sometimes everything that I have a right to expect from a heart that mine has been unable to deserve.

After so many days lost in pursuing a vain glory, by telling the public truths it was in no condition to understand, I finally see myself proposing a useful object, I shall carry out the efforts that you are demanding from me, I shall look after you, your duties, the virtues that suit you, the means of perfecting your happy natural disposition. I shall always have my eyes on you: no, if I passed my life seeking out a pleasant labor, I would not know how to find a better one according to my heart than the one you are imposing on me.

Never was a project formed under sweeter auspices, never did an undertaking promise a happier success. Everything that can set courage ablaze and nourish hope is joined to the tenderest friendship in order to incite my zeal. The path of perfection is open to you without obstacle; nature and chance have done so much for you that what you still lack no longer depends on anything but your will, and your heart answers to me for it in everything that relates to virtue. You bear an illustrious name that your fortune upholds and your merit honors; a newly formed family awaits only your efforts to make you the happiest of mothers someday; your Husband, received at court, esteemed in war, intelligent in business enjoys a constant happiness that began with his marriage.[14] The taste for pleasures is not alien to you; reserve and moderation are even more natural to you; you have the embellishments that make one succeed in the world, the enlightenment that makes one disdain it, and the talents that compensate for it; everywhere you will be where you want to be and always in your place.

That was not yet enough; a thousand others enjoy all these advantages and are only common women. More precious goods[15] are your lovable share. A precise and penetrating mind, an upright and sensitive heart, a soul smitten with love of the beautiful, an exquisite sentiment for knowing it, these are the warrants for the hopes that I have conceived for you. It is not I who want you to be the best, the most worthy, the most respectable of women; it is nature that wanted it, do not betray its intentions, do not bury its talents. I ask you only to interrogate[16] your heart, and to do what it recommends to you.[17] Do not listen to my voice, oh Sophie, except to the extent that you feel it confirmed by its voice.[18]

Among all these gifts that Heaven has dispensed to you shall I dare to count that of a faithful friend? There is one, you know, who, not content with cherishing you as you are, is filled with a keen and pure enthusiasm for everything that ought to be hoped for from you. With an eager eye he contemplates you in all the conditions in which you can be; he sees you at every moment of his life, in the past, in the present, in the future; he wants to gather all your being at the same time in the depths of his soul. He knows no other pleasure than to take care of you ceaselessly, his dearest desire is to see you perfect enough to[19] inspire the whole universe with the same feelings he has for you. Near the end of my short life, from the ardor with which I feel myself set ablaze, it seems that I am receiving a new life in order to use it for guiding yours. My mind is enlightened by the fire of my heart, I experience in myself the invincible impulse of genius. I believe myself sent from heaven to perfect its worthiest work; yes, Sophie, the occupations of my final days will honor my sterile youth[20] if you deign to listen to me, what I shall have done for you will redeem the uselessness of my entire life; and I shall become better for it myself, by exerting myself to give you the example of the virtues the love of which I want to inspire in you.[21]

We may very well have stopped seeing each other, we shall never stop loving each other, I feel it, for our mutual attachment is founded on relations that do not perish.[22] It is in vain that chance and the wicked separate us,[23] our hearts will always be close and if they agreed so well when two opposite passions inspired them with incompatible desires, what will they not do today, reconciled in the worthiest object that could fill them.

Recall the fine days of that summer, so charming, so short, and so suited to leaving long memories. Recall the solitary promenades that we loved to repeat on those shady hills where the most fertile valley in the world displayed all the wealth of nature to our eyes, as if in order to disgust us with the false goods of opinions. Consider those delightful conversations in which, in the effusion of our souls, the confiding of our troubles mutually relieved them, and in which you poured the peace of innocence over the sweetest feelings that the heart of man has ever tasted. Without being united with the same knot, without burning with the same flame, I know not what celestial fire still enlivened us with its heat and made us sigh jointly after unknown goods that we were made to enjoy together. Do not doubt it, Sophie, these so much desired goods were the same ones I have just offered you the image of today, the same inclination for everything that is good and decent attached us to each other and the same sensitivity brought together made us find more charms in the common object of our adorations. How changed we would have been and how necessary it would be to pity us if we could ever forget such dear moments, if we could stop recalling each other with pleasure, seated together at the foot of an oak tree, your hand in mine, your softened eyes fixed on mine and shedding tears purer than heaven's dew. Doubtless from afar the vile and corrupt man could interpret our speeches in accordance with the baseness of his heart; but perhaps the blameless witness, the eternal eye that one does not deceive at all, saw with kindness two sensitive souls mutually encouraging each other to virtue and, by means of a delightful effusion, nourishing all the pure feelings with which he filled them.

These are the warrants for the success of my efforts, these are my rights for daring to make them. In exposing my sentiments about the use of life, I am claiming less to give you lessons than to make my profession of faith to you, to whom better could I confide my principles than to the one who knows all my feelings so well?[24] Doubtless, along with some important truths of which you will know how to make use, you will find here some involuntary errors from which your rectitude of heart and mind will know how to cure me and preserve you. Examine, discern, choose, deign to explain the reasons for your choice to me, and may you be able to draw as much profit from these letters as the author expects from your reflections. If I sometimes take with you the tone of a man who believes he is teaching, you know, Sophie, with this air of a schoolmaster I am doing nothing but obeying you, and I would give you such lessons for a long time before paying you the value of those I have received from you.

If this writing had no use other than that of bringing us together sometimes and of reopening in absence those sweet conversations that filled my final days and made up my final pleasures, this idea would be enough to pay me for the labors of the rest of my life. I console myself in the midst of my ills by considering that, when I no longer exist, I will still be something to you, that my writings will take my place near you, that in rereading them you will reacquire the taste that you found in conversing with me and that, if they do not bring new enlightenment to your[25] mind, at least they will nourish in the depths of your soul the memory of the most tender friendship that ever existed.

These letters were not written to be made public and I do not need to tell you that they never will be without your assent. But if[26] circumstances allow you to grant it someday, how willingly would the purity of the zeal that attaches me to you[27] make its declaration public.[28] Without appearing in this work, perhaps neither your name nor mine would escape the suspicions of those who knew us;[29] as for myself, I would be more proud than humiliated by this acuteness and from it I would only obtain more esteem by showing the esteem that I have for you. With regard to you, lovable Sophie, although you do not need my approbation to be honored, I would like the entire earth to have its eyes on you, I would like to see the whole world informed about what I expect from the qualities of your soul, so as to inspire you with more courage and force to fulfill this expectation in the eyes of the public. They will say[30] that I have bestowed neither my attachment nor my esteem lavishly, particularly to women; because of this they will be more curious to examine the one who brought both of them together so perfectly. I charge you with my glory, oh Sophie, justify if possible the honor that I have received from good people. Make it be said one day in seeing you and recalling my memory: Ah, that man loved virtue and was a judge of merit.

Letter 2

The object of human life is the felicity of man, but who among us knows how to attain it? Without principle, without a sure goal, we flit about from desires to desires and those that we succeed in satisfying leave us as far from happiness as we were before we obtained anything. We have an invariable rule, neither in reason that lacks support, foothold, and consistency, nor in the passions that ceaselessly follow upon and destroy each other. Victims of the blind inconstancy of our hearts, the enjoyment of the desired goods does nothing but prepare us for privations and pains, everything we possess serves only to show us what we lack, and, for want of knowing how we should live, we all die without having lived. If there is some possible means for freeing oneself from this horrible doubt, it is to extend it beyond its natural limits for a time, to mistrust all one's inclinations, to study oneself, to carry the torch of truth to the depths of one's soul, to examine one time everything that one thinks, everything that one believes, everything that one feels, and everything that one ought to think, feel, and believe in order to be as happy as the human condition permits. That, my charming friend, is the examination that I am proposing to you today.

But what are we going to do, oh Sophie, but what has already been done a thousand times? All books speak to us about the sovereign good, all philosophers show it to us, each teaches others the art of being happy, none has found it for himself. In this immense labyrinth[31] of human reasoning you will learn to speak about happiness without knowing it, you will learn to speechify and not at all to live, you will lose yourself in metaphysical subtleties, the perplexities of philosophy will lay siege to you from every direction, you will see objections and doubts everywhere, and as a result of instructing yourself you will finish by not knowing anything. This method trains in speaking about everything, in shining in a social circle; it makes learned people, fine wits, talkers, arguers, happy people in the judgment of those who are listening, unfortunate people as soon as they are alone.[32] No, my dear child,[33] the study that I am proposing to you does not at all give a show of knowledge that one can display to the eyes of other people, but it fills the soul with everything that makes up the happiness of man; it makes not others, but ourselves, satisfied with it, it does not bring words to the mouth but feelings to the heart.[34] Upon abandoning oneself to it one gives more confidence to the voice of nature than to that of reason and, without speaking so emphatically about wisdom and happiness, one becomes wise inside and happy for oneself. Such is the philosophy about which I am seeking to instruct you; it is in the silence of your study that I want to converse with you. Provided that you feel that I am right, I care little about proving it to you; I shall not teach you to resolve objections, but I shall try to make it so that you do not have any to make to me; I trust your good faith more than my arguments and, without entangling myself with scholarly rules, in testimony for all I have to tell you, I shall summon nothing but your heart alone.[35]

Take a look at this universe, my lovable friend, cast your eyes on this theater of errors and miseries that makes us deplore the sad destiny of man when contemplating it. We live in the region[36] and the century of philosophy and reason. The lights of all the sciences seem to be gathered together at the same time to enlighten our eyes and guide us in this obscure labyrinth of human life. The finest geniuses of all ages gather their lessons together to instruct us, immense libraries are opened to the public, from infancy multitudes of schools and universities offer us the experience and meditation of 4000 years.[37] Immortality, glory, even wealth, and often honors are the reward for the most worthy in the art of instructing and enlightening men. Everything cooperates in perfecting our understanding and in lavishing on each of us everything that can form and cultivate reason. Have we become better or wiser from this, do we know any better from it what the path is and what the end of our short lifetime will be, are we in better agreement from it about the primary duties and the true goods of the human species? What have we acquired from all this vain knowledge other than quarrels, hatreds, uncertainty, and doubts? Each sect is the only one that has found the truth. Each Book exclusively contains the precepts of wisdom, each author is the only one who teaches us what is good. One proves to us that there is no body at all,[38] another that there are no souls at all,[39] another that the soul has no relation to the body,[40] another that man is a beast, another that God is a mirror.[41] There is no maxim so absurd that some author of reputation has not advanced it; no axiom so evident that it has not been combated by one of them; everything is good as long as one speaks differently than the others and one always finds reasons to maintain what is new in preference to what is true.

Let them admire as they please the perfection of the arts, the number and greatness of their discoveries, the extent and sublimity of human genius; shall we congratulate them for knowing all of nature except for themselves and for having found all the arts except the one of being happy? We are happy, they exclaim sadly, how many resources for well-being, what crowd of commodities unknown to our fathers, how many pleasures do we taste that they were unaware of. It is true, you have softness, but they had felicity; you are reasoners, they were reasonable; you are refined, they were humane; all your pleasures are outside of you, theirs were in themselves. And of what value are these cruel voluptuous pleasures that the small number purchase at the expense of the multitude?[42] The luxury of the cities brings misery, hunger, despair to the countryside, if some men are happier the human race is more to be pitied for it. By multiplying the commodities of life for some rich people one has done nothing but force the majority of men to regard themselves as miserable. Which is this barbarous happiness that one feels only at the expense of others? Sensitive souls, tell me, what is a happiness that is purchased at the price of money?[43]

Knowledge makes men gentle, they say again, the age is less cruel, we shed less blood. Ah, unfortunate people! Cause fewer tears to be shed, and would not the unlucky people that are made to die languishing during an entire life prefer to lose it once on a scaffold? For being gentler, are you less unjust, less vindictive, is virtue less oppressed, power less tyrannical, are the people less overburdened, does one see fewer crimes, are malefactors more rare, are the prisons less full? What have you gained then by making yourselves soft? For vices that show courage and vigor you have substituted those of small souls. Your gentleness is base and pusillanimous, you torment secretly and under cover those you would have attacked with open force.[44] If you are less bloodthirsty, it is not virtue but weakness, in you it is only one more vice.

The art of reasoning is not reason at all, often it is its abuse. Reason is the faculty of ordering all the faculties of our soul suitably to the nature of things and their relations with us. Reasoning is the art of comparing known truths in order to compose from them other truths that one did not know and that this art makes us discover. But it does not at all teach us to know these primitive truths that serve as elements of the others, and if we put in their place our opinions, our passions, our prejudices, far from enlightening us it blinds us, it does not exalt the soul at all, it enervates it and corrupts the judgment that it should perfect.[45]

In the chain of reasonings that serves to form a system the same proposition will return a hundred times with almost insensible differences that will escape the philosopher's mind. So often multiplied, these differences will finally modify the proposition to the point of changing it completely without him noticing it, he will say about one thing what he believes he has proved about another and his conclusions will be so many errors. This inconvenience is inseparable from the systematic spirit that alone leads to great principles and consists in always generalizing. Inventors generalize as much as they can, this method extends discoveries, gives an air of genius and force to those who make them and, because nature always acts by general laws, by establishing general principles in their turn they believe they have penetrated its secret. By dint of extending and abstracting one small fact, one changes it this way into a universal rule; one believes one is ascending to principles, one wants to gather together into a single object more ideas than human understanding can compare, and one affirms about an infinity of beings what often is barely found in a single one. Afterward, observers, less brilliant and colder, arrive ceaselessly adding exception upon exception, until the general proposition has become so particular that one can no longer infer anything from it and distinctions and experience reduce it to the sole fact from which it has been drawn. This is how systems are established and destroyed without discouraging new reasoners from raising upon their ruins others that will not last any longer.

Since everyone goes astray by various routes this way, each believes he reaches the true goal because no one noticed the trace of all the detours he made. What, then, will the one who sincerely seeks the truth do among these crowds of learned people who all claim to have found it and mutually give each other the lie? Will he weigh all the systems? Will he leaf through all the books, will he listen to all the Philosophers, will he compare all the sects, will he dare to pronounce between Epicurus and Zeno, between Aristippus and Diogenes, between Locke and Shaftsburi? Will he dare to prefer his intelligence to that of Pascal and his reason to that of Descartes?[46] Listen to a mullah speechify in Persia, a bonze in China, a lama in Tartary, a brahman in the Indies, a Quaker in England, a rabbi in Holland, you will be astonished by the force of persuasion that each of them can give to his absurd doctrine. How many people as sensible as you has each of them convinced? If you hardly deign to listen to them, if you laugh at their vain arguments, if you refuse to believe them, what resists their prejudices in you is not reason, it is your prejudices.

Life would have flowed away ten times before one might have discussed a single one of these opinions to the bottom. A bourgeois of Paris makes fun of Calvin's objections that frighten a doctor at the Sorbonne. The more deeply one goes into it, the more one finds subjects for doubt and though one opposes reasons to reasons, authorities to authorities, votes to votes, the more one advances the more one finds subjects to doubt; the more one instructs oneself, the less one knows, and one is completely astonished that instead of learning what one did not know one even loses the science that one believed one had.

Letter 3

We do not know anything, my dear Sophie, we do not see anything; we are a band of blind men, cast at random in this vast universe. Not perceiving any object, each of us makes for himself a fantastic image of everything that he afterward takes for the rule of the true, and since this idea does not resemble anyone else's, out of this appalling multitude of philosophers whose babble confuses us, not even two of them are found who are in agreement about the system of that universe that all claim to know, or about the nature of the things that all are careful to explain.

Unfortunately, what is precisely the least known to us is what it matters most for us to know, namely man. We do not see either anyone else's soul because it is hidden, nor our own, because we do not have any intellectual mirror.[47] We are blind men at every point, but born blind men who do not imagine what sight is, and, not believing that we lack any faculty, want to measure the extremities of the world while our short sight, like our hands, reaches only two feet from us.

By going deeply into this idea perhaps one would find it no less precise literally than it is figuratively. Our senses are the instruments of all our knowledge. It is from them that all our ideas come, or at least all are occasioned by them. Constrained and closed up in its envelope, human understanding cannot, so to speak, pierce through the body that compresses it and acts only through the sensations. These are, if one wishes, five windows by which our soul would like to give itself light; but the windows are small, the glazing is dim, the wall thick, and the house extremely badly lit. Our senses are given to us to preserve us, not to instruct us, to warn us about what is useful or the opposite to us and not about what is true or false, their purpose is not at all to be employed in inquiries into nature, if we make that use of them they are insufficient, they deceive us and we can never be sure of finding the truth by means of them.[48]

The errors of one sense are corrected by another; if we had only one of them they would deceive us forever.[49] Thus we have only defective rules for mutually setting right. Let two false rules come into agreement, they will deceive us by their very agreement and if we lack the third, what means is left for discovering the error?

Sight and touch are the two senses that serve us the most in the investigation of the truth because they offer us the objects more entirely and in a state of persistence more fit for observation than the one in which these same objects lay themselves open to the three other senses. The first two also seem to divide among them the whole philosophic spirit. Sight, which measures the entire hemisphere at a glance, represents the vast capacity of systematic genius. Slow and progressive touch that makes certain of one object before passing to another one resembles the spirit of observation. Both also have the defects of the faculties that they represent. The more the eye is fixed on distant objects the more it is subject to optical illusions, and the hand, always attached to some part, could not encompass a great whole.

It is certain that of all our senses sight is the one from which we receive the most instruction and the most errors at the same time, it is by sight that we judge about almost all of nature and it is sight that suggests to us almost all our false judgments. You have heard people speak about the famous operation on the born blind man; when not a saint but a surgeon had restored sight to him it took him much time to learn how to make use of it.[50] According to him everything that he saw was in his eye, in looking at bodies of unequal size in the distance he had no idea of either the sizes or the distances, and when he began to discern objects he could not yet distinguish a portrait from an original;[51] they forgot to ascertain whether he saw objects reversed.

With all acquired experience there is no man who is not subject by sight to putting forward false judgments about objects that are far away, to making false measurements about those that are under his eyes and, what is more surprising is that these errors are not even always within the rules of perspective.[52]

But if sight deceives us so often and touch alone corrects it, touch itself deceives us upon a thousand occasions. Who will assure us that it does not always deceive us and that there might not be a sixth sense to set it right? The experience of the small ball rolled between two crossed fingers shows that we are not any less slaves of habit in our judgments than in our inclinations.[53] Touch, which prides itself on judging shapes so well, does not judge any of them exactly, it will never teach us whether a line is straight, whether a surface is a plane, whether a cube is regular; it does not judge degrees of heat any better; the same cellar appears cool to us in the summer and warm in the winter without having changed temperature; expose the right hand to the air, the left to a great fire, then soak them both in tepid water at the same time, this water will appear hot to the right hand and cold to the left. Each person reasons about heaviness but no one feels its most general effect which is air pressure, we barely feel the fluid that surrounds us and we believe we are bearing only the weight of our body when we are bearing that of the whole atmosphere. Do you want to test some slight indication of this, when you are in the bath, slowly take your arm out of the water in a horizontal position and, to the extent that the air presses down the arm, you will feel your muscles growing tired from this terrible pressure, which you perhaps never suspected. A thousand other similar observations would teach us in how many ways the surest of the senses imposes upon us either by hiding or altering effects that exist, or by assuming some that do not exist. We might very well have united sight and touch in order to judge about extent, which falls within the competence of both; we do not even know what largeness and smallness are. The apparent largeness of objects is relative to the stature of the one who measures them. Some gravel that a mite finds in his path presents the mass of the Alps to it. A foot for us is a fathom in the eyes of a pygmy, and an inch in those of a Giant. If that were not so our senses would be out of proportion to our needs and we could not continue to exist. In every sense each takes upon himself the measure of all things. Where, then, is absolute size, does everyone deceive himself or no one? It is not necessary to say any more to you about it to make you glimpse how far one could push the consequences of these reflections. All of Geometry is founded only upon sight and touch and these two senses perhaps need to be rectified by others that we lack; the thing that is most completely demonstrated for us is then still open to question and we cannot know whether the *Elements* of Euclid are not a tissue of errors.

It is not so much reasoning that we lack as the foothold for reasoning. Man's mind is in a condition to do a great deal but the senses furnish him with few[54] materials, and our soul, active in its bonds, prefers to exert itself upon the chimeras that are within its reach than to remain idle and without movement. Let us not be surprised, then, at seeing prideful and vain philosophy[55] losing itself in its reveries and the finest geniuses exhausting themselves on puerile things. With what distrust should we abandon ourselves to our weak intelligence, when we see the most methodical of Philosophers, the one who has best established his principles, and reasoned most consistently, going astray from the first steps and plunging from errors to errors in absurd systems.[56] Wishing to cut the root of all prejudices, Descartes began by calling everything into question, subjecting everything to the scrutiny of reason; departing from this unique and incontestable principle: *I think, therefore I exist,* and proceeding with the greatest precautions, he believed he was going toward the truth and did not find anything but lies. Based on this first principle he began by examining himself, then finding in himself very distinct properties which also seemed to belong to two different substances, he first applied himself to knowing these two substances well and, setting aside everything that was not clearly and necessarily contained in their idea, he defined one as extended substance and the other as the substance that thinks.[57] Definitions all the more wise since they left the obscure question of the two substances as it were undecided, and since it did not absolutely follow that extension and thought were not able to unite and penetrate into an identical substance. Very well, these definitions that seemed incontestable were destroyed in less than one generation. Newton caused it to be seen that the essence of matter did not at all consist in extension, Locke caused it to be seen that the essence of the soul did not at all consist in thought. Farewell to all the philosophy of the wise and methodical Descartes. Will his successors be more fortunate, will their systems last any longer? No, Sophie, they are beginning to vacillate; they will fall the same way, they are the work of men.

Why can we not know what mind and matter are? Because we do not know anything except by our senses, and they are insufficient to teach it to us. As soon as we want to make use of our faculties we feel them all constrained by our organs; subjected to the senses, reason itself is in contradiction with itself as they are, geometry is full of demonstrated theorems that it is impossible to conceive. In philosophy, substance, soul, body,[58] eternity, motion, freedom, necessity, contingency, etc. are so many words that one is constrained to employ at every instant and that no one has ever conceived. Simple physics is no less obscure to us than metaphysics and morality, the great Newton, the interpreter of the universe, did not even suspect the prodigies of electricity, which appears to be nature's most active principle. Its most common operation[59] and the easiest to observe, namely the multiplication of plants by their seeds is still to be known and every day new facts are discovered that overturn all reasonings. Wanting to develop the mystery of generation, the Pliny of our century[60] found himself forced to have recourse to a principle that is unintelligible and irreconcilable with the known laws of mechanics and of motion; explain everything as we will, everywhere we find inexplicable difficulties that show us that we have no certain notion about anything.

You might have seen in the Abbé de Condillac's statue what degrees of knowledge would belong to each sense if they were given to us separately and the bizarre reasonings that would be made about the nature of things by beings endowed with fewer organs than we have.[61] In your opinion what would be said about us by beings endowed with other senses that are unknown to us?[62] How can it be proven that these senses cannot exist and that they would not clear up the darkness that ours cannot destroy?[63] There is nothing fixed about the number of senses necessary to give feeling and life to a corporeal and organized body. Let us consider the animals: numerous have fewer senses than we do, why would others not have more of them? Why would they not have some that will be eternally unknown to us because they offer no foothold to ours and by which one would explain what seems inexplicable to us in numerous actions of the beasts? Fish do not hear at all, neither birds nor fish have any sense of smell, neither snails nor worms have any eyes, and touch appears to be the only sense of the oyster,[64] but how many animals have prescience, foresight, inconceivable ruses that it would perhaps be better to attribute to some organ foreign to man than to that unintelligible word "instinct." What puerile pride to settle the faculties of all beings based on ours while to our own eyes everything gives the lie to this ridiculous prejudice. How can we be assured that, of all the reasoning beings that the various worlds might contain, we are not the least favored by nature, the least provided with organs suited to the knowledge of truth, and that it is not to this insufficiency that we owe the incomprehensibility that stops us at every moment over a thousand demonstrated truths?

With so few means for observing matter and sensitive beings how do we hope to be able to make judgements about the soul and spiritual beings? Let us assume that such things really do exist, if we do not know what a body is how will we know what a mind is? We see ourselves surrounded by bodies without souls, but who among us ever perceived a soul without body and can have the slightest idea of a purely spiritual substance? What can we say about the soul about which we know nothing except that it acts through the senses? How do we know whether it does not have an infinite number of other faculties that are waiting only for a suitable organization or the return of freedom in order to develop? Do our lights come to us from outside to the inside through the senses in accordance with the materialists, or do they escape from inside to the outside as Plato claimed? If the daylight enters the house through the windows the senses are the seat of the understanding. On the contrary if the house is lit up inside, you would close up everything but the light would not exist any less even though held in, but the more you open the windows the more lucidity will go out and the easier it will be for you to distinguish the surrounding objects. Thus it is a very puerile question to ask whether a soul can see, hear, and touch, without hands, without eyes, and without ears,[65] I would just as soon that a cripple ask how one can walk without crutches; it would be much more philosophic to ask how a soul can see, hear, and touch, with hands, eyes, and ears;[66] for the manner in which the body and the soul act on each other was always the despair of metaphysics and one is even more at a loss to give sensations to pure matter.

Who knows whether there are not minds of different degrees of perfections to each of which nature has given bodies organized in accordance with the faculties to which they are susceptible, from the oyster up to us on the earth and from us, perhaps, up to more sublime species in various worlds?[67] Who knows whether what distinguishes man from beast is not that the soul of the latter does not have any more faculties than its body has sensations, whereas the human soul compressed in a body that impedes the majority of its faculties at every moment wants to break open its prison and joins an almost divine audacity to the weakness of humanity? Is this not the way that those great geniuses, the astonishment and honor of their species, in some manner break through the barrier of the senses, soar into the celestial and intellectual regions, and raise themselves as far above the ordinary man as nature raises this latter above the animals? Why would you not imagine the vast bosom of the universe full of an infinite number of minds of a thousand different orders, eternal admirers of the play of nature and inevitable spectators of men's actions?[68] Oh my Sophie, how sweet it is for me to think that they witnessed our most charming conversations and that a murmur of applause was raised up among these pure intelligences, upon seeing two tender and honorable friends making sacrifices to virtue in the hidden depths of their heart.

That these are only conjectures without any probability, I agree, but it is enough for me that one cannot prove the opposite in order to deduce from them the doubts that I wish to establish. Where are we? What do we see, what do we know, what exists? We are only running after shadows that escape us. Some slight specters, some vain phantoms flit before our eyes and we believe we are seeing the eternal chain of beings.[69] We do not know one substance in the universe, we are not even sure of seeing its surface and we want to sound the abyss of nature. Let us leave such a puerile labor to those children who are called philosophers. After having proceeded through the narrow circle of their vain knowledge it is necessary to end where Descartes had begun. *I think therefore I exist.* That is all we know.

Letter 4

The more man looks at himself the smaller he sees himself to be. But the lens that makes things smaller is made only for good eyes.[70] Is it not, my dear Sophie, a strange pride that one gains by feeling all one's misery? That, nevertheless, is the only one that can be drawn from healthy philosophy. As for me, I would pardon the false learned person a hundred times for being vain about his so-called knowledge, rather than the true one for being so about his ignorance. Let a madman exalt himself as a Demi-God, at least his madness is consistent; but to believe oneself to be an insect and crawl proudly beneath the grass, that is, to my taste, the height of absurdity. What is, then, the first lesson of wisdom, oh Sophie? Humility! Humility, about which the Christian speaks and about which man knows so little, is the first feeling that ought to be born in us from the study of ourselves. Let us be humble about our species in order to be able to pride ourselves about our person. Let us not say in our imbecile vanity that man is the King of the world, that the sun, the stars, the firmament, the air, the earth, the sea are made for him, that the plants germinate for his subsistence, that the animals live so that he might devour them; with that manner of reasoning, that devouring thirst for happiness, for excellence, and for perfection, why will each not believe that the rest of the human race was created to serve him? And will he not regard himself personally as the sole object of all the works of nature?[71] If so many beings are useful to our preservation, are we certain of being less useful to theirs? What does that prove other than our weakness, and how do we know their destiny any better than ours; if we were deprived of sight, how could we learn that there exist birds, fish, insects almost insensible to touch; numerous of these insects in their turn appear to have no idea of us. What, then, might there not exist some other more excellent species that we will never perceive for lack of senses fit for discovering them, and for whom we are perhaps as contemptible as small worms are to our eyes? But this is discouraging the prideful man enough about gifts he does not have; there are enough of them left for him to nourish a worthier and more legitimate pride, if reason crushes and debases him, interior feeling lifts him up again and honors him;[72] the involuntary homage that the wicked man renders to the just in secret is the true title of nobility that nature has engraved in the heart of man.

Have you never felt that secret uneasiness that torments us at the sight of our misery and that becomes indignant about our weaknesses as about an insult to the faculties that exalt us? Have you never experienced those involuntary raptures that sometimes seize a sensitive soul in the contemplation of the morally beautiful and the intellectual order of things, that devouring ardor that suddenly comes to enflame the heart with love of the celestial virtues, that sublime going astray that raises us above our being, and carries us into the empyrean next to God himself? Ah, if this sacred fire could last, if this noble delirium animated our whole life what Heroic actions would frighten our courage, which vices would dare to draw near us, what victories would we not achieve over ourselves, and what great thing would there be that we could not obtain by our efforts? My respectable friend, the principle of that force is in us, it shows itself for a moment in order to incite us to seek it ceaselessly,[73] this holy enthusiasm is the energy of our faculties that detaches itself from their earthly bonds, and that perhaps it would depend only on us to maintain ceaselessly in this condition of freedom. However that might be, at least we feel in ourselves a voice that forbids us to have contempt for ourselves, reason crawls but the soul is exalted; if we are small by our intelligence, we are great by our feelings and whatever rank ours might be in the system of the universe,[74] a being that is a friend of justice and sensitive to virtues is not at all abject by its nature.

I have nothing more to demonstrate to you, oh Sophie, and if it were only a question of philosophizing I would stay at this point and, finding myself stopped in all directions by the limits of my intelligence, I would finish instructing you before I started; but I have already told you, my design is not to reason with you[75] and it is from the depths of your heart that I want to draw the only arguments that should convince you. Let me tell you then what is occurring in mine, and if you experience the same thing, the same principles ought to suit us, the same route ought to lead us in the search for true happiness.

In the span of a rather short life, I have experienced great vicissitudes, without leaving my poverty I have, so to speak, tasted from all stations, well- and ill-being have made themselves felt by me in all manners. Nature gave me the most sensitive soul, chance has subjected me to all imaginable affections, and I believe I can say along with one of Terence's characters[76] that nothing human is alien to me.[77]

In all these various situations, I always felt myself affected in two different and sometimes contradictory manners, one coming from the state of my fortune and the other from that of my soul, so that sometimes a feeling of happiness and peace consoled me in my disfavor and sometimes an intrusive malaise disturbed me during prosperity.[78]

These internal dispositions, independent of chance and events have made all the more lively an impression on me since my inclination for contemplative and solitary life gave them room to develop themselves better. I felt, so to speak, inside me the counterweight of my destiny. To console myself for my troubles I went into the same solitude in which I shed tears when I was happy. In seeking the principle of this hidden force that counterbalanced, so to speak, the empire of my passions, I found that it came from a secret judgment that, without thinking about it, I brought to bear upon the actions of my life and upon the objects of my desires. My ills tormented me less in considering that they were not at all my work. And my pleasures lost their value[79] when I saw coolly what I made them consist in. I believe I felt in myself a seed of goodness that compensated me for bad fortune and a seed of greatness that raised me above the good; I saw that it is in vain that one seeks one's happiness from afar when one neglects to cultivate it in oneself; for, come from outside as it may, it can make itself felt only to the extent that it finds inside a soul fit for tasting it.

This principle about which I am speaking to you did not serve me only for directing my present actions based on the rule it prescribed to me, but also for making a precise estimate of my past conduct, often blaming it even though it was apparently good, sometimes approving it even though it was condemned by men, and only recalling the events of my youth as a local memory of the various affections they occasioned in me.

To the extent that I advance toward the end of my course of life, I feel all the motions that have subjected me for so long to the empire of the passions weakening. After having exhausted everything that a sentient being can experience of good and of evil, little by little I am losing the sight and the expectation of a future that no longer has anything to gratify me. The desires are being extinguished along with hope, my existence[80] is no longer[81] anywhere but in my memory, I no longer see anything but my past life and its duration ceases to be dear to me since my heart no longer has anything new to feel.

In this condition it is natural that I love to turn my eyes toward the past from which I hold all my being from now on, it is then that my errors are corrected and good and evil make themselves felt in me without admixture and without prejudices.

All the false judgments that the passions have caused me to make have faded along with them. I see the objects that have affected me the most, not as they appeared to me during my delirium, but as they really are. The memory of my good or bad actions cause me a durable well-being or ill-being more real than the one that was their object; thus the pleasures of a moment have often prepared long repentances for me; thus sacrifices made to decency and justice compensate me every day for what they cost me one time and give me eternal enjoyment for short privations.

To whom could I speak better about the charms of these memories than to the one who makes me taste them so well again? It is to you Sophie that it belongs to make the memory of my final times of going astray dear to me by that of the virtues that have led me back from them. You have made me blush at my faults too much for me to be able to blush about them today, and I do not know what makes me more proud, victories won over myself, or the help that made me win them. If I had listened to nothing but a criminal passion, if I had been base for a moment and I had found you to be weak, how dearly I would be paying today for the raptures that would have appeared so sweet to me, deprived of all the feelings that have united us, we would have ceased to be united. Shame and repentance would have made us odious to each other; I would have hated you as a result of having loved you too much, and what intoxication of voluptuous pleasure could have ever compensated my heart for such a pure and such a tender attachment?[82] In place of that fatal estrangement, I do not recall anything about you that does not make me more satisfied with myself, and that does not add, to the friendship[83] that you inspired in me, honor, respect, and gratitude for having preserved me as worthy of loving you.[84] How could I consider without pleasure these moments that were painful to me only while sparing me eternal suffering? Today how would I not enjoy charm[85] at having heard in your mouth everything that can exalt the soul and give value to the union of hearts? Ah Sophie, what might I have become after having been insensible near you to everything that had acquired your esteem for me and having shown in the friend that you had chosen for yourself a wretch[86] whom you ought to despise?

It is everything that is most touching in the image of virtue that you set before my eyes, it is the fear of sullying so late a life without reproach, of losing in a moment the value of so many sacrifices; it is the sacred trust of friendship that I had to respect, it is from everything most inviolable in faith, honor, probity that was formed the invincible barrier that you ceaselessly opposed to all my desires.[87] No Sophie, there is not one of my days in which your speeches do not still come to rouse my heart and wrest delightful tears from me.[88] All my feelings for you are embellished by the one that overcame them. They make up the glory and the sweetness of my life, it is to you that I owe all that, at least it is by you that I feel their worth. My dear and worthy friend, I sought repentance and you have made me find happiness.

Such is the condition of a soul that, daring to propose itself to you as a model, is only offering you the fruit of your efforts in doing so. If that interior voice that judges me in secret and ceaselessly makes itself heard in my heart makes itself heard in the same way in yours, learn to listen to it and follow it, learn to draw your foremost goods from yourself; they are the only ones that do not depend on fortune at all [and] can take the place[89] of the others.[90] That is my entire philosophy and, I believe, the entire art of being happy that is feasible to man.[91]

Letter 5

The entire morality of human life is in man's intention.[92] If it is true that the good is good, it ought to be so at the bottom of our hearts as in our works, and the first reward for justice[93] is to feel that one is practicing it. If moral goodness is in conformity to our nature, man cannot be healthy or well constituted unless he is good. If it is not and man is naturally wicked, he cannot cease being so without corrupting himself. In him goodness would be only a vice against nature;[94] made to harm his fellows as the wolf is for slaughtering its prey, a humane man would be as depraved an animal as a wolf with pity[95] and only virtue would leave us with remorse.

Would you believe that there could be an easier question in the world to resolve? What is at issue in it but to return into oneself, to examine, all personal interest aside,[96] toward what our natural inclinations carry us? What spectacle gratifies us more, that of the torments or of the happiness of someone else; what is sweeter for us to do and leaves us a more agreeable impression after having done it,[97] an act of beneficence or an act of wickedness? In whom do you take an interest in your theaters:[98] is it from the heinous crimes that you take pleasure,[99] is it to their punished authors that you give tears;[100] between the unfortunate hero and the triumphant tyrant, to which of the two do your secret wishes ceaselessly draw you closer and who among you, if forced to choose, would not prefer to be the good man who suffers rather than the wicked one who prospers, so much does the horror of doing evil[101] naturally prevail in us[102] over that of enduring it?[103]

Does one see some act of violence and injustice in the street or on a path, instantly a movement of rage and indignation rises up in the depths of one's heart and brings us to take up the defense of the oppressed person, but a more powerful duty holds us back and the laws deprive us of the right to protect innocence.[104]

On the contrary, if some act of clemency or of generosity strikes our eyes what admiration, what love does it inspire in us. Who does not say to himself, "I would like to have done as much." The most corrupt souls cannot lose this first inclination completely: the thief who fleeces passersby nevertheless covers the nakedness of the poor,[105] there is no ferocious assassin who does not support a man falling in a faint, even traitors[106] in forming their plots among themselves touch each others' hands, give their word, and respect their faith. Perverse man, try as you might, I see in you only an inconsistent and awkward wicked man for nature has not at all made you to be one.[107]

One speaks about the cry of remorse that punishes hidden crimes in secret, and so often makes them public.[108] Alas! Who among us has never known that intrusive voice. One speaks from experience and one would like to erase this involuntary feeling that gives us so many torments. But let us obey nature, we shall know with what sweetness it approves what it has commanded and what charm one finds in tasting the internal peace[109] of a soul satisfied with itself.[110] The wicked man fears and flees himself, he cheers himself up by throwing himself outside of himself, he directs his anxious eyes around him and seeks an object that makes him laugh, without insulting raillery he would always be sad; on the contrary the serenity of the just man is internal; his laughter is not from malignity but from joy, he bears its source inside himself. He is as cheerful by himself as he is in the midst of a social circle; and he does not draw that unfailing contentment that one sees reigning in him from those who draw near him, he imparts it to them.

Cast your eyes on all the nations of the world, scour all the histories; among so many inhumane and bizarre forms of worship, among that prodigious variety of morals and characters, everywhere you will find the same ideas of justice and decency,[111] everywhere the same principles of morality, the same concepts of good and of evil. Ancient Paganism engendered abominable Gods[112] that one would have punished here below as scoundrels and who offered as the picture of the supreme happiness only heinous crimes to commit and passions[113] to satisfy. But vice, cloaked in a sacred authority descended in vain from the eternal abode; nature[114] repulsed it from the heart of humans. One celebrated Jupiter's debauchery but one admired Xenocrates' temperance,[115] the chaste Lucretia worshipped the lewd Venus, the intrepid Roman made sacrifices to fear, the great Cato was esteemed to be more just than providence; the immortal voice of virtue, stronger than that of the gods themselves made itself respected on the earth,[116] and seemed to relegate crime to Heaven along with the guilty ones.

There is then in the depths of all souls an innate[117] principle of justice and moral truth anterior to all national prejudices, to all maxims of education. This principle is the involuntary rule based on which we judge our actions and those of others as good or bad in spite of our own maxims, and it is to this principle that I give the name of conscience.

But at this word I hear being raised up from all directions the voice of the philosophers, "errors of childhood, prejudices of education," they all shout as if in a chorus. There is nothing in human understanding except what is introduced into it by experience and we judge nothing except on the basis of acquired ideas. They do more; they dare to reject this evident and universal agreement of all nations, and against this striking uniformity of men's Judgment they go to seek in the shadows some example that is obscure and known to themselves alone, as if all the inclinations of nature were annihilated by the depravity of some individuals and as soon as there are some monsters the human species is no longer anything. But what use to the skeptic Montaigne are the torments he gives himself to unearth in a corner of the world one custom opposed to the concepts of justice? What use is it to him to give the most contemptible and suspect traveler[118] an authority that he refuses to the most respectable writers; will some uncertain and bizarre practices, founded on particular causes that are unknown to us, destroy the general induction drawn from the convergence of all the peoples opposed in everything else and in agreement on this sole point? Oh Montaigne, you who pride yourself for frankness and truth, be sincere and true,[119] if a philosopher can be so, and tell me if there is some region on the earth where it is a crime to keep one's faith, to be clement, beneficent, and generous; in which the good man is contemptible and the scoundrel honored.[120]

I do not have the intention of entering here into metaphysical discussions that do not lead to anything. I have already told you that I do not want to dispute with philosophers, but to speak to your heart; if all the philosophers in the world prove that I am wrong, if you feel that I am right, I do not wish for anything more. For that it is necessary only to make you distinguish our acquired perceptions from our natural feelings; for we necessarily feel before knowing, and since we do not learn to wish for our personal good and to flee our harm, but obtain that will from nature, in the same way love of the good and hatred of the bad are as natural to us as our own existence; thus although ideas come to us from outside, the feelings that evaluate them are inside of us and it is by them alone that we know the suitability or unsuitability that exists between us and the things that we ought to seek out or flee.

For us, to exist is to feel; and our sensitivity is incontestably prior to our reason itself. Whatever the cause of our existence might be, it has provided for our preservation by giving us feelings in conformity to our nature; and one could not deny that at least those are innate. With regard to the individual these feelings are love of oneself,[121] fear of pain and of death, and the desire for well-being. But if, as one cannot doubt, man is a sociable animal by his nature, or at least made to become so, he can be so only by means of other innate feelings relative to his species. And it is from the moral system formed by this double relation to oneself and one's fellows that is born the natural impulse of the conscience.

Do not think, then, oh Sophie, that it is impossible to explain the active principle of the conscience by the consequences of our nature, independent of reason itself. And if that were impossible it would still not be necessary. For the philosophers who combat this principle cannot prove that it does not exist, but are satisfied with affirming it; if we affirm that it does exist, we are then as far forward as they are and we have in addition all the force of interior testimony[122] and the voice of conscience which testifies on its own behalf.

My dear friend,[123] how these sad reasoners are to be pitied, by effacing in themselves the feelings of nature they are destroying the source of all their pleasures, and do not know how to free themselves from heaviness of conscience except by making themselves insensitive to it.[124] Is it not a very clumsy system that does not know how to take remorse away from voluptuous pleasures[125] except by stifling both at the same time? If the faithfulness of lovers is only a chimera, if the modesty of the fair sex consists in vain prejudices, what will become of all the charms of love;[126] if we no longer see anything in the universe but matter and motion where then will be the moral goods for which our soul is always greedy, and what will be the worth of human life if we enjoy it only in order to vegetate?

I return to this feeling of shame, so charming and so sweet to conquer, perhaps even sweeter to respect, which combats and enflames the desires of a lover and returns so many pleasures to his heart for the ones he refuses to his senses. Why would we reject the interior reproach that veils with an impenetrable modesty the secret wishes[127] of a modest girl and covers her cheeks with a bewitching blush at the tender speeches of a lover who is loved? What, then, are attack and defense not among the laws of nature? Is it not nature that permits resistance to the fair sex which can grant as much as it pleases? Is it not nature that prescribes pursuit to the one it takes care to make discreet and moderate? Is it not nature that puts them, during their pleasures, under the care of shame and mystery, in a condition of weakness and forgetfulness of themselves that gives them over[128] to every aggressor? You feel then how false it is that modesty does not have its sufficient reason, and is only a chimera in nature, and how would it be the work of prejudices, if the very prejudices of education destroy it, if you see it in all its force among ignorant and rustic peoples and if, among more cultivated nations, its sweet voice is stifled only by the sophisms of reasoning?[129]

If the first gleams of judgment dazzle us, and at first confuse all objects for our gazes, wait until our weak eyes open again, strengthen themselves, and soon we shall see the same objects by the lights of reason such as nature first showed them to us.[130] Or rather, let us be simpler and less vain. In everything let us limit ourselves to the first feelings that we find in ourselves, since it is always to them that study leads us back when it has not led us astray.[131]

Conscience, conscience, divine instinct, immortal and celestial voice,[132] assured guide of a being that is ignorant and limited but intelligent and free,[133] infallible judge of good and evil, sublime emanation of the eternal[134] substance, which makes man similar to the Gods; it is you alone that makes up the excellence of my[135] nature.

Without you I feel nothing in myself that raises me above the beasts, except for the sad privilege of leading myself astray from errors to errors with the aid of an understanding without rule and a reason without principle.[136]

Apply yourself to doing things that you like to see done to others.

Letter 6

Finally[137] we have a secure guide in this Labyrinth of human errors, but it is not enough that it exists, it is necessary to know how to get to know it[138] and to follow it. If it speaks to all hearts, oh[139] Sophie, then why are there so few of them who hear it? Alas, it speaks to us in nature's language which everything has made us forget.

The conscience is timid and fearful, it seeks solitude, the world and noise scare it, the prejudices whose work they say it is are its most mortal enemies, it flees or keeps quiet before them, their noisy voices stifle its voice and prevent it from making itself heard.[140] As a result of being dismissed it finally gives up, it no longer speaks to us, it no longer responds to us, and after such long contempt for it, to recall it costs as much as banishing it did.

When I see each of us ceaselessly occupied by public opinion extending so to speak his existence entirely around him without reserving hardly any of it in his own heart, I believe I see a small insect form out of its own substance a great web by which alone it appears sensitive while one would believe it to be dead in its hole. Man's vanity is the spider's web that he spreads over everything that surrounds him. The one is as solid as the other, the slightest thread that one touches sets the insect into motion, it would die languishing[141] if one left the web tranquil, and if one tears it with a finger the insect completely exhausts itself rather than not remake it instantly. Let us begin by becoming ourselves again, by centering[142] ourselves in ourselves, by circumscribing our soul with the same limits that nature has given to our being; in a word let us begin by gathering ourselves together where we are, so that when we are seeking to know ourselves, everything that composes us comes to present itself to us at the same time. As for me, I think that the one who knows best what the human self consists in is the closest to wisdom and that,[143] just as the first stroke of a drawing is formed by lines that make up its boundaries, the first idea of man is to[144] separate him from everything that is not himself.

But how is this separation made? This art is not so difficult as one might believe, or at least the difficulty is not where one believes it to be, it depends more on the will than on intelligence, an apparatus of study and research is not at all necessary to attain it. The light illuminates us, and the mirror is in front of us; but to see it one must cast one's eyes and the way to fix them on it is to set aside the objects that turn us away from it. Commune with yourself, seek out solitude, there to begin with is the whole secret and by that one alone one soon discovers yours.[145]

Do you think in fact that philosophy teaches us to return into ourselves? Ah, under its name, how much does pride push us away from doing so! It is entirely the opposite my charming friend, it is necessary to begin by returning into oneself in order to learn to philosophize.

Do not be frightened I beseech you; I do not plan to consign[146] you to a cloister and to impose an Anchorite's life on a woman of the world. The solitude in question is less to have your door closed and to stay in your apartment than take your soul out of the throng as the abbé Terrasson said,[147] and first close it against the alien passions that assail it at every moment. But one of these means can aid the other, above all at the beginning; it is not the business of a day to know how to be alone in the middle of the social world and, after such a long habituation to existing in everything that surrounds you, the gathering together of your heart ought to begin by that of your senses. At first you will have enough of a job restraining your imagination without yet being obliged to close your eyes and your ears. Remove the objects that must distract you until their presence no longer distracts you. Then live ceaselessly in their midst, you will know very well when it will be necessary for you to find yourself with yourself again. Thus I am not at all saying to you: leave society; I am not even saying to you: renounce dissipation and the vain pleasures of the world. But I am saying to you: learn how to be alone without boredom. You will never hear the voice of nature; you will never know yourself without that. Do not fear that the practice of these short retreats might make you taciturn and unsociable[148] and detach you from habits that you do not wish to renounce. On the contrary,[149] they will only be sweeter to you for it.

When one lives alone one loves men better, a tender interest reconciles us to them. Imagination shows us society through its charms, and even being bored with solitude turns to the profit of humanity. You will gain doubly by the taste for this contemplative life, in it you will find more attachment for what is dear while you have it and less pain at losing it when you are deprived of it.

Every month, for example, take an interlude of two or three days from your pleasures and your business in order to dedicate it to the greatest one of all.[150] Make a law for yourself to live alone for those two or three days, even if you must get very bored at first. It is better to pass them in the country than at Paris;[151] this would be, if you wish, a visit that you would be going to pay: you would be going to see Sophie.[152] Solitude is always sad in the city. Since everything that surrounds us shows the hand of men and some object of society, when one does not have that society, one feels oneself out of one's place, and a room in which one is alone very much resembles a prison.[153] It is completely the opposite in the country, the objects there are cheerful and pleasant, they incite to meditation, gathering oneself together, and reverie; there one feels oneself in the open outside of the sad walls of the city and the shackles of prejudice.[154] Woods, streams, greenery keep the glances of men away from our heart; flitting about here and there in accordance with their caprice, birds[155] offer us the model of freedom in solitude, one hears their warbling, one smells the odor of the fields and woods.[156] Eyes struck only by the sweet images of nature bring it near to our[157] heart better.

Thus that is where it is necessary to converse with it and to consult its laws in its own empire. At least boredom will not come to pursue you so soon and it will be easier to bear in the practice of promenades and the variety of rustic objects than on a lounge-chair or an armchair. I would like you to avoid choosing times when your heart, acutely affected by some feeling of pleasure or pain, would retain its emotion in the retreat, or your imagination, too moved, would, in spite of yourself, bring near to you the beings that you would have thought you had escaped and in which your mind, too preoccupied, would refuse itself the slight impressions of the first returns to yourself.[158] On the contrary, so as to have less regret at going to being bored alone in the country, take the moments in which you would be reduced to being bored in the city; the life most occupied with cares or amusements still leaves only too many of such voids and this manner of filling the first ones that present themselves will soon make you insensitive to all the others. I do not ask that you abandon yourself to profound meditations at first, I ask only that you be able to keep your soul in a state of languor and calm that lets it fall back upon itself, and not bring back anything alien to you.

"In this state"; you will say to me, "what shall I do?"[159] Nothing. Do not interfere with that natural uneasiness that, in solitude, does not delay in making everyone occupied with himself whatever he might do about it.[160]

I do not say either that this state must produce a total prostration and I am very far from believing that we have no means of awakening the interior sentiment in ourselves. As one rouses up a numbed member with light rubbing, the soul, deadened in a long inactivity, revives from the gentle warmth of a moderate movement, it is necessary to rouse it by means of pleasant memories that are related only to itself, it is necessary to recall to it the affections that gratified it, not by the mediation of the senses, but by means of a suitable feeling and by means of intellectual pleasures.[161] If there existed in the world a being miserable enough to be unable to recall anything he had done in all the course of his life that could give him an internal satisfaction with himself and make him glad to have lived, that being, having only feelings and ideas that would turn him away from himself, would be in no condition ever to know himself; and for want of knowing in what the goodness suitable to his nature consisted, he would necessarily remain wicked and be eternally unhappy. But I maintain that there is not a single man on the whole earth depraved enough never to have yielded in his heart to the temptation of doing good; this temptation is so natural and so sweet that it is impossible always to resist it, and it is enough to give way to it a single time never to forget the voluptuous pleasure that one tastes through it. Oh dear Sophie, how many actions of your life will follow you into solitude in order to teach you to love it. I do not need to seek any that are foreign to me. Consider the heart that you preserved for virtue, consider me, you will love to live with yourself.[162]

These are the ways of laboring in the world to please yourself in retreat by preparing pleasant memories, by obtaining your own friendship for yourself there and making yourself into good enough company for yourself that you can do without any other. But what exactly must be done for that, on that point it is not yet the time here to enter into details that assume the knowledge that we are proposing to acquire. I know that one must not begin a treatise of morality at the end nor give for first precept the practice of what one wants to teach. But once again, in whatever state a soul might be, there remains a feeling of pleasure in doing good that is never erased and that serves as a first foothold for all the other virtues, it is by this feeling cultivated that one succeeds in loving oneself and in being pleased with oneself. The practice of beneficence naturally gratifies amour-propre by an idea of superiority,[163] one recalls all acts of beneficence as so many testimonies that, beyond one's own needs, one still has the force to relieve someone else's. This appearance of power causes one to take more pleasure in existing and makes one live more willingly with oneself. That is all that I ask of you at first.[164] Adorn yourself in order to present yourself to your mirror; you will more willingly look at yourself in it. Always consider providing yourself with a feeling of well-being when you are alone, and in the objects of your pleasures always give the preference to those one still enjoys when one no longer possesses them.[165]

A woman of quality is too much surrounded by her station, I would like you to be able to renounce yours for a few moments; this would be one more way to keep up a conversation with yourself more immediately. When you go on your retreats leave all of your house's retinue behind; do not take along either cook or butler. Take a lackey and a chambermaid.

That is still too much; in a word do not transport the life of the city to the country; go there genuinely to taste the retired and rustic life. But the proprieties. Ah! Always those fatal proprieties! If you want to listen to them endlessly, you do not need any other guide; choose between them and wisdom. Go to bed early, get up in the morning, approximately follow the march of the sun and of nature; no dressing table at all, no reading at all, take simple repasts at the same times as the people, in a word be a country woman in everything. If this manner of living becomes pleasant to you, you will be acquainted with one more pleasure, if it bores you, you will take back the one to which you have become accustomed with more relish.

Do even better. Out of these short intervals that you will want to pass by living in solitude, use one part of them in making the other pleasant for you. You will have long mornings empty of your ordinary occupations, destine them for errands[166] in the village. Inform yourself about the sick, the poor, the oppressed, seek to give each the aid he needs, and do not think that it is enough to assist them with your purse if you do not also give them your time and assist them with your efforts. Impose upon yourself that very noble function of causing several fewer evils to exist on the earth and if your intentions are pure and real you will soon find out how to accomplish them. I feel very well that at first a thousand obstacles will distract you from such an effort.[167] Unclean houses, brutal people,[168] objects of poverty will begin by disgusting you. But upon entering the homes of these unfortunates say to yourself: "I am their sister," and humanity will triumph over repugnance. You will find them to be liars, self-interested, full of vices that will rebuff your zeal, but interrogate yourself in secret about your own vices in order to learn soon to pardon those of others[169] and consider that by covering them with a more decent appearance, education only makes them more dangerous.[170] Above all boredom, that Tyrant of people of your station, which makes them pay so dearly for the exemption from labor, and to which one always makes oneself more prey by exerting oneself to avoid it, boredom alone will at first turn you away from these salutary occupations, and by making them unbearable to you will provide you with pretexts for dispensing yourself from them.[171] Consider that[172] to enjoy doing good is the reward for having done good, and one does not obtain it before having deserved it. Nothing is more lovable than virtue, but it shows itself that way only to those who possess it; virtue is similar to Proteus in the fable: at first when one wants to embrace it, it takes on countless terrifying forms and finally reveals itself in its own form only to those who did not let go. Resist the sophisms of boredom then. Do not set aside from you objects made for making you tender; detest that cruel pity that turns one's eyes away from other people's ills in order to dispense oneself from relieving them. Do not leave these honorable efforts in the hands of mercenaries.[173] Be assured that servants always lay the masters' benefits under contribution; that they know how to appropriate for themselves in one way or another a portion[174] of what one gives through their hands, and that they demand a very onerous gratitude for everything that the master has done for nothing. Make it a duty for yourself to bring everywhere, along with a real assistance, the interest and consolations that make the most of it and that often take its place of it. May your visits never be fruitless! May each thrill with joy at your approach, may public benedictions ceaselessly accompany you. Soon such a sweet retinue will enchant your soul and, in the new pleasures that you will learn to taste, if sometimes you lose the good that you believe you are doing, at least you will never lose the one that you will have drawn from it.

Notes on Helvétius's On the Mind[1]

P. 2: *In us we have two faculties, or if I dare to say it, two passive powers, whose existence is generally and clearly acknowledged.*

It seems to me that it would be necessary to distinguish purely organic and local impressions from the universal impressions that affect the whole individual. The former are only simple sensations, the others are sentiments.

P. 2: *memory is nothing but a continued, but weakened, sensation.*

not; memory is the faculty of recalling sensation, but sensation, even weakened, does not last continuously.

P. 6: to remember, *as I am going to prove, is properly only* to feel.

I do not yet know how he is going to prove that; but I know very well that to feel the present object and to feel the absent object are two operations whose difference very much deserves to be examined.

P. 6, note: *in sum up to the so-called miracles of Mohammed, up to those prodigies attested to by so many Arabs, and the falseness of which nevertheless is still very probable here below, where liars are so common and prodigies so rare.*

[Rousseau put bracket and a cross in the margin of this passage.]

P. 7: *then my internal organs must necessarily be found just about in the same position as they were at the sight of this oak tree.*

They are found in it in truth; but by the effect of a very different operation.

P. 7: *Now this position of the organs must incontestably produce a sensation . . .*

What do you call a sensation? If a sensation is the impression transmitted by the external organ to the interior organ, the position of the interior organ might well be assumed to be the same, when that of the external organ is lacking, this lack alone is enough to distinguish memory from sensation. Moreover it is not true that the position of the interior organ is the same in the memory[2] and in the sensation. Otherwise it would be impossible to distinguish the memory of the sensation from the sensation. Also the Author takes refuge in a *just about*. But a position of organs that is only just about the same ought not to produce exactly the same effect.³

P. 7: *it is then evident that to remember is to feel.*
there is this difference that the memory produces a similar sensation, and not the sentiment, and this other difference also that the cause is not the same.

P. 7: *Now this capacity [of perceiving the similarities and differences] is only the same physical sensitivity* . . .
This is something amusing! After having thoughtlessly affirmed that to perceive and to compare are the same thing, the author concludes with great display that to judge is to feel. The conclusion appears clear to me, but it is the antecedent that is the issue.

P. 8: *these objects [that nature presents us] have relations . . . among themselves; the knowledge of these relations forms what is called* Intelligence⁴ . . .
The greater or lesser aptitude for knowing them is what makes up greater or lesser intelligence.

P. 9: *Now, since judgment is only that perception itself [of similarities and differences], or at least pronouncement of that perception, it follows that all the operations of the mind are reduced to judging.*
To perceive objects is to feel; to perceive relations is to judge.

P. 9: *I can say equally, I judge or I feel that, of the two objects, the one that I call* fathom, *makes a different impression on me than the one I call* foot; *that the color that I name* red *acts differently on my eyes than the one that I name* yellow . . .
here there is a very subtle and very important sophism to take note of well. It is one thing to feel a difference between a fathom and a foot; and another thing to measure that difference. In the first operation the mind is purely passive, but in the other it is active. The one who has more precision in his mind to transport the foot upon the fathom by thought and to see how many times it is contained in it⁵ is the one who has the more precise mind on this point and judges the best.

P. 9: *I conclude from this that in a such a case* to judge *is never anything but* to feel.
it is a different thing; because the comparison of yellow and red is not the sensation of yellow nor that of red.⁶

P. 9: *In order to bring a judgment to bear on this subject [whether force is preferable to size of body], my memory must successively draw for me pictures of the different situations in which I can most commonly find myself in the course of my life.*

how! the successive comparison of a thousand ideas is also sentiment? One must not dispute over words; but the author is making a strange dictionary for himself.

P. 10: *this judgment [that justice is preferable to goodness] is really only a sensation.*

We have seen that it is a different thing.

P. 10: *one can, as experiment proves, by striking the ear with certain sounds, excite in us just about the same sensations that one experiences in the very presence of objects.*

here again is the same *just about* as the last one used in just as sophistical a manner.

P. 12: *It results, from what I have said, that judgments brought to bear on the means or the methods that chance presents to us for achieving a certain goal, are properly only sensations; and that, in man, everything is reduced to sensing.*

same sophism in this chapter, from one end to the other.

P. 12: *how up to this day has anyone assumed in us a faculty of judging distinct from the faculty of sensing? This assumption is owed, I shall answer, to the impossibility they believed they had up to the present of explaining certain errors of the mind in any other manner.*

not at all. It is that it is very simple to assume that two operations of different sorts are made by two different faculties.

P. 40: *I have shown that all the errors of the mind have their source either in the passions, or in ignorance, whether it be of certain facts, or about the true signification of certain words. Error is, then, not essentially attached to the nature of the human mind.*

you have not at all proven that your division[7] is precise; your conclusion is, then, not necessary, which does not prevent me from being of your opinion on this.

P. 41: *now nothing keeps me from putting forth that* to judge, *as I have already proven, is properly only* to sense.

you have not proven anything on this point except that you add to the sense of the word *to sense* the sense that we give to the word *to judge;* you unify under one common word two essentially different faculties.

P. 41: *mind, in this sense, is only sensitivity and memory* . . .
sensitivity, memory and judgment.

P. 54: *probity, in relation to a private individual, is, in conformity with my definition, only the habit of actions personally useful to that individual.*
If that private individual had to entrust a deposit or an important secret to some man of probity, would he go to look for the one who had only the habit of actions that have been[8] personally useful to him? Not at all, he would prefer to the good man who sold him justice the wicked man who did not want to let himself be corrupted. What gibberish!

P. 58, note e: *If people ordinarily are brought to certain excesses only in disputes about religion, it is because other disputes do not provide the same pretexts or the same means for being cruel.*
[Rousseau put a horizontal stroke next to this passage.]

P. 60: *Every idea too alien to our manner of seeing and feeling always seems ridiculous to us.*
[Rousseau put a horizontal stroke next to this passage.]

P. 69: *they [those who acknowledge more intelligence in others than in themselves] do nothing but give public opinion the preference over their own, and admit that these persons are more esteemed, without being inwardly convinced that they are more estimable.*
That is not true. I have meditated on a subject for a long time and I have drawn from it some notions with all the attentiveness that I was capable of putting into it. I make this same subject known to another man, and during our conversation I see coming out of the brain of this man crowds of new ideas and great notions about this same subject that had provided me with so few. I am not stupid enough not to feel the advantage of his notions and his ideas over mine; I am then forced to feel inwardly that this man has more intelligence than I do,[9] and to grant him in my heart a felt esteem superior to the one that I have for myself. Such was the judgment that Philip the Second made of the intelligence of Alonso Perez and what made the latter believe he was lost.[10]

P. 70, note g: *I assume . . . that this same Fontenelle was entreated to give, as regards poetry, the idea he had formed of perfection: it is certain that he would not have, in this genre, proposed any different expert rules than those that he himself had observed as well as Corneille . . .*

it is not a question of rules, it is a question of genius which finds great images and great feelings. Fontenelle could have believed himself to be a better judge of all that than Corneille, but not so good an inventor. He was made to feel Corneille's genius and not[11] to equal it. If the author does not believe that a man can feel the superiority of someone else in his own genre, certainly he very much deceives himself. I myself feel his, although I might not be of his sentiment. I feel that he deceives himself as a man who has more intelligence than I do. He has more notions and more brilliant ones, but mine are sounder. Fénélon has the upper hand over me in every respect; that is certain.[12]

P. 70, note *h: the woman who spends the evening with her cook believes she is as estimable as a scholar.*
she is much more so.

P. 71: *all three, perhaps, [three practitioners who leave the play] will cry out at the same time that Corneille is the greatest genius in the world: nevertheless, if, in order to unburden himself from the importunate weight of esteem, one of them adds that this Corneille is in truth a great man, but in a frivolous genre . . .*
the weight of esteem! Oh god! nothing is so sweet as esteem, even for those whom one believes superior to oneself.

P. 75: *to prevent the subdivision of a people into an infinity of families or small societies, whose interests, almost always opposed to the public interest, would in the end extinguish every sort of love for the fatherland in souls.*
to refute.

P. 79: *one cannot preserve a virtue as always strong and pure without having the principle of public utility habitually present to the mind, without having a profound knowledge of the genuine interests of this public, consequently of morality and politics.*[13]
to refute: by this reckoning there is no genuine probity except among philosophers. My faith, they do extremely well by paying compliments to each other.

P. 79, note *c: M. de Fontenelle defined lying:* Keeping silent about a truth one owes.[14] *A man leaves the bed of a woman, he encounters her husband:* Where are you coming from? *The latter says to him. What to respond* to him? does one owe him the truth then? No, *says M. de Fontenelle*, because then the truth is not useful to anyone.

amusing example! As if the one who did not have any scruple about sleeping with someone else's wife would have any about telling a lie! It may be that an adulterer is obliged to lie; but the good man does not want to be either a liar or an adulterer.

P. 81: *everything becomes legitimate and even virtuous for the public security.*

The public security is nothing if all the private individuals are not in safety.

P. 101: *people of high society being, in general, very much beyond needs, and having almost none to satisfy other than that of pleasure* . . .

[Rousseau put a horizontal stoke next to this passage.]

P. 110: *It is only by contemplating the earth from this point of view, by raising oneself up to this height, that it is gradually reduced, before a philosopher, to a small extent, and that it takes to his eyes the form of a large village inhabited by different families which bear the name of Chinese, English, French, Italian, in sum all those that are given to different nations.*

beautiful.

P. 113: *he [the great man] regards as a benefit all the evil that men do not do to him, and as a gift all that their iniquity leaves him* . . .

[Rousseau put a horizontal stroke next to this passage.]

P. 114: *he [the man of merit] has been tempted so many times, like Phocion, to turn back to his friend in order to ask him whether he has not said something very stupid* . . .

the author is forgetting that he said above that contempt of admiration is not true, and that the admirer is never stupid in the eyes of the person admired.

P. 114: *The last cause of the indulgence of the man of merit depends on his clear-sightedness about the necessity of human judgments . . . a superior intelligence could equally, and by means of the objects that have been presented to us, guess our thoughts; and, by means of our thoughts, guess the number and sort of objects that chance has offered to us.*

let the author not give this belief for a reason for indulgence toward other men. I am very much convinced that no man had ever said or believed that before him.

P. 115: *to insult him [the fool], is to reproach the oak for bearing an acorn rather than an olive . . .*

Doubtless the wicked man also bears crimes in the same manner, and to hang him is to punish the oak for bearing acorns.

P. 124: *That a dramatic poet writes a good tragedy based on an already known plot, is, they say, a contemptible plagiarism; but that a general makes use, in a campaign, of the order of battle and stratagems of another general, he often only appears more estimable for it.*

Truly I believe it very well! the first presents himself as the author of a new piece. The second does not present himself as anything. His object is to beat the enemy. If he was writing a book on battles he would not be pardoned for plagiarism any more than the dramatic author is.

P. 136: *It is then certain that theft, harmful to every rich people, but useful to Sparta, should have been honored there.*

yes in the children; is it said anywhere that the men stole?

P. 136, note *b: Everyone knows the deed that is recounted about a young Lacedemonion, who, rather than admitting his larceny, let, without crying, his belly be devoured by a young fox he had stolen and hid under his robe.*

it is said nowhere that he was questioned; it was only a question of not disclosing his theft, and not of denying it, but the author is very glad skillfully to put lying in the number of Lacedemonion virtues.

P. 158: *In the assumption that luxury is useful to a nation, is it not the flirtatious women who, by inciting the industry of the artisans of luxury, makes them more useful to the state from day to day? Well-behaved*[15] *women, by making generous gifts to beggars or criminals, are then less well counseled by their advisers,*[16] *than the flirtatious women are by the desire to please.*

the one is relieving people who are suffering, the other favors people who want to get rich. By inciting the industry of artisans of luxury she increases the number. By making the fortune of two or three she incites twenty to take on a station in which they will remain miserable. She multiplies the subjects in useless professions and causes them to be lacking in necessary professions.

P. 160: *[Moralists] should . . . feel . . . that it is modesty that put into the weak hands of beauty the scepter that commands force.*

[Rousseau underlined this passage beginning with *that it is . . .*]

P. 230: *the feeling of love of oneself is the only basis upon which one can cast the foundations of a useful morality.*
[Rousseau put a horizontal stroke next to this passage.]

P. 241, note *a*: *It must very much be the case that men feel in a confused way that intelligence is the foremost of gifts, since envy allows each to be the panegyrist of his probity, and not of his intelligence.*

it is not that, but it is that in the first place probity is indispensable and intelligence is not, and that in the second place it depends on us to be decent people and it does not to be intelligent people.

P. 256: *thus nature could not give men more or less disposition to intelligence, than by giving some in preference to others a little more subtlety of sense, extent of memory, and capacity for attention.*

The principle from which the author deduces the natural equality of minds in the following chapters, and which he tried to establish at the beginning of his work, is that human judgments are purely passive. This principle has been established and discussed with much philosophy and profundity in the Encyclopedia, article *Evidence*. I do not know who the author of that article is; but he is certainly a very great metaphysician. I suspect the Abbé de Condillac or M. de Buffon.[17] However that may be, I have tried to attack it and to establish the activity of our judgments, both in the notes that I have written at the beginning of this book, and above all in the first part of the profession of faith of the Savoyard Vicar. If I am right and the principle of M. Helvetius and of the above-mentioned author is false, the arguments of the following chapters, which are only its consequences, fall, and it is not true that the inequality of minds is the effect of education alone, although it can influence it very much.[18]

P. 276: *I see that, without sensitivity to physical pain and pleasure, men, without desires, without passions, equally indifferent to everything, would not have been acquainted with personal interest at all; that, without personal interest ... there would not have been any general interest at all, consequently no just or unjust actions at all; and thus that physical sensitivity and personal interest have been the authors of all justice.*

to reason as the author does, one can say that if men had not lived, they would not have acted at all, that without actions there would not have been any justice etc. from which one would conclude as he does that human life is the author of all justice.

P. 319: *the total absence of passions, if it could exist* . . .
[Rousseau struck out the masculine pronoun Helvétius had written for "it," and replaced it with the feminine to agree with "absence."]

P. 377: *If, among rich people, often less virtuous than indigent people, one sees few thieves and murderers it is because, for a rich man, the profit from theft is never proportionate to the risk of torture.*
what madness! it is not that at all, it is because they have a thousand more convenient ways of stealing and murdering.

P. 402: *to condemn ten soldiers to the ultimate torture as such [cowards]* . . .
[Rousseau crossed out the final letter in *supplicer* (torture), which was a misprint.]

P. 412: *Such a speech could not be spoken by a Roman.*
[Rousseau put a cross between *spoken* and *by*, and added in the margin "anyone but" (*que*).]

P. 474: *I believed that it was a citizen's duty to proclaim a truth suited to awakening attention about the means of perfecting this same education.*
[Rousseau put a diagonal stroke next to this passage.]

LITERARY WORKS

Queen Whimsical[1]

Bookseller's Foreword[2]

This little Tale, written in the past and on a sort of dare,* had not yet been printed at all as far as I know. Seven or eight years ago several of M. Rousseau's friends had copies that multiplied in Paris and the provinces; one of the less disfigured ones fell into my hands. I do not believe that the author will be annoyed with me for publishing a folly already well known and which he turned over to the public a long time ago.

Queen Whimsical[3]
A Tale

"Once upon a time there was a King who loved his people . . ."

"That begins like a Fairy Tale,"[4] interrupted the Druid. "It is one too,"[5] answered Jalamir, "There was, then, a King who loved his people, and who consequently was adored by them. He had made every effort to find ministers who would enter into his views:[6] but having finally recognized the folly[7] of such a search, he made the decision to do by himself everything he could rescue from their seething[8] activity. Obstinate about[9] the bizarre project of making his subjects happy, he acted consistently with that idea,[10] and such peculiar conduct held him up to an indelible ridicule among the Great: the people blessed him, but in the Court he passed for a madman. Aside from that he did not lack merit; also he was named Phoenix.

"If that Prince was extraordinary, he had a wife who was less so. Lively, giddy, changeable,[11] mad by her head, wise by her heart, good by temperament, wicked by capriciousness; there in a few words is the Queen's portrait. Whimsical was her name; a famous name, which she had received from her ancestors in the feminine line, and the honor of which she worthily upheld. This person, so illustrious and so reasonable, was the charm and the torture of her dear husband; for she also loved

---

* It was a question of trying to write a tolerable and even merry Tale, without intrigue, without love, without marriage, and without lewdness.

him most sincerely, perhaps because of the ease that she had in tormenting him. In spite of the reciprocal love that reigned between them, they passed several years without being able to obtain any fruit from their union. The King was pierced by sorrow at this, and the Queen set herself into fidgets about it which that good Prince was not the only one to feel: she blamed everyone for the fact that she did not have any children; there was not a courtier whom she did not giddily ask for some secret for having one, and whom she did not hold responsible for its poor success.

"The Doctors were not at all forgotten; for the Queen was uncommonly obedient to them, and there was not a drug that they prescribed that she did not have prepared very carefully in order to have the pleasure of throwing it in their faces at the moment that it was necessary to take it. The Dervishes had their turn; it was necessary to have recourse to novenas, to vows, above all to offerings; and bad luck to the priests in charge of the temples where Her Majesty went on pilgrimage: she rummaged through everything, and under the pretext of going to breathe a prolific air, she never failed to turn the monks' cells upside down. She also wore their relics, and decked herself out alternately in all their different outfits: sometimes it was a white cord, sometimes a leather belt, sometimes a long hood,[12] sometimes a scapular; there was no sort of monastic masquerade that her devotion did not take into its head; and since she had a little sprightly air, which made her charming in all these disguises, she did not leave any of them without taking care to have her picture painted in it.

"Finally as a result of devotions so well performed, as a result of doctors so wisely employed, heaven and earth heard the Queen's prayers; she became pregnant at the moment that they were beginning to despair of it. I leave the joy of the King and that of the people to be guessed: as for her own, as in all her passions she went to the point of extravagance: in her outbursts she broke and shattered everything; she embraced everyone she met indiscriminately; men, women, courtiers, valets, to find oneself in her path was to risk being smothered. She did not know, she said, any rapture comparable to the one of having a child to whom she could give a flogging entirely at her ease in her moments of ill humor.

"Since the Queen's pregnancy had been vainly[13] awaited for a long time, it passed for one of those extraordinary events, for which all the world wanted to have the honor. The doctors attributed it to their drugs, the monks to their relics, the people to their prayers, and the King to his love. Each took an interest in the child that was to be born as if it were his own, and all made sincere wishes for the fortunate birth of the Prince: for they wanted one, and the people, the Great, and the King united their desires on this point. The Queen found it extremely bad that they took it into their heads to prescribe to her whom she was to give birth to, and declared that she aspired to have a daughter, adding that it appeared rather singular to her that anyone might dare to dispute with her the right of disposing of a possession that incontestably belonged only to her alone.

"In vain did Phoenix wish to make her listen to reason, she told him clearly that this was none of his business, and closed herself up in her dressing room in order to sulk; a cherished occupation, for which she regularly used at least six months of the year.[14]

"The King understood extremely well that the mother's caprices would not determine the child's sex; but he was in despair that she might thus give her eccentricities as a spectacle to the whole Court. He would have sacrificed everything in the world for universal esteem to justify the love[15] he had for her, and the commotion that he made inappropriately on that occasion was not the only folly that the ridiculous hope of making his wife reasonable caused him to commit.

"Being at his wit's end,[16] he had recourse to the Fairy Discreet, his friend and the protectress of his kingdom. The Fairy advised him to take the routes of gentleness, that is to say, to ask the Queen for forgiveness. 'The sole end,' she told him, 'of all women's whims is to disorient masculine pomposity a bit, and to accustom men to the obedience that suits them. The best way that you have for curing your wife's extravagances is to extravagate along with her. As soon as[17] you stop contradicting her caprices, rest assured that she will stop having them, and that, in order to become wise, she is waiting for nothing but to have made you very completely mad. Thus do things with good grace, and give way[18] on this occasion so as to obtain what you will want on another.' The King believed the Fairy, and, to comply with her advice, having returned to the Queen's Circle, he took her aside, whispered[19] to her that he was sorry for having inappropriately disputed,[20] and that in the future he would try by his compliance to make up for the temper he might have put into his speeches in disputing against her impolitely.

"Whimsical, who feared that Phoenix's gentleness might cover her alone with ridicule[21] for this business, hastened to answer him, that under this ironic excuse she saw even more pride than in the preceding disputes, but that, since the wrongs of a husband did not at all authorize those of a wife, she was hastening to give way on this occasion as she had always done: 'my Prince and my spouse,' she added aloud, 'orders me to give birth to a boy, and I know my duty too well to fail to obey. I am not unaware that, when His Majesty honors me with marks of his tenderness, it is less for love of me than for that of his people, whose interest occupies him hardly less at night than during the day. I ought to imitate such a noble disinterestedness and I am going to ask the Divan[22] for an instructive memorandum about the number and the sex of the children that suit the royal family; a memorandum important to the happiness of the State, and upon which every Queen must learn to regulate her behavior during the night.'

"This fine soliloquy was listened to very attentively by the whole Circle, and I leave it to you to think how many outbursts of laughter were rather maladroitly stifled. 'Ah!' said the King sadly while shrugging his shoulders, 'I see very well that when one has a mad wife, one cannot avoid being a fool.'

"The Fairy Discreet, whose sex and name sometimes pleasantly contrasted in her character, found this quarrel so entertaining that she resolved to amuse herself with it to the end. She publicly told the King, that she had consulted the comets that preside over the birth of Princes, and that she could answer for it to him that the child who would be born of him would be a boy; but in secret she assured the Queen that she would have a girl.

"This notice suddenly made Whimsical as reasonable as she had been capricious up to then. It was with an infinite[23] gentleness and obligingness that she took all possible measures to distress[24] the King and the whole Court. She hastened to have the most splendid baby linen made, affecting to make it so suited to a boy that it might become ridiculous for a girl; in this plan it was necessary to change several fashions, but all that cost her nothing. She had a fine collar of the Order prepared, shining with precious stones and absolutely wanted the King to name in advance the governor and the preceptor of the young Prince.

"As soon as she was certain of having a girl, she spoke only of her son, and omitted none of the useless precautions that could cause those that should have been taken to be forgotten.[25] She laughed peals of laughter when she depicted for herself the astonished and stupid countenance that the Great and the magistrates who were to adorn her delivery with their presence would have. 'It seems to me,' she said to the Fairy, 'I see on the one side our venerable Chancellor sporting large glasses to verify the child's sex, and on the other His Holy Majesty lowering his eyes and saying in a stutter: "I believed . . . the Fairy nevertheless told me . . . Gentlemen, it is not my fault . . ." and other equally witty apothegms gathered together by the learned men of the Court, and soon carried to the extremities of the Indies.'

"She represented to herself with a mischievous pleasure the disorder and confusion into which this marvelous event was going to throw the entire assembly. She imagined in advance the disputes, the agitation of all the Ladies of the palace to lay claim to, to adjust, to reconcile the rights of their important charges at this unforeseen moment, and the entire Court set in motion for a baby bonnet.[26]

"It was also on this occasion that she invented the decent and witty custom of having the newborn Prince harangued by Magistrates in robes. Phoenix wanted to point out to her that this was to debase the Magistracy at a pure loss, and to cast an extravagant humor over the whole ceremony of the Court to go in great array to display Pretentious Nonsense to a little Brat before he could understand it, or at least respond to it.

"'And[27] so much the better!' chided the Queen in a lively manner, 'so much the better for your son! If only he were lucky enough to have the stupid things[28] they had to say to him exhausted before he understood them, and do you want them to save until the age of reason speeches suited to making him mad? For God's sake let them harangue him to their delight, while one is sure that he understands none of it and he has the less boredom from it.' You ought to know moreover that they were not yet out of it at such a bargain. It was necessary to go through that and by the express order of His Majesty the Presidents of the Senate and the Academies began to compose, study, scratch out, and leaf through their Vaumorière[29] and their Demosthenes in order to learn how to speak to an embryo.

"Finally the critical moment arrived. The Queen felt the first pains with transports of joy, which one hardly takes into one's head on such an occasion. She complained with such a good grace, and wept with such a laughing air, that one might have believed that the greatest of her pleasures was that of giving birth.

"At once there was frightful din throughout the palace. Some ran to look for the King, others the Princes, others the Ministers, others the Senate: the greatest number and the most in a hurry were moving in order to move, and rolling their barrel like Diogenes,[30] had nothing to do but to make themselves look startled. In the eagerness to assemble so many necessary people, the last person they thought of was the obstetrician; and the King, who was so upset that he was distracted, having by an oversight asked for a midwife, this inadvertence stirred up immoderate laughter among the Ladies,[31] which, joined to the Queen's good humor, made the delivery the most merry one that anyone had ever heard of.

"Although Whimsical had kept the Fairy's secret the best she could, it had not failed to leak out among the ladies of her house,[32] and these kept it so faithfully themselves, that the rumor took more than three days to be spread throughout the city; so that for a long time the King was the only one who did not know anything about it. Thus everyone was attentive to the scene that was looming, since the public interest provided a pretext[33] for all the curious to amuse themselves at the expense of the royal family, they made it into a festival[34] for themselves to spy out their Majesties' countenance, and to see how, with two contradictory promises, the Fairy could extricate herself from the affair and preserve her influence."

"Oh now Your Lordship,"[35] said Jalimir to the Druid while breaking off; "admit that it is entirely up to me to provoke you within the rules: for you are well aware that this is the moment for digressions, reflections, portraits, and those multitudes[36] of fine things, that every author who is a witty man never fails to employ appropriately in the most interesting spot in order to exasperate[37] his readers." "What by God!" said the Druid, "do you imagine that anyone is foolish enough to read all that wit? Learn that one always has the wit to do without it and that in spite of Monsieur the Author one has soon covered over one's display case with the[38] pages of his book. And you who are playing the reasoner here, do you think[39] that in order to avoid the imputation of a stupidity, it is enough to say that it is entirely up to you to commit it? Truly, saying so was the only thing needed for proving it: and unfortunately I do not have the resort of turning the pages." "Console yourself," Jalamir said to him softly, "others will turn them for you, if this is ever written down. Nevertheless, consider that there is the entire Court assembled in the Queen's room, that this is the finest occasion that I shall ever have to depict to you so many illustrious people who are one of a kind, and perhaps the only one that you will have to be acquainted with them." "May God hear you!" retorted the Druid jokingly, "I shall be only too well acquainted with them from their actions: thus make them act if your story needs them, and don't say a word about them if they are useless: I want no other portraits than the facts." "Since there is no way," said Jalamir, "to enliven my narrative by a little metaphysics, I am going to take up its thread again completely foolishly. But to tell for the sake of telling is so flat[40] ... you do not know how many fine things you are going to lose! Help me, I beg you, to find my bearings, because Philosophy[41] has carried me away so much that I no longer know where I was in the Tale."

"At that Queen," said the exasperated Druid, "whom you are having so much trouble in making give birth, and with whom you have been holding me in labor for an hour." "Oh, oh,"[42] responded Jalimir, "do you believe that the children of Kings are laid like a thrush's eggs? You are going to see whether it is not worth the trouble to hold forth. Thus after many cries and laughs the Queen finally removed the curious from pain and the Fairy from intrigue, by giving birth to a girl and a boy more beautiful than the sun and the moon, and who resembled each other so strongly that one could hardly distinguish them; which made it so that in their childhood people were pleased to dress them the same way.

"At this so much desired moment the King, departing from Majesty in order to return to nature, committed extravagances that he would not have allowed the Queen to commit at other times, and the pleasure of having children made him so much of a child himself, that he ran onto his balcony to shout to the people[43] as loud as he could: 'my friends, rejoice all of you, a son was just born to me, to you a father, and a daughter to my wife.' The Queen who found herself at such a festival for the first time in her life, did not notice at all the work she had done; and the Fairy who knew her whimsical mind, was content at first to announce a girl to her, in conformity to what she had desired. The Queen had her brought to her, and, what extremely surprised the spectators, she embraced her tenderly in truth, but with tears in her eyes and with an air of sadness, that squared badly with the one she had had until then. I have already said that she sincerely[44] loved her husband: she had been touched by the anxiety and the tenderness she had read in his glances during her suffering. Indeed at a singularly chosen time she had made reflections about how cruel it had been to distress such a good husband, and when her daughter was presented to her, she considered only the regret that the King would have at not having a son. Discreet, to whom the mind of her sex and the gift of fairyhood taught to read easily in hearts, penetrated on the spot what was passing in the Queen's, and no longer having any reason to disguise the truth from her, she had the young Prince brought. Having recovered from her surprise, the Queen found the expedient so funny, that she gave forth peals of laughter about it that were dangerous in the condition she was in. She fell ill, they had a lot of trouble in making her recover, and if the Fairy had not answered for her life, the keenest pain was going to take the place of transports of joy in the heart of the King and upon the faces of the courtiers.

"But here is what might have been most singular in this whole adventure. The sincere regret that the Queen had for having tormented her Husband caused her to acquire a more lively affection for the young Prince than for his sister, and on his side the King, who adored the Queen, marked the same preference toward the daughter for whom she had wished. The indirect caresses that these two unique spouses gave to each other this way soon became a very decided taste, and the Queen could not do without her son any more than the King could without his daughter.

"This double event gave a great pleasure to all the people, and at least for a time reassured them over the fear of lacking a master.[45] The freethinkers, who had made fun of the Fairy's promises, were made fun of in their turn. But they did not regard themselves as beaten; saying that they did not grant even to the Fairy the infallibility of her lie, nor to her predictions the virtue of making the things that she proclaimed impossible. Others, based on the predilection that was beginning to declare itself, pushed impudence to the point of maintaining that by giving a son to the Queen, and a daughter to the King, the event had given the lie to the prophecy at every point.

"While all were preparing themselves for the pomp of the baptism of the two newborn ones, and while human pride was preparing to shine humbly at the altars of the Gods . . ." "One moment," interrupted the Druid, "you are confusing me in a terrible manner: inform me, I beg you, in what place we are. First, in order to make the Queen pregnant you promenaded her among relics and hoods. After that you suddenly made us pass into the Indies. At present you just spoke to me about baptism, and then the altars of the Gods. By the great Tharamis, I no longer know whether in the ceremony you are preparing we are going to worship Jupiter, the holy Virgin, or Mohammed. It is not that it matters very much to me as a Druid whether these two kiddies are baptized or circumcised, but still one must observe the uniform, and not expose me to taking a Bishop for the Mufti and the Missal for the Koran." "The great misfortune!" said Jalamir to him, "for someone as subtle as you to be completely deceived. God keep from evil all those[46] Prelates who have seraglios and take the Latin of the breviary for Arabic. God grant peace to all those honest Sanctimonious People who follow the intolerance of the Prophet of Mecca, always ready to massacre the human race in a holy manner for the glory[47] of the Creator. But you ought to remember that we are in a country of Fairies, where no one is sent to hell for the benefit of his soul, where one does not at all take it into one's head to look at people's foreskin in order to damn or absolve them, and where the Miter and the green Turban equally cover sacred heads[48] in order to serve as a description in the eyes of the wise and as adornment in those of the fools.

"I know very well that the laws of Geography, which rule all the Religions of the World, want the two newborns to be Moslems, but they only circumcise the males, and I need both of my twins to be ministered to. Thus find it good that I baptize them." "Do it, do it," said the Druid,

"That, faith of a Priest, is the best-motivated choice I have heard spoken of in my life." Jalamir continued.[49]

"The Queen who was pleased to overturn all protocol wanted to get up at the end of six days and to go out on the seventh under the pretext that she was well: Indeed she nursed her children. An odious example, the consequences of which all the women represented to her in a very lively fashion. But Whimsical, who feared the ravages of spilt milk, maintained that there was no time more lost for the pleasure of life than that which comes after death, and that the bosom of a dead woman shriveled up even more[50] than that of a nurse, adding in the tone of a Duenna, that there was no more beautiful bosom[51] in the eyes of a Husband than that of a woman[52] who nursed her children. This intervention of Husbands in cares that regarded them so little made the Ladies laugh a lot, and after that the Queen, too pretty to be so with impunity, in spite of her caprices, appeared to them almost as ridiculous as her spouse, whom they called derisively the bourgeois of Vaugirard."[53]

"I see you coming," said the Druid right away, "you would like imperceptibly to give me the role of Schahbahan, and make me ask whether there is also a Vaugirard in the Indies, as there is a Madrid in the Bois de Boulogne, an Opera in Paris,[54] and a Philosopher at Court. But go on with your rhapsody and do not set any more of these traps for me; for not being either a husband or a Sultan, it is not worth the trouble to be a fool."

"Finally," said Jalamir, without responding to the Druid, "everything being ready, the day was set for opening the gates of heaven for the two newborn. The Fairy made her way to the Palace early in the morning, and declared to the august couple that she was going to give to each of their children a present worthy of their birth and of her power. 'I want,' she said, 'before the magic water screens them from my protection, to enrich them by means of gifts, and to give them names more efficacious than those of all the clods of the Calendar,[55] since they will express the perfections with which I shall have taken care to endow them at the same time: but since you ought to know better than I do the qualities that conform with the happiness of your family and your peoples, choose yourselves, and accomplish this way upon each of your two children by means of a single act of will what twenty years of education rarely do in youth and which reason does not do any more in an advanced age.'

"Immediately there was a great altercation between the two spouses. The Queen laid sole claim to ordering the whole family's character at her whim, and the good Prince, who felt all the importance of such a choice, was careful not to abandon it to the caprices of a woman whose follies he adored without sharing them. Phoenix wanted children who might someday become reasonable people; Whimsical preferred to have[56] pretty children, and provided that they shone at six years she troubled herself extremely little over their being fools at thirty. Try as the Fairy might to put their Majesties into agreement, soon the character of the newborn was no longer anything but the pretext for the dispute, and it was not a question of being right but of setting out to win the argument against the other.

"Finally Discreet imagined a way to arrange everything without laying the blame on anyone; this was that each might dispose of the child of his own sex to his liking. The King approved an expedient that provided for the essential by sheltering the heir[57] to the crown from the Queen's bizarre wishes,[58] and, seeing the two children on their Governess's knees, he hastened to seize hold of the Prince, not without looking at his sister with a glance of commiseration. But Whimsical, all the more mutinous because she had less reason to be so, rushed like someone carried away to the young Princess and also taking her into her arms, 'You are all uniting,' she said, 'in order to irritate[59] me; but so that the King's caprices might turn to the profit of one of his children in spite of himself, I declare that I ask for the one I am holding exactly the opposite of what he will ask for the other.' 'Choose now,' she said to the King with an air of triumph,[60] 'and since you find so much charm in controlling everything, decide the fate of your entire family with a single word.' The Fairy and the King tried in vain to turn her away[61] from a resolution that put this Prince into a strange perplexity, she never wanted to give in and said that she congratulated herself very much on an expedient that would reflect onto her daughter all the merit that the King would not know how to give to his son. 'Ah!' said this Prince indignant with vexation, 'you have never had anything but aversion for your daughter and you are proving it in the most important occasion of her life.' 'But,' he added in an outburst of rage of which he was not the master, 'in order to make her perfect in spite of you, I ask that this child resemble you.' 'So much the better for you and for him,' retorted the Queen sharply, 'but I shall be avenged, and your daughter will resemble you.' These words had hardly been blurted out on both sides with an unequaled impetuosity, when the King, despondent over his giddiness, would have very much liked to take them back: but it was done, and without any going back the two children were endowed with the requested characters. The Boy received the name of Prince Caprice, and the girl was called Princess Reason, a bizarre name that she illustrated so well that no other women has dared to bear it since.

"Behold then the future successor to the throne adorned with all the perfections[62] of a pretty woman, and his sister the Princess destined one day to possess all the virtues of an honorable man, and the qualities of a good King; a division that did not appear to be one of the best stipulated, but upon which there was no going back. The amusing thing was that the mutual love of the two spouses, acting at that moment with the whole force that essential occasions always—but often too late—returned to it, and, the predilection not ceasing to act, each found the one of his children that ought to resemble him the more ill endowed of the two, and thought less about congratulating it than pitying it. The King took his daughter in his arms, and clasping her tenderly, 'Alas,' he said to her, 'what use would the very beauty of your mother be to you, without her talent for setting it off? You will be too reasonable to make anyone's head turn!' Whimsical, more circumspect about her own truths, did not say everything that she was thinking about the wisdom of the future King, but, from the sad air with which she caressed him, it was easy to doubt that at the bottom of her heart she had a high opinion of his share. Nevertheless the King, looking at her with a sort of confusion, made her several reproaches about what had happened. 'I feel my wrongs,' he said to her, 'but they are your work; our children would have been much more worthy than we are, you are the cause that they will only resemble us.' 'At least,' said she immediately falling upon her Husband's neck, 'I am sure that they will love each other as much as possible.' Touched by what was tender in this flash, Phoenix consoled himself by this reflection, which he so often had the occasion to make, that in fact natural goodness and a sensitive heart were enough to atone for everything."

"I can guess all the rest so well," said the Druid to Jalamir, interrupting him, "that I would finish the tale for you. Your Prince Caprice will make everyone's head turn, and will be the imitator of his Mother too well not to be her torment.[63] He will turn the Kingdom topsy-turvy while wanting to reform it. In order to make his subjects happy he will put them into despair, always finding fault with others for his own wrongs: unjust for having been imprudent, he will commit new faults in order to atone for the former.[64] Since wisdom will never lead him, the good that he will want to do will aggravate the evil that he will have done.[65] In a word, although at bottom he might be good, generous, sensitive, his very virtues will turn to his harm, and his giddiness alone, united to all his power, will make him more hated than a rational wickedness would have done. On another side, your Princess Reason, new Heroine of the country of the Fairies, will become a prodigy of wisdom and prudence, and, without having adorers, will make herself so much adored by the people, that each will make prayers to be governed by her: her good conduct advantageous to everyone and to herself, will do wrong only to her brother, to whose foibles her virtues will be ceaselessly opposed, and to whom the public bias will give all the defects that she does not have, even if he does not have them himself. It will be a question of inverting[66] the order of the succession to the throne, of subjecting jester's cap and bells to the distaff and fortune to reason. Scholars will emphatically set forth the consequences of such an example, and will prove that it is better for the people to obey blindly the rabid men that fate[67] can give them as masters, than to choose reasonable leaders for themselves, that although one prohibits to a madman the government of his own possessions, it is good to leave him the supreme disposition of our possessions and of our lives, that the most insane of men is still preferable to the wisest of women, and that, even if the male or the firstborn is a monkey or a wolf,[68] it would be a good policy for a Heroine or an Angel born after him to obey his wishes. Objections and replies on the part of the seditious, in which God knows how one will see your sophistic eloquence shine: for I know you; it is above all in casting aspersions on what is done that your bile gives vent with extreme pleasure, and your bitter frankness seeks to rejoice in men's wickedness by the pleasure it takes in reproaching them for it."

"Zounds, Father Druid, how you do go on," said Jalimir completely surprised! "What a flood[69] of words! Where the devil did you find such fine tirades? Never in your life have you preached so well in the sacred wood, although you did not speak any more truly there. If I let you do it, you would soon change a Fairy tale into a treatise of politics, and someday one would find in Princes' studies Bluebeard or Donkeyskin[70] instead of[71] Machiavelli. But do not go to such expense to guess the end of my Tale.[72]

"To show you that I am not lacking in denouements at need, in four words I am going to dispatch one of them, not as learned as yours, but at least[73] as natural and surely more unforeseen.[74]

"You will know then that the two twin children, as I remarked, having extremely similar faces, and moreover, dressed the same way, the King, believing he had taken his son, was holding his daughter between his arms at the moment of the influence, and the Queen deceived by her husband's choice, having also taken her son for her daughter, the Fairy took advantage of this error to endow the two children in the manner that suited them best. Caprice was then the Princess's name, Reason that of her brother the Prince, and in spite of the Queen's peculiarities, everything found itself in the natural order. Having attained the throne after the King's death, Reason caused much good and extremely little commotion; seeking rather to fulfill his duties than to acquire glory for himself, he caused neither war for foreigners, nor violence for his subjects, and received more benedictions than encomiums. All the plans formed under the preceding reign were executed under this one, and by passing from the dominion of the father to that of the son, the peoples—twice happy—believed they had not changed master. The Princess Caprice, after having caused multitudes of tender and lovable lovers to lose their life or reason, was finally married to a neighboring King, whom she preferred because he had the longest moustache and hopped on one foot the best. As for Whimsical, she died from an indigestion from a stew of chicken[75] feet, which she wanted[76] to eat before getting into bed where the King was cooling his heels while waiting for her one night when, as a result of flirting, she had induced him to come to pass the night with her."

The Loves of Claire and Marcellin[1]

In the village of Orival in Dauphiné resided a Farmer who was quite well-off[2] named Germon. This Country Fellow had an only child named Marcellin: A young man happily born and of a merit all the more true since he had not received the cosmetic of education. Sorry at having only him, his Father wanted to marry him early in order to assure himself of a larger family: for the multitude of children, who among Country Folk add to the misery of the Poor, increase the wealth of those who are well-off. Thus having come to an agreement for this marriage, Germon concluded it less as a villager than as a rich man, that is to say based only on suitability of possessions and without consulting his son's taste very much.

Marcellin, whose heart did not say anything in favor of his Father's choice, but who did not have anything reasonable to oppose to it either, made the decision to obey without muttering; and the marriage was going to take place if the fiancé had not been found to be attacked by a very extraordinary illness two days before the Wedding. Continuous vomiting accompanied by convulsions and dangerous symptoms made them fear for his life. They called for the Surgeon of the village who, knowing nothing about such a singular malady,[3] did not fail to give a long explanation of it and to make many bad prescriptions for lack of knowing how to find a good one. Fortunately for the poor Marcellin the genuine cause of his malady was discovered before his Aesculapius's Drugs gave him a more dangerous one.

This secret cause was Love, but along with such singular circumstances that they will make the innocent simplicity of this young man known better than all the descriptions[4] that I could make of him.

A young girl from Orival named Claire had been brought up at Valence with a Lady who had taken a liking to her and whom her Mother had nursed as a Child. This Lady had died at just about the time that the marriage about which I was just speaking had been decided, and several days after this event Marcellin, having gone to Valence with his Mother to do his Wedding shopping, had had the occasion to see Claire for several commissions with which that girl's family had charged him for her.

Claire was charming without being beautiful, or at least her beauty had less elegance than regularity; she did not incite admiration, but she had an effect without one knowing why: This "why" was that, with ordinary features, her glances, her movement, her physiognomy proclaimed a sensitive Soul, and that, for those who feel[5] it, a sensitive soul is the first and the most powerful of all charms. As for those who have this internal sense less exquisitely, and who are affected, so to speak, only by rule and method, Claire was for them nothing but an ordinary person whom one is surprised to find it hard to forget even though one does not see any reason at all to remember her. Upon seeing her a good Observer might have said: It is very possible that she will never incite passion, but it is certain that she will never incite a mediocre one.

As for Marcellin; calm on the exterior and with a Temperament that was cold in appearance, one would have believed him to be little made to feel all of Claire's merit. Nevertheless he had very lively passions and was all the more tormented by them because, under a calm air, the Storm was concentrated in the depths of his heart. The indolence and cold senses that one believed one noticed in him were often the work of his very sensitivity. Numerous objects affected him little because they acted upon an extremely preoccupied soul. Others affected him so keenly that he was ashamed of so much emotion and used all his force to overcome it or at least disguise it.[6] The sort of rough and coarse education he had received from his Father had contributed not a little to making him take on this forced habit of moderation that gentler Lessons would perhaps have never given him.[7]

There, perhaps some will say, is a lot of subtlety for Country folk. I answer[8] that I have not at all undertaken to depict their habits here. I might also answer that there are Souls whose place is not in any rank because they are superior to all, and such were those of Claire and Marcellin. Princes, Country folk, and even Philosophers think and feel the same way; education changes the names and the appearances, but the depths of hearts never changes. Now Nature does not have different molds for Kings and farmers. Let us return to our story.

These two persons saw each other, then, and one can easily guess what occurred because of it;[9] Marcellin came back to his village extremely pensive and found his fiancée even more sullen than before. However indifferent he was about his adornment and that of his Spouse, he found that I know not how many necessary things had been and always were forgotten, for which it was necessary to make successively so many trips to Valence, without ever failing to receive Miss Claire's commissions.[10]

After the loss of her protectress, Claire had not at all considered leaving the city where she could live comfortably from her labor and from a[11] pension which that Lady had left her. During Marcellin's errands she changed her mind, and reflecting that at her age it was more suitable to[12] live under her Parent's eyes, she made the decision to return to her Father's home;[13] as soon as she was at Orival, Marcellin no longer had anything to do at Valence.

Claire learned with surprise that Marcellin was ready to get married. In all the visits that he had made to her he had never spoken to her about it, and since she did not find that the tone he had taken with her was that of a man ready to marry someone else, she believed she had a right to reproach him for his dissimulation; even some tears escaped her which she made efforts to hide; nevertheless Marcellin noticed them; he was moved by them to the bottom of his heart, and two almost imperceptible drops of water were the source of many storms.

In despair and a hundred times more in love than he believed he was, Marcellin resolved to break off or at least to put off his marriage, on various occasions he was at the point of speaking to his Father about it, but this rough and coarse Country Fellow who pushed paternal severity to the point of brutality was so stubborn that nothing could bring him around; the son, who feared to approach him and believed he foresaw the uselessness of his representations, renounced it less from reason than from timidity. He would willingly[14] have spoken to his Mother, but she had more kindness toward him than influence over Germon's mind. Moreover she had been sick for a long time, he feared to distress her and to harm her cure. Finally, in spite of this malady which kept being dragged out and upon which Marcellin had founded the hope of a delay, the day for the wedding having been fixed by the Parents,[15] who were annoyed at waiting, Marcellin took an expedient into his head in order to put off the moment of his unhappiness, and this expedient was to procure for[16] himself a passing malady suited to[17] giving a little alarm on his account and to causing the marriage to be suspended. He had found a packet of an Emetic that contained numerous doses and that had been prepared for his Mother; he swallowed the whole thing without skimping. I do not know whether his love had foreseen the greatness of the peril into which he was going to rush; but the too strong dose joined to the lack of precautions necessary for making the effect of this dangerous drug gentler and easier put him in a condition to make them fear for his life and that is what had produced so many learned dissertations on the part of the Surgeon.[18]

The son's danger revived the Mother and roused her from her bed. And this event, which might perhaps have deprived her of health if it had happened to her, restored it to her against all appearance; so much does

Nature have resources unknown to art. This good woman suspected something extraordinary in her son's malady; the eyes of a Mother are very penetrating in such a case. She noticed with fright that the fatal drug had disappeared. Full of agitation she questions her son, he hesitates, she presses him, and appropriately using those tender maternal caresses that are so powerful over good natural dispositions, she finally extracted his secret and he ended his Confession by declaring to her that he could love life only in order to pass it with Claire.

Once the causes of the Illness were known there was no longer any difficulty in the selection[19] of remedies. The youth and vigor of the Sick Man very much promised the prompt healing of the body, but the soul's wound had to bleed for a long time.

Germon learned the secret of his son's malady with surprise,[20] nevertheless for a long time his natural obstinacy counterbalanced the fright that such a desperate resolution caused him. He looked at it more as the simplicity of a Young man than as an excess of love. For the phenomena of this strange passion are mysteries inconceivable to[21] all hearts that are not made to feel it.[22] Claire was not deceived in the same way; the secret had leaked out; although the good Mrs. Germon was a mother, that did not keep her from being a woman. And one conceives very well that in such a case, an uneasy lover is not the last to be informed about the events that concerned her. Claire flew to Marcellin's bedside; she had the good fortune not to be the slave of those ridiculous proprieties that make the proceedings [of the politeness][23] of cities into a perpetual commerce of constraint and falsehood. Thus, without scruple, she abandoned herself to all the sensitivity of her soul; her eyes said more about it than her mouth and she could express herself with all the more assurance since the language of feeling, so lively, so energetic, so well understood by her and by Marcellin, was hardly understood by the other spectators.[24]

She found him almost out of danger and her presence completed putting him out of it so that she enjoyed[25] her triumph without having anything to fear for the outcome. This so decisive proof of Marcellin's feelings[26] did not make any less of an impression on her,[27] than his tears had made on her and she did not delay in returning to him in just as unequivocal a manner the testimonies of love that she had received.[28]

Claire had well noticed that Marcellin's Father and Mother saw her with a sort of pain.[29] They had made plans based on their son's marriage.[30] They were rich: that was a very strong reason to want to be even more so. And although the girl[31] they had chosen[32] was not much so by herself, they counted on the influence that her Father had at the chateau to obtain its farm, and for other advantages that would have made them the foremost people in the place. The marriage could not be broken off without renouncing such seductive views. They did not want to make Marcellin unhappy, for ambition does not silence nature in such a low[33] rank, but they were saddened that his taste was an obstacle to their plans. Plans of villagers![34] Why not?[35] Did not Caesar himself prefer to be the first in a hamlet than the second at Rome?

While Germon and his wife were disputing among themselves whether their son would be happy or rich, the fiancée's father came to put them into agreement in the most unexpected manner. He told them that his daughter, vexed by Marcellin's disdain and by his love for Claire,[36] was renouncing this marriage and that he was coming to give them back their promise and to take back his own: but he did not say[37] the genuine cause of this change.[38] It was the tender Claire who had found the rare secret of winning over her rival and of obliging a girl who was wise and without any other love voluntarily to break off a suitable marriage.[39] Claire went to find the fiancée.[40] "I loved Marcellin," she said to her, "before I knew that he was promised to you and I can no longer keep myself from still loving him; your marriage and my love will make both of us unhappy. With this contract of two hundred pounds of income that I am giving you, you can choose[41] just as good a portion, and find in addition a husband who loves you. Grant to me then at this price a heart that you also would have difficulty taking away from me; it suits you better to bring some possessions to a man by whom you will be loved than to receive it from a man who loves another." To the fiancée, what was clearest in this speech was the two hundred pounds of income, and this was[42] the motive that determined her. She sold her future husband who suited her rather badly in order to purchase another[43] more interested and whose temper promised more. Marcellin, in fact a modest Boy and not very fertile in stupidities, always passed among the connoisseurs for having rather little wit.[44]

Never was Claire so satisfied as at the moment that she no longer had anything; never was her love so sweet to her as after having cost her everything.[45] On his side, Marcellin was thrilled with joy at this happy news.[46] He felt how much he was loved and how worthy Claire was of being at his side. Proud of the pallor and weakness that remained with him[47] he seemed to fear seeing the testimonies of his tenderness[48] disappear along with his convalescence, while Claire's indigence[49] was a continuing proof of hers. One would have said[50] that all the privations that cost others the most were for them new means for wealth and happiness. Young Lovers, savor[51] with long draughts those delightful feelings that make up the charm and the value of life.[52] Poor, infirm, forgotten or despised by all the earth, but content with your heart[53] and with the one who is dear to you, you are happy by means of everything that causes other people's unhappiness. Hasten to enjoy the purest pleasures[54] that are known to men. Alas! someday you will perhaps know the price of wealth, of greatness, and of consideration,[55] but you will no longer find true happiness.

In fact, the very means that made it so sweet to them already were delaying the fulfillment. The proofs of Claire's tender and disinterested love did not increase the repugnance of old Germon any less than the eagerness of Marcellin and in the same event where the son saw only his mistress's sacrifice, the miserly Father saw only the loss of the two hundred francs.

Such a singular adventure, even in the village, caused something of a stir in Orival.[56]

The Little Savoyard; or, The Life of Claude Noyer[1]

I was born in the mountains of Savoy. My Father was a good Country Fellow rich enough to live at his ease[2] in his station, too poor to be exposed to the torments of covetousness, for one cannot desire very ardently what one judges to be impossible to acquire: happy not only at having what was necessary, but above all of having it only by his labor which kept him from considering what was superfluous. Heaven seemed to have destined me to be an honest Farmer like him. The first and the greatest of the evils that fortune did to me is to have betrayed my vocation.[3] Each step that I have made in the world took me away from innocence and true happiness. In my mountains[4] perhaps I would have studied the duties of man less but I would have followed[5] them better and instead of being reduced to regret, overburdened with troubles and infirmities, a long and unhappy life given over to the tumult of the passions and to games of chance I would be a merry, happy, robust old man, honored in my hamlet and respected among all men, for having worthily filled a station by means of an innocent and laborious life and deserved well of Society.[6]

Although devoid of interesting events, the first years of my life will always be present to my memory from the singularity of the ideas with which I was occupied. For example, almost as soon as they spoke to me about God I represented him to myself under the shape of my Parish Priest, that is to say old, deformed, sometimes drunk, and always fretful. The good vicar was younger and of better humor, for me he was a sort of subordinate deity whom I put up with better, because I was less afraid of him. I was attached to him, he also acquired friendship for me and in exchange for the services that I did for him he taught me to read. I had also heard much talk about the Marquis d'Argentière whose farmer my Father was, and who, like all the lords of a Village who lived in the Capital passed onto his Land in order to be in great favor at Court.[7] My imagination did not delay in laboring[8] after the ideas of nobility, wealth, and power that I had conceived from him, I portrayed for myself a tall and handsome man of more than 6 feet of height, of a majestic bearing, of a robust temperament, and endowed with all the perfections of body, mind, and soul the ideas of which could pass into a Child's head.

What was my surprise, when this gentleman, having come to pass several months[9] at his chateau, I perceived only a little precocious old man, 38 years of age, worn-out, gouty, decrepit, crippled in half his members,[10] and to whom from his youth one could have said as Caesar did to an old solider covered with wounds[11] who asked him for permission to kill himself: "And what! you imagine that you are still alive." This man, who was so sated, had a son and this son, who did not yet feel his Father's ill health, was taking the road to attain it just as promptly, and to lose the faculties and the taste for pleasure early by the immoderate use of pleasures.

This young man, who will reappear more than one time on the stage of my life, was its scourge; if he had had a part only in the first event that moved me away from my fatherland he is the one I ought to blame for all the unhappiness that has been its sequel.[12] I hasten to come to this first period[13] from which I date the history of my misfortunes.

I had a sister who was several years older than I was and who,[14] barely out of childhood,[15] already captured attention and made herself noticed advantageously in a province so rich in beautiful girls. She was a lively and sprightly brunette who abandoned herself to all her playful moods with all the less discretion since she had not received those dangerous instructions of modesty and reserve along with which well brought up young girls always and early[16] acquire the enlightenment which they hardly delay[17] in turning secretly to advantage.[18] My sister was not one of those apparent automatons, artificial idiots in whom the calm exterior only concentrated the storm inside, she was giddy because she was wise and, in order to be much more modest, she needed only a little less innocence.[19] My mother, a woman full of sense, had never considered repressing this gaiety, and my Father, who was crazy about his daughter, was convulsed with joy at seeing her enliven all the young people of the place and bring together to herself alone all boys' efforts to get married. But the Marquis d'Argentière arrived with his son, and it is the fate of Gentlemen to be killjoys everywhere. The satiated courier forgot the gout at the sight of the young Claire.[20] That was my sister's name; he teased her, he made her promises and propositions with more ardor for being taken at his word than faculties[21] for availing himself of it, and, since his head had turned completely, he lavished on her all the politeness of the old court and for this he was always treated[22] as an old fool who was good only for making one laugh. She also laughed with the son, but, sometimes claiming to take the game too far,[23] this one received corrections whose memory he kept for more than a day and that taught him that village girls commonly have a different method, as well as more vigor for that sort of defense, than the girls of the city. Nevertheless, perceiving that these very frequent games[24] could degenerate into quarrels or into worse than quarrels,[25] my Father and my Mother several times gave lessons to my sister of which, to tell the truth, she did not take much notice and everything went on just about as before; the games continued with the same liberty that should have been enough to prove to them that they were in fact only games, but good people do not pride themselves on so much refinement, they took alarm in earnest, they made some severe reprimands, Claire wept,[26] promised everything they wanted; and two hours later began her follies again, either with the young Argentière or with the first comer, for everyone was good for that and no one was preferred;[27] that is, she followed her natural mood without any particular taste getting mixed up in it. Thus my Parents should have blessed Heaven for the very thing that was making them uneasy. It has been said a thousand times, the natural disposition does not change, or at least in order to succeed in changing it there is only a remedy much worse than the evil. Unfortunately for me that is precisely what corrected Claire. Suddenly she was seen to change bearing and carriage; all her giddiness stopped, she became dreamy and melancholy.[28] With young people she took on an air of reserve[29] and circumspection that had never been seen in her, she blushed at a word and sharply[30] repressed the slightest liberty that anyone wanted to take with her. My Father and my Mother blessed Heaven at a change that they attributed to their lessons and hardly suspected that it was precisely the effect[31] of an evil that they had wanted to prevent. Love had caused this miracle. How many Readers are already casting their suspicions upon the young Argentière?[32] But it was not a fop[33] full of his nobility and of his vanity who was to subject a heart all the harder to vanquish since[34] the side that seemed to show an easier approach was precisely the one by which it was invincible. Bantering and giddiness could do nothing there. Interest even less. A woman[35] can sell her person but hearts are not sold and Claire was not the girl to abandon one without the other.

Several lines more[36] and there we are at the loves of a Country Girl and a Country Fellow. But I am not fooling anyone and as far back as my title one must have expected it. Delicate readers,[37] people of high society, close my book, it is not written for you, and I warn you that I am going to speak a language that you pride yourself on not understanding at all[38] and that I pride myself even more on making unintelligible to you.

The young Argentière, without society, without dissipation, abandoned to the solitude of his chateau, to his tutor's pedantry, and to his Father's old stories[39] genuinely acquired a taste for Claire. From this impetuous taste⁴⁰ without delicacy and without restraint, to run after possession without even considering⁴¹ pleasing and such, in a word, as a young man of his station could take on for a country fellow's daughter.⁴² Thus not having been able to obtain anything at his pleasure he resolved to made use of surprise at the first occasion. He had noticed that every morning my sister went to bring milk to the chateau. For that it was necessary to cross⁴³ a corner of the Park very suited to harboring amorous thefts. It was there that one day he came early to wait for her, well resolved to draw⁴⁴ from the tête-à-tête a better advantage than he had done from all his teasing. He ran to her as soon as he perceived her and, taking advantage of the awkwardness in which the preservation of her pot of milk put her for her own defense, he caused much disorder in her attire before she had found the way to protect herself. Finally with the danger increasing and the young man still gaining ground in spite of her repeated threats, she made the decision to make a weapon for herself out of what was serving her adversary and covered his face with the receptacle and all the milk it contained.⁴⁵ Bathed and even wounded, D'Argentière only became more animated from it but disencumbered of her obstacle Claire soon put herself in a condition to be disencumbered of her enemy and that madman, more angry at a defense.⁴⁶

I take up my sister's story again, or rather my own. Our whole family had been invited to the wedding of one of our relatives who resided several leagues from our village. We all prepared ourselves for it with that ardor that one has for pleasure when it is relaxation from labor. Festival clothes were all set out. Claire above all did not neglect her adornment, a simple adornment, but elegant in its manner, and all the more piquant to vanity since it disguised nature less. The little minx knew all that she had to hope from her charms, certain that they were worth more than all the ornaments that would have covered them. From her proud and merry air it was seen that⁴⁷ she was tasting in advance all the pleasure⁴⁸ that her presence was going to inspire, that of setting the tone for the festivities and of easily finding in one wedding something to become the subject for another wedding soon.

[On Eloquence][1]

You ask why at certain times eloquence falls into corruption, and how it happens that minds throw themselves into bad taste . . . why for example bold and excessive figures of speech sometimes please—and that at other times people like brusque and equivocal speeches that leave more to be understood than they say . . . why some times have been seen in which they were not ashamed to commit injustices.

As the life of a man has been so have been his speeches.

In the same way that each one's actions are depicted in his speeches, thus it sometimes happens that the oratorical taste is related to present morals.

If the discipline of a state is enervated and degenerates into pleasures, this is an argument for believing that eloquence will soon contract that soft and effeminate taste there; . . . The mind cannot be tinctured differently than the heart.

When the mind becomes accustomed to despising the things that are in practice, and to regard them as base and vile, it also takes on the taste for novelty in speech.

And it is not such a great defect in speeches to use puerile or bad words,[2] and more free than modesty allows, as to make use of a too florid and too sweet style if, moreover, it means nothing and cannot produce any effect other than the very sound of the words.

Idea of Method in the Composition of a Book[1]

When one undertakes to write a work, one has already found the subject and at least a part of the substance, so that it is a question only of enlarging upon it and giving it the organization most suited to convincing and to pleasing. This part, which also includes the style, is the one that ordinarily determines the work's success and the Author's reputation; it is the one that makes up, not exactly a good or a bad Book, but a well or badly written Book.

It is difficult to form a good working plan unless one has a precise Mind and a perfect knowledge of one's material. On the contrary, with these two qualities it is difficult to make a bad one when one gives it all the attention necessary. By means of the one, one encompasses all the parts of one's subject, by means of the other, one puts them in the order most favorable and most suited for making the most of them and of supporting them with each other.

There is no doubt that one can form a multitude of different plans, each one of them good in relation to its particular object: without going into this inexhaustible detail, here is approximately the general order that I would like to follow in the construction of a work of reasoning: I select this genre as my example, as the one that requires the most method and proportion in its parts.

First I would begin by clearly explaining the subject I am proposing, carefully defining the new or equivocal ideas and words that I would need to use, not one right after the other and in the form of a dictionary the way mathematicians do, but as if for the occasion and skillfully inserting my definitions into the exposition of my subject. When one undertakes a Book, one intends to instruct the public with something it did not know which is done by teaching it some new truths, or by disabusing it of some false opinions with which it was possessed; in such a case, the author's duty is first to explain the common sentiment, to show by what foundations it is supported, and by what arms it is defended; when one sets about it well this always prepossesses the reader favorably, from the beginning he sees, on the one hand, an informed man who does not adopt an opinion out of ignorance of reasons advantageous to the other side, and, on the other, an upright and sincere man who does not at all seek to conceal his adversaries' reasons from the eyes of his readers by means of surreptitious ruses.

Upon entering into the substance, I would put what I had to prove in such a light that at first I would appear to grant to the opposite sentiment many more things than I would actually grant it, leaving to the force of my reasons in what followed the right of laying claim to the excess of what I had granted at first. This skill is also of great effectiveness for gaining the Reader's esteem. It seems that, from an overabundance of proofs, an Author finds himself constrained to retract the concessions that his natural moderation had caused him to make.

In the examination of a question one ordinarily has several sorts of proofs; first one destroys the opposite sentiment, then one establishes one's own. In both cases one draws one's arguments from the very basis of the thing, or from its relations with other objects. It is the entire selection of one's proofs, the arrangement that one gives them, and the light in which one puts them that shows the judicious Writer and skillful Dialectician. Most of the propositions that one can make upon a single subject have among them a subtle analogy, a hidden connection that escapes the vulgar Mind but that the true genius always grasps. Once one holds one end of this chain one guides oneself with a marvelous facility and one is quite astonished that an infinite number of routes that seemed either not to have anything in common, or to cut across each other in a thousand ways, nevertheless successively lead you to the end that you have proposed for yourself by the surest and shortest path. The books of Philosophers are full of Laws and maxims on this subject that are related to two general methods. One, that they call synthesis or method of composition, by which one passes from the simple to the composite and that serves to teach others what one knows; the other, that they call Analysis or method of resolution, and that one uses to instruct oneself about what one does not know; when, for example, one is researching the genealogy of a house, one traces back from the present time from relation to relation and ancestor to ancestor up to the origin of that house, that is the Analytic way. Afterward, one draws up a table at the head of which one places the found progenitor, from whom one descends from generation to generation up to the one that exists at present; that is synthesis. These methods have extremely numerous and extremely extensive rules which the Mind follows without thinking about it when it has capacity and precision. With Books it is the same as with Pieces from the Theater; it is impossible to begin them too simply, but it is necessary to raise oneself up ceaselessly until the final moment; not with an elevation of style, for it ought to be always the same; but with an increase in abundance in the matter and of force in the reasoning. After a lively and animated Reading, the slightest relaxation throws the reader into distaste or boredom; one has all the difficulty in the world in drawing him out of this lethargy, and in this indolence he often lets an infinite number of good things pass before he gets back the attention and taste they should have inspired in him. I would like, then, always to begin my discussions with the weakest order of proofs. There are matters in which the most convincing arguments are drawn from the very basis of the subject; such are questions of Physics. For example, the knowledge of the nature of plants can be very much aided by that of the terrain that produces them, the saps that nourish them, and their specific virtues, but one will never know the mechanism and the springs very well unless one examines them in themselves, unless one considers the entire internal structure, the fibers, valvules, tracheae, bark, pith, leaves, flowers, fruits, roots, and, in a word, all the parts that enter into their composition. In moral researches, on the contrary, I would begin by examining the little that we know about the human mind taken in itself and considered as an individual, from this, by groping along I would draw some obscure and uncertain pieces of knowledge, but soon abandoning this shadowy labyrinth, I would hasten to examine man by his relations, and it is from that, that I would draw a crowd of luminous truths that would soon make disappear the uncertainty of my first arguments, which would receive more light by comparison.

Art consists, not only in selecting one's proofs well, and in placing them in a fine order: but also in giving them the light that suits them. There are simple and solid reasonings whose force consists in their very simplicity, and which one would enervate with the slightest ornamentation; others, more composite, weaker, or less perceptible by themselves, need the help of images and comparisons: there are some that receive an air of precision and vivacity only as a result of flowers and figures of speech. It is necessary for art to labor everywhere, but it ought to redouble its efforts to conceal itself in the places where it is most necessary. If the reader notices it, it is a warning for him to keep himself on guard. It is also necessary to study the value of one's proofs in order to present them only with the degree of confidence that suits them. Make the ones upon which you are counting the least pass first, by all means: but they might have such a degree of weakness that it would be dangerous to begin with them unless one gives them a turn that proclaims that they are there only to anticipate and prepare more solid arguments.

The final part of a Work can be employed in resolving objections and citing examples: but there are defects to avoid in both of these cases.

As to objections, it is necessary to present them in good faith and with all the solidity they can have; on this point most Authors follow the worst policy in the world: They give forces to their adversaries only in proportion to the ones they feel in themselves; they measure out the objections based on their responses, and they believe they have accomplished wonders when they have overturned these weak obstacles. But soon they have to deal with people who do not handle them the same way, and these sorts of disputes often result in convicting an author of ignorance or bad faith. One forestalls that by expediting matters: When one makes one's adversaries speak it is necessary to give them all the intelligence that one might have oneself, put oneself in their place, clothe oneself in their opinion, tackle and not spare oneself; even if the solutions should be of less value than the difficulties, that would still make a better effect than the ruses of an insincere Writer who leads astray and seeks to impose on one.

It is necessary to know what one is doing when one cites examples, to cite simply to cite is a Pedant's profession: I laugh when in so many books and in almost all conversations I see some particular facts alleged as proof of general propositions. This is a Schoolboy's sophism into which a judicious writer is not allowed to fall. What! because every day two or three madmen kill themselves in London, the English are not afraid of death? Thus I do not know how many contradictory propositions it would be necessary to accept on the same subject every day.

When one cites, one must reckon; otherwise it is wasted erudition. Let us assume that I wanted to prove that in general women have as much merit as men, or more. If I cited Semiramis, Alexander would be cited to me, to Judith, Scaevola would be opposed to me, to Lucretia, Cato of Utica, Anacreon to Sappho, and so on from example to example the list of great men would soon exhaust that of women. But if one established a proportion between the number of persons on each one side who have governed States, commanded Armies, and cultivated Letters, and the number of those who shone in these different Genres, then it is evident that the side in which the relative quantity outweighed would really deserve the advantage.

When I said that one could set aside objections and examples to the final part, I did not claim to make this practice a universal rule. On the contrary, it is what I would not want to put into practice except in those sorts of matters in which one could not break the thread without misdirecting the reader and moving him away from the principal object. If your subject requires this variety you will do well to blend all this into the very body of the work and to exhaust on each point the matter that relates to it and that you intend to use. But it is dangerous to make a Book cold and long by this method. A prudent Writer combines everything and does not settle upon the form of his work until after having weighed the advantages and inconveniences on all sides.

The final part of a work can also be used to compare: above all if it is a question of substituting some hypotheses or systems for others, and one must not ask whether authors are careful to show the old one in a disadvantageous aspect in order to make their own shine. I do not stop on that point at all, I would only be saying things known to everyone.

Above all it is necessary to know how to conclude. Today it is fashionable to find all Books too long; I find numerous of them too short, but it is the ending that always appears strung out to me. The Ancient Playwrights often enervate their denouements in order to submit to I know not what bad rules that they had imposed on themselves. Remove the final two or three scenes of the majority of Terence's Plays, their climax will be much sharper and the ending more pleasant. It is the same thing in numerous modern books. Peroration is a Rhetorician's practice; if you have said what was necessary and as was necessary, in the body of the work, the reader will know how to draw the conclusion well.[2]

[Lexicological Remarks.][1]

Danger risk peril. The first word is vague and is applied to all sorts of inconveniences. The last, more precise, is hardly said except about danger to one's person and when it reaches the life or even worse, for it will be extremely well said of a sick person that his life is in danger and his health in peril.

It can also be said that peril is the highest degree of danger. It is dangerous to go to sea, but one is in peril during the storm.

With regard to risk, it is a danger to which one voluntarily exposes oneself and with some hope of escaping from it, with the intention of obtaining something that tempts us more than the danger frightens us.

It is also said rather improperly, at one's perils and risks, but the first word in this sense passes only in favor of the second.

A phrase in which the word, peril, serves only to go one better over that of risk and passes only in its favor.

At peril of life is an improper expression but authorized where the word peril is taken for risk.

the word pain applying more to privations assumes a lasting feeling. When

[On Women.][1]

Another subject of admiration[2] for me is the air of confidence with which we make the brilliant enumeration of all the great men that History has celebrated in order to put them into parallel with the small number of Heroines whom it has deigned to remember, and we believe we find our advantage very well in this comparison. Ah, Gentlemen, let[3] the whim of transmitting their annals to posterity come to women, and you will see in what rank you can be put[4] and whether, perhaps based on reasons that are more just,[5] they will not award themselves the preeminence that you usurp with so much pride.

And after all, if we entered equitably into the details of all the fine actions that times have brought about and if we examine the genuine reasons that might have increased or diminished the number, I do not at all doubt that we would find much more proportion there than we find at first and that the scale might stay just about in equilibrium.

Let us consider at first women deprived of their freedom by the tyranny of men, and the latter masters of everything, for crowns, offices, employments, command of armies,[6] everything is in their hands, from the earliest times they have taken hold of them by I know not what natural right which I have never been able to understand very well and that might very well have no other foundation than superior force. Let us also consider the character of the human mind, which wants only what is brilliant, which admires virtue only in the midst of greatness and majesty, which despises everything greater[7] and more admirable that subject and dependent people can do in their station.[8]

After having speculated about all that, let us enter into the details of the comparison, and, for example, put into parallel[9] Mithridates with Zenobia, Romulus with Dido, Cato of Utica with Lucretia one of whom gave himself death for the loss of his liberty and the other for that of her honor, the Count de Dunois with Joan of Arc, finally Cornelia, Arria, Artemisia, Fulvia, Elisabeth, the Countess de Tekeli, and so many other Heroines of all times with the greatest men,[10] in truth we shall find that the number of the latter outnumber infinitely, but in recompense we shall see in the other sex models as perfect in all sorts of civic and moral virtues. If women had had as great a[11] share as we do in the handling of business, and in the governments of Empires, perhaps they would have pushed Heroism and greatness of courage farther and would have been displayed in greater number. Few of[12] those who have had the good fortune to rule[13] states and command armies have remained in mediocrity, they have almost all distinguished themselves by some brilliant point that has deserved our admiration for them. It is far from being the case that one could say as much of so many Monarchs who have governed nations, how many of them have there been, as Voltaire also said[14] whose name deserved to be found anywhere but in chronological tables where they are only to serve as an epoch? I repeat it, all proportions maintained, women would have been able to give greater examples of greatness of soul and love of virtue and in greater number than men have ever done if our injustice had not despoiled, along with their freedom, all the occasions to manifest them to the eyes of the world.

I reserve another time[15] for speaking to you about the women who have had a share in the republic of letters and who have adorned it by their works that are ingenious and full of delicacy.

[A Household on rue Saint-Denis][1]

The woman makes more noise, the man does more harm.

In Paris I saw a woman who was very much the most wicked Prude of the whole rue St. Denis and whose husband passed for the neighborhood Saint; when they had some quarrel together, which happened rather frequently, the wife spewed out torrents of insults against her husband with frightful shouts and this uproar lasted for two to three hours and more, but admire if you please the easygoingness of the gawper who was no more disturbed than a rock and listened to this beautiful litany from beginning to end with an angelic patience; it is true that when his better half found it appropriate to conclude he coolly took up a stick, rained blows on her, left her lying for dead, and calmly went to drink with his friends, overwhelmed with insults and weariness.

Just because an example is drawn from the dregs of the people, it is no less conclusive, men show themselves everywhere, the lower the level they are in, the less nature is disguised.

Essay on the Important Events of Which Women Have Been[1] the Secret Cause[2]

Roman History, Catrou and Rouillé, Tome 4, p. 169[3]

I am not claiming to speak here about all the affairs that women have[4] managed by themselves, either by virtue of their birth, or even by virtue of the posts to which their merit and their talents had raised them, I shall limit myself solely to giving some idea of the memorable events the production of which peoples have attributed to the most sublime[5] causes and which nevertheless owed their origin only to[6] the secret instigation of women. This is what my title proclaims, and that is simply what I shall limit myself to, very satisfied at giving[7] some general perspectives on a completely new subject which the abundance and attractiveness of the matter will doubtless engage[8] someone to push farther afterward.

I am even sorry in good faith at not having been anticipated and that some delicate pen has not had the whim of treating the subject I am undertaking;[9] from it someone would have written a seductive book for every reader who is not a fool. As for me, I frankly admit that I have only precisely the amount of genius that is necessary to feel perfectly all the attractiveness that my matter would provide in the hands of an intelligent man.

One does too much honor to men, or perhaps sometimes[10] not enough, by attributing solely to their ambition, their courage, their love for glory, their vengeance, or their generosity the majority of the striking actions that have made a commotion in history, and that often have no other principles than the passions that, for being less resounding on the exterior, only more securely produce the most prodigious effects, and that the vulgar[11] certainly do not suspect to have as much ascendancy over great men as they have in fact.[12]

It is easy to understand[13] what I am driving at.

I shall give rise to the idea.[14] It will be the fault of private individuals, perhaps that of the public, if no one undertakes to execute it. Moreover, it must not be believed that intelligence is enough to fulfill such a project well. I dare to say that knowledge added to intelligence is not enough. How many people are there who imagine themselves to be well-informed about the intrigues of courts, the plans of Princes, the motives that make them act, in a word, about history, politics, and negotiations and who hardly know any more about them than what they read in the gazette? It is the same for the past. I would very much like someone to tell me whether ninety percent of our historians have been[15] adequately informed to fulfill the task they have imposed on themselves;[16] what posts they have filled, what negotiations they have handled, what mistresses they have had who might have unveiled these great mysteries to them, these primitive[17] springs—always hidden, sometimes very frivolous—that are the motive forces of almost all the proceedings of the great and consequently of the events[18] that depend on them, and in the circle of which almost the entire history of the human Theater is restricted. It is so little true that it is enough to be a man of letters, an intelligent man, a scholar in order to be in a condition to write history as I am conceiving it well, that even a Prime Minister would sometimes not be too good to succeed in it: but let a favorite,[19] retired from the Court and who stayed in a position for a long time, occupy[20] his leisure by describing what he has seen and the business of his time; purchase his memoirs, have them recast by a skillful hand who knows how to put them into order and to fill their gaps with the particulars of events that he did not deign to insert there because they were too common, that is a history.

But they propose only to write the history of what has come into the public's knowledge; may the[21] advantages of history no longer be vaunted and may it be admitted that this is only a history of pretexts and likely-looking appearances with which one is dazzling the public.[22]

The public events that I do not want to mention here. The taking of Troy. The Burning of the Palace at Persepolis. The Establishment of the Roman republic. The deliverance of Rome by Coriolanus's mother. The changing of England under Henry VIII. etc.

Division of the Work

In 3 Books. The 1st will contain the great events in Ancient history caused by women.

The establishment of a Plebian consulate, etc.

The 2d in modern history. Charles VII recovering France, etc.

The 3rd some observations on the great men who let themselves be governed by women. Themistocles. Antony, etc.

Fulvia, the wife of Antony, stirs up war for not having been capable of being loved by Caesar.

Advice to a Curate[1]

Finally, my dear abbé, now you are a Curate: I rejoice at it with all my heart and am charmed to have been for you *Vates*[2] in all regards. Believe, I beg you, that my friendship is proof against fortune. In spite of my disdain[3] for titles and for the fools that bear them, in spite of my hatred for everything that is called positions[4] and for the scoundrels who occupy them, I believe that I would even see you become a Bishop without ceasing to love you.

Enough other people will be paying you compliments without caring about you; as for myself who am your friend, I want to give you advice. I believe I am showing you my attachment much better by that than by lavishing on you all the praises that flattery does not dare to refuse to those who are unworthy of it, but which seemliness forbids toward those who do deserve them.[5] I will be Gros-Jean[6] if you wish; but unfortunately for the people, there are many fewer of these Gros-Jeans than of Curates who might need them.

Behold you free, at last, that is to say subjected to a single master, but the most imperious of all, which is duty, for,[7] although it is less subject to caprice,[8] the yoke of reason is no less harsh than the Tyranny of men, and there is no slave who has more trouble satisfying his master than a decent man finds in satisfying himself. It is even worse when one has other people[9] under one's guidance. Then the freedom is only apparent; it is enough for the free man to have to govern himself, but whoever commands others necessarily has engagements to fulfill and is no less subjected than the very ones who obey him.

Of all the sad bonds that bind a man above others, to me yours appears the most tolerable. You are going to be beneficent by station, a peaceful Magistrate, a Father. You will have a right to do all the good that you want without anyone daring to find it bad and no one will have the power to constrain you to do evil.

These prerogatives, Sir, are great, rare, and perhaps belong only to a country Curate. For aside from the fact that city Curates appear to me already very great lords for being decent people, they are too far away from finding in their parishioners the simplicity, the docility necessary in order to be able to make them live wisely.[10]

* * *

for no one is unaware[11] that by obliging the clergy to continence they have made[12] chastity impossible for them.

I consent for you to teach them[13] all the rubbish of the catechism, provided that you also teach them[14] to believe in God and to love virtue.[15] Make Christians out of them[16] since you must, but do not forget[17] the more indispensable duty of making them into decent people.

Funeral Oration for His Most Serene Highness Monseigneur the Duke of Orléans, First Prince of the Blood of France[1]

Modicum plora supra Mortuum, quoniam requievit.
Weep moderately for the one that you have lost for he is in peace.
—Ecclesiasticus 22: 11.

M.

The profane Writers tell us that a powerful King,[2] considering with pride the imposing and large Army he was commanding, nevertheless shed tears, upon considering that in a few years, out of so many thousands of men, not a single one would remain alive. Doubtless he was right to grieve: For a Pagan, death could only be a subject for tears.

The funereal spectacle that strikes my eyes and the Assembly that is listening to me, draws forth the same reflection from me today; but with motives of consolation capable of moderating its bitterness and of making it useful for the Christian. Yes, Gentlemen, if our souls were pure enough to subdue earthly affections and to raise themselves up to the abode of the Blessed by means of contemplation, we would perform the sad duty that brings us together without suffering and without tears, in a sacred joy we would say to ourselves: He who has done everything for Heaven is in possession of the recompense that is due to him; and the death of the Great Prince which we lament, would be only the triumph of the just in our eyes.

But, weak Christians still attached to the earth, how far we are from that degree of perfection necessary to judge about genuinely desirable things without passion! And how would we dare to determine what can be advantageous to others, we who do not even know what is good for ourselves? How could we rejoice along with the saints about a happiness whose value we feel so little? Let us not try to stifle our just suffering. God forbid that a guilty insensitivity give us a constancy that we ought not to receive except from Religion. France has just lost the first Prince of the Blood of its Kings, the Poor have lost their Father, Scholars their Protector, all Christians their model: Our loss is great enough to have acquired for us the right to weep, at least over ourselves. But let us weep with moderation, and as it suits Christians: Let us not consider our losses so much that we forget the inestimable reward that they have acquired for the Great Prince whom we mourn. Let us bless the holy name of God and the gifts he has given us, and those he has taken back from us. If the tableau that I must set forth to your eyes offers you just subjects for pain in the death of the Most High, most Powerful, and most Excellent Prince, Louis, Duke of Orléans, First Prince of the Blood of France, you will also find in it great motives for consolation in the legitimate hope for his eternal felicity. Humanity, our interest allows us to grieve at no longer having him; but the sanctity of his life and Religion console us for him; For he is at peace. *Modicum plora supra mortuum; quoniam requievit.*[3]

First Part

In the homage that I come to render today to the memory of Monseigneur the Duke of Orléans, it will be easier for me to find the praises that are due him, than to subtract from that number all of those that his virtue does not need in order to appear with all its luster. Such are those that have for their object the rights of birth, rights about which those who are called Grandees are ordinarily so jealous, and which only too often betray their pettiness by their very attentiveness to turning them to account. He was born from the most illustrious blood in the world, next to the foremost throne in the Universe, and from a Prince who was its support. These advantages are doubtless great; he counted them for nothing. May this great Prince's modesty reign even into his eulogy, and since he remembered his rank only in order to study its duties, let us remember it ourselves only in order to see how he fulfilled them.

It must be admitted, Gentleman, that if these duties consist in the affectation of an empty display often more suited to revolt Hearts than to dazzle eyes; in the luster of an unbridled Luxury that substitutes the marks of wealth for those of greatness; in the imperious exercise of an authority whose rigor commonly shows more pride than justice: if those are, I say, the duties of Princes; I am pleased to agree, he did not fulfill them at all.

But if genuine Greatness consists in the exercise of beneficent virtues, after the example of God who manifests himself only by the goods that he lavishes upon us; if the foremost duty of Princes is to labor for men's happiness; if they are raised above them only in order to be attentive to anticipating their needs; if they are allowed to make use of the authority that Heaven gives them only in order to force them to be wise and happy; if the invincible inclination of the People to admire and imitate the behavior of its Masters is for them only a means, that is to say, an additional duty to lead them to do good by means of their example, always stronger than their laws; Finally if it is true that their virtue ought to be proportionate to their elevation: Grandees of the earth, come to learn that science which is rare, sublime, and so little known by you, of making use of your power and your wealth, of acquiring the Greatness that belongs to you, and which you can bear off with you while leaving all the others behind.

The first duty of man is to study his duties; and that knowledge is easy to acquire in private conditions. The voice of reason and the cry of conscience make themselves heard there without obstacle, and if the uproar of the passions sometimes keeps us from listening to these importunate counselors, the fear of the Laws makes us just, our impotence makes us moderate; in a word, everything that surrounds us warns us about our faults, forestalls them, corrects us of them, or punishes us for them.

On this point Princes do not have the same advantages. Their duties are much greater and the means of instructing themselves about them much more difficult. Unfortunately in their loftiness everything seems to cooperate in banishing light from their eyes and virtue from their hearts. The vile and dangerous retinue of flatterers beleaguers them from their most tender youth; having an interest in feeding their ignorance, their false friends put all their care into keeping them from seeing anything with their eyes. Passions which nothing restrains, a pride which nothing humbles inspire them with the most monstrous prejudices and cast them into a fatal blindness which all who draw near them do not fail to increase: For in order to be powerful over them[4] they spare nothing to make them weak,[5] and the master's virtue is always the Courtier's dread.

This is how the faults of Princes come from their blindness even more often than from their ill will, which does not make these faults any less criminal and only makes them more irreparable. Imbued with this great truth from his childhood, the Duke of Orléans labored early to strip away the veil that his rank put in front of his eyes. The first thing that he had been taught is that he was a great Prince; his own reflections also taught him that he was a man, subject to all of humanity's weaknesses; that in the rank he occupied there were great duties to fulfill and great errors to fear. He understood that these first pieces of knowledge imposed on him the obligation to acquire many others. He ardently gave himself over to study, and, in good Authors and above all in our Sacred Books, he labored to make for himself some faithful Friends and sincere

Councilors who, without ceaselessly considering their self-interest, might sometimes speak for his. The success was such as one might expect from his intentions. He cultivated all the sciences; he learned all languages, and Europe saw with astonishment a still very young Prince knowing all by himself, and having his own understanding.

Such were the first sources of the virtues with which he adorned and edified the world. Almost as soon as he was left to himself, he put them all into practice. Tied by sacred bonds to a Wife who was cherished and worthy of being so,[6] he made it seen from his gentleness, from his regards, and from his tenderness for her that genuine piety does not at all harden hearts, removes nothing from the pleasures of an honorable association, and only causes more charm and fidelity to be added to conjugal affection. Death deprived him of this virtuous Wife in the flower of her youth, and, if he testified by his suffering how dear she had been to him, he showed by his constancy that the one who does not misuse happiness does not let himself be beaten by adversity either. This loss taught him to know the instability of human things and the advantage that one finds in joining together all one's affections in the one who does not die. It is in these circumstances that he chose a pious solitude for himself in order to abandon himself more tranquilly to his just grieving and his Christian meditations,[7] and if he did not absolutely take leave of the Court and the World, where his duty still held him, at least he made it well enough known that the only commerce that henceforth could be pleasant to him was the one that he wished to have with God.[8]

The Education of his son was the principal motive that drew him from his retirement.[9] He spared nothing to fulfill this important duty well. Success dispenses me from expanding upon what he did in this regard, and we would be even less allowed to forget that today we are enjoying the fruit of his efforts.

If he was a good Father and a good Husband, he was not any less a faithful subject and a zealous Citizen. Impassioned for the glory of the King, that is to say for the prosperity of the State, it is known how zealously he was animated everywhere he believed it to be concerned: It is known that no consideration could ever make him dissimulate his feeling as soon as it was a question of the Public good; Rare and perhaps unique example at Court, where these words of public Good and of service of the Prince, hardly signify anything but personal interest, jealousy, and greed in the mouth of those who use them.

Summoned into the Counsels, I shall not say by his rank, but even more honorably by the esteem and confidence of a King who grants them only to merit; It is there that he made both his talents and his virtues shine equally: It is there that the rectitude of his soul, the wisdom of his advice, and the force of his Eloquence, consecrated to the service of the Fatherland, more than once brought all opinions around to his own: It is there that he might have astonished by the solidity of his reasons those Minds, more subtle than judicious, who cannot understand that to be just is the supreme Policy in the government of States: It is there, to state it all in a word, that, seconding the beneficent perspectives of the Monarch who makes us happy, he cooperated in making him happy himself by laboring with him for the happiness of his Peoples.

But respect stops me, and I feel that I am not allowed to bring indiscreet glances to bear upon these Cabinet Mysteries in which the Destiny of the State is balanced in secret in the scale of equity and reason; And why want to learn more about them than is necessary? I have already said it; in order to honor the memory of such a great man we have no need to count all the duties that he fulfilled or all the virtues that he possessed. Let us hasten to reach those sweet moments of his life in which, completely retired from the world, after having discharged what he owed to his birth and his rank, in his solitude he gave himself over entirely to the inclinations of his heart and to the virtues of his choosing.

It is then that one saw him deploying that beneficent Soul whose Love of humanity made up its principal character, and which sought its happiness only in that of others. It is then that, raising himself up to a more sublime Glory, he began to show to men a rarer and infinitely more admirable spectacle than all the Masterpieces of Politicians[10] and all the triumphs of Conquerors. Yes, Gentlemen, on this day of sadness pardon me for this afflicting remark. History has established the memory of a multitude of Heroes in all genres; Great Captains, Great Ministers, and even Great Kings; But we could not conceal from ourselves that all these Illustrious Men have labored much more for their Glory and for their private advantage than for the happiness of the human Race, and that a hundred times they sacrificed the peace and repose of Peoples to the desire of extending their Power or of immortalizing their names. Ah! how much rarer and more precious Gift from Heaven is a genuinely beneficent Prince whose first and unique care is the public felicity; whose helpful hand and admired example makes happiness and virtue reign everywhere. For so many Centuries a single one deserved immortality by this claim; still did not the one who was the glory and the love of the world only appear like a flower that shines in the morning and perishes before the closing of day. You are mourning a second one, Gentlemen, who without possessing a Throne was no less worthy of one; or who, rather, exempt from the insurmountable obstacles that the weight of the

Diadem ceaselessly opposes to the best intentions, perhaps caused even more good, more happiness, in the depths of his retirement than Titus did governing the Universe.[11] It is not difficult to settle which of the two deserves the preference. Titus as a Christian; Titus virtuous and beneficent from his earliest youth; Titus not wasting a single day, might have been equal to the Duke of Orléans.

I have said that he had retired from the world, and it is true that he had taken leave of that frivolous, brilliant, and corrupt world in which the wisdom of the saints passes for folly, where virtue is unknown and despised, where its very name is never pronounced, where the prideful Philosophy for which they vaunt themselves consists in some sterile maxims, reeled off in a tone of haughtiness, and the practice of which makes anyone who would dare to attempt it criminal or ridiculous: But he began to familiarize himself with that world, so new for his peers, so unknown, so disdained by the other one,[12] where the suffering members of Jesus Christ draw Heavenly indignation upon the happy people of the Age, where Religion, probity, doubtless too neglected, are at least still held in honor, and where it is still permitted to be a man of good without fearing the raillery and hatred of his equals.

Such was the new Society that he gathered around him in order to pour the Treasures of his charity over it like a beneficent dew. Every day in his retreat he gave an audience and relief impartially to all unfortunate people, reserving for the Palais-Royal[13] more formal audiences where Rank and birth took back their rights, where Nobility found again a Protector and a great Prince in the one whom the Poor had just been calling their Father. It was the very tenderness of his soul that forced him to accustom his eyes to the afflicting sight of human miseries. He did not at all fear seeing ills that he could relieve, and did not at all have that criminal repugnance that comes only from a bad heart, or that barbarous[14] pity about which numerous people dare to boast, which is only a disguised cruelty and[15] an odious pretext for withdrawing from those who are suffering;[16] and how can it be, my God! that those who are not courageous enough to face the sores of a poor person are enough so to refuse alms to the wretch who is covered with them?

Shall I enter into the immense details of all the good that he poured forth, of all the happy people that he made, of all the unhappy ones whom he relieved, and of those even more unhappy blind people whom he did not disdain to call back from their aberrations by means of the same motives that had plunged them into them, so that, having once tasted the pleasure of being decent People, they henceforth did out of love of virtue what they had begun to do out of Self-Interest? No, Gentlemen, respect holds me back and keeps me from raising the veil that he himself put over so many heroic actions, and my voice is not worthy of extolling them.

Oh you, chaste Virgins of Jesus Christ, you reclaimed spouses whom the helpful hand of the Duke of Orléans[17] drew out of or protected from the dangers of opprobrium and seduction, and for whom he procured holy and inviolable refuges: You pious mothers of families whom he united with a sacred bond in order to bring up children in the fear of the Lord; You indigent Literary People, whom he put into a condition to dedicate your talents solely to the glory of the one from whom you receive them; You Warriors grown old and grey under arms, for whom the care of your duties has made you forget that of your fortune, whom the weight of years forced to have recourse to him, and whose scarred brows did not have to blush from the shame of his refusal: Raise all your voices; weep for your Benefactor and your Father. I hope that from the height of Heaven his pure soul will be aware of your gratitude; may it be immortal like his Memory: The blessings of your Hearts are the only eulogy worthy of him.[18]

Let us not conceal it from ourselves, Gentlemen, we have had an irreparable loss. Without speaking here about Monarchs, too occupied with the general good to be able to descend into the details that would make them neglect it; I know that Europe does not lack great Princes; I believe that there are still truly beneficent Souls; even more enlightened minds who would know how to dispense wisely the benefits that they ought to love to pour forth. All these things taken separately can be found: But where shall we find them joined together? Where shall we look for a man who, being able to see our needs with his eyes and relieve them with his hands, gathers together in himself alone the power and the will to do good along with the enlightenment necessary always to do good appropriately? Those are the qualities joined together that we would admire and that we loved above all in the one whom we have just lost, and there is the only too just motive for the tears that we ought to shed upon his tomb.

Second Part

I feel it well, Gentlemen, the Picture that I have just offered you should not make me flatter myself for calming a suffering that is only too legitimate; and the image of the virtues of the great Prince whose memory we are honoring is suitable only for redoubling our grief. It is, nevertheless, by depicting him adorned with much more sublime virtues that I am undertaking to moderate your just affliction. God forbid that an insane presumption about my capacities be the principle of that hope! It is established on more reasonable and more solid foundations: I am drawing my confidence from the piety of your hearts, from the consoling maxims of Christianity, from the edifying details that I still have to give to you. Holy Religion! Refuge ever safe and ever open to afflicted Hearts; come imbue ours with your divine truths; make us feel all the nothingness of human things; inspire us with the disdain that we ought to have for this vale of tears, for this short life which is only a passage for arriving at the one that does not end at all, and fill our souls with that sweet hope that God's servant, who has done so much for you, enjoys in peace in the abode of the Blessed as the reward for his virtues and his labors.

How consoling these ideas are! How sweet it is to think that after having tasted the affecting pleasure of doing good in this life, in the other one we shall also receive its eternal recompense! It is true that, to lay claim to it, more than good actions are necessary; and that is the very thing that should enliven our confidence. With the virtues that I have spoken of, the Duke of Orléans might only have been a great man, but along with them he received the faith that sanctifies them, and nothing was lacking in him for being a good Christian.

This powerful faith that is, however, nothing without works, but without which works are nothing, sprang up in his heart from his first years, and, like the mustard seed in the Gospel, there it soon became a tall Tree that extended its beneficent branches afar.* This was not at all that sterile and frigid faith of a mind convinced by reason, in which the Heart has no share at all, and equally destitute of hope and love. This was not at all the dead faith of those bad Christians who vainly say each day, *Lord, Lord;* and will not enter into the Kingdom of Heaven. It was that pure and lively faith that made the Apostles walk on water and about which the Lord himself said that a single grain would be enough for finding nothing impossible. It was so ardent in his soul and so present to his memory that he regularly made an Act of it at the beginning of all his Actions, or rather his entire life was only a continuous Act of faith, since one has reliable witness that he never had a single moment of doubt over the truths and the mysteries of the Catholic Religion.[19] And how, then, with so much faith, did he not perform any miracles? Christians, does God owe you an account of his favors, and do you know what point the humility of a Just person can reach? Why ask for Miracles; did he not do a greater and more edifying one than moving Mountains? What

---

*Luke 13: 19.

is this miracle, then, you will ask me? The Sanctity of his life in such a sublime rank and in such a corrupt age.

The Duke of Orléans believed; and that says enough. One can be surprised that men are to be found capable of offending against a God whom they know died for them: But who will ever be surprised that a Christian has been humble, just, temperate, humane, charitable, and that he accomplished to the Letter the precepts of a Religion so pure, so holy, and of which he was so intimately persuaded. Ah! no, without a doubt; one did not notice that monstrous opposition between his maxims and his behavior that dishonors our morals or our reason, and one could not, perhaps, cite a single one of his actions that did not show, along with the force of that great soul made to subject his passions to the empire of his will, the more powerful force of Grace made to subject his will to that of his God in all things.

All his virtues bore that divine imprint of Christianity; that says enough how much they blotted out the luster of human virtues always so eager to attract to themselves that vain admiration that is their sole recompense, and which, however, they still lose compared to those of the true Christian. The greatest men of antiquity would be honored at seeing his name inscribed beside theirs, and they would not even need to believe as he did, in order to admire and respect those heroic virtues that he consecrated or sacrificed entirely to the triumph of his faith.

He was humble; not with that false and deceptive humility that is only pride or baseness of soul; but with a pious and discreet humility, equally suitable to a Christian sinner and to a great Prince who, without debasing his title, knows how to humble his person. You have seen him, Gentlemen, modest in his elevation and great in his private life, simple like one of us, renouncing the Pomp consecrated to his rank without renouncing his dignity: You have seen him, disdaining that apparent Greatness about which no one is so jealous as those who do not have any real greatness at all, not keeping the honors due to his birth except for what was painful for him in them, or what he could not neglect without offending himself. Each day prostrate at the foot of the Cross, the affecting image of a suffering God, even more present to his heart than to his eyes, did not allow him to forget at all that it is in his Love alone that *consist, wealth, glory, and justice;** and he was not unaware, either, in spite of so many empty speeches, that if the one who knows how to maintain Greatness is worthy of it, the one who knows how to despise it is above it. Vulgar men, who are dazzled by a frivolous luster, even when you

---

*Proverbs 7: 18.

pretend to disdain it, read in your hearts one time, and learn to admire what none among you is capable of doing.

He was beneficent, I have already said it, and who could be unaware of it? May I be permitted to return to it again; I cannot take leave of such a sweet object. A beneficent man is the honor of humanity, the genuine image of God, the imitator of the most active of all his virtues, and one cannot doubt that he will one day receive the reward for the good he will have done, and even for the good that he will have wanted to do, nor that the Father of humans will reject with indignation these harsh souls that are insensitive to the pain of their brother and who take no pleasure in relieving it. Alas! This virtue, so worthy of our love, is perhaps even much rarer than one thinks. I say it with pain, if, from the number of those who seem to lay claim to it, one were to set aside all those prideful minds who do good only to have the reputation for doing it, all those weak minds who grant favors only because they do not have the force to refuse them; there would remain few of those truly generous Hearts whose sweetest recompense for the good that they do is the pleasure of having done it! The Duke of Orléans would have been at the head of that small number. He knew how to pour out his favors with selection and proportion; his tender and compassionate, but firm and judicious heart might even have been able to refuse them to those he did not believe worthy of them, if he did not recall ceaselessly that we have too great a need ourselves of celestial mercy to have the right to refuse our own to anyone.

Did I say that he was beneficent? Ah! he was more than that. He was charitable. And how could he not have been? With so lively a faith how could he not have loved that God who had done so much for him? How could the holy ardor with which he burned for his God not have inspired him with Love for all the men whom Jesus Christ redeemed with his blood, and for the Poor whom he adopted? The glory of the Lord was his first desire, the salvation of Souls his first care, on his part to relieve the unfortunate was only an occasion for doing greater goods for them by laboring for their sanctification. He blushed at the negligence with which the sacred Dogmas and the holy morality of Christianity was learned and taught. He could not see without pain numerous of those who were charged with the respectable care of instructing and edifying the faithful pride themselves at knowing everything, except for the only thing they needed to know, and to prefer the study of a prideful philosophy to that of the Holy Literature that they could not neglect without making themselves guilty of their own ignorance and of ours. He overlooked nothing to procure greater enlightenment for the Church, and better instruction for the People. Everyone knows with what ardor he showed the example, even on this point. Similar to a favorite[20] Child, who, imbued with a tender gratitude, leafs through his father's testament with a pleasure mixed with tears, he ceaselessly meditated on our Sacred Books; he ceaselessly found in them new motives to bless their divine Author and to be saddened over the terrestrial bonds that kept him far away from him. He was master of the Holy Scripture better than anyone in the world; he knew all its languages, and was acquainted with all the texts. The Commentaries that he made on Saint Paul and on Genesis are not any less reliable testimony of the precision of his criticism and the depth of his erudition than of his zeal for the glory of the holy spirit who dictated these Books, and the Chair for a Professor of Hebrew Language that he founded at the Sorbonne will not be any less of a monument to the enlightenment the need for which he caused to be noticed, than of the Christian munificence that brought him to provide for it.[21]

But of what use is it to enter into all these details here? Is it not enough for us to know that he had a single one of these virtues to this high degree in order to be assured that he had them all? The Christian Virtues are indivisible like the principle that produces them. When they are sufficiently perfect, faith, Charity, hope, call forth each other, sustain each other mutually; everything becomes easy for great souls with the will to do everything to please God, and the very rigors of penitence almost no longer have anything painful in them for those who know how to feel their necessity and consider their value. Shall I undertake, Gentlemen, to describe to you the austerities that he practiced on himself? Let us not frighten the softness of our century to that point. Let us not dishearten the penitent souls who, with many more offenses to atone for, are incapable of bearing such rough labors. His were too much beyond ordinary strengths to dare to propose them as models. Ah! My God I almost have to justify their excessiveness before this effeminate world so little made to judge the gentleness of your yoke! How many reckless people will dare to reproach him for having cut short his life as a result of mortifications and fasts, who would not blush at all for cutting their own short in the most shameful excesses? Let us allow them to proclaim the maxims of their so-called wisdom with pride in the bosom of their aberrations; and nevertheless the day will come in which each will receive the wages for his works. Let us content ourselves with saying here that this great and virtuous Prince mortified his flesh as Saint Paul did, without having to weep for the blindness of his youth as he did. Doubtless he did sin; and what man is exempt from it? Also, although his heart was not at all hardened, although he could say like that man of the Gospel for whom Jesus conceived an affection: *Oh my Master, I have observed all these things since my Childhood;** he was not unaware that he, nevertheless, had faults to expiate or prevent; he was not unaware that in order to arrive at the end he was proposing for himself, the safest road was the most difficult; in accordance with this great Precept of the Lord: *Strive to enter by the narrow gate, for I tell you that many will ask to enter and will not obtain it at all,*** he was not unaware, finally, of these awesome words of Scripture: *In vain would we escape from the hands of men, if we do not penance, we shall fall into those of God.****

In the final moments of his life when his exhausted body was ready to leave that pure soul in freedom to be reunited with his Creator, we saw him still refuse to moderate those holy rigors that he practiced on his flesh.[22] Up to the eve of his death we saw him, and all those People in tears saw him along with us, get up with effort and, holding himself up with difficulty, drag himself to Church every day, pronouncing these words whose fulfillment he felt to be approaching with joy: *We shall go into the house of the Lord.***** Very different from that Pagan Emperor[23] who wanted to die standing up for the frivolous pleasure of proclaiming a sententious remark, he wanted to die standing up in order to render to his Creator, up to the final day of his life, that public homage that he had never neglected to render to him; he wanted to die as he had lived, by serving God and edifying men.

Let us not doubt that such a holy life would obtain the recompense due it. Let us admit without murmur that the one who loved men's happiness so much would see his own crowned in the end. Let us hope that the desire of pouring benefits over us, which was the object of all his actions on earth, will become that of all his prayers in heaven. In sum, let us labor to sanctify ourselves as he did, and let us act so that, no longer being able to be useful to us by his good works, he might still be so by his example.

While waiting for him to share upon our altars the honors of his holy and glorious ancestor Louis IX, while waiting for his name to be inscribed in the sacred annals of the Church, as it already is in the book of life, let us invoke divine mercy for him: let us address in his favor the prayers to the Saints that we shall someday address to him: let us ask the Lord for him to take part in his glory for which he had so much zeal, that he pour out his blessings on the whole Royal house whose honor this virtuous Prince maintained so worthily, and that the august name of Bourbon be great forever, both in heaven and on earth.[24]

---

*Mark 10: 20.
**Luke 12: 24.
***Ecclesiasticus 2: 22.
****Psalms 121: 1.

Letters to Sara[1]

Jam nec spes animi credula mutui.[2]
—Horace

It will not be hard to understand how a sort of dare could have caused these four letters to be written. Someone asked whether it was possible for a half-century-old lover not to make people laugh. It seemed to me that one could be caught by surprise at any age, that a Greybeard could even write as many as four love letters, and still be interesting to decent people, but that he could not proceed to six without dishonoring himself. I do not need to state my reasons here, one can feel them upon reading these letters; after reading them, one will judge about it.[3]

First Letter

You[4] read in my heart, young Sara; you have seen through me, I know it, I feel it. A hundred times a day your curious eye comes to spy out the effect of your charms. From your satisfied manner, from your cruel kindnesses, from your scornful flirting, I see that you are secretly enjoying my misery; you are congratulating yourself with a mocking smile for the despair into which you are plunging a wretch, for whom love is no longer anything but a disgrace.[5] You are mistaken, Sara; I am to be pitied, but I am not at all to be scoffed at:[6] I am not at all worthy of scorn, but of pity, because I do not deceive myself either about my appearance or about my age, because, while loving, I feel myself to be unworthy of pleasing,[7] and because the fatal illusion that is leading me astray keeps me from seeing you as you are, without keeping me from seeing myself as I am.[8] You can deceive me about everything aside from myself: you can persuade me of anything in the world, except that you can share my insane ardors.[9] To see myself as you see me is the worst of my tortures; for me your deceiving caresses are only a further humiliation, and I love with the horrible certainty of not being capable of being loved.

Be content then. Ah well, yes, I adore you; yes, I burn for you with the cruelest of passions. But try, if you dare, to chain me to your chariot, as a suitor with grey hair, as a greybeard lover[10] who wants to play the pleasant fellow,[11] and, in his extravagant delirium, imagines himself to have rights over a young object. You will not have that glory at all, oh Sara, do not flatter yourself about it: you will not see me at your feet wishing to amuse you with the jargon[12] of gallantry, or to soften you with languid words. You can wrest tears from me, but they are less of love than of fury. Laugh if you will at my weakness:[13] at least you will not be laughing at my credulity.

I am speaking to you about my passion with a quick temper, because humiliation is always cruel, and disdain is hard to bear: but my passion, completely mad as it is, is not at all quick-tempered; it is lively and sweet at the same time, as you are. Deprived of all hope, I am dead to happiness and live only from your life.[14] Your pleasures are my only pleasures; I cannot have any enjoyments other than yours, nor form any wishes other than your wishes.[15] I would love my Rival even if you loved him; if you did not love him, I would want him to be able to deserve your love;[16] to have my heart in order to love you more worthily, and make you happy.[17] This is the only desire permitted to anyone who dares to love without being lovable. Love and be loved, oh Sara. Live satisfied, and I shall die satisfied.

Second Letter

Since I have written to you,[18] I want to write to you again. My first fault attracts another one; but I shall know how to stop, be sure of it; and it is the manner in which you will have treated[19] me during my delirium that will determine my feelings in your regard when I have recovered from it. Pretend though you do that you have not read my Letter: you are lying, I know it, you have read it. Yes, you are lying without saying anything to me, by the equable[20] air with which you believe you are deceiving me about it: if you are the same as before, this is because you have always been false,[21] and the simplicity that you are putting on with me,[22] proves to me that you never had any. You are dissimulating about my folly only to increase it; you are not satisfied for me to write to you unless you still see me at your feet: you want to make me as ridiculous as I can be; you want to make a spectacle of me for yourself, perhaps for others, and you do not believe yourself to be triumphant enough unless I am dishonored.

I see all that, wily girl, in that feigned modesty by which you are hoping to deceive me, in that feigned equality by which you seem to want to tempt me to forget my fault, by appearing to know nothing about it yourself. Once again, you have read my Letter; I know it, I have seen it.[23]

I saw you, when I was entering your room, hurriedly put down the Book in which I had put it; I saw you blush[24] and appear upset for a moment. Seductive and cruel upset that perhaps is yet another of your traps, and that has done me more harm than all your glances. What do I divine from that aspect that still agitates me? A hundred times in a moment, ready to throw myself at the feet of the proud one, what struggles, what efforts to hold myself back! I left, nevertheless,[25] I left palpitating with joy at escaping from the unworthy base action that I was going to commit. This sole moment avenged me for your[26] insults. Be less proud, oh Sara, of an inclination that I can conquer, since once in my life I have already triumphed over you.

Unlucky one![27] I impute to your vanity[28] some fictions of my amour-propre. Why do I have the happiness of being able to believe that you are concerned about me? Isn't it only in order to tyrannize over myself! But to deign to tyrannize over a greybeard lover would still be doing him too much honor. No, you have no art other than your indifference; your disdain makes up all of your coquetry, you devastate me without thinking about me.[29] I am unfortunate to the point of not being able to concern you even with my ridiculousness,[30] and you despise my folly to the point of not deigning even to make fun of it. You have read my Letter, and you have forgotten it; you did not speak to me at all about my ills, because you were no longer thinking about them. What! am I nothing for you then? Far from exciting your pity, my raging, my torments do not even excite your attention? Ah! where is that sweetness that your eyes promise?[31] Where is that so tender feeling that appears to enliven them? . . . Barbarian! . . . insensitive to my condition, you ought to be sensitive to every decent feeling. Your face promises a soul; it lies, you have nothing but ferocity . . . Ah Sara! From your good heart I would have expected some consolation in my misery.

Third Letter

Finally, nothing more is lacking to my shame,[32] and I am as humiliated as you wanted. To what then have my spite, my struggles, my resolutions, my constancy led? I would be less debased if I had resisted less. Who, me! I have displayed love like a young man? I have passed two hours at a child's knees? I have shed torrents of tears upon her hands? I have put up with her consoling me, with her pitying me, with her wiping my eyes dimmed by age? I have received lessons of reason, of courage, from her? I have profited very well from my long experience[33] and my sad reflections! How many times have I blushed at having been at twenty years what I have become again at fifty! Ah, I have, then, lived only in order to dishonor myself! If only a true repentance were bringing me back to more honorable feelings: but no; in spite of myself I take delight in those you inspire in me,[34] in the delirium in which you plunge me, in the humiliation into which you have reduced me. When I imagine myself at my age on my knees before you, my entire heart rises up, and becomes angry;[35] but it forgets itself and loses itself in the raptures I felt there. Ah! I did not see myself then; I saw nothing but you, adored girl: your charms, your feelings, your speeches filled, formed my entire being: I was young with your youth, wise with your reason, virtuous with your virtue.[36] Could I disdain the one that you honored with your esteem? Could I hate the one that you deigned to call your friend?[37] Alas! that father's tenderness that you asked me for in such a touching tone, that name of daughter that you wanted to receive from me soon made me return to myself: your remarks so tender, your caresses so pure enchanted me and tore me apart, tears of love and rage flowed from my eyes. I felt that I was happy only from my misery, and that if I had been more worthy of pleasing I would not have been treated so well.[38]

No matter. I have been able to make tenderness enter your heart.[39] Pity closes it to love, I know it, but for me it has all its charms. What! I have seen your beautiful eyes become moist for me? I have felt one of your tears fall upon my cheek? Oh that tear, what a consuming[40] blaze it caused! And I am not the happiest of men? Ah, how much so I am beyond my most prideful expectation.[41]

Yes, let those two hours return endlessly, let them fill the rest of my life with their return or their memory.[42] Ah, what has my life had to compare with what I felt in that posture? I was humiliated, I was insane, I was ridiculous; but I was happy, and in that short space I tasted more pleasures than I have had in the whole course of my years.[43] Yes, Sara, yes, charming Sara, I have lost all repentance, all shame; I no longer remember myself, I feel only the fire that is devouring me; in your chains I can brave the hoots of the entire world. What does it matter to me how I might appear to others? I have the heart of a young man for you, and that is enough for me. Winter might well have covered Etna with its ice, its bosom is no less set aflame.[44]

Fourth Letter

What! it was you of whom I stood in fear,[45] it was you whom I blushed at loving? Oh Sara, adorable girl, soul more beautiful than your face! Henceforth if I esteem myself for anything,[46] it is for having a heart made to feel your worth. Yes, doubtless, I blushed from the love that I had for you, but that is because it was too fawning, too languid, too weak, too little worthy of its object. For six months my eyes and my heart have been devouring your charms, for six months you alone have been occupying me and I have not seen anything but you: but it is only yesterday that I learned to love you. While you were speaking to me and speeches worthy of Heaven were leaving your mouth, I believed I was seeing your features, your air, your bearing, your face change; I know not what supernatural fire was gleaming in your eyes, rays of light seemed to surround you. Ah Sara, if you are really not a mortal, if you are the Angel sent from Heaven in order to bring round a heart that is going astray, tell me so; perhaps there is still time. May your image no longer[47] be profaned by desires formed in spite of myself. Alas! if I am deceiving myself in my wishes, in my raptures, in my reckless homage, cure me of an error that offends you, teach me how you must be adored.[48]

You[49] have subjugated me, Sara, in all ways and if you make me love my folly, you make me feel it cruelly. When I compare your behavior to mine, I find a wise man in a young girl, and in myself I feel only an elderly child. Your sweetness, so full of dignity, reason, seemliness, has told me everything that a more severe reception would not have told me; it made me blush more over myself than your reproaches would have done; and the slightly more serous accent that you put into speeches yesterday easily made me know that I should not have exposed you to making them to me twice. I understand you, Sara, and I hope also to prove to you that, even if I am not worthy of pleasing you by my love, I am by the feelings that accompany it.[50] My going astray will be as short as has been great, you have shown it to me, that is enough; I shall know how to get out of it, rest assured of it: however insane I might be, if I had seen its entire extent, I would never have made the first step. When I deserved censures you only gave me advice, and you wanted very much to see me merely as weak when I was criminal.[51] What you have not said to me, I know how to say to myself; I know how to give my behavior toward you the name that you have not given it and if I have been capable of committing a base act without knowing it, I shall make you see that I do not at all bear a base heart. Doubtless it is less my age than yours that makes me guilty. My contempt for myself[52] kept me from seeing all the indignity of my proceeding. Thirty years of difference showed me only my shame and hid your dangers from me. Alas! what dangers?[53] I was not vain enough to assume any: I did not imagine that I was capable of laying a trap for your innocence and if you had been less virtuous, I was a suborner without knowing anything about it.

Oh Sara! Your[54] virtue is proof against more dangerous trials, and your charms have better to choose from. But my duty does not depend on either your virtue or your charms, its voice speaks to me and I shall follow it. May an eternal oblivion hide[55] my errors from you! May I forget them myself! But no, I feel it, I have them for life, and the dart buries itself deeper from my efforts to tear it out. It is my fate to burn until my last breath with a fire that nothing can extinguish,[56] and from which each day removes a degree of hope and adds one of unreasonableness.[57] That is what does not depend on me, but here, Sara, is what does depend on me.[58] I give you[59] my word as a man who has never broken it, that never again in my life shall I speak to you about that ridiculous and unfortunate passion that I perhaps could have kept from being born, but which I can no longer stifle. When I say that I shall not speak to you about it, I understand that nothing in me will speak to you about what I ought to keep silent. I impose the same silence upon my eyes as upon my mouth: but, as a mercy, impose it upon yours not to come to wrest this sad secret from me. I am proof against everything, aside from your glances: you know too well how easy it is for you to make me forswear myself. Could such a triumph, so sure for you and so stigmatizing for me, flatter your beautiful soul? No, divine Sara, do not profane the Temple[60] in which you are adored, and leave at least some virtue in this heart from which you have removed everything.

I am neither able nor wish to take back the unfortunate secret that escaped from me; it is too late, it must remain with you, and it is of so little concern for you that it would soon be forgotten if the admission were not ceaselessly renewed. Ah! I would be too much to be pitied in my misery[61] if I could never tell myself that you pitied it, and that you ought to pity it all the more since you will never[62] have to console me for it. You will always see me as I ought to be, but know me always as what I am: you will no longer have to censure my speeches, but put up with my Letters; that is all that I ask of you. I shall draw near you only as a Divinity before which one imposes silence on one's passions. Your virtues will suspend the effect of your charms; your presence will purify my heart; I shall not at all fear being a seducer while telling you nothing that it does not suit you to hear; I shall cease to believe myself ridiculous[63] when you no longer see me as such; and I shall no longer want to be guilty when I shall be able to be so only far from you.

My Letters? No. I ought not even desire to write to you, and you ought not ever to put up with it. I would esteem you less if you were capable of it. Sara, I give you[64] this weapon, in order to use it against me. You can be the depositary of my fatal secret, you cannot be its confidante. It is enough for me that you know it, it would be too much for me to hear it repeated. I shall keep silent: what more would I have to say to you? Banish me, despise me henceforth, if you ever see your lover again in the friend you have chosen for yourself. Without being able to flee you,[65] I bid you farewell for life. This sacrifice was the final one that I had left to make to you. It was the only one that was worthy of your virtues and of my heart.

[Fifth Letter][66]

No, there is no peace at all on the earth, since my heart does not enjoy it. It is not your fault, dear[67] Sara, it is mine; or rather it is fate's that puts so far from me the sole good that could make me happy.[68] This good was the possession neither of your heart nor of your person.[69] My imagination leaves you always too far from my hope to ever expose you to my desires. My passion, my fatal passion never blinds[70] me to that point, it led me astray without seducing me, and I let myself[71] be dragged by its force alone without seeing any goal that could attract me. The height of my wishes was that you might see my folly and that it might not excite your disdain. You became acquainted with it[72] you pitied it,[73] you consoled me: I was satisfied. I will be so if that condition, so sweet, could last forever:[74] my happiness would last the same. If you could love nothing and let yourself be adored in silence, I would pass my days in that delightful occupation, without desiring anything, without perceiving anything beyond it. But I enjoy my passion without being able to give you any. But[75] my heart is full, yours is empty, it cannot be so for very long and I am not the one who can fill it. You will love, Sara, if you do not love already; that is the horrible torment that is reserved for me, and that the certainty of experiencing some day already causes me to feel in advance. I have known too well how to do justice to myself in order not to submit to my fate, but I feel with fright[76] that yours will depend on someone else. No, my despair is not from not being loved at all, but that another must be loved. It is by you, angelic girl, that I am afflicted. Let him have my heart and I shall forgive him; but who will know how to love you as I do?

[Remarks on the
Letters on the English and the French
by Beat de Muralt.][1]

Letters on the English. Paris 1747

1.

[... my remarks will principally concern the Inhabitants of London. I believe that by making you acquainted with them I shall make you acquainted with the English ...]

T. I, p. 3   and I do not think along with M. de Muralt that by making one acquainted with the inhabitants of the capital, one makes one acquainted with those of the country.

2.

p. 146   *The French cannot bear freedom in anything; what the Prince leaves them of it, they sacrifice it to custom.*

m.[2]   and they so little conceive of what it is to be free, that if you put them on this subject they will maintain to you that they are free.

3.

p. 146   *It is true that they have a certain French freedom ...*
m.   A freedom for which they pride themselves more is that of bad morals; it is true that they do enjoy it but that is because it is the greatest instrument of slavery.

4.

p. 146   *Hospitality practiced toward the foreigner, which makes up one of the greatest objects of praise of the ancients, has something so sweet and so human in it, that everything that is related to it in some way, the entire welcome that one gives to the foreigner, serves to give a value to the nation where one has some inclination for it, and distinguishes it from the ones in which the foreigner is neglected.*

m.   to which one must add that the abundance of Foreigners, who almost always decrease the zeal of hospitality, has not at all rebuffed the French among whom one sees more foreigners than in any other nation in the world.

5.

p. 175   *The French are, I think, the best friends in the world, or if that is saying too much, they are at least the friends who are most sensitive to the duties of friendship, and perhaps the nation in which there are the most friends.*

Muralt praises them for many virtues which the effects of the system have destroyed.

6.

p. 204   *[The goal which the majority propose in conversations is to show oneself off well . . .]*

m.   Each exerts himself to make pass his faults, his vices in maxims of morality, and to do so props them up with all the most subtle sophisms with which his mind can provide him.

7.

With this easy means of showing oneself off well one neglects those that really make us worth something.

And ordinarily a polite man is nothing but a polite man.

8.

M. de Muralt says that the women of France are the best known of all the women in the world. m. I have reported this saying to numerous among them with some fear, but I was soon reassured and all have taken it for praise. The women of quality regard modesty as a consideration for someone else rather than for themselves and because of that they do not want to have any. Also one sees at first from their manner that, of all the women of the Kingdom, they are the ones who must be esteemed least, that is precisely what they claim, for honor and public esteem are in their eyes only the substitute for nobility and they have nothing to do with the substitute.

9.

p. 301 *I would prefer to meet a French man of merit than an English one; just as there would be more pleasure in finding a treasure in coins than in ingots.*

m. in putting it into coins it has been alloyed a bit, the gold in it is a little less pure, but on the other hand its use is more convenient.

10.

p. 304 *The French make wit into an essential thing (...) and nature has not distributed it to everyone.*

m. I see that here all men are rather generally divided into two classes, the witty people and the fools. With regard to the sensible man, he is counted for nothing or put in the latter class. In this country it would be just as good to be dead as to be without wit, and since everyone wants to have some, one must not be surprised if one finds only witty people or fools there.

11.

p. 304 *In order to put wit to its genuine use, it is necessary, then, to husband it very much and to make it as it were, imperceptible: it is necessary that the truth that it should embellish overshadow it, to the point of not owing to it anything but embellishments drawn from itself, as a beautiful person sets off her face by an agreeable arrangement of hair that naturally goes with it.*

Each in turn serves as a doll for himself whom he is pleased to dress up in the beautiful clothes he knows how to make.

12.

Comedy and Tragedy:[3] *Here the relations go to the man but, since the goal of the Dramatic is solely to give us pleasure (...) The Theater is not at all made to give men what they do not have, the great feelings that make the subject of Tragedy; it is suited only, at the very most, to make them lose what they have too much of, and what is lost easily, the follies that make them ridiculous.*

m. The Theater can correct manners, never morals.

13.

[*Let us say boldly that the character of mind of the author of the* Critical Dictionary, *is that of a Charlatan,*[4] *and that, of all the Charlatans who has ever appeared, he is perhaps the most noteworthy (. . .) There is no role that he does not play, nor character that he does not take on, in order to enlarge the crowd of Spectators, as well as to satisfy them: and the fruit of all that, is to make them envisage all things as made for serving as matter for Reasoning and Reasoning as made for making sport of everything.]*

Baile.⁵ m.   No one has so well proved that reasoning is made for making sport of everything and has taught us better to despise that lying art; the only wrong with which one can reproach him on that, but it is grave, is to have employed four folio volumes to demonstrate that to us.

14.

T. 2   Letters on Voyages.⁶ *The life that one leads in cities has something too agitated about it (. . .) I understand that the country alone puts us into our natural situation (. . .) That is where we become calm and where we succeed in knowing ourselves (. . .)*

m.   In the cities only an external and apparent order reigns, disorder and fatal passions reign there in the depths of all hearts; it is only in the peace of solitude that one learns to order one's soul and one's will in accordance with the genuine laws of universal harmony.

15.

[It is my sentiment henceforth, that just as one should make war only in order to have peace, and to consolidate it further, in the same way one should travel only in order to be able reside tranquilly at home afterward and enjoy repose without growing tired of it.]

a little m.   I think that just as one should make war only in order to have peace, one should live in the social world only in order to learn to love solitude and to enjoy repose without growing tired of it.

Various Fragments.[1]

1.

You did not at all want to be my protectors, my patrons, but my consolers and my true friends; and I, I did not address praises to you at all but I loved you tenderly.

M. the Mareschal and Mme. the Mareschale, receive with kindness this homage from my heart; and may my writings, victors over time, transmit to other ages this monument of my respect and my attachment for you.[2]

2.

Before taking, as I am doing now, this leave from the public after which I sighed for twenty years, I wanted to present it a complete and correct collection of the same writings that it welcomed separately, hoping that it will still be willing to welcome them united and purged of those multitudes of faults and absurdities with which swarm all the editions done up to now by various booksellers, and who have not let them go out of print easily. This is the first Edition that I have been involved in: this will be the last, it contains everything I have left in manuscript and presentable and since I am doing it only upon putting down the pen . . .[3]

3.

I am sparing the readers, or rather myself the tender verses that slipped out of me formerly and at which I blush today. For aside from the fact that these would be bad lessons to give to the young people who perhaps will read these writings, it suits only corrupted hearts to dare to show off in the age of reason the going astray of their youth.

4.

I do not call this collection my works because the works of a man are not what he says but what he does, and unfortunately I am very far from having to make a book out of mine.

5.
For the large Edition

1. Similar to those fruits eaten into by an insect that are golden to the sight, perfumed to the smell; and that would flatter the senses less if the heart were healthier.
2. Like those so richly dotted fields in which the abundance of flowers proclaims a bad harvest.

6.

How debased the station of man of Letters, formerly so honorable, has been in the eyes of the People since it has seen those who fill it close at hand. The name of Poet, a name formerly venerable and sacred, is an insult in our times and hardly one man who wants to preserve a sort of dignity dares to admit himself to be an author. Whence is this disdain and this ignominy born? Oh truth, when our interest is nothing in front of you what will become of literary pride? What can the People think of all the academies upon observing what takes place in those that are within its scope; it sees with astonishment bands of imbeciles becoming academic subjects in the provinces and literary honors lavished on imbeciles[4]
when the vulgar sees drawn from its bosom so many academic subjects, when it learns upon how many frivolous pieces of research these societies authorized by the approbation of the Prince exert themselves. When so many assemblies of men of letters barely offer it several man of sense.

7.

Whether literary societies are necessary; a question that I do not have to resolve and that I do not wish to stir up. It is certain at least that they could not be in too small a number for[5] the honor of Letters and the progress of the sciences.

8.

What use are so many academies open to the small number of those who honor them? Less to distinguish these great men than to give them equals. One lowers them by raising up beside them so many weak talents, and true merit, forgotten or blended into the crowd, becomes indignant at seeing lavished on the vulgar a reward that is due only it.

9.

If chance gathers together three Scholarly men in a small town, right away an Academy of twenty or thirty members is set up of which these three make up the entire substance. Nevertheless these Scholarly men die, the academy continues to exist and, equally void of intelligence and knowledge, the thirty scientists are not lacking there any more than the ten generals were lacking in Athens.[6]

10.

this effeminate, puerile, affected language, stripped of warmth and force, this web of labored phrases, these extravagant and bizarre turns of phrase that are taken for wit and that vile tone of pleasantry that profaned the most serious subjects and turned reason itself to ridicule.[7]

11.

What a difference from our authors who are ceaselessly obliged to praise aloud what they blame in a whisper, to think in one manner and to speak in another.

12.

Impetuous and halting style; short sentences, never Maxims.

13.

For aside from the fact that there is more than what is Physical in the constitution of our souls, there is a great deal of difference between what the mind of a man is when it departs from the hands of nature and what it can become from habit, education, and prejudices.

14.

The moral has a great reaction upon the physical and sometimes changes even the features of the face. There was more feeling and beauty in the faces of the Ancient Greeks than there is in those of today, there is more wiliness and less greatness in the physiognomies of the modern Romans than in those of the Ancients.

15.

Vengeance, says Plato, is equally harmful to the offender and to the offended; to the one because he is the slave of his passion; to the other because he is the victim.[8]

16.

The noblest of the created beings is man, man is the glory of the earth he inhabits; if God takes pleasure in some one of his works, it is certainly in the human race. For everything in us that is from nature is admirable, it is only by his own work that man is disfigured.

17.

Reflections

Do you want to know the interior of a disguised man? Ask him for advice.

18.

Each, says a celebrated Author, *hates praise, when he believes it to be false.* He is mistaken. Numerous people love praise less as a flattering truth, than as a sign of the desire that one has to please them, as an act of the dependence in which one puts oneself upon them. It matters little to them that one is lying as long as one flatters them. The baseness of the praises that one gives them compensates them for the truth.[9]

19.

There is this difference between jealousy and emulation, that emulation tends to raise us up to the level of others and jealousy to lower others to our level.

20.

Among us it is the body that works, among the Orientals it is the imagination. Our promenades come from the need to rouse our too stiff fibers, and to go looking for new objects. Among them the motion of the brain takes the place of that of the person, they stay immobile and the universe promenades in front of them.

21.

Immortal and sentient Beings have a manner of existing about which we have no idea and about which, consequently, we could not reason. For, as to us, our sensitivity is related to the desire for our preservation. The natural State of a being subject to pain and mortal as man is, is to take pleasure in the feeling of its existence, to feel with pleasure what tends to preserve it and with pain what tends to destroy it, it is in that natural and simple state that it is necessary to seek the source of our passions.

One imagines that the first is the desire to be happy, one is mistaken. The idea of happiness is very composite, happiness is a permanent state the appetite for which depends on the extent of our knowledge, whereas our passions are born from a present feeling independent of our intelligence. The development is accomplished with the aid of reason, but the principle existed before it. What is this principle, then: I have already said it; the desire to exist. Everything that seems to extend or consolidate our existence gratifies us, everything that seems to destroy or restrict it afflicts us. Such is the primitive source of all our passions.

This extent of existence or, to state it better, of life, is not always the same, it has a certain latitude for us, it is susceptible to increase or diminution. It is in the feeling that evaluates it; but this sentiment itself is passive, it depends on many things, the senses, imagination, memory, understanding, even habit affects and modifies it, but nothing affects it except by its relation with our existence or by the judgment that this affection makes us bear on it.

22.

to pour flowers and tears over your honorable ashes.[10]

She had a great deal of intelligence without being in a hurry to show it. It was too solid for frivolous people, too subtle for lengthy reasoners. What she said was too precise for the first and too delicate for the others.

But her gentleness was not a weakness, it was a virtue. She knew how to be firm without being obstinate, full of sense and accommodating at the same time; her will gave way to everyone, her judgment gave way only to reason.

23.

Depart this unhappy earth, pure soul pass into the abode of eternal peace. Young and virtuous woman you are not in your place here below.

You were in a hurry to fulfill the duties of your station here in order to be able to depart from life after having deserved the reward for doing so. Go in the flower of youth to seek the recompense for lengthy virtues; but give way to[11] tender friendship.

Isabelle's character was better than modest, it was simple, she did not display her merit at all and it was hardly known; others might have seen her to be less lovable precisely because of what should have made her loved more. She had talents, that was known; but she made so little account of them herself that one was tempted to take her at her word. Those who, penetrating beyond, see more precious qualities in her knew very well how to give her the tribute of the esteem that was due to her.

24.

Alas, few have seen her and none will see her again.

25.

The majority of men, my dear Paulin, grumble against the nature that has given them such limited days, and against the time that flows with such a rapidity that, with the exception of a very small number, all the others pass their lives in preparing themselves to live. And these complaints are not only, as is thought, those of people of vulgar minds, even great men have been seen daring to repeat it. Art is long, say the doctors, and life is short; and Aristotle[12] makes to nature a reproach hardly suitable for a wise man when he accuses it for having lavished centuries of life upon low animals while man, destined for great things, sees his course limited to such a small number of years. He should not have said that we have little time, but that we waste very much of it, for we would find our life long enough to do great things if we knew how to employ it well. But by passing it in luxury and idleness without making any useful use of it, it is hardly astonishing that, before noticing its length we feel ourselves at its end. Our life is too short, it is true, not by nature's fault, but by ours, and it is a good with which we are more wasteful than poor. A wise economy can preserve and turn to good account a slender[13] substance while immense wealth perishes in the hands of a spendthrift, it is the same with the employment of time and that which is granted to us suffices for many things for whoever knows how to use it well.

Why, then, do we complain about nature? Let us know how to take advantage of life and we shall find it long enough.

And we do not live for the quarter of our life.[14]

26.

What did you say to me young man? How alarmed I am for you, how I pity you! You are afraid to love; you love, then, and that fear never comes until after the evil. But when one loves
is one afraid to love[15]
no. The first attack of love seduces more than it frightens, without examining what one is feeling one abandons oneself to it. The sweeter one's raptures are, the less one seeks to know them out of fear of being obliged to vanquish them after having known them. Thus you cannot give yourself an account of state of your heart: it neither fears nor hopes, it is uneasy. Your naïve innocence would like to be enlightened about your true feelings; you come to consult a friend of the truth to whom the passions are not unknown, you do not fear to trouble his repose to secure your own. Young Madman what are you asking me? Is it necessary to lead me astray in order to lead you, and warm up my half-frozen blood by means of dangerous images that one never contemplates with impunity? Alas; I feel it too much, by seeking out their features effaced by age, I am renewing their charming impression in myself and in order to grant your indiscreet wishes I am perhaps[16] giving way more to my inclination than to your importunity.

At least take advantage of the risks to which you are exposing me[17] and become wise by my experience.

I was happy

Oh my child, I loved, and my happiness began where my pleasures ended.

27.

less discontent with what I had given to you than with what I did not ask in return

28.

on the Wise man   essays on Morality: XII p. 8[18]

Since the Christian life is opposed to the torrent of nature, the one who does not make any effort against this torrent is necessarily swept away by it, it is enough to lack force in order soon to lack virtue and by weakness to become as unhappy as the majority of men.

29.

The first Philosophers were virtuous, I admit it, and even much more so than ours who are nevertheless much more learned than any of them ever was.

30.

thus the one who pardons while being able to punish brings together the pleasures of vengeance and clemency; but the one who punishes does not bring them together.

31.

with that exception the past no longer interests us except by the inductions that we draw from it for the future.

32.[19]

Man is induced by nature to follow his appetites; that is his first active principle which he has in common with all the animals. The feeling that one experiences in satisfying an appetite is called pleasure, and the opposite feeling is called pain or distress.

The continuity of our being makes us distinguish our appetites into present, past, and future. The first are the only ones of which we have the current feeling, the second act upon us only by memory, the third only by foresight.

I call concordant pleasures those that combine with each other and that the same individual can taste. I call discordant pleasures those that are incompatible and are mutually exclusive. I made the same distinction in the pains.

The concordance or discordance of pleasures and pains is simultaneous or successive. The first is that of the appetites that one can or cannot satisfy. The second is that of those that combine with each other or are mutually exclusive in different times.

It is doubtful whether animals are susceptible to numerous truly simultaneous pleasures. For example, that one might be able to lend the sense of sight to lovely objects and that of taste to delicious dishes at the same time without one of these sensations[20] distracting us from the other; but that one might be able truly to join together at the same time two opposite feelings such as a true pleasure and a genuine distress, that is even more doubtful.

I say that these questions are doubtful, for we would not know how to resolve them by experience, given the multitude and inconceivable rapidity of the moments in which our attention is divided among two or numerous sensations that strike us at the same time in order to lend ourselves successively to their various impressions and that keep us from distinguishing whether their effect is successive or simultaneous.

As to successive pleasures, it seems that all those of which human nature in general is capable can be tasted by each man in particular. But that is not true without distinction; for the appetites common to the species do not fail to vary very much among the individuals. All have neither the same tastes in everything nor the same degrees of sensitivity. So that one has distaste for what[21] pleases another and so that such a pleasure that gratifies one by its delicacy is, from the same thing, insipid to the one whose senses are coarser.

There are appetites, tastes from age, sex, temperament, situation, habit, over which one should not dispute because they pertain to certain modifications of our being which do not at all depend on us and which are not the same in all individuals or in each individual at all times.[22]

There are more or less durable sensual pleasures. There are some that wear out with habit; others that resist it, others whose sharpness it softens but which it transforms into true needs so that, without being gratified by their enjoyment, one is tormented by their privation.

33.

Read, Sir, the Dialogues of Plato and you will find that you were playing the role of the prideful sophist and your adversary that of Socrates. He crushed you modestly with fearsome arguments which you very haughtily answered with insults as reasons.

34.

Without being a great Prophet I believe I can easily predict to you the fate you are preparing for yourself. You will perish like a scatterbrain by your best friend's sword, or someday you will be seen as a low and belated penitent in the arms of a monk[23] stuggling against the fear of death and of the Devil.

35.[24]

"If only I had some hope of making myself more comfortable, I would willingly cut back on the necessities in order to procure them more abundantly for my family some day: but I am barely able to earn enough to maintain it. In twenty years the little that I would save each week would not make up a foundation adequate to procure me a perceptible revenue:

I need it in order to amuse myself or console myself,[25] in order to revive my courage and my forces and to bear without complaining a continuous labor that will have no other terminus than the end of my life. On Sundays I come to tavern with my wife, for I do not have the means to raise myself above my station and get involved in corrupting decent girls or to frequent bad spots." "My friend," his wife said to him with a manner that pierced me, "I know very well that you do not have the desire either." "No," he said, "for my family would suffer from it and let's drink."

36.
Solitude

Inanimate beings which I preferred to the society of men.[26]

37.

If under the oak where my ashes will rest

38.

In the bosom of superstition where reason has no force philosophy must necessarily take on a mysterious air in order to gain credence. Without which all the truths that are merely demonstrated would not find any sectaries at all.

39.

Doubtless it was necessary to say some good things, but in order to say them usefully it was necessary to begin by[27] getting oneself listened to.

40.

The two sexes will be better off for it, will esteem themselves more, and rest assured that genuine love will lose nothing in it.

41.

Hardly anyone but fools can present themselves as professors of wisdom, also the times of the crowd of Philosophers are also those in which one sees the fewest wise men.

42.

Oh Greeks, set your mind at rest. The fleet[28] that is coming under full sail is one of ours. I recognize the flag of the invincible Achilles. Lesbos is taken. He draws up to us with victory following.[29] The Gods are going to deliver Hector and Phrygia to the blows of this Hero.

43.

I wandered in thick shadows, the sudden burst of daylight dazzled me and removed the light from me again. My heart languished hopelessly.[30] I learn of my happiness and do not dare to believe it.

44.

A preference very suited to order, for expiring nature needs help more than aroused nature does.

45.

Again often that softening is not at all the work of reflection, but only of memory, which, recalling to us the idea of our past ills, serves to identify us more strongly with the one who is suffering similar ones at present.

46.

The tears that one sheds at the representation of an engaging tragedy, as well as the interior feeling that makes us pity the unfortunate, have an extreme sweetness for us, etc. etc. . . . The abbé du Bos says that at extremely great length,[31] but it seems to me that reason is not very satisfied with the manner in which he claims to explain it; he says that the pleasure comes from the emotion. But why do certain emotions give pleasure, while others do not give it at all, as in seeing a sick person suffer or a man unjustly mistreated?

Why does the emotion caused by pity give pleasure in certain cases and not give it at all in others?

The soul finds it hard to identify itself with contemptible men whom one would be sorry to resemble and whatever ills they suffer, the pity that they inspire is never extremely vivid, but one loves to put oneself in the place of an unfortunate hero who by means of his courage triumphs over a barbarous persecutor and displays to our gazes a virtue that one appropriates for oneself all the more willingly since its practice costs nothing. If the Tragedy of Atreus[32] gives less pity than horror, it is because Thyestes is a weak man, whom one even knows to have been guilty and in whom the spectators, hardly touched, take only a mediocre interest. But one does not envisage without lively alarm the dangers of the virtuous—because the pride that we bear in willingly identifying ourselves with that great soul to which we strive to elevate ours.

Notes

Collected Writings   Jean-Jacques Rousseau. *Collected Writings of Rousseau*, Volumes I–X. Edited by Roger D. Masters and Christopher Kelly. Hanover, N.H.: University Press of New England, 1991–.
Emile   Jean-Jacques Rousseau. *Emile; or, On Education*. Edited by Allan Bloom. New York: Basic Books, 1979.
Leigh   Jean-Jacques Rousseau, *Correspondance complètes*. Volumes 1–52. Edited by R. A. Leigh. Geneva: Institute et Musée Voltaire, 1965–1998.
Pléiade   Jean-Jacques Rousseau. *Oeuvres complètes*, Volumes 1–5. Paris. NRF–Editions de la Pléiade, 1959–1995.
Response   *Réponse aux Lettres Ecrites de la Montagne; Publiée à Genève, sous ce titre: Sentiment des Citoyens*. Paris: Duchesne, 1765.

Introduction

1. Leigh, 1, 33–34.
2. *Collected Writings*, V, 199.
3. "The Banterer," 26 below.
4. Ibid., 28.
5. See *Collected Writings*, X, 191–196.
6. See *Collected Writings*, II, 8.
7. Leigh, 1, 138–139.
8. 16 below.
9. 10 below.
10. 11 below.
11. 14 below.
12. *Collected Writings*, II, 5.
13. 16 below.
14. 18 below.
15. *Collected Writings*, V, 201.
16. Friedrich Melchior Grimm, *Correspondance littéraire, philosophique et critique* (Paris: Michaud, 1813), première partie, tome troisième, 176. The selection is from June 15, 1762.
17. In recent years a group of French scholars have done the groundwork for understanding Rousseau as a scientific thinker. See the following: *Rousseau et les sciences,* sous la direction de Bernadette Bensaude-Vincent et Bruno Bernardi (Paris: L'Harmattan, 2003); the issue of the journal *Corpus* no. 36 (1999),

devoted to "Jean-Jacques Rousseau et la chimie" and the reedition of Rousseau's *Institutions chymiques* (Paris: Fayard, 1999). The latter two were also done under the direction of Benadette Bensaude-Vincent and Bruno Bernardi.

18. *Collected Writings,* V, 101.

19. For a more extensive discussion of the "Fiction" in the context of Rousseau's literary career, see Christopher Kelly, *Rousseau as Author: Consecrating One's Life to the Truth* (Chicago: University of Chicago Press, 2003), 155–171.

20. 178 below.

21. 183 below.

22. 190 below.

23. 199 below.

24. For an excellent account of Rousseau's use of this form in relation to his predecessors and followers, see William Ray, *Story and History* (Oxford: Basil Blackwell, 1990), 240–269.

25. 215 below.

26. Leigh, 5, 193.

27. 239 below.

28. See Victor Goldschmidt, *Anthropologie et politique: Les principes du système de Rousseau* (Paris: Vrin, 1974), 21–22.

29. 284 below.

30. 284 below.

Autobiographical Poems

1. This poem was published anonymously in 1739 with a title page indicating that it was published in London by the publisher Jacob Tomson, whereas it was in fact published in either Chambéry or Lyon. The part contained in brackets was first published in 1776. Rousseau also included it in a manuscript called "The Allobrogian Muse," which has as its epigraph: *Barbarus hic ego sum, quia non intelligor illis / Et redent stolidi verba Latina Getae* (Here I am the barbarian, because no one understands me / The stupid Getae laugh at Latin words), from Ovid's *Tristia,* Book V, Elegy X, 37–38. Rousseau later used the first of these lines as the epigraph of his *First Discourse* and also of the *Dialogues.*

2. "Rare the house that takes on a friend without fortune, and rare the palace where a client without birth is not humbled." This is from the anonymous *Laus Pisonis,* written in the first century A.D.

3. The manuscript gives the title as "The Orchard of Les Charmettes." Les Charmettes is the name of the house in Chambéry where Rousseau lived with Mme. de Warens.

4. Rousseau read La Bruyère's *Characters* when he was very young. He mentions Mme. de Warens's preference for La Bruyère over La Rochefoucauld in the *Confessions* (*Collected Writings,* V, 8 and 93.) He regarded Montaigne as a defective predecessor in writing autobiography.

5. Just before committing suicide after his defeat by Caesar, Cato the Younger is said to have read Plato's *Phaedo,* which recounts the death of Socrates.

6. Philippe de La Hire (1640–1718) was a French mathematician and astron-

omer. Jean-Dominique Cassini (1625–1712) and his son, Jacques Cassini (1677–1756) were French astronomers. On Rousseau's study of astronomy, see *Confessions*, in *Collected Writings*, V, 201–202.

7. Christiaan Huyghens (1629–1695) was a prominent mathematician and astronomer. He was an early proponent of the view that the earth was flattened at the poles. See 84–90 below. Bernard Le Bovier de Fontenelle (1657–1757) wrote many works popularizing modern science. Rousseau read his *Conversations on the Plurality of Worlds* when he was very young (*Collected Writings*, V, 8).

8. The manuscript reads, "base hearts."

9. Titus and Trajan were Roman emperors noted for their liberality. On Titus, see 256–257 below.

10. The manuscript omits "And."

11. This verse begins a passage not in the original publication.

12. See 163 below. The reference is to the pension given to Mme. de Warens by the king of Sardinia, Charles-Emmanuel III.

13. This verse concludes the passage not in the original publication. In the 1739 published version the text continues here, but the next four verses read:

> But you who honor me with the tender name of mother,
> Accept today this sincere homage,
> This legitimate and perhaps too much owed tribute
> That my gratitude offers to your virtue.

14. The manuscript reads, "Yes!"

15. The manuscript reads, "Precious times, Alas!"

16. John Wallis (1616–1703), Isaac Barrow (1630–1677), and Father Charles Reyneau (1656–1716?) were all prominent mathematicians.

17. This could also be translated as "I am." The original edition read, "I flee," which appears to be a misprint.

18. This footnote occurs only in the manuscript.

19. Bernard Nieuwentyt (1654–1718) was a Dutch philosopher who wrote *The Existence of God demonstrated by the marvels of nature*.

20. The reference is to the novel by Fénélon.

21. The novel of this name by the abbé Terrasson was published in 1731.

22. The abbé Prévost's novel *The History of Cleveland* was published in 1731.

23. Jacob Spon (1647–1685) was the author of *The History of the Republic of Geneva*.

24. Civil unrest broke out in Geneva in 1734 and again in 1737. The French intervened and established peace in 1738.

25. Charles-François-Nicolas Lemaître de Claville (1670–1740) wrote *Treatise on the True Merit of Man*. Gilbert-Charles Legendre, marquis de Saint-Aubin (1688–1746) wrote *Treatise on Opinion*. François-Eudes de Mezeray (1610–1683) wrote a multivolume history of France.

26. Nicolas Boileau-Despréaux (1636–1711), Alexander Pope (1688–1744). Charles Rollin (1661–1741) wrote a multivolume history of France. The Pléiade editors suggest that Barclai is Jean Barclay (1582–1621), who wrote the novel *Argenis*. Rousseau sometimes uses this spelling for George Berkeley whose name could have been listed with the philosophers mentioned earlier in the poem.

27. Antoine Houdar de La Motte (1672–1731) was an author of lyric tragedies.

28. The manuscript reads, "amusing."

29. A later copy of the poem reads, "M. de Bordes." This was probably written in 1741 when Rousseau was living in Lyon. The first thirty verses of the poem are in the collection, *The Allobrogian Muse*. The poem was first published in 1743. Charles Bordes (1711–1781) was one of Rousseau's closest friends, but the two did not maintain contact when Rousseau moved to Paris. Bordes later wrote an attack on the *First Discourse*. This attack and Rousseau's responses can be found in *Collected Writings*, II, 93–129 and 182–185. There is also another copy of the entire poem in the hand of Rousseau's young friend François Coindet. Coindet's copy gives the title as *Letter to Monsieur de Bordes*.

30. Coindet's copy reads, "doubtless."

31. The word translated as "rouse up" is *révolter*, and the word translated as "disgusted" is *révolté*. Coindet's copy replaces the second of these with *irrité*, "irritated."

32. Coindet's copy reads, "by luck."

33. Coindet's copy reads, "foolish."

34. Coindet's copy reads, "upright."

35. Coindet's copy reads, "Too frank, perhaps too true, and not criminal."

36. Here Rousseau switches from the informal to the formal second-person pronoun.

37. Coindet's copy reads, "limited, whose wise indigence."

38. Coindet's copy reads, "will."

39. Coindet's copy reads, "no longer."

40. Coindet's copy reads, "pious."

41. In Coindet's copy this verse is followed by,
> No, for a wretch the excess of knowledge
> Beyond his own ills increases his suffering
> And for the indigent it is the summit of horror
> If he still dares to keep a Heart in his misery.

42. The four verses ending here are not in Coindet's copy.

43. Coindet's copy adds the following verses at this point.
> Let us leave, sad plaything of vulgar prejudices
> This somber Jansenist and his austere errors
> Which assume that a rich man is damned
> By the fact that he does not live as an unfortunate does;
> That the slightest sweet things are the devil's traps,
> And here below want a wretched Croesus
> To suffer like Tantalus surrounded by pleasures
> Whose prohibition further irritates desires.
> As the sacred character of virtue
> Is not at all graven in manna so as to support
> That invincible inclination for innocent pleasures
> Is not given to us in order to torment our senses,
> God would not have left its knowledge in us
> If he had forbidden its sweet enjoyment;

> What relish would a tender Father dare to find
> In showing us goods of which he wished to deprive us?

44. Coindet's copy reads, "by."

45. In Coindet's copy the note reads, "Mr. The intendant of Lyon, Director of the Academy of Fine Arts whose good taste and Enlightenment are acknowledged. Those who are acquainted with me know very well that even though he is Intendant, I would never have praised him if he did not deserve to be."

46. In Coindet's copy the note reads, "*Blanche of Bourbon,* a Tragedy by Mr. De Bordes, full of fire, elevation, and feeling; and which, to the great regret of his Friends, he refuses to let be staged."

47. This is contained in *The Allobrogian Muse* and was probably written in 1740 or 1741. The answer to the riddle is generally regarded as: A Portrait.

48. Gabriel Parisot (1680–1762) was a surgeon and member of the Academy of Lyon.

49. Rousseau is apparently referring to his plan to go to Paris to make his fortune.

50. A lustrum is five years. The date given in the title for the completion of this poem is two weeks after his thirtieth birthday. Rousseau would certainly have arrived in Paris by this time.

The Banterer

1. Around 1749 Rousseau and Diderot planned to coauthor a periodical patterned after such works as *The Spectator.* Rousseau wrote this draft of what was meant to be the first issue.

2. Abbé Jean-Antoine Nollet (1700–1770) was a well-known experimental physicist.

3. This appears to be a note to Diderot, who had written extensively on the natural sciences. In the version published in 1782, the gap is filled with the remark, "that of doing without reasoning with the help of several formulas." It is not know whether Rousseau wrote this remark or whether it came from Du Peyrou, who edited the work.

4. Denis Petau (1583–1652) was the author of an *Abridged Chronology of Sacred and Profane Universal History,* which Rousseau had studied. See *Confessions* (*Collected Writings,* V, 201). Bernard de Montfaucon wrote numerous scholarly volumes on ancient and French history. The contemporary works Rousseau is referring to are popular novels, including *The Skimmer; or, Tanzaï and Néadarné* by Crébillon fils (1734); *Grigri, an Authentic History Translated from Japanese* by De Cahusac (1734); *Angola, Indian Historical Account* by La Morlière (1746); and *The Sultan Misapouf* by Voisenon (1746). These are all exotic novels, more or less influenced by Montesquieu's *Persian Letters.*

5. There is, in fact, no epigraph to this sheet.

6. Aristarchus of Samothrace was a famous critic and editor in the third and second centuries B.C. In announcing his break with Diderot, in the *Letter to d'Alembert,* Rousseau referred to his former friend as his Aristarchus. See *Collected Writings,* X, 256.

7. The Pléiade editors suggest *Satire* IV as Rousseau's source.
8. This is the flying machine for traveling to the sun and the moon in Cyrano de Bergerac's *Comical History of the States and Empires of the Sun*.
9. The hypogriff appears in Strophe XVIII of Ariosto's *Orlando Furioso*.
10. This appears to be a note to Diderot.

Biographical Fragment

1. This series of fragments was probably written in 1755–1756 in the midst of Rousseau's dispute over music with Rameau. We are following the Pléiade editors in putting passages crossed out by Rousseau in brackets.
2. Rousseau is referring to King Stanislas of Poland, who wrote *Reply to the Discourse which was awarded the prize of the Academy of Dijon* in 1751 responding to Rousseau's *First Discourse*. Rousseau responded the same year with *Observations by Jean-Jacques Rousseau of Geneva on the Reply Made to his Discourse*. These works can be found in *Collected Writings*, II, 28–54.
3. Rousseau is referring to *Discourse on the Advantages of the Sciences and Arts* (1751) by Rousseau's acquaintance, Charles Bordes. Rousseau responded the next year with his *Final Reply*. These works can be found in *Collected Writings*, II, 93–129. Bordes later responded with a *Second Discourse on the Benefits of the Sciences and the Arts*.
4. This is almost certainly Diderot.
5. See the *Letter on French Music* in *Collected Writings*, VII, 141–174.
6. The work is *Errors on Music in the Encyclopedia*, published anonymously by Rameau in August 1755. Rousseau is probably merely pretending to believe that the work was falsely attributed to Rameau by his enemies. In his response to the work Rousseau referred to it as simply *Errors on Music* or simply M. Rameau's *Errors*. See *Collected Writings*, VII, 222–250 and 260–289.
7. The philosopher is d'Alembert, who wrote *Elements of Music Following the Principles of M. Rameau*.
8. In the *Errors on Music* Rameau accuses Rousseau of having plagiarized parts of his opera.

My Portrait

1. These fragments are found on separate sheets in a single folder with the title in Rousseau's hand. It is unclear when they were written, although the majority probably date from 1758 to 1762.
2. Rousseau's work was copying music.
3. This footnote is crossed out in the manuscript.
4. Rousseau leaves the name blank. The Pléiade editors suggest that he is thinking of Adeimantus, but it seems at least as likely to be Glaucon, who also gives a speech contrasting justice and the appearance of justice.
5. Before settling on the final version Rousseau wrote successively, "that they did not conceive that one could be alone and content," "that they do not know

my compensations," and "that having always judged me from themselves they cannot believe that."

6. Rousseau originally wrote, "believe."

7. Rousseau originally wrote, "that not having been able to enjoy them in the city."

8. The work is probably the *Social Contract.*

Response to the *Letters Written from the Mountain*

1. The *Sentiment of the Citizens* was published anonymously by Voltaire in December 1764, immediately after Rousseau's publication of the *Letters Written from the Mountain*. Rousseau mistakenly concluded that the work had been written by the Genevan clergyman Jacob Vernes, who had been giving sermons in which Rousseau was attacked. In the *Confessions* Rousseau says that he decided to have the work reprinted in Paris along with notes in which he responded to personal attacks (*Collected Writings*, V, 529–531). It was published by the bookseller Nicholas-Bonaventure Duchesne, who had been one of the publishers of *Emile*. For an account of these events, see Christopher Kelly, *Rousseau as Author: Consecrating One's Life to the Truth* (Chicago: University of Chicago Press, 2003), 9–12.

2. The *Letters Written from the Country* by Jean-Robert Tronchin were published in September and October 1763. This work was a justification of the Genevan condemnation of *Emile*. Rousseau responded with the *Letters Written from the Mountain*.

3. Rousseau had renounced his citizenship after the condemnation of *Emile*.

4. Voltaire is referring to Rousseau's career as a composer of operas, which began with rejection, but was ultimately immensely successful. In his play *Le Cercle,* Charles Palissot de Montenoy portrayed Rousseau as walking on all fours in a parody of the views in the *Second Discourse*. In a letter to Rousseau (*Collected Writings*, III, 102), Voltaire said, "One acquires the desire to walk on all fours when one reads your book."

5. *Letters Written from the Mountain* in *Collected Writings*, IX, 151. In the context Rousseau argues that if those who criticize his books read the Gospel as carelessly they would arrive at the criticism he puts into the mouth of a critic.

6. Julien Offray de la Mettrie (1709–1751) was the author of numerous works of materialism, including *Man a Machine*.

7. *Letters Written from the Mountain,* in *Collected Writings*, IX, 178. Voltaire changes the quotation slightly.

8. Ibid., 158. The term Rousseau uses is *Amphigouri*.

9. Ibid. Again, Voltaire shortens the quotation.

10. Rousseau had converted to Catholicism in 1728. He was accepted as a Calvinist again in 1754.

11. Rousseau's claim in his note to this passage that he did not have his children exposed outside the foundling hospital is true in a literal sense: it appears that he had the children put in the hospital rather than exposing them outside as many other people did.

12. *Letters Written from the Mountain*, in *Collected Writings*, IX, 172–173.
13. Ibid., 292–293. Voltaire shortens the quotation.
14. Ibid., 254.
15. Ibid., Voltaire changes the quotation slightly.

Notes for the *Reveries*

1. These notes are found on playing cards that Rousseau carried with him on his walks.
2. An illegible word follows.
3. The story is from Plutarch, *Life of Solon*. It can also be found in Montaigne's *Essays*, I, xix.
4. Rousseau originally wrote, "Who consult self-interest before justice and do not crown the one who has spoken best, but the one who has supported the side that suits them best and ask for flattery much more than eloquence."
5. This passage is struck out by two diagonal lines.
6. This list is sometimes taken as a preliminary outline of the *Reveries*.
7. This is the title of a work that Rousseau planned, but did not complete. His draft has been lost. See *Confessions*, in *Collected Writings*, V, 343–344.
8. The Pléiade editors read an addition to this passage as "leave me for love of *écry*." The writing here is almost illegible. The word "écry" does not exist in French.
9. This fragment is crossed out. It also appears on the same card with a passage from *Emile and Sophie*. Accordingly, it may not have been intended for the *Reveries*.

On the Art of Enjoying and Other Fragments

1. It is not clear that these fragments were all written in the same period. It has been suggested that the longest of them were written in 1758–1759. The last ones were clearly written after 1768.
2. This could also be translated as "spirits."
3. *Iliad*, IV, 141.
4. Presumably these preferences would be that others prefer you to themselves.
5. The word here is *evidence*, which means certitude or obviousness rather than evidence in the sense of the English word.
6. This is very close to a passage in the *Dialogues* (*Collected Writings*, I, 92).
7. Choiseul was the prime minister of France at the time. Rousseau had come to believe that he was an ardent enemy.
8. Alexandre Deleyre (1726–1797) was later active during the French Revolution. On Deleyre's correspondence, see *Confessions* (*Collected Writings*, V, 508–509).
9. The actual date of this ceremony was August 30, 1768. It was not, in fact, a legal ceremony because Rousseau (a Protestant) could not legally marry Thérèse (a Catholic) in France.

Various Writings

1. For Rousseau's description of this trip, see *Collected Writings,* V, 330. It took place September 22–28, 1754. It is unclear whether this itinerary was the planned one, the actual one, or based on recollection.
2. This town is the setting for *Julie.*
3. This defense against Hume's charge that Rousseau had rejected a pension from the king of England simply out of vanity was never published. It would have been written at the end of 1766.
4. This was probably written in April 1768 at a time when Rousseau believed that he was being accused of being a poisoner.
5. The Chateau at Trye belonged to the Prince de Conti. After his return from England, Rousseau stayed there from June 1767 to June 1768 under the name of Renou. Deschamps was the caretaker of the chateau.
6. Manoury (or Maunoury) was also employed at the chateau.
7. The warrant for Rousseau's arrest that had been issued in 1762 was still in force.
8. Reading "n'" rather than "m'" as in Pléiade.
9. By adding a "de" to Mme. Manoury's name here, Rousseau sarcastically elevates her to a higher social status.
10. Rousseau wrote this in 1768. In a letter, he says that he had amused himself by writing this list in pencil, had left it in a room, and then found that some changes had been made in it by ill-intentioned people. He made an accurate copy of the original so that changes could be identified.
11. The "Speech Planned or Pronounced in Order to Introduce the Reading of the *Confessions,*" which is fifth in the Pléiade can be found in *Collected Writings,* V, 592–593.
12. Rousseau wrote this, perhaps after a quarrel with his publisher, Rey. After several journals refused to print it, Rousseau made numerous copies and passed them out on the streets.
13. Rousseau kept this memorandum along with copies of letters.
14. At this time Rousseau was receiving from annuities the sum of 1,440 francs each year. He had also been earning an average of about 850 francs by copying music.
15. It is unclear when Rousseau wrote this. Possible dates range from 1772 to 1777. Its content is very similar to parts of the first one of the *Dialogues,* written in 1772–1773. See, in particular *Collected Writings,* I, 55.
16. Le Mierre might be Antoine-Marin Le Mierre (1723–1793) who had worked with Rousseau as secretary to the Dupin family in the 1740s and attended the first reading from the *Confessions* in 1779.

Course on Geography

1. This essay dates from the period of Rousseau's study of astronomy in Chambéry in the late 1730s.

2. The technical terms that Rousseau uses here are now somewhat archaic. His meanings are clear enough from his descriptions.

3. For an account of the Cartesian astronomy used by Rousseau here, see Richard B. Carter, *Descartes' Medical Philosophy: The Organic Solution to the Mind-Body Problem* (Baltimore: Johns Hopkins University Press, 1983), 159–166.

4. These are all the planets discovered by the time Rousseau wrote this. The next one, Uranus, was discovered in 1781.

5. Newton's figure is the correct one.

6. This idea can be found, in particular, in the *Treatise on the Existence of God*.

7. Rousseau left the page blank. The list can be found on 78 above.

8. Also known as Auriga.

9. Also known as Lyra

10. The manuscript breaks off here.

Response to the Anonymous Memorandum

1. The anonymous memorandum to which Rousseau refers was published in the *Mercury of France* in 1738. The issue being discussed is whether the earth is elongated or flattened at the poles; the first being the position of the Cartesians and the second, that of the Newtonians. The issue was settled in favor of the flatness of the poles by expeditions sent to make astronomical observations in Lapland and Peru. At the time of publication the first expedition had returned to Paris, but the second was not completed until 1744. For a very helpful discussion of the expeditions and the scientific controversy, see Mary Terrall, *The Man Who Flattened the Earth: Maupertuis and the Sciences in the Enlightenment* (Chicago: University of Chicago Press, 2002), 88–172. Rousseau refers to the expeditions in the *Second Discourse* (*Collected Writings*, III, 85).

2. Father André Tacquet (1612–1660) was a Jesuit mathematician and astronomer who is cited in the anonymous memorandum.

3. Rousseau is referring to Nicolas Fizes (1648–1718).

4. Jean Picard (1620–1682), Philippe de La Hire (1640–1718), and Jacques Cassini (1677–1756) were prominent mathematicians and astronomers.

5. In other words, on circular reasoning.

Memorandum Presented to M. de Mably on the Education of His Son

1. Rousseau was employed as tutor for the two sons of Jean Bonnot de Mably in Lyon from April 1740 through May 1741. The older of the two boys was not yet six years old when Rousseau became his tutor. For an account of this period see *Confessions*, Book VI, in *Collected Writings*, V, 223–228. The internal evidence of this memorandum indicates that it was written toward the end of 1740.

2. In the first draft Rousseau wrote, "by all the efforts."

3. Rousseau originally wrote, "over them."

4. Rousseau originally wrote, "neither."

5. Rousseau originally wrote, "him."

6. This refers to M. de Mably's brother Gabriel Bonnot, abbé de Mably, who wrote a number of important works on politics and history.

7. *Les Femmes savants,* IV, iii, line 1296.

8. Marcus Ternetius Varro (116–27 B.C.) was one of the most prolific writers of antiquity.

9. Rousseau originally wrote, "in making them regard."

10. Rousseau originally wrote, "explaining."

11. In the first draft Rousseau wrote, "natural things."

12. Rousseau originally wrote, "wit" (*esprit*).

13. Rousseau originally wrote, "accidents."

14. In the first draft Rousseau wrote, "their hearts."

15. Jean-Philippe Rameau (1683–1764) was the leading French composer of the century. Michel Blavet (1700–1768) was a musician. The Coypels were a family of painters. François Girardon (1628–1715 was a sculptor.

16. Rousseau originally wrote, "in others."

17. Rousseau originally wrote, "perfect oneself."

18. Rousseau originally wrote, "to society."

19. In the first draft Rousseau wrote, "in the soul."

20. Rousseau originally wrote, "with honorable people."

21. Rousseau originally wrote, "taste."

22. Rousseau originally wrote, "transported."

23. Rousseau originally wrote, "him."

24. In the earlier version Rousseau wrote, "the effects."

25. Both Molière and La Bruyère were among the authors Rousseau read when he was very young. See *Confesssions,* in *Collected Writings,* V, 8 and 93. Abbé Jean-Baptiste Morvan de Bellegarde published *Curious Letters on Literature and Morality* in 1701.

26. Rousseau originally wrote, "tone."

27. Rousseau originally wrote, "such thing."

28. Rousseau originally wrote, "in place of."

29. This is a sphere filled with water which is raised to a boiling point. The steam escapes through vents causing it to revolve.

30. On Hiero fountains, see *Confessions,* in *Collected Writings,* V, 85.

31. Rousseau began to write, "by the addition of."

32. In his *Treatise on Studies.*

33. *Abstract of the Principles of French Grammar* by Pierre Restaut published in 1732.

34. *Treatise on French Grammar* by abbé François-Séraphin Regnier-Desmarais was published in 1705. The other two authors are Claude Favre, baron de Péroges, seigneur de Vaugelas, and Father Dominique Bouhours.

35. The abbé de Mably was M. de Mably's brother.

36. Father Bernard Lamy's *The Art of Speaking* was published in 1675.

37. Rollin published his Quintillian's *Institutes* in 1715 and *On the Manner of Teaching and Studying Belles-lettres,* referred to below, from 1726 to 1728.

38. Published in 1687.

39. See Tacitus, *Annals,* VI, 47–48.

40. Rousseau originally wrote, "that air of Candor and truth."
41. Abbé Noël-Antoine Pluche published this work in eight volumes from 1732 to 1750.
42. Bernard Nieuwentyt wrote, *The Existence of God Demonstrated by the Marvels of Nature*, which was published in French translation in 1725.
43. Chevalier Jean-Charles de Folard pulished his commentary on Polybius from 1727 to 1730.
44. Abbé de Mably.

Plan for the Education of Monsieur de Sainte-Marie

1. Jean de La Bruyère, *Characters*, XI.
2. This refers to M. de Mably's brother Gabriel Bonnot, abbé de Mably.
3. *Les Femmes savants*, IV, iii, line 1296.
4. Abbé de Mably.
5. Abbé de Mably.

Rousseau to the abbé Guillaume-Thomas-François Raynal

1. This letter appeared in the *Mercury of France* in July 1753.
2. Guiluame-François Ruelle (1703–1770) gave courses on chemistry that Rousseau attended in the 1740s.
3. François Thierry was Rousseau's doctor.
4. Camille Falconet (1672–1762) was a consulting doctor for the king and presided over the faculty of medicine.
5. Joseph Paris Duverney (1684–1770) was the first intendant of the Ecole Militaire in Paris.
6. Louis-François de Bourbon, prince de Conti later became one of Rousseau's protectors. On the beginning of their relations, see *Confessions*, Book X (*Collected Writings*, V, 453–454).
7. The Senator is Carl Fredrik Scheffer and the lady is Mme. Dupin, who had been Rousseau's employer.
8. Joseph Amy developed the domestic fountains that Rousseau mentions in his letter. He wrote a pamphlet promoting the use of these as an alternative to copper receptacles for water.

Treatise on the Sphere

1. This work appears to have been written sometime around 1767.
2. The copy of the manuscript, which is not in Rousseau's hand, reads *meme*, which editors have replaced with *méne*.
3. The edition published in 1861 reads, "it is necessary to study men, and to study men it is necessary to do it at various times, in various places."
4. This discussion can be compared with the one in *Emile*, Book III.
5. Since Rousseau lived at the Prince de Conti's home at Trye from June 1767 until June 1768, this reference is evidence that he wrote this work during that period.
6. The manuscript actually reads, "position," which appears to be a slip.

7. Greenwich was not agreed upon as the location of the prime meridian until late in the nineteenth century.

8. Editors have corrected the manuscript, which disrupts the parallel by saying, "the East."

9. By North Sea, Rousseau indicates the Atlantic Ocean and by South Sea, the Pacific.

10. The 1861 edition erroneously reads, "West."

11. The 1861 edition reads, "immense seas, whose salt water keeps them from corruption."

12. The words, "Providence has," are omitted from the manuscript.

The New Daedalus

1. This work was originally published as a pamphlet in 1801, apparently from a manuscript that had passed through several hands. The manuscript has been lost. At the time of publication it was claimed that Rousseau wrote it in 1742. This date would correspond with his arrival in Paris with his system of musical notation. Dates as late as 1752 have also been suggested. The date of 1742 is suggestive because it corresponds to the marquis de Bacqueville's attempt at flight in which he succeeded in gliding for approximately three hundred meters. A very good discussion of the work and its background can be found in Jean-Jacques Rousseau, *Le Nouveau Dédale: A Reproduction of the First Edition,* with an Introduction by Members of the Staff of the Aeronautics Division, Library of Congress (Pasadena, Calif.: Institute of Aeronautical History, n.d.).

2. The edition reads "the eyes and reason," but Rousseau's parallel and the sense of the sentence seem to require the reading given here.

3. It is likely that the first time Rousseau saw a seagoing vessel was in 1743 when he traveled to Venice to become secretary to the French ambassador. Having spent his earliest years in Geneva, he was very familiar with small boats.

4. In his opera *Discovery of the New World,* composed in 1741, Rousseau has an Indian refer to these ships as "winged monsters" (*Collected Writings,* X, 24).

5. Andrea Doria (1466–1560) was a Genoese admiral who fought numerous sea battles against the Turks.

6. The Black Sea.

7. At this point the published version interrupts the text with the note.

8. The fable of the tortoise and the two ducks is from La Fontaine's *Fables,* Book X, Fable 2. The tortoise is taken aloft by two ducks by means of a stick held in her mouth. In the air she proclaims herself to be the queen of all tortoises and lets go of the stick, falling to the ground.

9. Leander was a young man from Abydos who fell in love with Hero who lived in Sestos. Each night she placed a light in a tower and Leander swam across the Hellespont to meet her. One night the light went out and he drowned. She then committed suicide.

10. Alfonso Borelli was the author of *De Motu Animalium* (1680) in which, based on comparisons between the anatomy of birds and of humans, he argued that men were not strong enough to fly on their own power, even if they were equipped with wings.

11. Honoratus Fabri (1607–1688), a Jesuit, was the author of *Physica Rerum Corpoerearum*, in which he argued that rockets could be adapted to make flight possible.

12. For Rousseau's experience with Hiero-fountains, see *Confessions*, in *Collected Writings*, V, 85–86. A Hiero-fountain has two chambers, one of which is filled with wine and the other with water. It uses air pressure to move the contents of one chamber into the other.

13. A quintal weighs a hundred pounds.

14. The pamphlet misspells Fabri here.

15. In effect Rousseau translates this quotation in the sentences preceding and following it as "One could not see anything more wonderful than someone wandering for a long time through the medium of the air." This is an approximate translation of the passage. I thank Jim Nendza for his assistance with Fabri's Latin.

16. At this point the published version interrupts the text with the note.

17. Rousseau discusses air pressure in the *Moral Letters*, 185 below and in *Emile*.

18. This is reminiscent of the frontispiece of the *First Discourse* and Rousseau's explanation of it in the "Letter to Lecat" (*Collected Writings*, II, 179).

Fragments on God and Revelation

1. It has been suggested that this fragment was written around 1735; in other words, when Rousseau was in his early to mid-twenties.

2. Editors place this prayer, and the following one, between 1736 and 1738, when Rousseau was living at Les Charmettes.

3. The manuscript actually reads "our," which most editors consider to be a slip.

4. Rousseau first wrote, "all the beings," which was then crossed out and replaced (perhaps in someone else's hand) with "this universe," which was crossed out and replaced with "the whole world."

5. After this Rousseau added and then crossed out, "today I make the firm resolution to."

6. Rousseau originally wrote "deign to have pity on my weakness and on all the vices into which." The passage is replaced (perhaps in someone else's hand) by the one in the text.

7. Rousseau originally wrote, "the neighbor"; the alteration appears to be in someone else's hand.

Memorandum Delivered April 19, 1742, to Monsignor Boudet, Antonine

1. For the story behind this memorandum and its consequences for Rousseau, see *Confessions*, in *Collected Writings*, V, 101.

2. For Rousseau's account of these events, see *Confessions*, in *Collected Writings*, V, 41–42.

Fiction or Allegorical Fragment on Revelation

1. Numerous suggestions have been made about the date of this work ranging from the beginning of Rousseau's literary career to the very end of his life. Most recent critics place it around 1756–1757. For a discussion of the "Fiction," see Christopher Kelly, *Rousseau as Author: Consecrating One's Life to the Truth* (Chicago: University of Chicago Press, 2003), 155–171.

2. Rousseau originally wrote "life," rather than "heat."

3. Rousseau discusses the "great chain of beings" in the "Letter to Voltaire," *Collected Writings,* III, 114.

4. The form of the French possessive pronoun used by Rousseau requires a plural noun, but his manuscript gives a singular. The Pléiade editors have supplied the plural ending of the noun in brackets.

5. Rousseau originally wrote, "ideas," rather than "lights."

6. Rousseau originally wrote, "divine," rather than "new."

7. Given the description of four of the statues that follows, it seems clear that the statues represent the seven deadly sins.

8. Rousseau originally wrote, "Everyone come to serve," and then, "Everyone hasten and serve," before settling on the formulation in the text.

9. At this point in the manuscript occurs the following passage, which has been crossed out: "Depicted on its visage was seen ecstasy with fury; death and hell were under its feet, but its eyes were turned toward heaven. In the left hand it was holding a blazing heart and in the other it was sharpening a dagger." A passage closely resembling this appears several paragraphs below in the final version.

10. The manuscript alternates between "perceived" and "saw uncovered" before settling on the former. After this sentence comes the following passage, which has been crossed out: "The Philosopher who had approached without being observed dared to draw aside the veil with a reckless hand but—frightened by a thousand menacing cries—he let it fall back and hastily withdrawing, he contented himself with examining in secret everything that struck his eyes." In this passage between "fall back" and "and hastily" the following passage was struck out: "The veil drew itself aside for the philosopher but he soon closed it himself seeing himself threatened by a dagger."

11. Rousseau first wrote and then crossed out "the phantom of his own mind," rather than "the idol of his own heart."

12. Rousseau originally wrote, "Pythagoras," and then "The Philosopher," each of which is crossed out.

13. Here and several places below the manuscript gives only the letter "h," which Rousseau frequently used as an abbreviation for *hommes* (men).

14. This sentence is an addition to the original draft.

15. The manuscript gives a singular verb that has been corrected by the Pléiade editors.

16. At this point in the margin of the manuscript occur the words "and all the most sublime ideas that we attached to this word, *God,* presented themselves to his mind." The words have been crossed out and appear a few paragraphs earlier in the final version.

17. Rousseau originally wrote and then crossed out, "infamous and barbarous" and then, "execrable and barbarous," before settling on horrible.

18. Rousseau originally wrote and then crossed out, "a man who was accompanying him" and then "a man he suddenly noticed close to him," before settling on "the invisible being who had already spoken to him." There is no such figure earlier in the story as it stands.

19. Numerous attempts have been made to identify this figure. It seems quite likely that the figure is the philosopher himself. The man attempts to do what the philosopher had been planning on doing before he fell asleep. The dream is a warning not to do it.

20. All the details of this section suggest that the old man is Socrates.

21. Rousseau first wrote and then crossed out, "the hope for a miracle made the priests not very fastidious about verifying the blindness."

22. For a useful account of the "son of man" in the Bible, see Henri Gouhier, *Les Méditations métaphysiques de Jean-Jacques Rousseau* (Paris: J. Vrin, 1970), 202–203.

23. Rousseau first wrote and then crossed out, "his bearing, modest and grave without being base or imperious."

24. Rousseau originally wrote and crossed out, "the purest divine morality."

25. In place of "for his defense" some editors beginning with Streckeisen-Moultou have put "and neglected to defend him seeing that he did not want to attack at all." This phrase occurs at the bottom of the manuscript page without any indication of where or if it belongs in the manuscript. At that point Rousseau first wrote and then crossed out, "did not any longer defend the one who did not want to attack at all.

26. Rousseau first wrote and then struck out "robust people," instead of "men."

27. This word is unclear in the manuscript. Rousseau originally wrote and then struck out, "raised up."

28. The manuscript ends here.

Fragments on the Infinite Power of God

1. It is not known when Rousseau wrote this. The subject matter has some resemblance to the *Essay on the Origin of Languages* or the *Letter to d'Alembert*.

2. See *Daniel*, 25–28. God causes a hand to write these words on a wall in front of Balthasar. Rousseau discusses this in the *Letter to d'Alembert*, in *Collected Writings*, X, 340.

Moral Letters

1. These letters were written around 1756. Rousseau did not give theme letters any title. Letters 2, 3, and 4 were published for the first time in 1861 under the title of *Letters on Virtue and Happiness*. Letters 1, 5, and 6 were published for the first time in 1888.

2. Rousseau first wrote, "the voice of your friend."

3. Rousseau first wrote, "at least my mouth was not the accomplice of my going astray."

4. The term is "travestie," which means cross-dressed. In the *Confessions* Rousseau says that he fell in love with Sophie when she paid him a visit dressed like a man. See *Collected Writings,* V, 369.

5. In the first draft Rousseau wrote, "reason did not prostitute itself to shameful sophisms for the defense of the error.

6. In the margin Rousseau added and crossed out numerous phrases, the most significant of which read, "humiliated vice did not aspire to usurp."

7. Instead of "Sophie," Rousseau originally wrote, "Sophism." Sophie is Elisabeth-Sophie-Françoise Lalive de Bellegarde (1730–1813) who married the Comte d'Houdetot when she was eighteen. Rousseau first met her shortly after her marriage. For his account of his relations with her, see *Confessions,* Books IX–X.

8. Rousseau originally wrote, 'those of which you are unaware."

9. Rousseau originally wrote and crossed out, "at that time."

10. Rousseau first wrote, "noble."

11. Rousseau first wrote, "a love such as mine could be vanquished only by itself."

12. Rousseau first wrote, "ceasing to love you."

13. After this Rousseau originally added, "not less charming and more durable."

14. At the time Rousseau wrote this letter, Sophie had two daughters and a son. Her husband had a brilliant military career, but in the *Confessions* Rousseau says that, in spite of his merits, he was "a gambler, argumentative, hardly lovable at all" (*Collected Writings,* V, 370). He also says that Sophie never loved him.

15. Rousseau first wrote, "gifts."

16. Rousseau first wrote, "listen to."

17. Rousseau first wrote, "and to be what it asks of you," and then "and to be what it wants you to be."

18. Rousseau first wrote, "confirmed inside of you by the very voice of nature."

19. After this Rousseau originally wrote and then crossed out, "authorize everything that he has felt for you."

20. Rousseau first wrote, "honor the rest of my life."

21. After "yes, Sophie," Rousseau first wrote, "and if my presentiments do not deceive me in this undertaking, my efforts, your progress will one day make it seen how far zeal and courage can take the place of talent for instructing and redouble that of learning."

22. Rousseau wrote several versions of this phrase, including, "on relations the least perishable of all," "on human relations," and "on relations that pertain to the soul and can perish only with it."

23. Rousseau first wrote, "It is in vain that fortune and the wicked keep us apart from each other."

24. Rousseau first wrote, "who knows so well the state of my heart."

25. Rousseau first wrote, "my."

26. Rousseau first wrote, "if ever."

27. Rousseau first added, "would be gratified in making."

28. Rousseau first added, "it seems to me that I would be much more esteemed myself for it if the whole world knew how much I (my heart) honors you."

29. Rousseau first wrote, "the suspicions of the curious."

30. Rousseau first wrote, "They know."

31. The term translated as "labyrinth" here is "*dédale*," from Daedalus. Below, Rousseau uses the word "labirinthe."

32. Rousseau first wrote, "wise people when one listens to them, insane people when they are all alone."

33. Sophie was eighteen years younger than Rousseau. She was twenty-seven at the time these letters were written.

34. Rousseau originally wrote "depths of the soul," rather than "heart."

35. In the margin of this passage Rousseau wrote, "Reason is the faculty of making use of all the faculties of our soul in the manner most suitable to the nature of things and their relation with us." This sentence is found on p. 182 below.

36. The word is "climat," which could also be translated as "climate."

37. In the margin of this passage Rousseau wrote, "now the true relationship of things to man is not at all known to him by reasoning but by feeling; for if he does not feel anything, all the reasoning in the world could not teach him to order anything in relation to himself. But, such as he is, he has no need of reasoning to judge what is good or bad in relation to himself, and feeling alone teaches him that better than all arguments."

38. Rousseau is probably referring to George Berkeley (1685–1753). In the *First Discourse* Rousseau makes a similar statement, saying, "This one holds that there are no bodies and that everything is appearance" (*Collected Writings*, II, 20). In the "Letter to Franquières" (*Collected Writings*, VIII, 264) he says "[W]hile all of modern philosophy rejects spirits, suddenly Bishop Berkley arises and maintains there is no body. How has anyone managed to respond to this fearsome logician?"

39. This could refer to any number of materialists.

40. This refers to Malebranche and his doctrine of occasional causes.

41. As Pléiade indicates, this is a somewhat imprecise reference to Leibniz.

42. Rousseau first wrote, "these cruel sensual pleasures in which the small number swim and which are purchased at the expense of a crowd of unhappy people."

43. After this paragraph Rousseau wrote and crossed out, "We have said a thousand times, Sophie, one is happy only by feeling and all these things give none at all. What use is it for reasoning to build us ingenious systems of felicity that the heart ceaselessly gives the lie to? Reason holds back more than it incites." Beneath this he wrote, "and if man were only reasonable he would remain in an eternal inactivity." In the margin, he wrote, "the art of reasoning is a very different thing than reason."

44. In the margin next to this passage Rousseau wrote, "what then, will it

be necessary to pass our lives in learning how to live, and will we know what we ought to do only at the moment it is necessary to die?"

45. After this Rousseau originally wrote and then crossed out, "and leads from errors in errors to crime and to the misfortune of the mad man (proud man) who gives himself over to it." In the margin Rousseau wrote, "finally by dint of study they arrived at no longer knowing whether man has a body and a soul or one of the two, whether he is a machine, a God, or a beast: neither why he comes, nor why he stays, nor why he goes, nor what he is, nor what he will be, nor what he ought to do to make the best possible use of his existence.

"All these so-called wise men who still philosophize in old age are children who have wasted their whole lives in vain meditations. Observe them and you will find that after so many studies they are not worth any more at a hundred years than at thirty. A citizen of Sparta having found one of these old men in a school of philosophy, completely surprised asked him what he was doing there. 'He is learning,' they told him, 'wisdom.' 'When will he practice it then?' retorted the indignant Spartan."

46. Each of the pairs in these two sentences represents philosophic opponents.

47. Rousseau originally added, "that shows it to us."

48. In the margin Rousseau wrote, "to prove that shame is natural in the article on the conscience."

49. Rousseau originally wrote, "eternally."

50. This case formed the basis of Diderot's *Letter on the Blind* in 1749. The hypothetical case had been raised by the blind geometrician William Molyneux and discussed in Locke's *Essay on Human Understanding*, II, ix, par. 8.

51. Rousseau first wrote, "distinguish a picture from a true countryside," then "a painted object from the original."

52. This paragraph replaces the following one: "Without reflecting about it well, one has difficulty conceiving how many false judgments we would put forward by our eyes if our hands and our feet did not correct these blunders: the entire universe would not be any larger than the eye, there would not be any absolute size for us, we would not imagine any difference between moving objects away and making them smaller, and the same body carried twice the distance would be smaller by half."

53. Rousseau discusses this example in Book III of *Emile*.

54. Rousseau first wrote, "do not furnish him with enough," and then " no longer furnish him with."

55. Rousseau first wrote, "philosophy, greedy to explain everything."

56. Rousseau first wrote, "the most absurd systems."

57. In the margin of this passage Rousseau wrote, "what do you think my dear Sophie of a system in which one preferred to give feeling to rocks than to grant a soul to man?"

58. In place of "soul, body," Rousseau first wrote, "mind, matter."

59. Rousseau first wrote, "The most common phenomenon," then "the most common operation of nature."

60. Buffon, the first several volumes of whose *Histoire naturelle générale et particulière* had been published by the time Rousseau wrote this, presents a very tentative mechanistic account of generation.

61. Condillac's statue is described in his *Treatise on Sensations,* published in 1754. Rousseau had assisted Condillac in the publication of the *Essay on the Origin of Human Knowledge.* In *Emile,* he says, "I do not doubt that posterity will give him an honorable and distinguished place among the best reasoners and the most profound metaphysicians of his age" (*Emile,* Bloom ed., 107).

62. Rousseau first wrote, "endowed with other senses about which we have no idea," then, "endowed with more senses than we have."

63. Rousseau first wrote, "clear of the darkness that hides from us the essence of the things by which we feel ourselves surrounded."

64. Rousseau originally added, "Let us not imagine, then, that the senses are fixed at the number five for all animals."

65. In the margin Rousseau wrote, "oh my Sophie what a dreadful abyss for reason."

66. In the margin Rousseau wrote, "and we want to get mixed up with reasoning about the nature of beings! In truth I would barely pardon this foolishness in children."

67. In the margin Rousseau wrote, "Plato's idea about those that come back."

68. Rousseau first wrote, "eternal admirers of the order of nature, spectators and righteous judges about men's actions."

69. On the chain of beings, see above 165.

70. Rousseau first wrote, "The more man sounds himself, the smaller he sees himself. That is what his best study leads to."

71. Rousseau first wrote, "works of God?"

72. At the bottom of the page, in the margin Rousseau wrote, "But I feel in myself a secret murmur that rouses me up against such debasement." This is followed by the following, crossed out: "without being a philosopher, I feel myself a man and still find myself great enough for Sophie." The passage proceeds, "To what eyes can a being sensitive to the beautiful be contemptible? No Sophie the one that the contemplation of . . . animated near you by a holy enthusiasm is not at all an insect."

73. In the margin next to these lines Rousseau wrote, "I would be ashamed of you and of myself; I would feel that we had been contemptible, that we would have unworthily abused everything most inviolable and sacred in esteem, friendship, confidence, without a doubt I would hate you for having let me debase myself, you would hate me even more justly."

74. Rousseau first wrote, "universe: we feel that a being capable of justice."

75. In the margin of this passage Rousseau wrote, "If we had been, myself more lovable or you weaker, could the memory of my pleasures be as sweet as that of your innocence." After "weak" Rousseau first wrote, "would the witness of the innocence that your fidelity has preserved in me be so sweet in my heart." The passage proceeds, "would I shed the delightful tears that escape me while writing these letters, would you be as dear to me after having satisfied my wishes

as you are after having made me wise." On a separate sheet this passage continues, "and nevertheless amid the pleasures that I am tasting, I still lack the sweetest of all, I do not have that of making my resistance into a merit, I am as guilty as if I had succumbed, without you I was lost, I was the least of men, and it is you who have forced me to vanquish myself."

76. Rousseau originally wrote, "and I believe I can say better than that character, Chr[emes]."

77. The line "Homo sum, humani nihil a me alienum puto" is in Terence's *Hautontimorumenos*.

78. After this sentence Rousseau originally wrote, "desires, by degrees extinguished along with hope, I no longer see anything but my past life, and its duration ceases to be dear to me since my heart no longer has anything new to feel." A very similar passage occurs three paragraphs below.

79. Rousseau first wrote, "My disfavors were less bitter when I could say to myself that I did not deserve them. And my happiness lost all its value."

80. Rousseau first wrote, "my happiness," and then, "pleasure."

81. Here Rousseau first added and then struck out, "so to speak."

82. Some editors insert the passage in note 72 above here.

83. At this point Rousseau successively wrote and struck out, "friendship," "inclination," and "interest" before settling on "friendship."

84. Some editors insert the passage in note 75 above here.

85. Rousseau first wrote, "charm," then, "honor," before settling on "charm."

86. Rousseau first wrote, "disgraceful man."

87. Rousseau first wrote, "barrier: that you ceaselessly put between you and me."

88. In the margin of this passage Rousseau wrote, "what a horrible knowledge is the one that serves only to remove scruples, stifle remorse, and multiply the number of wicked people on the earth."

89. The word translated as "take the place," is *suppléer*, which can also have the sense of "add on to."

90. After "fortune," Rousseau originally wrote, "and console us for our . . ." In crossing out the phrase and adding the end of the sentence he crossed out "and" without replacing it as the sense of the sentence seems to require.

91. At the bottom of this sheet of paper Rousseau wrote and crossed out the following remarks, which appear to be drafts of the beginning of the next letter. First, "All the morality of human life is in intentions." Previously he had written, "The entire morality of human actions is in the estimation of those who do them." Then he wrote, "is in men's wills." Second, "If it is true that the good is good, it ought to be so at the bottom of our hearts as in our works." He fist wrote, "in the actions of our life." The remark continues, "and the first reward for virtue is to feel that one is practicing it."

92. Rousseau vacillated between "will" and "intention." In the margin of this passage he wrote, "Even his good actions lose their worth at the bottom of his soul from the lack of this motive."

93. Rousseau vacillated between "virtue" and "justice."

94. Rousseau originally wrote, "In him goodness would be a vice of conformation."

95. After this Rousseau originally added, "Does it seem to you, oh Sophie, that that could be a question?"

96. In the margin of this passage Rousseau wrote, "Oh Let us return into ourselves oh my good friend. Let us examine . . ."

97. After this point Rousseau first wrote and then crossed out, "a crime or a good action."

98. From this point in the paragraph Rousseau originally wrote in the first-person plural. In changing it to the second person he did not always change the verbs. Nor did he always change the pronouns. Most editors correct the text. It should be noted that when he addresses Sophie directly Rousseau uses the more intimate second-person singular.

99. At this point Rousseau added and then crossed out, "do the malefactors have all our secret wishes."

100. After "tears," Rousseau successively wrote and then crossed out, "of tenderness," "of pity," and "of emotion."

101. Rousseau first wrote, "the horror of crime."

102. After "us," Rousseau first wrote, "over that of all other evils."

103. This paragraph should be compared with the argument of the *Letter to d'Alembert,* where Rousseau grants the reality of the theatrical experience of pity, but insists upon its sterility. See *Collected Writings,* X, 268–269.

104. This paragraph was added in the margin. In it Rousseau made many changes. The original version is put in parentheses. The passage read, "One of the torments (of the greatest tortures) that the civil state imposes on well-born people (private individuals) is always to see evil, and not to dare either to oppose it or to pity it (and to leave the wicked all-powerful) but a more powerful duty holds us back and it is a crime in the social order to make opposition to the evil one sees being done."

105. After this Rousseau originally wrote, "some murderer on the highway who takes pity."

106. Rousseau first wrote, "even traitors and the perfidious."

107. In place of this sentence Rousseau first wrote, "Oh man whoever you might be, sound your heart, however perverse you are capable of being sound your heart."

108. Rousseau first wrote, "One speaks very much about the voice of remorse that punishes hidden crimes in secret and so often makes them public by means of the terror of the guilty people."

109. Rousseau first wrote, "in feeling the applause."

110. In the margin Rousseau wrote, "Picture of the happiness of the just."

111. Rousseau first wrote, "morality," then "virtue," before arriving at "decency."

112. Rousseau originally continued, "that were worshipped."

113. Rousseau first wrote, "disgraceful passions."

114. Rousseau made numerous changes to this passage. The first versions are in parentheses. He wrote, "But crime seemed to descend in vain from Olympus

(from Heaven) on the earth; the holy voice of nature (holy imprint of virtue) repulsed it."

115. Rousseau made numerous changes to this passage. The first versions are in parentheses. He wrote, "Never has one seen a Religion so impure (depraved) and of such holy maxims, such contemptible divinities were never implored by such great men and virtue triumphed over the example of the gods (triumphed in the hearts of mortals). Jupiter could commit incest, Xenocrates was not any less temperate (chaste)."

116. Rousseau originally added, "in spite of them."

117. Rousseau first wrote, "eternal," then "immortal," before settling on "innate."

118. Rousseau first wrote, "give to the first liar."

119. Rousseau first wrote, "be of good faith."

120. Rousseau first wrote, "or virtue be punished and heinous crimes rewarded."

121. On the love of oneself see *Collected Writings III*, 91.

122. Rousseau originally added, "that sustains (confirms) our feeling."

123. Above these three words, the manuscript reads, "Good young man." As the word "friend" is in the feminine, it appears that Rousseau considered adapting this letter for a male audience (as is the case for equivalent passages in *Emile*).

124. After "pleasures" Rousseau originally wrote, "and in order to free themselves from heaviness of conscience, they deprive themselves of the very sensual pleasures into which it would be sweet to immolate oneself."

125. The word translated as "voluptuous pleasure" is *volupté*, which has a primary meaning of sensual pleasure, but can mean exquisite pleasure of any sort. Rousseau's point is that the pleasure involved in sexuality is not primarily or simply one of sensation.

126. In the margin Rousseau added, "If virtue is nothing, if friendship is only habit, personal interest, what true pleasures (moral) can we taste on the earth?"

127. Rousseau originally wrote, "desires."

128. Rousseau vacillated between "give them over" and "would give them over."

129. Rousseau first wrote, "sophisms of reason."

130. Rousseau first wrote, "as the instinct of nature alone first showed them to us."

131. The letter stops here and the following passages are notes written on the same sheet of paper.

132. Instead of "divine instinct," Rousseau successively wrote, "sublime voice," "pure voice," "celestial voice," and "intimate voice."

133. In place of this, Rousseau first wrote, "model of the true (beautiful)" and then "unique guide of an intelligent and free but ignorant and limited being."

134. Rousseau first wrote, "divine."

135. Rousseau first wrote, "its."

136. Rousseau first wrote, "with the aid of my reason."

137. In the "Profession of Faith," equivalent passages to this and the next paragraph occur in *Emile* (Bloom ed.), 291.

138. Rousseau first wrote, "but it is not enough that it speaks to us, it is necessary to hear it, it is necessary to distinguish its voice, to learn to be acquainted with it."

139. Rousseau added and then struck out, "my dear," between "oh" and "Sophie."

140. Rousseau first wrote, "keep it from daring to raise itself in our hearts (souls)."

141. Rousseau originally wrote, "of exhaustion."

142. Rousseau first wrote, "return," then, "becoming again."

143. Rousseau first added here, "the first way of knowing ourselves well consists in gathering ourselves together well."

144. Rousseau first wrote, "know well the limits of human nature."

145. The word here is "*votres*," but numerous editors think this is a slip on Rousseau's part and should read "*autres*," which would be "others."

146. Rousseau first wrote, "confine."

147. This remark is actually taken from Montaigne (*Essays*, III, 3) and is quoted by d'Alembert in his preface to Jean Terrasson's *Philosophy Applicable to All the Objects of the Mind and Reason*.

148. The word translated as "unsociable," is *sauvage*.

149. Rousseau first wrote, "No, Sophie."

150. Rousseau originally added, "which is to know yourself" at the end of this sentence.

151. Rousseau first wrote, "in the city."

152. Rousseau first wrote, "this will be if you wish a visit to make, you will be going to see Sophie."

153. In the margin of this passage Rousseau wrote, "do not deny to your own hands the honor of being beneficent."

154. In the margin of this passage Rousseau wrote, "soon a secret voice will speak to your heart and will say to you: you are not alone, your good actions have a witness."

155. Rousseau first wrote, "singing without rule and flying here and there, birds."

156. Rousseau first wrote, "odor of the grass and flowers."

157. In the margin Rousseau repeats this sentence with "your," rather than "our." He also wrote "pure" rather than "sweet," but struck it out and replaced it with "sweet."

158. In the margin of this passage Rousseau wrote, "in the most profound solitude your heart tells you that you are not alone."

159. In the margin Rousseau wrote, "To that, I have nothing to say to you but that I have employed the same means, that they have led me by the same route, that I believe I have a healthy soul and I am certain of my good faith."

160. In the margin Rousseau wrote, "and in (the search for) the objects of your pleasures give preference to the things that one still enjoys when one no longer possesses them."

161. The passage that begins here is a version of a part of the "Profession of Faith." See *Emile* (Bloom ed.), 291.

162. Rousseau first wrote, "you will be satisfied with your self," and then, "you will be pleased with yourself."

163. Rousseau vacillated between the passage as it stands and "an idea of force and superiority," before settling on the version in the text.

164. After this Rousseau originally added, "I can restate my precept in fewer words: lead yourself back to yourself."

165. In the margin Rousseau wrote, "N.B. divide or shorten the sentence."

166. Rousseau first wrote, "promenades."

167. Rousseau first concluded the sentence, "so noble an effort but the desire (zeal) for doing good will easily smooth them."

168. Rousseau first wrote, "coarse people."

169. After "in secret," Rousseau first wrote, "ask yourself: 'and I, am I perfect?'"

170. The clause beginning "consider . . ." originally read, "Ah, if you take an interest only in people without fault go to bring your benefits somewhere else rather than among men. Are the coarse vices of the peasant more odious than those that a little education covers with a more decent appearance?"

171. Rousseau first wrote, "boredom alone will turn you away more from these salutary occupations than humanity will be able to lead you to them and will tell you a thousand sophisms in order to dispense you from them."

172. A version of the passage that begins here and ends "did not let go," can be found in the "Profession of Faith," *Emile* (Bloom ed.), 291.

173. Rousseau originally wrote, "Do not dispense yourself from these honorable efforts to have them fulfilled by Servants."

174. Rousseau first wrote, "half."

Notes on Helvétius's *On the Mind*

1. *On the Mind* by Claude-Adrien Helvétius was published anonymously in 1758 and was quickly censored. In the *Letters Written from the Mountain* Rousseau explains that, prior to the prosecution of Helvétius, he had planned on writing a refutation, but decided against it "judging that no duty could authorize the baseness of join the crowd to overwhelm an oppressed man of honor" (*Collected Writings*, IX, 138). He goes on to explain that he addressed these issues in later writings without naming either Helvétius or his book. The italicized passages in the text represent the passages in *On the Mind* commented on by Rousseau. The page references are to the first edition, which is the one owned by Rousseau.

2. The term here is *mémoire*, but Rousseau also uses *souvenir*. The distinction seems to be between memory in the sense of a faculty and memory in the sense of a particular thing remembered.

3. This note was apparently added later than the others and is crossed out.

4. The word here is *esprit*.

5. Rousseau originally added and then crossed out, "exactly."

6. Rousseau first wrote, "because the comparison of yellow and red is independent of the sensation of yellow and of that of red."

7. Rousseau first wrote, "your conclusion."

8. Rousseau first wrote, "that are."

9. The statement actually reads, "more of my intelligence," which editors take to be a slip.

10. This statement was apparently added later and is crossed out. Rousseau's reference is to the relations between Philip II and his secretary, Antonio Perez. Philip condemned Perez to death, but Perez found refuge in France in the court of Henri IV.

11. Rousseau first wrote, "but not."

12. These last two sentences are a later addition.

13. Rousseau underlined this passage.

14. Rousseau discusses a version of this maxim in the *Reveries,* See *Collected Writings,* VIII, 29.

15. The word translated as "well-behaved" is *sages.*

16. This can have the connotation of spiritual adviser, or confessor.

17. This article appeared in 1756. Its author is unidentified and it has been suggested that it was François Quesnay.

18. This note was apparently added later than the others. Its reference to the "Profession of Faith" indicates that it was written after Rousseau completed *Emile,* which was published in 1762.

Queen Whimsical

1. Rousseau probably completed this work in the spring of 1756. It was printed without his permission in 1758. In the preface to this edition it was denounced, perhaps facetiously, as a dangerous work attacking the laws, morals, and religion. The publication of such a work was justified by the desire to unmask the false philosophy of the author. Rousseau gave permission for it to be published in a collection of his writings, although he later said that he regretted having done so.

2. This foreword was written by Rousseau.

3. At the top of the manuscript Rousseau wrote, "N.B. have this recopied by someone who knows how to follow and who is very attentive.

4. Rousseau originally wrote, "This is doubtless a Fairy Tale that you are making up."

5. Rousseau originally wrote, "Precisely."

6. The manuscript reads, "as well intentioned as he."

7. Rousseau originally wrote, "imbecility."

8. The manuscript reads, "maleficent."

9. The manuscript reads, "since he was extremely intoxicated."

10. The manuscript reads, "he acted as a consequence."

11. The manuscript reads, "capricious."

12. The manuscript reads simply, "a hood."

13. The manuscript reads, "uselessly."

14. At this point the manuscript adds, "I say six months, not in succession; that would have been so much rest for her husband; but taken in the intervals suited to annoy him."
15. The manuscript reads, "all the love."
16. Literally, "not knowing which saint to devote himself to."
17. The manuscript reads, "From the moment."
18. The manuscript reads, "try to give way."
19. The manuscript reads, "to comply with the Fairy's advice, returned to the Queen's Circle and taking her aside said to her."
20. The manuscript reads, "disputed against her."
21. The manuscript reads, "all the ridicule."
22. The Divan was the Turkish council of state presided over by the Grand Vizier.
23. The edition of 1758 reads, "unheard of," rather than "infinite."
24. The manuscript adds, "as best she could."
25. The manuscript reads, "that could cast ridicule upon (make extravagant) the forgetfulness of the others."
26. The manuscript reads, "quilt (cornet)."
27. The manuscript reads, "Eh."
28. The manuscript reads, "all the stupid things."
29. Pierre d'Ortigues de Vaumorière (1610–1690) wrote novels and *Harangues on All Sorts of Subjects, with the Art of Composing Them.*
30. Diogenes the Cynic rolled his barrel upon noticing the furious activity of his fellow citizens when their city was under siege.
31. The manuscript reads, "Ladies of the palace."
32. The manuscript reads, "she had not failed to communicate it with the greatest precautions to all the Ladies (women) of her house."
33. Rousseau originally added, "convenient."
34. Rousseau originally wrote, "mischievous pleasure."
35. The manuscript reads, "Monsieur Druid."
36. The manuscript reads, "digressions, portraits, and that multitude."
37. The manuscript reads, "provoke (amuse)."
38. Rousseau originally wrote, "one hastens to cover one's display case with the."
39. The manuscript reads, "that your words are worth more than others' wit and that in order to avoid."
40. The manuscript reads, "it is a great pity (is so boring)."
41. The manuscript reads, "the essential."
42. Rousseau originally wrote, "truly."
43. The manuscript omits, "to the people."
44. Rousseau originally wrote, "tenderly."
45. The manuscript reads, "masters."
46. The manuscript reads, "the."
47. The manuscript reads, "the greater glory."
48. Rousseau originally wrote, "cover the heads of scoundrels."
49. Rousseau originally wrote, "was content to have."

50. The manuscript reads, "did not shrivel up any less."
51. The manuscript reads, "no bosom so beautiful."
52. The manuscript reads, "Mother."
53. Vaugirard was a suburb of Paris, but has been absorbed into the city.
54. This is a reference to the argument of Rousseau's "Letter on French Music," which denies that there is any French music. See *Collected Writings*, VII, 141–174.
55. In other words, saints. The reference is to the practice of naming children after saints to obtain their intercession with God.
56. Rousseau first wrote, "was content to have."
57. The manuscript reads, "presumptive heir."
58. Rousseau first wrote, "plans."
59. The manuscript reads, "exasperate."
60. Rousseau originally wrote, "triumphantly."
61. The manuscript reads, "dissuade her."
62. Rousseau originally wrote, "caprices."
63. Rousseau originally wrote, "torture."
64. The manuscript reads, "regret for his faults will cause him to commit even greater (new) ones."
65. Rousseau originally wrote, "will not have any better success."
66. Rousseau originally wrote, "perverting."
67. The manuscript reads, "chance."
68. Rousseau originally wrote, "bear."
69. Rousseau originally wrote, "what abundance."
70. These two fairy tales were put into verse by Charles Perrault (1628–1703). Perrault was a participant in the "quarrel between the ancients and the moderns," referred to by Rousseau (23–24 above). It should be noted that the two fairy tales referred to by Rousseau here are notable for involving murder and incest. The contrast with Machiavelli made in the text is not based on the innocence of the fairy tales.
71. Rousseau originally wrote, "in the place of."
72. Rousseau originally wrote, "tale: for," and then continued with the following couplet:
I tell you Lord, and you will acknowledge
The more you believe you foresee, the more you go astray.
73. The manuscript reads, "Perhaps."
74. The manuscript reads, "in four words I am going to dispatch this one, and I very much wager that this for you and perhaps for many others this will be in a very unforeseen manner."
75. The manuscript crosses out "chicken" and replaces it with "partridge."
76. Rousseau originally wrote, "had wanted."

The Loves of Claire and Marcellin

1. From correspondence it is clear that Rousseau was working on this piece of fiction in 1756. It would appear that he abandoned it in order to concentrate on *Julie*.

2. Rousseau originally wrote, "extremely rich."
3. Rousseau originally wrote, "about the malady."
4. Rousseau originally wrote, "portraits."
5. Reading "sentent," rather than "sont" as in Pléiade.
6. Rousseau originally wrote, "he was ashamed of the emotion that he received from them and (believed himself obliged to) give all his efforts to hiding it carefully."
7. On an isolated sheet, a version of this passage ends, "this habit of moderation which a gentler and more polished education does not always give."
8. Rousseau originally added, "to that."
9. In the margin to this passage Rousseau wrote, "to extend. —Genuine love increases on the one hand and the other the difficulties of possession. Countries where debauchery reigns with the greatest excess where one is least acquainted with love, etc."
10. Rousseau originally wrote, "so many trips to Valence, in which they had much more attention to going to receive Miss Claire's commissions than to do his own. And nevertheless after many errands."
11. Rousseau originally added, "small,"
12. Rousseau originally wrote, "return to live."
13. Rousseau originally wrote, "Marcellin's business was found."
14. Rousseau originally wrote, "more willingly."
15. Rousseau originally wrote, "on the one side and the other."
16. Rousseau originally wrote, "give."
17. Rousseau originally wrote, "alarming his parents."
18. Rousseau originally wrote, "that is what the Surgeon had not been able to guess and what had caused him to make so many learned dissertations."
19. Rousseau originally wrote, "administration."
20. Rousseau originally added, "and pain."
21. Rousseau originally wrote, "for."
22. Rousseau originally wrote, "them."
23. The bracketed words were struck out without being replaced.
24. Rousseau originally wrote, "by any of the spectators."
25. Rousseau originally added, "internally."
26. Rousseau originally wrote, "her Marcellin's feelings."
27. Rousseau originally wrote, "her heart."
28. Rousseau originally wrote, "that she had received from him, and if, as one is going to see, she did not put the same simplicity into it, this is because there is naturally less of it in women's hearts."
29. Rousseau originally wrote, "that Marcellin's Parents did not look favorably in the fami . . . (only some pain)."
30. Rousseau originally wrote, "They had made plans of fortune and ambition based on Marcellin's marriage."
31. Rousseau originally wrote, "portion."
32. Rousseau originally added, "did not add much to their possessions."
33. Rousseau originally wrote, "inferior."
34. Rousseau originally wrote, "Plans of a Villager! The ambition of a country fellow."

35. Rousseau originally wrote, "Ambition speaks the same language to the heart.... I would prefer, said Caesar, to be the first."
36. Rousseau originally added, "which was not unknown to anyone."
37. Rousseau originally added, "to them."
38. Rousseau originally wrote, "step."
39. This sentence originally read, "Claire, the amorous Claire, had done in secret what few lovers would have done in her place and to oblige a moreover honest girl without any other lover to voluntarily break off a suitable marriage." The passage then proceeded, "Interest (avarice) that had accomplished this miracle in the fiancée..." The term translated here and in the text as "suitable marriage" could also mean simply "arranged marriage."
40. Rousseau then added, "Marcellin loves me, she said to her, and I loved him before..."
41. Rousseau originally wrote, "find a better portion, and I will be poor with Marcellin."
42. Rousseau originally added, "also."
43. Rousseau originally wrote, "her future husband in order to have something (for the pleasure of) to buy another at her whim."
44. Rousseau originally wrote, "Also Marcellin, always modest and introspective, passed for having little wit in the village."
45. Rousseau originally wrote, "was sweeter to her only after having sacrificed so much to it."
46. Rousseau originally wrote, "thrilled with the sacrifice that his mistress had made for him."
47. Rousseau originally wrote, "that the malady left him."
48. Rousseau originally wrote, "he saw with regret the return of a health that must erase the testimony of his love."
49. Rousseau originally wrote, "poverty."
50. Rousseau originally wrote, "It seems."
51. Rousseau originally wrote, "Happy Lovers, taste."
52. Rousseau originally wrote, "you possess nothing of what men seek and you are happy, you are poor and your hearts are content."
53. Rousseau originally wrote, "yourself."
54. Rousseau originally wrote, "most perfect happiness."
55. Rousseau originally wrote, "public consideration."
56. There are three fragments that may relate to the continuation of the story:

"hardly was he at the door."

"to tear (and throw) his Maltese cross throw it (impetuously) on the ground and throw himself at the feet of his Spouse were only a single and identical motion. Before he could say a word."

"Feeling, when it is true, always has its rights over beautiful souls."

"Learn Mylord d'Orival that country fellow though I may be, I do not want to survive an affront, and that your life (is not) cannot be safe (as long as I make any account) when I no longer make any account of mine."

The Little Savoyard; or, The Life of Claude Noyer

1. This work was probably written in the first half of 1756. There are two manuscript copies of it.

2. The other manuscript reads, "comfortably."

3. A fragment gives a different version of this passage: "I was born in the midst of the mountains of Savoy in a family of poor country folk. Heaven seemed to have destined me to be an honest farmer. By what (cruel) fatality could I have betrayed my vocation."

4. The other manuscript reads, "hamlet."

5. The other manuscript reads, "practiced."

6. The other manuscript reads, "to regret an agitated and tumultuous life and to feel in my old age all the infirmities that are its fruit, I would enjoy a calm mind in a still robust body and I would be a good old man honored by good people and respectable among all men for having . . ." A fragment gives the following version, "to weep over a long and unhappy life abandoned to the tumult of the passions and to the caprices of fortune, I would be a good old man honored in my hamlet and respectable among all men for having by means of a long and laborious life and by means of pure and simple morals worthily filled my functions on the earth and deserved well of society. Alas, I was born for such a sweet fate! Heaven is my witness that it was not at all by my choice that I have followed a completely different career. My intentions have always been healthy, the bottom of my heart always upright! And it will sometimes be seen that the vices (to which I was abandoned) that seduced me are born much more from the circumstances of my situation than from bad inclinations of my heart."

7. The other manuscript reads, "at the Court of Turin." Turin was the capital of Savoy.

8. The other manuscript adds, "soon."

9. The other manuscript reads, "weeks."

10. The other manuscript adds, "and deprived from his youth of the enjoyment of life for having wanted to enjoy it too much."

11. The other manuscript reads, "to one of his veteran soldiers."

12. The other manuscript reads, "This is the young man I ought to blame for all the unhappiness of life from the part he had in the first event that led to all of them."

13. The other manuscript reads, "catastrophe."

14. The other manuscript reads, "and who, in the first gleam of a hardly formed beauty."

15. The other manuscript reads, "already made herself noticed (distinguished) by her beauty."

16. The other manuscript adds, "in cities," here.

17. The other manuscript reads, "do not fail to put."

18. The other manuscript reads, "as early as they can. It was the very innocence of her heart and the purity of her senses that gave my sister that little air of vivacity and giddiness."

19. The other manuscript reads, "she needed only a little less innocence in order to have much more modesty."

20. In *Julie,* Claire is the name of the heroine's cousin. The description given above of this Claire would also fit the one in *Julie.*

21. The other manuscript reads, "possibility (means)."

22. The other manuscript reads, "for it was treated only as."

23. The other manuscript reads, "pushing things seriously the banter sometimes went too far. As price for his small liberties he often carried off."

24. The other manuscript reads, "these sorts of games pushed too far."

25. The other manuscript reads, "or into better terms than was suitable."

26. The other manuscript adds, "a lot."

27. The other manuscript reads, "what do lessons serve against natural mood."

28. The other manuscript reads, "dreamy, melancholy, and circumspect."

29. The other manuscript adds, "and pride."

30. The other manuscript reads, "severely."

31. The other manuscript continues, "of what they had feared."

32. The other manuscript reads, "already suspect that the young Argentière was the object."

33. The other manuscript reads, "to a fop that was destined the honor (belonged)."

34. The other manuscript reads, "the approach appeared easier to me."

35. The other manuscript reads, "I know that a woman."

36. The other manuscript reads, "I want to forestall the reflection, several more pages."

37. The other manuscript reads, "Good company."

38. The other manuscript reads, "that you do not understand."

39. The other manuscript reads, "to political lessons of point of honor."

40. The other manuscript reads, "delightful, very lively, and impetuous taste."

41. The other manuscript reads, "without caring at all about."

42. The other manuscript reads, "for a country girl."

43. The other manuscript reads, "to pass by."

44. The other manuscript reads, "to profit."

45. The other manuscript reads, "Disencumbered of the obstacle, she was soon disencumbered of the enemy. This suspended the attack for a moment, but the truce did not last long. Bathed in milk and marked by a contusion, D'Argentière only laughed and still wanted to pursue his undertaking."

46. The other manuscript adds, "which he had not at all expected, and desperate at having failed in his blow." The following paragraph is on a separate sheet.

47. The other manuscript reads, "that she felt herself made to attract eyes and hearts."

48. The other manuscript reads, "that all the youth of the canton was going to take at seeing her."

On Eloquence

1. This fragment apparently dates from 1735.
2. Rousseau originally wrote and then crossed out, "puerile and trivial or ill-adapted words."

Idea of Method in the Composition of a Book

1. This essay was written around 1745 when Rousseau was employed as a secretary by the Dupin family.
2. In the margin of this paragraph Rousseau wrote, "Conclusion too long."

Lexicological Remarks

1. It is not known when Rousseau wrote these two fragments. The fragments, on "pronunciation" that come before this one in Pléiade can be found in *Collected Writings*, VII, 333–336.

On Women

1. Most editors have suggested that this was probably written around 1735, but it is quite possibly from the 1740s when Rousseau was working for the Dupin family.
2. Rousseau first wrote and then crossed out, "Another subject of admiration for me, is the air of triumph with which we (we embellish—compare) exalt all the great men. I do not see up until now that we found our advantage very much in the comparisons."
3. Here Rousseau added and then crossed out, "a little."
4. Rousseau originally wrote and then crossed out, "Perhaps they will correctly put you in the place that you have unjustly deprived them of."
5. Rousseau originally wrote and then crossed out, "with some reason."
6. Rousseau originally wrote and then crossed out, "scepters."
7. Rousseau originally wrote and then crossed out, "brilliant."
8. Rousseau originally wrote and then crossed out, "condition."
9. Rousseau originally added and then crossed out, "for civil and military virtue."
10. Zenobia was the queen of Palmyra in the third century A.D. Lucretia committed suicide in 510 B.C. after being raped by Sextus Tarquin. Rousseau began a play devoted to her. Cornelia (second century B.C.) was the mother of the Gracchi brothers. Arria was the wife of Caccna Paetus and committed suicide under the reign of the Emperor Claudius. Artemisia (fourth century B.C.) built the famous Mausoleum as the tomb of her husband. Fulvia denounced the Catiline conspiracy. Elisabeth was the queen of Hungary and the regent of Poland. The Countess of Thököly was a leader of Hungarian resistance to Austria in the seventeenth century.
11. Rousseau originally wrote and then crossed out, "an equal."

12. Rousseau originally wrote and then crossed out, "All."
13. Rousseau originally wrote and then crossed out, "possess."
14. This is from the Preliminary Discourse of Voltaire's *Charles XII*.
15. Rousseau originally wrote and then crossed out, "in another letter."

[A Household on the Rue Saint-Denis]

1. This fragment is said to have been written around 1735. Rousseau's first visit to Paris had been several years earlier. It is not unlikely that it dates from the period that Rousseau worked with the Dupin family some years later.

Essay on the Important Events of Which Women Have Been the Secret Cause

1. Rousseau originally wrote, "have occasioned."
2. Although some editors have suggested that this was written in the 1730s, the editors of Pléiade reasonably suggest that it dates from the 1740s when Rousseau was working for the Dupin family.
3. Rousseau is referring to *Roman History* by Catrou and Rouillé, published in 1731. The passage in question involves the two daughters of Fabius Ambustus, one of whom married a plebian and the other, a patrician. The former complained that she was being shown too little consideration. As a result, her father worked to have certain offices opened to plebians. The authors conclude, "It seems that it was the destiny of Rome, that the great events always were begun by women."
4. Rousseau originally added, "only."
5. Rousseau originally wrote, "elevated."
6. Rousseau originally wrote, "intrigues, Policy, ambition, or."
7. Rousseau originally added, "only."
8. Rousseau originally wrote, "will be able to engage."
9. Rousseau originally wrote, "that I am taking into my head."
10. Rousseau originally wrote, "rather."
11. Rousseau originally wrote, "even."
12. Next to this paragraph Rousseau drew a line and wrote, "good."
13. Rousseau originally wrote, "feel."
14. Rousseau originally added, "perhaps someone will execute it."
15. Rousseau originally wrote, "in a condition to write."
16. Rousseau originally wrote, "to write what they have undertaken."
17. Rousseau originally wrote, "secret."
18. Rousseau originally added, "slightly important."
19. Rousseau originally added, "who having been disgraced."
20. Rousseau originally wrote, "use."
21. Rousseau originally added, "specious."
22. In the margin of this paragraph Rousseau drew a line and wrote, "to correct."

Advice to a Curate

1. On the reverse of one of the sheets of this manuscript is a draft of a part of the *Response to Bordes,* which Rousseau wrote in 1752. It is not clear which of the works Rousseau wrote first, but it is not unlikely that they were written close to the same time, although it has also been suggested that Rousseau wrote this in 1749.
2. An inspired poet.
3. Rousseau originally wrote and then crossed out, "whatever disdain I might have."
4. Rousseau originally wrote and then crossed out, "for all positions."
5. Rousseau originally wrote and then crossed out, "praises which mawkishness lavishes upon those who deserve them the least, and which seemliness itself forbids for all those who are worthy of them."
6. To play Gros-Jean means to be an ignorant person giving advice to a learned person.
7. Rousseau originally added and then crossed out, "it must be admitted."
8. Rousseau originally wrote and then crossed out, "less capricious."
9. Rousseau originally wrote and then crossed out, "men."
10. Rousseau originally wrote and then crossed out, "to make them into decent people."
11. Rousseau originally wrote and then crossed out, "we are not unaware."
12. Rousseau originally wrote and then crossed out, "for, Sir, you know it better than I do that by obliging you to continence they have made for you."
13. Rousseau originally wrote and then crossed out, "teach them if you wish."
14. Rousseau originally wrote and then crossed out, "but try to teach them rather."
15. Rousseau originally wrote and then crossed out, "and to be decent people."
16. Rousseau originally wrote and then crossed out, "I consent for you to make them Christians (Catholics)."
17. Rousseau originally wrote and then crossed out, "provided that you do not forget (do not neglect) to make out of them."

Funeral Oration for S.A.S. Monseigneur the Duke of Orléans

1. Louis, Duke of Orléans was the son of the regent. He was born in 1703 and died in 1752. Rousseau composed this oration at the request of abbé Alexis-Armand d'Arty, the nephew of Mme. Dupin, but the abbé was not chosen to make the oration. Above the title of the manuscript, Rousseau wrote, "This speech should not be published at all, given that it was done by commission and I was paid for it. But it is intended for Monsieur Moultou, minister from Geneva, and I ask that it be sent to him after my death." In fact, Rousseau sent it to Moultou in 1761.

2. The king is Xerxes. See Herodotus, *History*, VII.46.
3. See the epigraph, which Rousseau translated.
4. Rousseau originally wrote, "great near them."
5. Rousseau originally wrote, "small themselves."
6. The duke married Augusta-Marie-Jeanne, princess of Bade, in 1724. She died two years later.
7. The duke acquired an apartment in an abbey in Paris in 1725 and moved there permanently in 1742.
8. Rousseau originally wrote, "his God."
9. The son, Louis-Philippe, had been born in 1725.
10. This term can be translated as "political thinker," as well as "politician."
11. Titus was emperor of Rome from 79 to 81 A.D.
12. Rousseau originally wrote, "the first." In one of the manuscripts he wrote, "in that world so new for his peers, so unknown, so disdained by the other one, where the suffering members of Jesus Christ attract Heavenly indignation against the happy people of the age, where Religion and probity . . ."
13. The Palais-Royal was his official residence.
14. Rousseau originally wrote, "false" and then added "pity."
15. Rousseau originally wrote, "which is only a genuine cruelty, a pretext."
16. One manuscript gives the following version of this passage: "Such was the new society that he gathered around himself in the place of the one he had taken leave of and, wanting to pour out the treasures of his charity in a beneficent dew over the immense crowd of unfortunate people. It was the tenderness of his heart that obliged him to accustom his eyes to the sight of human v( ), for he did not at all imitate the false and cruel compassion of society people and did not at all fear facing the ills that believed he could relieve."
17. Rousseau originally wrote, "his helpful hand."
18. The duke, in fact, was famous for establishing many charitable institutions for a variety of purposes.
19. The Pléiade editors take this remark as a defense against the charge that the duke held Jansenist opinions. On the duke's deathbed a priest wished to deny him communion unless he retracted these opinions. The duke refused and had the sacrament administered by his chaplain. (Pléiade II, 1946).
20. Rousseau originally wrote, "favored."
21. The duke knew numerous ancient languages and wrote literal translations of several books of the Bible.
22. Rousseau originally wrote, "on himself."
23. Vespasian.
24. The last two paragraphs are in the first published version, but not in the manuscript. They are presumed to have been lost.

Letters to Sara

1. It is thought that Rousseau wrote this when he was approximately fifty, as the presumed author of the letters is. That would place the composition around 1762. The text of the first four letters is from the final draft done by Rousseau.

The fifth is from the earlier draft. The draft has the title, "The Greybeard in Love," which is crossed out. Only the final version has the epigraph and introductory notice.

2. "Neither the credulous hope for a soul that responds to me" (Horace, *Odes*, IV, 1, 30).

3. This statement has led some readers to belief that these letters were not written as a dare, but were intended by Rousseau as love letters from himself to a younger woman.

4. The writer uses the second-person familiar to address Sara here and below.

5. The draft reads, "a wretch who is longer in the age for loving."

6. The draft reads, "I am not at all ridiculous."

7. The draft reads, "that I love while feeling myself unworthy of pleasing."

8. At this point the draft has in the margin, "but these tears are less of love than of rage," which also occurs below.

9. What follows is not in the draft, which resumes at "I love with the horrible certainty . . ." In the margin Rousseau wrote, "good."

10. The draft reads, "superannuated lover."

11. Rousseau originally wrote, "gallant," and replaced it with "pleasant fellow."

12. The draft reads, "exhausting the foolish jargon of gallantry in order to amuse you."

13. The draft reads, "and if you amuse yourself with my weakness."

14. The draft reads, "it is not I, it is you that I love; deprived of all hope, I forget myself in order to be occupied with you alone."

15. The draft reads, "nor other happiness than your happiness."

16. The draft reads, "I desire everything that you desire; I would even love my rival, if his heart could satisfy all your wishes; if you did not love him, I would want him to be worthy of (deserve) your love."

17. After this the draft reads, crossed out, "I would like him to be able to soften you in order to make you feel all the charms of love. I would like to make all my feelings pass into you, even for someone else. I have only one desire: to form . . ." In the margin, Rousseau wrote, "My final desire . . ."

18. In this part of the letter the writer uses the formal second person.

19. The first published edition reads, "you have treated me."

20. The draft reads, "simple."

21. After this the draft reads, crossed out, "and you are only deceiving me one more time." Rousseau then added, and struck out, "You wanted to take on a simple air with me and you still want to keep it."

22. The draft reads, "the simplicity that you wanted to keep with me in my weakness."

23. In the margin the draft reads, "Ah Sara, from your good heart I would have expected some consolation in my misery."

24. In the margin the draft adds, "This blushing was still another of your acts of faithlessness."

25. The draft reads, "I vanquished."

26. At this point the writer reverts to the familiar second person.
27. The gender makes it clear that the writer is referring to himself here.
28. The draft reads, "I accuse your vanity."
29. The draft reads, "you make me despair by not thinking about me."
30. The draft reads, "I am very miserable not even to be able to concern you with my ridiculousness."
31. After this the draft has, crossed out, "Barbarian, ingrate, your ferocious heart . . ."
32. In the draft this letter begins, crossed out, "You have won, Sara, that was not difficult."
33. The draft reads, "from the years I have lived."
34. The draft reads, "you make me experience." It then adds in the margin, "Wretch! You put on so much pity only to make me feel how worthy of it I was."
35. The draft reads, "gets indignant and revolts."
36. After this the draft adds, crossed out, "How much I would honor the one who deigned to console you."
37. In the margin the draft reads, "If you disdained me, I am done for."
38. The draft reads, "I would have been less well caressed."
39. The draft reads, "I have been able to touch your lovable heart."
40. The draft reads, "inextinguishable."
41. The draft omits, "prideful."
42. In the margin the draft reads, "It is certain that I would have wished in vain to stop loving you. You will put good order into it."
43. In the margin the draft reads, "One could not have either more virtue or more coquetry."
44. In the margin the draft reads, "for being a superannuated lover I am not at all a faint-hearted lover."
45. The draft reads, "you whom I feared so strongly?"
46. The first published edition reads, "henceforth if I esteem myself to be anything."
47. The draft has, "your sublime essence," crossed out and replaced by, "your celestial essence," also crossed out and replaced by, "your sublime image," with "sublime" crossed out.
48. After this the draft reads, crossed out, "In a heart like mine love cannot either be born or endure without esteem and respect."
49. The writer reverts to the second-person formal.
50. After this the draft reads, crossed out, "Your manner of handling me full of indulgence and friendship did not fail to be humiliating because it showed me as guilty where I least believed myself to be, that is to say less toward myself than toward you."
51. The draft reads, "when in fact I was vile."
52. The draft adds here, "even the humiliation of the feeling that was dragging me."
53. The draft adds here, "could one make run."
54. The writer resumes the informal second person here.

55. The draft reads, "(cover) veil my errors from you." The copy reads, "veil from me," corrected to "hide from you."
56. The draft reads, "stifle."
57. The draft reads, "each day adds a new degree of despair and ignominy."
58. The draft reads, "That is what does not depend on me, and what in reason's eyes makes me more unfortunate than guilty; but here, Sara, is what does depend on me and what can give me back my esteem in my misery even in the eyes of the one who is causing it."
59. The writer reverts to the formal second person.
60. The draft reads, "No redoubtable girl, do not debase the temple."
61. The draft reads, "Ah I would be too overwhelmed by my misery."
62. The draft adds, "even."
63. The draft reads, "I shall be only halfway ridiculous and guilty when I shall no longer be under your eyes."
64. The writer resumes the familiar second person.
65. The draft reads, "without (being able) (needing to) without wanting to flee you."
66. This letter exists only in the draft.
67. Rousseau originally wrote, "lovable."
68. Rousseau wrote, successively, "fate's which caused me to be born so far from you with a heart that could belong only belong to you alone," then, "which put into a man to whom you cannot belong a soul made to be yours," then "a heart that can only be yours," finally, "(caused to be born) put so far from me."
69. After this the draft reads, crossed out, "I swear it to you and you must believe me!"
70. Rousseau originally wrote, "leads me astray."
71. Rousseau originally wrote, "and if I let myself be dragged."
72. Rousseau originally wrote, "You saw my heart."
73. Rousseau originally wrote, "you pitied me."
74. Rousseau originally wrote, "my entire life."
75. Rousseau originally added, "dear Sara."
76. Rousseau originally wrote, "I cannot think without dying."

Remarks on the *Letters on the English and the French*

1. Rousseau wrote extracts and remarks from the *Letters on the English and the French* by Louis Béat de Muralt during the winter of 1756–1757. He refers to this work frequently in *Julie* and the *Letter to d'Alembert*. The extracts, or relevant passages, from Béat de Muralt are given in italics.
2. Rousseau uses this to distinguish his own comments.
3. Rousseau copied a long passage only the first and last parts are given here.
4. The reference is to Pierre Bayle.
5. Rousseau's spelling for Bayle.
6. Rousseau copied out two long passages from this work by Béat de Muralt. Several sentences are given in this and the next fragment.

Various Fragments

1. These fragments were written at various, often undetermined, dates.
2. Rousseau met the duke and duchess of Luxembourg in 1759 and lived in a house provided by them for two months while repairs were being made to his house. He stayed in very close relations with them for the next three years. See *Confessions* (*Collected Writings*, V, 433–489).
3. This fragment, and the next several, are probably concerned with the collection of his writings that Rousseau was planning around 1765.
4. "Imbeciles" is crossed out.
5. Rousseau first wrote and then crossed out, "to proceed usefully to their ends."
6. After this Rousseau wrote and then crossed out, "With what, however, is such a society occupied? With little gallant verses that Cotin would have disavowed, with resolving some [ ] in honor of the Ladies; who would ever have the courage to skim through these insipid memoranda." Cotin is the abbé Charles Cotin.
7. This fragment is on the back of a draft of a passage from the "Letter to Philopolis," which was written in 1755.
8. See Plato, *Gorgias*.
9. After this Rousseau wrote and then crossed out, "Tu m'aduli ma tu mi piace." (You adulate me but you please me). It is likely that the author is Helvétius. See 208–210 above.
10. The editors of Pléiade suggest that this and the next two fragments concern Isabelle Guyenet who almost died while giving birth in February 1765. Rousseau describes his relations with her (under her maiden name, d'Ivernois) in the *Confessions* (*Collected Writings,,* V, 503–506).
11. Here Rousseau wrote and crossed out "the most."
12. No passage in Aristotle has been found stating this.
13. Rousseau originally wrote and crossed out, "a very mediocre."
14. At the bottom of the page Rousseau wrote "half of life."
15. Rousseau wrote and crossed out, "perhaps also you do not love at all."
16. Rousseau originally wrote and then crossed out, "in spite of myself."
17. Rousseau originally wrote and then crossed out, "the risks that you are making me run and the ills you have recalled to me."
18. This is a citation to Pierre Nicole's *Essays on Morality* in *Moral Reflections on the Epistles and the Gospels: On the Epistle of the 14th Sunday after Pentecost*. In the sentence following, the part before the second comma is from Nicole and the completion is from Rousseau.
19. The watermark of the sheet of paper bearing this fragment has the date 1759. That, then, is the earliest possible date of the fragment.
20. Between this line and the one above Rousseau wrote, "I say the same thing about pains."
21. The manuscript reads, "for what it pleases another," which would not be grammatically correct.
22. After this Rousseau wrote and crossed out, "The sensuality of a child is

limited to eating sugar and as sovereign good he imagines only never-never land. It is not the same thing at twenty, the sensuality of a child is no longer that of a young man, and the tastes of a young . . . that of an old man are not the same."

23. Rousseau originally wrote, "capuchin."

24. From other things written on the same sheets, it would appear that fragments 33, 34, 35, 38, 39, 41, 42, and 43 were written near the end of 1764.

25. After this Rousseau added and then crossed out, "from time to time on Sundays."

26. From other things written on the same sheet, it would appear that fragments 36 and 37 were written in the winter of 1758–1759.

27. After this Rousseau wrote and then crossed out, "finding the secret of."

28. Rousseau first wrote and then crossed out, "It is a friendly fleet."

29. After this Rousseau wrote and then crossed out, "It is also to the blows of this Hero that."

30. After this Rousseau wrote and then crossed out, "Suddenly."

31. In this fragment and the preceding one, Rousseau is referring to *Critical Reflections on Poetry and Painting,* by Abbé Jean-Baptiste Dubos. The subject of this fragment is addressed at greater length in the *Letter to d'Alembert.*

32. *Atreus* was written by Crébillon.

Index

Achilles, 285
Adeimantus, 292n4
Aesculapius, 228
Alembert, Jean le Rond d', 292n7, 310n147
Alexander, 242
Allobrogians, xvii
amour-propre, 30, 39, 40, 42, 106, 154, 176, 201, 266
Amy, Joseph, 133, 298n8
Anacreon, 242
Antony, 249
Archimedes, 8
Ariosto, 28, 292n9
Aristarchus, 25, 291n6
Aristippus, 183
Aristotle, 23, 85, 280
Arria, 245, 319n10
Arruntius, 113
Artemisia, 245, 319n10
Arty, Alexis-Armand, abbé d', 321n1
Atreus, 286

Bacqueville, marquis de, 299n1
Bade, Augusta-Marie-Jeanne, princess of, 322n6
Balthasar, 302n2
Barclay [Barclai], Jean, 9, 289n26
Barrow, Isaac, 8, 289n16
Bayle [Baile], Pierre, 274, 325nn4 and 5
Bellegard, Jean-Baptiste Morvan, abbé de, 109, 297n25
Bensaude-Vincent, Bernadette, 287–288n17
Berkeley, George, 289n26, 304n38
Bernardi, Bruno, 287–288n17
Bernex, 162–164
Blavet, Michel, 102, 297n15
Boileau, Nicolas, 9, 26, 289n26
Bordes, Charles, 9–13, 290n29, 292n3
Borelli, Alfonso, 151, 299n10
Boudet, Father Claude, 162
Bouhours, Father Dominique, 112–113, 297n34
Buffon, George-Louis Leclerc, 211, 306n60

Caccna Paetus, 319n10
Caesar, Julius, 112–14, 128, 232, 235, 249, 288n5, 316n35

Cahusac, Louis de, 291n4
Calvin, Jean, 183
Carter, Richard B., 296n3
Cassini, Jacques and Jean-Dominique, 4, 77, 85–87, 288–289n6, 296n4
Catiline conspiracy, 319n10
Cato of Utica, 4, 195, 242, 245, 288n5
Catrou, Father François, 320n3
Champagneux, Luc-Antoine-Donin de, 61
Charles VII, 249
Charles-Emmanuel III, 6, 289n12
Choiseul, Etienne-François, duc de, 60, 294n7
Christianity, 49, 95, 259–261
Cicero, 9, 23, 112–113, 128
Claudius, 319n10
Claville, Charles-François-Nicolas Lemaître de, 9, 289n25
Coindet, François, 29
Columbus, Christopher, 136, 147
commerce, xviii, 12, 18, 57, 102, 147
Condillac, Etienne Bonnot, abbé de, 187, 211, 306n61
conscience, 39, 54, 119, 160, 195–198, 254, 309n124
Conti, Louis-François de Bourbon, prince de, 64, 132, 295n5, 298nn6 and 5
Copernicus, Nicolas, 86, 141
Coriolanus, 349
Corneille, Pierre, 102, 208
Cornelia, 245, 319n10
Cotin, Charles, 326n6
courage, 49, 50, 179, 190, 246, 248, 266, 284, 286
Coypel, 102, 297n15
Crébillon, Claude-Prosper Jolyot de, 291n4, 327n32
Croesus, 10, 51, 290n43
Cyrano de Bergerac, Savinien, 28, 292n8

Deleyre [De Layre], Alexandre, 60, 294n8
Demosthenes, 219
Descartes, René, 8, 86, 183, 186, 189
Deschamps, 63–66, 295n5
Desmarais, François-Séraphin Regnier, abbé, 112, 297n34
Despréaux. See Boileau

329

Diderot, Denis, xvi, 60, 291nn1, 3, and 6, 292n10 and 4, 305n50
Dido, 245
Diogenes, 183, 219, 313n30
Don Quixote, 17
Doria, Andrea, 147, 299n5
Dubos, Jean-Baptiste, abbé, 285, 327n31
Duchesne, Nicholas-Bonaventure, 293n1
Dunois, Count de, 245
Dupin, Louise-Marie-Madeleine, 298n7, 321n1
Duras, duc de, 132
Duverney, Joseph Paris, 298n5132

Elisabeth, Queen of Hungary, 245, 319n10
Epictetus, 9, 17
Epicurus, 183
Euclid, 186
existence, feeling of, 279

fables, 81, 96, 202
Fabri [Fabre], Honoratus, 151, 300nn11, 14, and 15
Falconet, Camille, 130, 298n4
fanaticism, 149
fatherland, 8, 11, 17, 46, 48, 161, 163, 208, 235, 256
Fénelon, François de Salignac de la Mothe, 81, 208, 289n20
Fizes, Nicolas, 86, 296n3
Folard [Follard], Jean-Charles, 114, 298n43
Fontenelle, Bernard Le Bovier de, 4, 207–209, 289n7
freedom, 14, 21, 34, 49, 69, 85, 101, 103, 107, 166, 187, 188, 190, 200, 245, 246, 250, 263, 271
Fulvia, 245, 249, 319n10

Girardon, François, 102, 297n5
Glaucon, 292n4
God, gods, 6, 18–20, 54, 95, 136, 157–161, 167, 169, 171, 181, 190, 195, 197, 208, 219, 222, 226, 234, 251, 252–263, 278, 285, 290n43, 301n16, 302n2, 304n45, 306n71, 309n115, 314n55
Goldschmidt, Victor, 288n28
Gospel, 46, 47
Gouhier, Henri, 302n22
Gracchi brothers, 319n10
Grimm, Friedrich-Melchior, xx, 287n16
Grotius, Hugo, 114, 129

Hector, 285
Hell, 146

Helvétius, Claude-Adrien, xxiii, 204–212, 311n1, 326n9
Henri IV, 312n10
Henry VIII, 249
Heraclitus, 27
Hero, 299n9
Herodotus, 148, 322n2
Holbach [Holback], Paul-Henri Dietrich or Thiry, Baron d', 60
Homer, 44, 58, 62, 136
Hôpital, marquis de l', 8
Horace, 9, 264, 323n2
Houdetot, Elisabeth-Sophie-Françoise, countess d'. See Sophie
Hume, David, 295n3
Huyghens, Christiaan, 4, 289n7

imagination, 43, 100, 101, 150, 169, 170, 174, 199, 200, 234, 270, 278, 279
injustice, 42, 107, 110, 194, 238, 246
instinct, 187, 197, 309n130
Ivernois, Isabelle d', 279–280, 326

Jesus, 46, 47, 96, 257, 258, 261, 262, 322n12
Joan of Arc, 245
Judith, 242
justice, 6, 53, 60, 62, 70, 110, 157, 159, 172, 190, 192–194, 207, 211, 253, 260, 292n4, 294n4, 307n93

Kelly, Christopher, 288n19, 293n1, 301n1
Kepler, Johannes, 8

La Bruyère [La Bruiére], Jean de, 4, 109, 119, 288n4, 297n25, 298n1
La Fontaine, Jean de, 299n8
La Hire, Philippe de, 4, 87, 288–289n6, 296n4
La Mettrie [La Métrie], Julien Offray de, 46, 293n6
La Morlière, Charles-Jacques-Louis-Auguste Rochette de, 291n4
La Motte, Antoine Houdar de, 9, 290n27
Lamy [Lami], Father Bernard, 113, 128, 297n36
La Rochefoucauld, François, duc de, 288n4
Laubel, Dr., 63, 65, 66
laws of nature, 197, 200
Leander, 150, 299n9
Leibniz [Leibnitz], Gottfried-Wilhelm, xviii, 8, 304n41
Le Mierre, Antoine-Marin, 71, 295n16
Le Vasseur, Thérèse, 61, 294n9
Livia, 37
Locke, John, 8, 28, 183, 186, 305n50

Louis IX, 263
Louis XV, 9
love of oneself, 196
Lucretia, 195, 242, 245, 319n10
Luxemburg, Mareschal and Mareschale de, 275, 326n2
luxury, xviii–xix, 11, 15, 181, 210

Mably, Gabriel, Bonnot, abbé de, 94, 113, 120, 128, 297nn1 and 35, 298nn44, 2, 4, and 5
Mably, Jean Bonnot de, xx, 91–129, 296n1, 297n6, 298n2
Machiavelli, Nicolo, 226, 314n79
Maecenas, 10
Malebranche [Mallebranche], Nicolas de, 8, 28, 304n40
Manory, 63–66, 295n6
maxim, 111, 240, 257, 259, 260, 272, 277
Mazarin, Cardinal, 53
Mezeray [Mezarai], François–Etudes de, 9, 289n25
miracles, xxi, 47, 259–260, 316n39
Mithridates, 245
moderation, 176, 229, 240, 253
modesty, 196–197, 210, 272
Mohammed, 204, 222
Molière, 33, 94, 102, 109, 121, 297n25
Molyneux, William, 305n50
Montaigne [Montagne], Michel de, 4, 43, 195, 288n4, 294n3, 310n47
Montesquieu, 291n4
Montfaucon, Bernard de, 24, 291n4
morality, 50, 56, 95, 96, 98, 114, 121, 123, 129, 173, 175, 187, 193, 195, 200, 208, 211, 261, 272, 307n91, 308n111
morals, 11, 46, 75, 94, 97, 115, 119, 121, 122, 195, 238, 260, 271, 273, 312n1
Moultou, Paul, 321n1
Muralt, Louis Béat de, 271–274, 325nn1 and 6

natural equality, 211
natural laws, 7
natural right, 114, 129, 245
nature, 8, 11–13, 31–34, 43, 48, 100, 101, 135, 150, 159, 165, 168, 170, 172, 176, 177, 180–184, 187–202, 205, 206, 211, 221, 229, 231, 232, 247, 273, 277, 278, 280, 281, 285, 304n35, 305n59, 309n130, 310n144
Newton [Neuvton], Isaac, 8, 77, 85, 86, 186–187, 296n5
Nicole, Pierre, 326
Nieuventyt [Nyeuventit, Nyeuwentit, Niuventyt], Bernard, 8, 289n19, 298n42

Nollet [Nolet], Jean-Antoine, abbé, 23, 291n2

original sin, 95
Orléans, Louis, Duke of, 252–263, 321n1
Ovid, xvii–xviii, 288n1

Palissot de Montenoy, Charles, 293n3
Pallu, Bertrand-René, 12
Parisot, Gabriel, 13–21, 291n48
Pascal, Blaise, 8, 183
Paul, Saint, 262
Perez, Antonio [Alonso], 207, 312n10
Perrault, Charles, 314n70
Petau, Denis, 24, 291n4
Philip II, 49, 207, 312n10
philosophers, philosophy, xxii, xxv, 11, 24, 30–32, 34, 67, 101, 104, 113, 128, 132, 135, 136, 165, 167, 170–172, 180, 182, 183, 186, 189, 195, 196, 199, 208–211, 219, 223, 229, 240, 257, 261, 282–284, 289n26, 292n7, 301nn10 and 12, 302n19, 305nn45 and 55, 306n72, 312n1
Phocion, 209
Picard [Picart], Jean, 87, 296n4
Plato, 4, 28, 40, 188, 278, 283, 288n5, 306n67, 326n8
Pliny, 8, 148, 187
Pluche, Noël-Antoine, abbé, 298n41
Plutarch, 9, 294n3
Polybius, 114, 298n43
Pope, Alexander, xviii, 9, 289n26
Prévost, Antoine-François, abbé, 289n22
pride, 7, 10, 11, 15, 17, 98, 123, 127, 167–169, 187, 189, 190, 199, 217, 219, 252–254, 276
providence, 56, 58, 158, 159, 161, 163, 195, 299n12
prudence, 105, 118, 122, 225
Ptolemy, 85, 141
Pufendorf [Puffendorf], Samuel, 114, 129
Pythagoras, 301n12

Quesnay, François, 312
Quintilian, 113, 297n37

Rabelais, 35, 47
Racine, Jean, 9, 102
Rameau, Jean-Philippe, 34–35, 102, 292nn1, 6, and 8, 297n15
Ray, William, 288n24
Raynal, Guillaume-Thomas, François, abbé de, 130–133
religion, xxi, 34, 47, 48, 75, 95, 96, 121, 149, 157, 207, 252, 253, 257, 259, 260, 309n115, 312n1, 322n12
Restaut, Pierre, 112, 297n33

Rey, Marc-Michel, 68
Reynaut [Rainaud], Charles, 8, 289n16
Rollin, Charles, 9, 112, 113, 128, 289n26, 297n37
Romulus, 245
Rosière, M. de, 61
Rouillé, Father Pierre-Joseph, 320n3
Rousseau, Jean-Baptiste, 44
Ruelle [Rouelle], Guilaume-François, 130, 298n2

Saint-Aubin, Gilbert-Charles Legendre, marquis de, 9, 289n25
Sallust, 113
Sappho, 242
Scaevola, Gaius Mucius, 242
Schahbahan, 223
Scheffer, Carl Fredrik, 298n7
science, 75, 94–96, 98, 103, 114, 121–123, 125, 129, 153, 180, 254, 255, 276, 291n3
Semiramis, 242
Sextus Tarquin, 319n10
Shaftesbury [Shaftsburi], Anthony Ashley Cooper, Count, 183
shame, 192, 197, 268
Socrates, 4, 40, 283, 288n5, 302n20
Solon, 51
Sophie, 175–203, 303nn4, 7, 14, and 21, 304nn33 and 43, 305n57, 308nn95 and 98, 310nn139, 149, and 152
soul, 16, 18, 20, 21, 28, 30, 37, 42, 50, 54, 55, 57, 95, 100, 102, 103, 106, 150, 158–160, 165, 168, 172, 173, 175–203, 208, 222, 229, 231, 234, 246, 252, 256–263, 266–268, 274, 277, 279, 286, 297n19, 304n35, 305nn57 and 58, 306nn65 and 72, 307n92, 310nn140 and 159
sovereign, xix, 14, 32, 52, 161
Spon, Jacob, 8, 289n23
Stanislas, King, 292n2

Tacitus, 37, 113, 297n39
Tacquet, Father André, 86, 296n2

Terence, 191, 243, 307n77
Terrall, Mary, 296
Terrasson, Jean abbé, 199, 289n21, 310n147
Themistocles, 249
Thierry [Thierri], François, 130, 298n3
Thököly [Tekeli], Countess of, 245, 319n10
Thyestes, 286
Tiberius, 37
Titus, 5, 113, 256–257, 289n9, 322n11
Titus Livius, 112, 128
Trajan, 5, 289n9
Tronchin, Jean–Robert, 293n2
tyranny, tyrant, 49, 194, 202, 250

vanity, 10, 22, 33, 34, 37, 97, 98, 123, 125, 189, 198, 236, 266, 295n3
Varro, Marcus Ternetius, 94, 121, 297n8
Vaugelas, Claude Favre, baron de Péroges, seigneur de, 112, 297n34
Vaumorière, Pierre d'Ortigues de, 219, 313n29
Vernes, Jacob, 45, 293n1
Vespasian, 322n23
vice, 21, 39, 45, 52, 104, 105, 115, 160, 175, 182, 190, 195, 202, 272, 300n6, 308n94, 317n6
Virgil, 44, 113
Voisenon, Claude-Henri de Fusée, 291n4
Voltaire, 9, 67, 102, 246, 293nn1, 4, 7, and 9, 294nn13 and 15, 301n3, 320n14

Wallis, John, 8, 289n16
Warens, Louise Eleonor de, xix, 3–9, 162–164, 289n12
wisdom, 7, 11, 15, 18, 19, 28, 93, 103, 104, 118, 134, 157, 160, 165, 168, 173, 175, 180, 181, 189, 198, 202, 225, 262

Xenocrates, 195, 309n115
Xerxes, 322n2

Zeno, 17, 183
Zenobia, 245, 319n10

The Collected Writings of Rousseau

Roger D. Masters and Christopher Kelly, series editors

1. Rousseau, Judge of Jean-Jacques: Dialogues
2. Discourse on the Sciences and Arts (First Discourse) and Polemics
3. Discourse on the Origins of Inequality (Second Discourse), Polemics, and Political Economy
4. Social Contract, Discourse on the Virtue Most Necessary for a Hero, Political Fragments, and Geneva Manuscript
5. The *Confessions* and Correspondence, Including the Letters to Malesherbes
6. Julie, or the New Heloise: Letters of Two Lovers Who Live in a Small Town at the Foot of the Alps
7. Essay on the Origin of Languages and Writings Related to Music
8. *The Reveries of the Solitary Walker*, Botanical Writings, and Letter to Franquières
9. *Letter to Beaumont, Letters Written from the Mountain,* and Related Writings
10. *Letter to D'Alembert* and Writings for the Theater
11. *The Plan for Perpetual Peace, On the Government of Poland,* and Other Writings on History and Politics
12. Autobiographical, Scientific, Religious, Moral, and Literary Writings
13. *Emile* or On Education (Includes Emile and Sophie; or The Solitaries)

www.ingramcontent.com/pod-product-compliance
Lightning Source LLC
Chambersburg PA
CBHW030302080526
44584CB00012B/405